JAPANESE PHILOSOPHY IN THE MAKING 3
ALTERNATIVES WITH TRACKS THROUGH ZEN

Studies in Japanese Philosophy
Takeshi Morisato, General Editor

1. James W. Heisig, *Much Ado about Nothingness: Essays on Nishida and Tanabe* (2015)
2. Nishitani Keiji, *Nishida Kitarō: The Man and His Thought* (2016)
3. Tanabe Hajime, *Philosophy as Metanoetics* (2016)
5. Nishida Kitarō, *La logica del luogo e la visione religiosa del mondo* (2017)
6. James W. Heisig, *Filosofi del nulla. Un saggio sulla scuola di Kyoto* (2017)
7. Nishitani Keiji, *Dialettica del nichilismo* (2017)
8. Ueda Shizuteru, *Zen e filosofia* (2017)
9. Nishida Kitarō, *Autoéveil. Le système des universels* (2017)
10. Jan Gerrit Strala, *Der Form des Formlosen auf der Spur. Sprache und Denken bei Nishida* (2017)
11. Nishitani Keiji, *La religione e il nulla* (2017)
13. John C. Maraldo, *Japanese Philosophy in the Making 1: Crossing Paths with Nishida* (2017)
14. Nishitani Keiji, *Zen, filosofia e scienza* (2017)
15. Nishitani Keiji, *La religión y la nada* (2017)
16. Nishitani Keiji, *Nishida Kitarō. L'uomo e il filosofo* (2018)
17. Nishida Kitarō, *La Détermination du néant marquée par l'autoéveil* (2019)
18. Andrew Feenberg, *Nishida, Kawabata, and the Japanese Response to Modernity* (2019)
19. John C. Maraldo, *Japanese Philosophy in the Making 2: Borderline Interrogations* (2019)
20. Taitetsu Unno, ed., The Religious Philosophy of Nishitani Keiji (2019)
21. Nishida Kitarō, Intuition and Reflection in Self-Consciousness (2020, reprint)
22. Taitetsu Unno and James W. Heisig, ed., *The Religious Philosophy of Tanabe Hajime: The Metanoetic Imperative* (2020, reprint)
23. Jacynthe Tremblay, *Le lexique philosophique de Nishida Kitarō: Japonais-français, Français-japonais* (2020)
24. John C. Maraldo, *The Saga of Zen History and the Power of Legend* (2021)
25. Myriam-Sonja Hantke, *Mística en la filosofía alemana y japonesa Schelling, Hegel, Nishitani* (2020)

Japanese Philosophy in the Making 3

Alternatives with Tracks through Zen

JOHN C. MARALDO

CHISOKUDŌ

Cover graphic: Claudio Bado
Cover calligraphy of "Japanese Philosophy in the Making": Mary Jo Maraldo

Copyright © 2023, Chisokudō Publications

ISBN: 979-8370916489

Nagoya, Japan
http://www.chisokudo.org/

*For Mary Jo Maraldo
ever clearing the way for
my paths through philosophy*

Contents

Acknowledgments *ix*
Lead-in *1*

UNDERSTANDING RELIGIONS IN PRACTICE

1. Three Stories That Invite Us to Rethink Religious Relativism *15*
2. Outsiders and Insiders of Zen, Turned Inside Out *39*
3. Understanding: An Alternative to the Hermeneutical Model *56*

PRACTICE

4. Practice: An Alternative Mode *105*
5. Four Things and Two Practices: Taking Heidegger Farther East *125*
6. Practice, *Samādhi*, Realization: Three Innovative Interpretations by Nishitani Keiji *153*

SELF AND OTHERS AND IN-BETWEEN

7. Writing the Self: The "Autobiographic" Practices of Rousseau, Hakuseki, and Hakuin *171*
8. Finding the Self in Mountains: Zen Landscapes of the Mindful Heart *200*
9. Personal Autonomy: An Alternative View *218*
10. Alternative Configurations of Alterity in Dialogue with Ueda Shizuteru *237*

11. History from a Buddhist Perspective: Nishitani's Account and Accountability *266*

12. The Alternative Normativity of Zen *294*

DŌGEN'S ZEN

13. The Study of Body-Mind: Dōgen's Alternative *321*

14. Negotiating the Divide of Death in Japanese Buddhism: Dōgen's Difference *351*

Follow-up: Ante-Originality and the Alternative Creativity of Japanese Pathway Arts *387*

Bibliography *403*

Index *439*

Acknowledgments

This book is dedicated to you, Mary-san, for faithfully encouraging and enabling my long plunges into recondite matters that matter little to most people who cross our path. For more than fifty years you have helped turn my solitary excursions into conversations we can share with others. You've taught me how to *notice* what often escapes my attention and then to articulate it, so that I might know better what I am talking about. You endured every sentence of this book's drafts (and the first two volumes of this trilogy); you inferred words that were supposed to be there but were not, and discovered redundancies in words what were. You noticed abrasive phrases and snags in sentences and then helped smooth them into more transparent prose. When we debated, your uncanny instinct for wordplay lightened my ponderous thoughts, and when together we composed the final essay in this book your experience with Japanese pathway arts grounded my airy ideas. If readers of this volume find their way through it to insight, it is no doubt due to your patience with my writing. And if they do not, let them admonish me.

Once again, Wayne Yokoyama put his eagle eye to work in proof-reading and copy-editing, correcting both minutiae and gross errors, and tracking down quotations and references to ensure accuracy. Mistakes that remain can reliably be laid at my door. Many colleagues heard or read versions of the papers that grew into this book and contributed incisive remarks. James W. Heisig unselfishly gave the books in this trilogy their typographical design, and Claudio Bado contributed their cover design. Heisig, Morisato Takeshi, and Pierre Bonneels brought Chisokudō Publications to life and made the entire series, *Studies in*

Japanese Philosophy, easily accessible to a wide audience. I AM deeply grateful to all these friends.

Versions of all the chapters in this book have appeared previously in various volumes and journals, but all have been updated and revised or expanded for this volume. I am grateful to the publishers of the following articles for permission to reprint.

A shorter version of Chapter 1 appeared as "Religion and Relativism: A Reappraisal," in *Zen Buddhism Today: Annual Report of the Kyoto Zen Symposium* 9 (1992), 30–45.

A version of Chapter 2 was published under the title, "Can Scholars Understand Zen? A Re-examination of the Opposition Between Objective Study and Religious Practice," in H. Eisenhofer-Halim, ed., *Wandel zwischen den Welten: Festschrift für Johannes Laube*. Frankfurt, Berlin, and New York: Peter Lang (2003), 439–50.

Chapter 3 appeared in a shorter version as "A Call for an Alternative Notion of Understanding in Interreligious Hermeneutics," in C. Cornille and C. Conway, eds., *Interreligious Hermeneutics*. Eugene, OR: Cascade Books (2010), 89–115. Reprinted with the permission of Wipf and Stock Publishers (www.wipfandstock.com).

A shorter version of Chapter 4 was published as "An Alternative Notion of Practice in the Promise of Japanese Philosophy," in Lam Wing-keung and Cheung Ching-yuen, eds., *Frontiers of Japanese Philosophy 4: Facing the 21st Century*. Nagoya: Nanzan Institute for Religion and Culture (2009), 7–21.

Chapter 5 was published in a previous version as "Four Things and Two Practices: Rethinking Heidegger Ex Oriente Lux," *Comparative and Continental Philosophy* 4/1 (2012), 53–74.

Chapter 6 appeared under the same title, "Practice, Samādhi, Realization: Three Innovative Interpretations by Nishitani Keiji," in *The Eastern Buddhist* 25/1 (Spring 1992), 8–20.

A version of Chapter 7 appeared as "Rousseau, Hakuseki, Hakuin: Understanding Self in Three Autobiographers," in Roger T. Ames, ed.,

Self As Person in Asian Theory and Practice. State University of New York Press (1994), 57-79.

Chapter 8 appeared as "A Walk Through Some Zen Landscapes of the Heart," in Hans-Georg Möller and Andrew K. Whitehead, eds., *Landscape and Travelling East and West: A Philosophical Journey*. London and New York: Bloomsbury (2014), 111–25.

A shorter version of Chapter 9 appeared as "Personal Autonomy: An Alternative View," in Jason Dockstader, Hans-Georg Möller and Günter Wohlfart, eds., *Selfhood East and West: De-Constructions of Identity*. Nordhausen: Verlag Traugott Bautz (2012), 221-36.

Chapter 10 was published under the same title, "Alternative Configurations of Alterity in Dialogue with Ueda Shizuteru," in *Comparative and Continental Philosophy* 14/2 (2022), 178–95.

A shorter version of Chapter 11 appeared as "Emptiness, History, Accountability: A Critical Examination of Keiji Nishitani's Standpoint," in *Zen Buddhism Today: Annual Report of the Kyoto Zen Symposium* 15 (1998), 97–117.

A version of Chapter 12 appeared as "The Alternative Normativity of Zen" in Raquel Bouso and James W. Heisig, eds., *Frontiers of Japanese Philosophy 6: Confluences and Cross-Currents*. Nagoya: Nanzan Institute for Religion and Culture (2009), 190–214.

Chapter 13 was published as "The Practice of Body-Mind: Dōgen's *Shinjingakudō* and Comparative Philosophy," in William R. LaFleur, ed., *Dōgen Studies*. Honolulu: University of Hawai'i Press (1985), 112–30.

Chapter 14 was published under the same title, "Negotiating the Divide of Death: Dōgen's Difference," in Steven Heine, ed., *Dōgen and Sōtō Zen*. Oxford: Oxford University Press (2015), 109–37.

A shorter version of the "Follow-up," co-authored by Mary Jo Maraldo, appeared as "Ante-originality in Japanese Pathway Arts," in the *American Philosophical Association Newsletter on Asian and Asian-American Philosophy* (Spring 2022), 7–11.

Lead-in

Alternatives open up the perspective we have on things and the words that depict theem. They shift our focus from things singled out to the relations existing among things, and from one-to-one relationships—twosomes—to a third that loosens their binding on our minds. They depolarize our thinking. Alternatives to binaries throw them into relief and reveal their premises and the limits of their relevance. They release the potency of distinctions to clarify problems, or of oppositions to solve them. Alternatives do not always have these fortuitous effects; they are not necessarily bound to be either good or bad. They do not replace the need for discernment, but their consideration can enable wider perspectives and wise choice. Those I have chosen to present in this book will earn their keep if they display these advantages.

The alternatives proposed here invite a re-examination of philosophical oppositions often taken for granted—those that pit mental against physical, normative against descriptive, agency against passivity, practice against theory, and others still. They seek options and reasons to prefer them. Often, the alternatives I advance complement rather than replace an opposition; sometimes they are meant to displace it, or to disengage a choice between two mutually exclusive possibilities. In no case do they dissolve traditional oppositions by reducing one side to the other, or combine parts of each side to form a new notion. Just as they deter any overarching synthesis, taken together they do not derive from any single principle, system, or unitary whole. The chapters of this book derive rather from lectures and papers given over the past three decades, and may be read in any order. My transitions between them now appear as an afterthought. If readers find other connections and contrasts, that too will fill the intention of these alternatives.

I find one non-linear link between them more prominent than others, and that is the thinking associated with Zen. As controversial as the meaning of that name is—and presented often enough as the negation of thought—Zen literature and Zen teachers have inspired me to examine a number of conceptual oppositions. While the alternatives presented here cannot be said to originate with Zen, I found their traces or tracks in Zen teachings that helped me identify them and locate counterparts in other philosophical traditions. The title of this book links these alternatives to "Zen tracks" precisely in order to indicate the open nature of their evidence in that tradition and others. But this is not a book about Zen. It neither takes the effects of that Buddhist tradition as its object of inquiry (as did my *Saga of Zen History*) nor presumes to teach Zen from the inside. Still, the understanding of Zen as self-investigation (己事究明), as the Japanese philosopher Nishitani Keiji amplified it, proved to be particularly expedient in tracking down the alternatives, which often range far beyond conceptions of selfhood. The philosophy of Nishitani's successor, Ueda Shizuteru, and the much earlier teachings of Zen abbots Dōgen and Hakuin, also served as sources that frequently expanded my focus.

If I place the principal resources of my alternatives in Japanese philosophical and religious traditions, it is only as I have tried to engage these traditions in interactions with others. I include this book in the series *Japanese Philosophy in the Making* because it draws from the font of resources I identify as Japanese philosophy. Like the previous two volumes, it includes interpretations and applications of philosophical texts in Japanese and other languages, but it focuses in particular on their potential to present alternatives. That, in turn, allows us to re-read volumes 1 and 2 as a series of alternatives. For example, in Volume 1, Japanese philosophy in contrast to Greco-European thought appears as an alternative to the usual "Japanese thought" versus "Western philosophy." Nishida's placing of *mu* (無) displays it as the obscure and indeterminate source of clear, determinate distinctions, and that placing also gainsays a translation like *nothingness* by undermining our tendency to substantialize everything. Nishida's notion of self-reflecting awareness presents an alternative to both the "pre-reflective" and the "nonreflective" self-awareness we read about in current philosophical literature. Volume 2 presents intercultural philosophy as an alternative to "comparative philosophy" and its usual contrary, "Western philosophy," for intercultural philosophy transgresses the divide between "East and West." Watsuji's ethics promotes an alternative to the priority of the individual and supports relational conceptions of dignity and human rights. Tanabe's metanoetics leads to alternative notions of responsibility and autonomy. The final essay alters the popular conception of "nature" as whatever is not human. And so forth.

As did the first two volumes, this third collection resists an attempt to weave the proposed alternatives into an overarching system of relations that would allow a test of their consistency with one another. Instead, it continues the momentum of altering familiar patterns of thinking. And, like the previous volumes, this collection seeks alternatives via the path of trans-lation, the transformation of textually-embedded problems, methods, and terminologies both across and within natural languages. Translations are modeled after their sources but inevitably alter them. (The Italian saying "*traduttore, traditore*" expresses a negative view of this alteration.) The alternative proposed at the end of this book regards a source as an "ante-original" that gives way to creativity. It presents an alternative way to understand repeated patterns and to release the creativity of modeling what has come before. I continue to advocate trans-lation (with a hyphen) as a mode of modeling the significance, of carrying on the import, of what has moved previous generations of thinkers. But this volume also intimates the source of creative language in silence—the silence known through forms of practice that first leave language behind and then evoke its disclosures. And so this book occasionally ventures beyond trans-lation to question the limits of interpretation and application, of language and text.

Each of the chapters presents a controversial topic or problem and develops an alternative to commonplace approaches or solutions. This lead-in will leave it to your reading to discovery what, precisely, the alternatives are. They are grouped in four sections.

The first section considers a way to understand religion in practice. Chapter 1, "Three Stories That Invite Us to Rethink Religious Relativism," frames the problem of relativism as it occurs when advocates of one religious tradition encounter challenges to the truth of their beliefs or the validity of their practices. Religious relativism conceives religious truths and moral values as necessarily relative to something, some external, variable condition such as their time in history, their cultural context, the language in which they are expressed, the gender or social class or singular experience of their adherents, the changing identity of "religion." Relativism would undermine claims to any singular, unchanging truth or moral conviction by demonstrating its absolute reliance on variable conditions. In modern, pluralistic cultures thoughtful religious people, seeking tolerance as an alternative to violence, have recognized three options to face the challenge of religious difference. They can conclude that such differences remain irreconcilable and can continue to insist on the singular truth of their own beliefs and practices; they can attempt to discover a common core of ultimate truth among the differences; or they can embrace difference as a sign of the common vitality of religions and the limitation of human understanding. All three options are unstable and reactive, likely to ensure continued challenges both personal and social. I invite us to take an alternative approach that inquires into the conditions under which the problem of religious relativism arises. If elements of religion are relative, what is the nature of the factors that condition them? We approach an answer via the third story that begins this chapter, recounting a dialogue between a Zen Buddhist philosopher and Christian theologians.

Where religious people rise to the challenge posed by significant differences in what they hold to be true and morally imperative, other thoughtful people step back from such convictions in order to assess them from a distance. They take a position that views the elements of religions objectively, as parts of the life or society in which they do not participate. They remain "outsiders," committed to truthful description, analysis, and critique that does not depend on the claimed truths or validity of their subject matter. Alternately, those that do commit themselves to one religion may remain outsiders to other religious communities or institutions. Controversies arise over the reliability of an outsider's stance or an insider's credibility—and over the possibility of belonging to two, seemingly incompatible religious traditions. Particularly when religious truths are conceived as matters of faith and religious ethics as matters of obligation, a detached, objective understanding seems to insiders to miss the point, and that point seems to outsiders to invite self-delusion and historical ignorance. Chapter 2, "Outsiders and Insiders of Zen, Turned Inside Out," takes a different tack. It begins with a focus on an exemplary case of what is supposed to be incommensurate: the stance of objective scholars of Zen and the viewpoint of Zen "insiders." For all the diversity within each stance, a clear opposition seems to unite one against the other (and it has been proclaimed by advocates on both sides): being a follower of Zen either enables or prevents an understanding of what Zen really is. We might say that it all depends on the definition of "Zen," but in the alternative I propose, the relevant meaning of "Zen" (or of Buddhist practice in general) remains the same, however unsettled its definition. What is altered is the mode of understanding, and what counts is the sort of practice that sustains this understanding.

Modes of understanding are the concern of hermeneutics. Traditionally, hermeneutics aims to clarify the conditions and presuppositions of the various ways that humans understand the world. Some of its practitioners placed understanding at the base of both scientific explanation and humanistic explication; others have made understanding to be the very way we have a world in the first place. The object of hermeneutics—what is to be understood—expanded from the texts we write and read to the formation of culture and to world-making in general. Its early proponents intended hermeneutics ideally to clarify how we make sense of the world and of whatever might enter the world from a transcendent source, as religious texts are often read to do. But our critical reading of twentieth-century hermeneutical theory undercuts this expansion and reveals it to be overly reliant on the understanding of texts in particular. Just how hermeneutics has oriented our understanding of worldly and world-transcending religion to discursive textual understanding—and how it has modeled language in general after textual language—is the concern of Chapter 3, "Understanding: An Alternative to the Hermeneutical Model." Our examples of religious and interreligious practices lead to an alternative that engages embodied rather than text-based understanding.

Chapter 4, "Practice: An Alternative Notion," opens the second section of this book. It delves deeper into the specific mode I find at the heart of "Zen practice" but certainly not exclusive to it alone. We will follow the tracks of a notion of practice that is exemplified in Dōgen and in Nishida, but is also traceable in Aristotle as well as Confucius (using these personal names to stand for a body of work). That notion offers an alternative to the conceit that Zen is unique among traditions of Buddhism or that Buddhist practice is unique among religious traditions. It helps clarify mystifying ideas such as Nishida's intuition that is action (and vice versa), and Dōgen's practice that is realization (and conversely). This alternative also directs us to a field of inquiry that undermines the traditional opposition between theory and practice, and makes more relevant the practice of philosophizing together.

A nuance of the alternative mode of practice shows up when we contrast it with descriptions in Martin Heidegger's early philosophy. Early on, Heidegger modeled our engagements in the world after goal-oriented activities; Heidegger's later work, where we find echoes of Daoist and Zen Buddhist thinking, does intimate the alternative. The mode of attentive practice that engages a carpenter, a cleaver, a potter, and a calligrapher variously exemplify the alternative and release it from its home in East Asian thought. This is the theme of Chapter 5, "Four Things and Two Practices: Taking Heidegger Farther East."

Within Buddhist thought, the emphasis on practice takes an intriguing turn in the interpretations of Nishitani Keiji. We may be familiar with how the medieval Zen master Dōgen weans us from understanding practice as a means to enlightenment. But Nishitani delves deeper into the usual summaries of Dōgen's view when he makes sense of saying that clouds moving across the sky, water flowing, leaves falling, and blossoms scattering are all forms of practice. Here, the alternative model, invoking purely "natural" phenomena, shifts our understanding of practice from the action of a willful subject to an activity released from subjective intention. Nishitani similarly intrigues us with his descriptions of *samādhi*, usually taken to mean an elevated state of mind, a practice of mental concentration that can lead to an understanding of things and conditions as they truly are. In contrast, Nishitani speaks of burning fire being fire-*samādhi*, and of falling leaves, flying birds, and swimming fish as manifestations of "*samādhi*-being." Then there is Nishitani's talk of "realization," which no longer refers simply to Buddhist enlightenment or awakening but expresses the "self-realization of reality." What all this might mean is the topic of Chapter 6, "Practice, *Samādhi*, Realization: Three Innovative Interpretations."

Reading Nishitani entices us to rethink a theme he seems to displace in his focus on selfless, embodied practice. The third section of this book, "Self and Others and In-between," draws his philosophy into the wider world. With his innovations in mind as a contrast, we return with new eyes to textual language and practices, and to the forms of selfhood they express. Chapter 7, "Writing the Self: The 'Autobiographic' Practices of Rousseau, Hakuseki, and Hakuin," follows the paths through which three writers explicitly construct themselves as authors of their own lives, and the paths by which practices of self-referential writing reconstruct and deconstruct senses of authorship. The chapter frames these three authors between two seeming extremes: the modern novelist Tōson's claim that he first discovered he had a self upon reading Rousseau's *Confessions*, and Zen master Hisamatsu's astonishing claim, "I do not die." As alternatives to one another, the examples together illuminate three areas: divergent senses of self along with their conceptual background, the controversial identity of autobiography, and the ways in which writing functions as an authorizing practice.

While diverse autobiographic practices virtually "write" different senses of self into being, certain startling expressions we find in Nishitani and Dōgen (such as "the practice of clouds moving, water flowing, and leaves falling") seem to empty any notion of a willfully practicing self. Other expressions like "heart" and "mind" (*kokoro* or 心) can indicate the core of the self in Zen traditions, but often in classical Zen literature it is a description of a natural landscape (山水) that expresses this "mindful heart." Some expressions are clearly metaphors, yet a metaphor is not merely a substitute word when it transposes a self-center into an environing world. How might we understand poetic verses that tell us mind *is* mountains, waters, and the great earth? Or sayings in indigenous traditions that echo the refrain: self and place are inseparable? If this kind of talk does not simply commit the "pathetic fallacy" of attributing human mind to unminded "natural" objects, what then might the mindful heart of a mountain mean? This is the question that provokes Chapter 8, "Finding the Self in Mountains: Zen Landscapes of the Mindful Heart."

The identities pondered in the chapters on self are two-sided. Poetic identifications of self with environing place initiated our inquiry in Chapter 8; one's identity as an autonomous self set up the questions in Chapter 7. One side conjoins; the other separates. If we consider them together, what happens to the meaning of personal autonomy? After all, autonomy defines the sort of self-determination and independence that characterizes our individual undertakings and makes ethical responsibility possible—whereas the notion of (non)self in Zen seems to empty selfhood of self-subsistence and so to undermine personal responsibility. Key to both sides is the question of what it means to be free. Drawing from examples in the Zen *Record of Linji* and in Nishitani, with surprising parallels in Confucius, Chapter 9, "Personal Autonomy: An Alternative View," follows the freedom of "according with all things."

If autonomy and selfhood are to be understood as relational, then the status of others as different from oneself is in question. In recent literature, the singular name for otherness is *alterity*, but its connotations make this term a two-faced Janus word. Otherness subjugates people when it is imposed on them; otherness can empower people whose difference is recognized. At times, the sense of alterity expands from the difference between singular selves to a totality in difference from any one of them—to the entire world that is "not self." Chapter 10, "Alternative Configurations of Alterity in Dialogue with Ueda Shizuteru," shows how this Kyoto School philosopher intimates four different configurations of alterity. Where Nishida's *Inquiry into the Good* seems ultimately to undermine difference by stressing "pure experience"—the "sole reality" that would explain everything—Ueda's reconstruction introduces a factor barely mentioned by Nishida. Ueda focuses on language, often claimed to differ from (pre-linguistic) pure experience, but shows us how it is (in my words) nothing other than pure experience. The rather abstract configuration of alterity in the guise of language becomes more concrete when we differentiate language from silence and then come to understand silence as both a source and a resting place for language. Ueda's interpretation of a poem by Rainer Maria Rilke illustrates the movement between the two, once again recognizing but contradicting difference. In a third excursion into alterity, Ueda interprets the familiar Zen Oxherding Pictures that begin with the difference between boy and ox, self and other, and that end (in Ueda's view) with an imagined conversation in a marketplace. Here, for a reason the chapter exposes,

Ueda's rendition of the classical Buddhist "not-two, not one" allows difference to emerge but not quite come to fruition. The chapter concludes by showing how Ueda's presentation of *renku* or linked verse offers a more dynamic model of alterity.

Chapter 11, "History from a Buddhist Perspective: Nishitani's Account and Accountability," examines another way that selves and communities have been differentiated—in terms of their histories. If it takes a landscape to define the self, Nishitani's work also places that self in time, and Buddhist practice and realization take on an uncommonly wide significance. "In bottomlessly embracing the endless past and endless future, we bring time to the fullness of time at each and every moment of time." Nishitani's conviction offers a fresh alternative to views of inevitable historical conditioning, not to speak of historical determinism. At the same time, it seems to flatten historical accounts that select some events as important and neglect others as a matter of course. It also seems to deflate the accountability we usually want to preserve. This chapter first explains the modern-day nihilism that Nishitani's proposal is intended to address, then interprets its meaning in contrast to Nietzsche's solution and to seeming parallels in postmodern deconstructions of history. We then can discern more clearly the problem of accountability: how can Nishitani's bare equivalence of moments allow for the possibility of value judgments that discriminate actions as well as events? An old Zen story points the way to a resolution, but only when we pursue the question of ethical normativity in Zen.

Chapter 12, "The Alternative Normativity of Zen," examines standard assumptions in normative ethics that (quite naturally) divides *is* and *ought*. The focus on this division may seem to narrow the scope of Nishitani's alternative sense of non-discriminating history, but it also offers a way to understand it more deeply. Stereotypes of Zen traditionally depict its ethical dimension as reliant on Mahāyāna precepts regulating individual monks and on Neo-Confucian mores governing society—all more or less in tension with Zen's proverbial freedom from ethical strictures— its (sometimes self-proclaimed) amoral antinomianism. This chapter takes another look at the nature of the ethical *ought* invoked by precepts and by ideals in general. Two discussions regarding the precept against killing—one by a contemporary Zen teacher, the other between Dōgen and his successor—bring the alternative into focus. For now, we may call it *declarative* in contrast to both *descriptive* and *imperative*. Its realization through practice is the crux of the matter.

The alternative notion of practice sketched in Chapter 4 is at the heart of Dōgen's Zen, the theme of section four. Dōgen's way to study the nature of body and mind, as presented in his *Shinjingakudō* (身心學道), opens our inquiry. In a manner that allows qualified comparison with Anglo-European philosophies, Dōgen takes the mind-body duo one facet at a time; he probes the manifestation called "body" (身) after that called "mind" (心)—the same heart-mind that offered us views of its landscapes. But Dōgen's way (道) to study (學) is the "Buddha Way" of practice that realizes the nondual nature of our being, rather than a method that reflects on conceptual and phenomenal identities and differences. It may seem utterly incongruent to place a medieval Japanese Buddhist sermon alongside contemporary Anglo-European analyses. Yet that very setting proves expedient when we see the power of contrast to illuminate unnoticed assumptions in classical and contemporary versions of the mind-body problem. We come to see how both sides avoid dogmatism—philosophers by continued questioning, Zen teachers by calling for continual practice, and both by bringing into play metaphors that connect phenomena and belie fixed, univocal concepts. Still, what might it mean to say that "mind [is] mountains and rivers, earth, sun, moon, and stars" or "fences and walls, tiles and stones"? This is the question that engages us in Chapter 13, "The Study of Body-Mind: Dōgen's Alternative."

For most of us, death appears as the end of one's life—the closure of the self's existence as a unique body-mind. For Dōgen, too, death seems to appear this way—until he turns our head around to see life as its own time, not passing away, and death as its own time, not an end, not coming and not taking one away. Dōgen's intriguing view aligns him with a few other philosophically-minded Buddhist teachers and divides them all from the Buddhism that takes care of the concerns of the populace, Dōgen's alternative also leaves my mind reeling. It apparently goes beyond the Mahāyāna equation of samsara (生死, birth and death) with nirvana. Indeed, it contradicts the cliché that the Japanese view life and death together when it intimates that birth or arising is independent of perishing or death, and vice versa. Perhaps the problem lies in the point of view from which we think of these realities—the first-, second-, and third-person perspectives. How Dōgen would liberate us from all three personal perspectives is the question that engages us in Chapter 14, "Negotiating the Divide of Death: Dōgen's Difference."

This book ends with a "Follow-up" that might re-turn perplexing philosophical problems to pleasant everyday pastimes. "Ante-Originality and the Alternative Creativity of Japanese Pathway Arts" describes a kind of modeling that contrasts with the typical goal of artistic practices. Neither mere copying nor original innovation, the mode of creativity practiced in many Japanese pathway arts (and elsewhere, too) can be called "ante-original," for it follows a model that precedes and takes priority over the production of original works. A look at how this occurs, and how art work is performance as much as artifact, brings the book to a temporary close. Its goal will be realized when you, the reader, thoughtfully engage and appraise its proposals.

Understanding Religions in Practice

1
Three Stories That Invite Us to Rethink Religious Relativism

One day in 552 CE, during the reign of Emperor Kinmei, a group of imperial attendants stood on the banks of a canal southwest of where the city of Nara stands today and heaved a statue of Shakyamuni Buddha into the current. The statue was, according to the story, the only Buddhist image in the land of Yamato, ancient Japan, and had been presented a few months before to the Emperor by emissaries from the Korean kingdom of Baekje. It must have been a daring act for these officials to throw this image into the water. I imagine their bodies shaking as much from fear as from the sheer weight of the gilt bronze figure. The superb craftsmanship that could embody the image of a superior being would have been awesome in itself, but, in addition, its presence was deemed powerful enough to rouse the wrath of indigenous deities who brought pestilence upon the land. The Emperor had allowed the Soga clan, who were managers of his estates and foreign affairs, to worship the foreign deity or *kami*, and soon afterwards plague struck and scores of people died. Rival clans to the Soga, the military Mononobe and the ritual specialists Nakatomi, persuaded the Emperor that the alien worship was at fault. Buddhism was officially disposed of, at least for a few years, until its proponents turned the table and attributed the illness of a Soga leader to the curse of the spurned Buddha-kami. Soga members convinced the successor Emperor Bidatsu to allow a Buddha image again. "Let thy forefather's god be worshipped," the Emperor proclaimed, but he withdrew his word when pestilence struck once more and the Mononobe clan blamed it on the alien worship. Officials flung the remains of another burnt Buddha image into the canal.[1] The next emperor, Yōmei, had a Soga mother, however, and the chronicles report that he "believed in the Law of the Buddha and reverenced the Way of the Gods." When he himself fell ill, he ordered that an image of the healing buddha Yakushi be made. Before it was finished Yōmei died, in 587, the year that the Soga clan drove the Mononobe and Nakatomi from power. Yōmei's sister, Empress Suiko, had the image completed and enshrined; this time it was not thrown into the canal. Buddhism, the textbooks tell us, was established as a state religion.[2]

The ancient chronicles tell of these events from the victor's point of view. Empress Suiko and her successors had the stories compiled and written down in an act that not only recorded events to legitimize their rule, but also helped to institutionalize the technology of writing, which must have been an astonishing advance in communication for preliterate Yamato people. Books were produced for the first time. What we call Buddhism was part of an imported cultural complex that included written language and formal iconography. The novel category of the Way (*dō* or *dao* 道), was introduced and allowed writers to represent a vast array of phenomena for the first time as Shintō, "the Way of the Kami," in contradistinction to the Way or the Law of the Buddha. New things were also represented in older, familiar categories. The Buddha at first was just a new if rival kami, and Buddhist temples were effectively shrines to house the new deity. Buddhism appeared as a superior technology (or magic) of healing and havoc-wreaking, medicine and meteorology, before it appeared as an ethical vision and

1. NIHON SHOKI, 102–3.
2. MATSUNAGA 1974, 11. Historians now relate a more complicated story, putting in question, for example, precisely which parties—the Mononobe and Nakatomi or Emperor Kinmei's family itself—were reluctant to accept the Buddha, a new foreign god, after all, whose recognition might imperil the emperor's claim to divine ancestry. See COMO 2008, 18–20. In any case, Suiko's successor was the regent Prince Shōtoku, who, according to the legends, secured the imperial connection to Buddhism.

a set of doctrines concerning salvation. Even after these dimensions of Buddhism became clear, to Yōmei's son Prince Shōtoku, for example, we cannot speak of a conversion to Buddhism and repudiation of Shintō, for there was no sense of one being right and the other wrong.[3] It would be misleading to see the conflict between the Buddhist Soga clan and the Shintō clans as a disagreement about doctrinal or ethical systems; it may even be anachronistic to call them Buddhist and Shintō. Certainly it is an anachronism to refer to this conflict principally as one between two "religions." It concerned rivalry over imperial control and the perceived threat or appeal of a foreign civilization. It did involve elements we regard as religious, but the compromise of Yōmei who "believed in the Law of the Buddha and reverenced the Way of the Gods" was not a relativistic stance that regarded two religions as equivalent in value or function.

One morning in 1549, in Kagoshima, the southernmost city of Japan, Francis Xavier, leader of a missionary team to Japan, is strolling through the grounds of a Zen temple with his new friend Ninshitsu, the abbot. The Spanish Jesuit has had no trouble in locating a site of Japanese religious practice. He notices some Zen monks seated in silent meditation, marvels at their unmoving concentration, and asks the abbot what they are doing. Ninshitsu grins and says, "Oh, some are calculating the contributions received from their followers during the past months. Others are thinking about how they might get better clothing and personal care. Still others are thinking of vacation and pastimes. In short, no one is thinking of anything important."[4] I imagine the Jesuit Father furrowing his brow, as puzzled by this remark as the Zen abbot was by Xavier's incessant questions about his beliefs. Is

---

3. "The Shōtoku Constitution" (JPSB, 35–9) exhibits an innovative attempt to harmonize the sources of early Japanese religiosity.
4. DUMOULIN 2005, 263. Dumoulin's source is P. Louis Frois, *Die Geschichte Japans*, translated and annotated by G. Schurhammer and E. A. Voretsch, Leipzig: Verlag der Asia Major, 1926, 7.

the soul immortal or does it perish with the body? Who created the world? What attributes does your god have? How can we win redemption from evil? Xavier and his Jesuit missionary successors attempted to debate their fundamental issues with Zen monks during the next four decades. Their letters report of several converts, but also of much consternation with the inconsistent or incomprehensible views of the Buddhists. One (temporary) convert, who became the Jesuit Brother Fabian, cites a typical baffling response: "The true law [Dharma] of the law is no law; this law—no law, is nonetheless law...."[5]

I suspect that most of the early converts were impressed by the kindness and concern of the Christian missionaries rather than persuaded by arguments that appealed to "the person's natural knowledge of God and... the moral law revealed in one's conscience," as one missionary, Cosme de Torras, put it. In *Zen Buddhism, A History: Japan,* Heinrich Dumoulin intimates the point I want to make when he writes of one nobleman, Ōtomo Yoshihige, who finally "reached a decision and became a Christian." Baptism meant repudiation of his practice of Zen; there could be only one true faith. When the Buddhists appealed to *upāya* or expedient means and tried to explain that teachings were adapted to the hearers' level of understanding, the Jesuits took this as a kind of irresponsible evasion, "contrary to one's obligation to recognize the truth."[6] Nevertheless, the subsequent persecution of Christians that began in 1587 had little to do with their exclusivist truth claims. The shogunate banned Christianity for nearly three hundred years because it was perceived as a precursor to Western colonization. Christianity was in fact part of a cultural complex that

---

5. DUMOULIN 2005, 268; based on the translation of Pierre Humberclaude in *Monumenta Nipponica* 1 (1938), 529. Fabian was the Jesuit name of Fukansai Habian, who as a convert first insisted that religious teachings were mutually exclusive and defended the singular truth of Christianity against Buddhism, Confucianism, and Shintō in 1605; then, in his *Deus Destroyed* of 1620, completely reversed his conclusions and propounded the total falsity of Christian teachings. See JPSB, 1038–46.

6. DUMOULIN 2005, 267, 264 and 268.

valued accelerated trade with foreign nations and presented Japan with gunpowder, rifles, and the might of great ships armed with cannons.

In the fall of 1981, in a small seminar room at the School of Theology in Claremont, California, a group of scholars gather around a table and engage in polite but animated conversation. They have been talking together for two days, and one of them repeatedly presses the others for clarification of their stance on a passage in Paul's Epistle to the Philippians, the famous *kenosis* passage about Christ emptying himself, becoming man, and dying on the cross. Later in the conversation, someone else questions that person's understanding of Buddhism. The group consists of a Zen Buddhist philosopher, Abe Masao, and several Christian theologians; it is the Buddhist who is interested in the *kenosis* passage and whose understanding of Buddhism is being questioned. Through the years since then their dialogue has grown in frequency, scope, and participants.[7] One outcome is the book, *The Emptying God*, containing a presentation by Abe, responses by the others, and Abe's rejoinder.[8] For the book, three more theologians, representing Roman Catholic, Jewish, and feminist traditions, have joined the discussion.

Abe presents their common ground as the task of overcoming irreligion, scientism, and ideologies that negate the significance of religion. Yet even that point does not go unquestioned. Catherine Keller finds that project anachronistic, and proposes that the real threat today is not irreligion but "barbaric rereligion," the religious reintrenchment of oppressive values.[9] But everyone agrees that this interreligious dialogue is no longer confined to mutual understanding and tolerance. For this group it is about the mutual transformation of religions. Abe thinks that Christianity must come to terms with the kenotic passage,

---

7. The discussions that continue and expand the conversation reported here take place in venues such as the Society for Buddhist-Christian Studies, its journal and newsletter, and the Japan Society for Buddhist-Christian Studies.
8. COBB and IVES 1990.
9. KELLER 1990, 104.

which suggests, to him at least, that it is of the very nature of God to be self-negating. Repeating a variation of his favorite formula, Abe says God is not God and precisely because God is not God, God is truly God. This formula applies not only to Christ as the Son of God, but to God Godself and by extension to the human self.[10] Abe is urging the Christian theologians to recognize in their own tradition something close to the Buddhist philosophy of the emptiness and relationality of all things.

David Tracy, the Catholic theologian, responds, "I am not persuaded that [this] is the way for Christians... to think about God." Tracy does suggest that the Christian tradition is deeply conditioned by its geography and history, but he backs off from a full-fledged relativism: "If Christian speculative thought had emerged in East Asia rather than West Asia, might it not have taken a course very like the one which Abe suggests.... It might have. But it did not." Tracy thinks it possible to abandon the Greco-Roman conceptuality, but not the Jewish religious roots, of the Christian tradition and still retain "ultimate theism," as he calls it.[11] He invokes the notion of an "Ultimate Reality" whose relational structure might be commonly affirmed by Buddhists and Christians even while they disagree about its personal nature. Abe, for his part, is adamant that Buddhism cannot accept the notion of a transcendent ruler of the universe or savior outside

---

10. The locus classicus of this formula, stating that self-identity requires self-negation, is a passage in the Diamond Sutra; as adapted by NISHITANI (1961, 118) it becomes: Fire is not fire, therefore it is fire. Abe's own formulations are: "The Son of God is not the Son of God (for he is essentially and fundamentally self-emptying); precisely because he *is not* the Son of God, he *is* truly the Son of God (for he originally and always works as Christ, the messiah, in his salvational function of self-emptying." "Self is not self (for the old self must be crucified with Christ); precisely because it is not, self is truly self (for the new self resurrects with Christ)." "God is not God (for God is love and completely self-emptying); precisely because God is not a self-affirmative God, God is truly a God of love (for through complete self-abnegation God is totally identical with everything including sinful humans)." ABE 1990, 11, 12 and 16.

11. TRACY 1990, 135–6.

one's self.[12] In effect, he focuses on doctrines implicit particularly in the Japanese Zen Buddhist tradition, and he disregards the functional significance of devotional practices in Buddhism that are directed to a transcendent Other.[13]

WHAT IS THE PROBLEM WITH RELIGIOUS RELATIVISM?

Abe Masao and his dialogue partners were in a position to be relativists. They might have reached the conclusion that their doctrinal differences were ultimately reconcilable, or were due to contingent factors that left intact a common core of ultimate truth. In fact, they did recognize how radically conditioned their respective traditions and understandings are, and they could have denied that differences remain ultimate and decisive. In spite of much mutual influence and personal change, however, they continued to adhere to the truth they found in their own tradition and to regard relativism as problematic. Francis Xavier and his Japanese acquaintances, on the other hand, were not in a position to be relativists. They lacked comprehension of each other's views, comparative knowledge of their own tradition, and willingness to discover truth in the other. Ancient Emperor Yōmei's accommodation of the Law of the Buddha and the Way of the gods was not a relativist concession because he did not think in terms of a possible equivalence or a possible incompatibility of the two. He promulgated a division of labor in the work of the gods, as it were.

What then is required for relativism to arise as a problem? The answer to this question will, I think, significantly displace religious relativism as an intractable problem. Relativism appears as a problem that undermines the truths of a religion, the beliefs it advances,

12. ABE 1990, 29.
13. One example of a doctrinal and devotional stream of Buddhism ignored by Abe is the "Pure Land" tradition directed to Amida Buddha as "Other-power." See MARALDO 2019A, 178–208 and 264–85, for interpretations of Other-power by the twentieth-century Japanese philosophers Tanabe Hajime and Kuki Shūzō.

the moral codes it promotes, the practices it advocates—when these beliefs, morals, or practices conflict with others that demand equal recognition and validity. Relativism threatens to reduce unchanging, unconditional truths to contingent and variable factors. But relativism itself essentially depends upon prior conditions and assumptions. Our three stories suggest the kind of contrast necessary for understanding when and why religions appear to be relative and problematic. The stories serve as a lead-in to analyze the conditions of religious relativism in a very general sense. Within the wide array of phenomena we associate with religion, just what elements are subject to the problem of relativism? Under what circumstances? For whom? What are the proposed solutions, or what might obviate the problem? And taking a step back from these questions, we may first of all ask about the *referents* of relativism: the nature of *that to which* elements of religions are said to be relative.

WHAT ARE RELIGIONS SUPPOSED TO BE RELATIVE TO? UNDER WHAT CIRCUMSTANCES?

In order for relativism to arise as a problem to be (re)solved, four basic conditions are discernible. There must be (1) an awareness of differences among things grouped together, but there must also be (2) an interest in reconciling the differences, so that (3) they must appear incompatible in some sense. Truth claims exhibit these qualities, of course, but so also do beliefs, interpretations, values, and perhaps methods and practices. Finally, there must be (4) a distinction between what is taken to be different and what is meant to explain its difference from other alike things. Taking the element of religious beliefs, for example, we can be aware of differences among them; we can recognize that they seem incompatible, and we can be interested in reconciling the differences, not merely noticing that they exist. For us to consider these different beliefs as a problem of relativism, we must also refer them to some factor that is meant to explain, in part at least, why one belief differs from another.

The most commonly named factors are the particular society, culture, language, and history in which the belief emerges. We may see a religious belief as relative to, or deeply conditioned by, a particular culture, history, or language.[14] Each of these factors names a set of conditions that both differentiate the belief from others and render it comparable to others. My belief, for example, may differ from yours not only because of evidence available to me and what I admit as evidence, but also because of my cultural, linguistic, and historical background. Yet the fact that culture, language, and history also condition your belief makes it all the more possible for us to compare our beliefs. What sets our beliefs apart also provides the terms for placing them together. The factors can both divide and unite because they both differentiate and universalize human behavior.

Take the factor of culture, for example. In the past, the anthropological notion of culture has been a way of distinguishing humans from other animal species, and therefore of naming something that is universally human. Anthropologists and ethologists today may dispute the view that only humans exhibit culture, where culture refers to the learned behavior and tool-making that some species generally are capable of but not others.[15] In either case, culture is not only a generalizing factor; it is at the same time a way of differentiating one group—human or nonhuman—from another. Culture in fact exists only in a plural form, as cultures, which is to say that structured group *diversity* is what

---

14. I mention religious beliefs as the type of thing that can be relative, but I do not take it for granted that all religions have "ultimate sacred propositions" as anthropologist Roy RAPPAPORT (1971) maintained, or even have postulates that can be called true or false according to some standard. Certainly not all "religions" place primary importance on dogmas or doctrines.

15. For example, SAFINA (2020, 33) rhetorically asks, "isn't it obvious that other animals don't have human culture? Whales have whale culture. Elephants have elephant culture." The question then is "What are the cultures of various species…? Who are we here with?"

is universal. "Culture" is a universal concept that primarily denotes *difference*, the difference that distinguishes some biological classes of animals from others as well as the differences between one group and another within the same species. Different groups of humans display different cultures, we say, or different groups of elephants exhibit different cultural traits. We might even say that the more cultures there are, the better the term "culture" applies to humans or the respective species, notwithstanding the idea of an emerging "global culture."

The category of language follows a similar logic. Language is cited as something that differentiates humans, in degree or in kind, from other animals, but it also differentiates one group of humans from another. Language exists as languages, and any universal theory of language must be tested against the plurality of actual languages. History as a category, however, seems to be dissimilar. We are used to speaking not only of the distinct histories of divergent peoples and states, but also of one human history, especially since the nineteenth-century idea of universal history. Ideas, too, have their history, and so also do natural phenomena, at least insofar as history refers simply to progressive change through time. But human history, not to speak of natural history, does not seem to exist necessarily in the plural form in the way that culture and language do. Nevertheless, the category of history functions as a factor in relativism insofar as it differentiates human groups, that is, insofar as there are different histories or distinct sets of historical conditions. The categories of history, language, and culture all attempt to name factors that multiply human common denominators. A practical consequence of the use of such categories is that the description of any particular culture will depend upon its interaction with other cultures; and we can say the same of any history or language as well. We could also mention gender and social class as frequently named factors that relativize, and we could show that these categories follow the same logic.[16]

16. Anthropologists have long made us aware of the diversity of gender classifications

A consideration of factors should not omit the *personal* conditions often said to relativize a religious position. To regard something as relative to the person, however, is to refer to gender and social class, to cultural, linguistic, and historical conditions as they are particularized in an individual. Unless there is some unconditioned essence to the individual that could serve as a referent, any reference to something personal inevitably involves the other factors we have mentioned. Each of the named factors seems to involve all the others. To say that a belief is relative to a particular culture is to imply that it is relative, in some degree, to the history and language of a particular group of individuals. The choice of which factor to name as the relativizing factor seems to be a matter of focusing on certain kinds of conditioning but not in principle excluding others. The factors that make a religious position relative are themselves relative to one another. What a particular culture *is* depends in part upon its history and the language(s) of its members; a people's history depends in part upon cultural and linguistic conditions, and so forth.

What about appeals to a religious experience that would ground religion in something prior to layers of conceptual beliefs and social conditions? "Religious experience," however vague its identity and disputed its occurrence, frequently names an element of religion that is supposed to be sui generis yet basic to the root source of religions, and that is thought to be undergone subjectively and personally yet directed to something taken as objective and real for all. Many depictions of religious experience describe it as coming upon the person from a source transcendent to or independent of one's personal life— and not a necessary consequence of one's beliefs or, as one scholar says, "not as the result of some deliberate practice undertaken to produce

---

in different cultures. There are often more than two recognized genders, and sometimes when a people speaks of two genders, they are not the ones we might expect. D. TAYLOR (1977, 61) notes that for the Arawak peoples of South America, the genders are (1) male Amerindian and (2) everybody and everything else.

an experience."[17] Debates about religious experience are complicated by the circularity of the term: empirically-minded scholars treat it as a concept, but regard concepts as deriving from experience. The controversy is further challenged by claims that some experiences cannot be grasped conceptually at all. Any analysis would then pertain at best to descriptions and not to the experience itself. Yet the content of experiences identified as religious does seem to depend upon factors both shared and variable. People raised in Buddhist traditions do not have visions of the Virgin Mary, and Christians do not have deathbed visions of the Buddha Amida.[18] Supposedly ineffable mystical experiences, as one variety of religious experience, seem to depend upon the personal history and memory of the subject, as do other subjective and more mundane experiences that defy clear description in words. What a cup of coffee tastes like to me will change radically if I think I am about to drink a cup of wine. Critics are quick to point out the factors that relativize religious experience and explain it away as the result of contingent variables. They often seek to undermine its status as a sui generis foundation for non-relative religious beliefs.[19] What goes unnoticed is the fact that the more mediated one's experience is, by factors such as language, culture, and history, the more likely it is to be similar to the experiences of others, and therefore more ascertainable and empirically valid. And again, these generalizing factors are themselves all interdependent.

As a consequence of the interdependence of relativizing factors, formulations that *relativize* something are unlike those that *reduce* it to something else. A reductive description is one that refers a phenomenon to some more basic factor that allegedly provides an adequate

17. WEBB 2017.
18. BECKER (1984) invokes the notion of religious experience to validate Pure Land Buddhism in the way that other religious traditions are validated.
19. See, for example, RUNZO (1986, 101), who argues contra Rudolf Otto that a sui generis experience (and indeed all supposedly ineffable mystical experiences), requires some conceptual schema to be intelligible at all.

explanation by itself. A Freudian reductive strategy, for example, attempts to explain religious beliefs by interpreting them solely as illusory wish-fulfillments. In contrast, a relativist depiction of beliefs might very well refer them to psychological motivations among other things. To relativize is not to reduce.

WHAT, IF ANYTHING, IS RELATIVE TO A RELIGION?

The category of religion itself seems to be like the other general factors that relativize things. Religion purportedly names something universally human, but it exists only in plural form. The description of any religion must take into account its history as well as the cultures and languages of its adherents, and its relation to other religions.

To be sure, these statements about religion are not beyond controversy. Some scholars dispute the universality of religion. Clifford Geertz, for example, questions whether "religion" and other cultural phenomena such as "marriage," "kinship," and even "shelter," are meaningful universals.[20] We may agree with him that the category of "religion" is empirically not well defined. Yet it is not clear whether the lack of definition means that this category is inapplicable to some cultures, or merely that some cultures do not have a category like religion. In any case, Geertz does employ the singular term "religion" as a construct to orient a line of inquiry into human behavior; religion is a certain kind of symbol system.[21] Wilfred Cantwell Smith has argued that it is an invention of the European Enlightenment to identify religions as distinct and supposedly incompatible doctrinal systems, such as Christianity, Buddhism, and Islam.[22] Cantwell Smith's thesis finds support in the work of Samuel Preuss, who demonstrates how the concept and study of religion historically emerged from the criticism

20. GEERTZ 1973, 43.
21. Ibid., "Religion as a Cultural System," 90 ff.
22. W. C. SMITH 1962 and 1967.

of religious faith.²³ Their work points to the fact that the very notion of religion is relative to history and culture. Yet other scholars suggest that if religions have become relativized, the category of religion has not. Peter Homans argues that the "history of religions" movement implies a defense of the idea that religion is a universal phenomenon,²⁴ and Roland Robertson claims that "religion" as a Western, recently globalized, category "encapsulates the modern sense of 'what we have lost.' It is part of modernity's *nostalgia*."²⁵ The critiques suggest that the supposed universal of "religion" is more like a phantom beneath a vast array of diverse phenomena that could be organized quite differently, destroying the common ground of comparison. Even so, the critiques admit that the category of religion is at least one historical way of representing and studying human experience.

Ironically, and at the other end of the spectrum, the twentieth-century Japanese philosopher Nishida Kitarō wrote idealistically of the essence of religion, an essence he identified with a religious awareness as universal and as individual as the awareness of death.²⁶ Nishida wrote of the great historical religions, in the plural, as manifestations of one basic human awareness that transcends cultural conditioning. I find his view ironic because the category of religion entered Japanese culture relatively late, in the 1860s. Japanese intellectuals resurrected an old term, *shūkyō* (宗教), and gave it a new meaning as a translation of the Western category in their attempt not only to organize patterns in Japan, but also to introduce the Western ideal of the separation of religion and state and to place Japanese culture on a par with Western powers. Nevertheless, this historical context shows only that the notion of religion is culturally and historically relative, not that it is inapplicable to times and peoples that did not have the concept.

23. PREUSS 1987, 152.
24. HOMANS 1987, 71.
25. ROBERTSON 1988, 128.
26. For elaboration, see MARALDO 2017, 127–57.

Scholars do differ radically about the universality and plurality of religion, and we would do all a disservice by attempting a definition that would encompass all views. In fact, all of the factors or categories I have named—history, culture, language, gender, social class—are similarly controversial, unsettled, and polysemic. But as terms used in discussions about relativism they function in an equivalent manner. What about the term "religion"? Does it also function to relativize human expressions and behavior? We speak of religious beliefs as relative to history, culture, language, class, and sometimes even gender. Why is it that we do not ordinarily speak of other factors as relative to religion?[27]

There are, to be sure, legal precedents of naming a religion as a reason to relativize a law or edict that otherwise unconditionally binds a population in general. In the United States, for example, the Supreme Court has ruled that a religious group can use certain substances ("drugs") in their "worship services" that are otherwise generally proscribed. And courts of law grant "religious exemptions" to generally binding regulations in the name of "religious freedom." In these examples, something promulgated as generally valid or binding is made relative to a religion. But that is the exception.

I suspect that religion is not commonly named as a relativizing factor because of a tendency to emphasize the normative aspect of religions over other, more symbolic aspects. On the one hand, the normative dimension of doctrines and expressed values deals with matters that can easily be considered compatible or incompatible, conflicting or harmonious, right or wrong—thus making them likely candidates for relativizing. But on the other hand, the normative dimension sets standards *relative to which* things are compared. It provides guidelines or measures that are meant to be applied equitably and uniformly if not universally. A measure cannot function if it

---

27. MARALDO 2021 examines the notion of history relative to Buddhist and, in particular, Zen traditions. The essays in NEUSNER 1990 also explore the religious relativity of concepts of history.

is relative to the things it measures. The problem of relativism arises, rather, when we compare measures and norms with each other and seek to determine which are better, or which one is the right one. That problem becomes more manageable but also more challenging when we ask what sorts of things are amenable to a particular measure, and what that measure overlooks. What indeed does the emphasis on the normative dimension overlook when it comes to religion? I suspect it overlooks a tacit assumption that religion is not supposed to exist in plural form, that there *should* be only one expression of truth corresponding to one ultimate reality, that if religions do in fact provide differing measures, then it is sad fact. In other words, matters are not supposed to be relative to a *religion*, because there ought not be different religions. At least, that seems to be the underlying assumption that takes doctrines and ethics as the core of a religion. When we focus on other dimensions of religion, on ritual, myth, art, music, practice, etc., we do not suppose that the more uniform or univocal, the better. On the contrary, we may come to see that, in these areas, the more variety there is, the more descriptive or true to experience the expression is. Wendy Doniger O'Flaherty sees myths as an example of a matter where variation is needed to express truth.[28] The same may be supposed of other narrative forms, and of rituals, religious practices, and material embodiments of religion in art, architecture, and music, perhaps also in the institutionalized organization of religious communities.[29]

It would seem that socio-cultural approaches to the study of religion would be most aware of the value of variation, insofar as the

---

28. PANDIAN (1991, 140) summarizes O'Flaherty's view in this way: "To the believer, the repetition of the myth in several versions renders the myth true in conveying the meaning." See O'FLAHERTY 1973, 36.

29. Variation may be an aspect of dogmatic truths as well. The variation in (Roman Catholic) Christian dogma appears in the form of the history of dogma, which for Karl Rahner is not primarily the sequence of different dogmas but rather the necessity of continually re-interpreting and re-stating the truth of dogmas defined in the past. Similarly, we might ask why there are (canonically) four gospels and not merely one; and why there is a plurality of theologies within the gospels.

socio-cultural sciences seek adequate description and not adjudication of claims and values. Why is it then that these approaches, which would seem to relativize things the most, rarely specify things as relative to a religion? Could it be that a mirror image of the European Enlightenment construction of religion is still operative in these approaches? The work of Wilfred Cantwell Smith and J. Samuel Preuss suggests again that the Enlightenment created the category of religion as a foil to attack the notion of revealed truth. We may hypothesize that Enlightenment scholars attacked the notion of revealed truth in the same breath as they constructed a model of the one true scientific method. It may be a sign of the prevailing value of unitary truth today that pluralism appears as a problem and that so-called postmodernism is seen as fragmentation. In this context, it is not so much that sacred religious truths are debunked as vulnerable, contingent phenomena. Rather, religion appears as debunked science.

So far, our reflections have connected the problem of relativism in religion with an emphasis on its normative dimension. More specifically, the emphasis has been on the doctrinal side of the normative dimension, to the relative neglect of the ethical side. Even the debate about the status of religious experience is often skewed toward the doctrinal, normative dimension of religions.[30] To what degree does the problem of ethical relativism similarly arise due to an emphasis on the doxastic side of ethics? Does the perceived incompatibility of ethical values arise from a tendency to express values in the form of doctrinal statements and to ignore the more symbolic and experiential dimension of social values? These are questions that deserve further investigation.

For now, we may note that an emphasis on any one of the dimensions of religion is bound to deemphasize other aspects, and that therefore a variety of approaches best suits the study of religion. Similarly,

---

30. PROUDFOOT (1985), for example, claims that religious experience must be understood in the context of doctrines. See also the essays in RUNZO AND IHARA 1986.

the normative dimension itself is subject to a variety of interpretations, only some of which see the normative as providing a measure. Feminist ethics, for example, provides normative role models other than measurement, namely, relationship and care.[31] Other models that are normative but not a matter of measure are also evident, as we shall see.

FOR WHOM IS RELIGIOUS RELATIVISM A PROBLEM? AND WHAT IS THE WAY OUT?

Let us next refocus the question of what makes religious relativism a problem by asking *for whom* it becomes problematic, and what are their possible responses. Again, we may confine the discussion to the normative, doctrinal dimension of religions. Who considers the relativism of religious beliefs a problem? Not the staunch believer, utterly convinced of the truth of his or her belief—unless outwardly unwavering conviction is also a sign of inner insecurity about the relative status of one's beliefs within a pluralistic culture. Nor is relativism a problem for the indifferent atheist or agnostic, or the person simply unconcerned with religion—unless indifference towards religious belief is a symptom of avoidance of problems one would rather not face. Insecurity and avoidance may indeed be responses, on a psychological level, to a perceived threat of relativism. To pursue this possibility, we would need to establish two sorts of connections: between conviction and insecurity, or indifference and avoidance, on the one hand; and, on the other hand, between cultural pluralism and the cultural value placed upon being right.

To some, the relativism of religious beliefs may appear not as a psychological threat but as a conceptual and social challenge. Thoughtful believers and theologians may take one of several stances toward the pluralism of belief. Logically, they may insist on the existence of some absolute truth under pain of being incoherent otherwise. If we claim

---

31. See, for example, the essays in GILLIGAN et al. 1990.

that there are no absolute truths, then that statement as well cannot be unconditionally true, it is argued. This argument depends upon confining truths to logical propositions or statements, and upon disallowing contradiction as something that defeats the purpose of argumentation. When the argument is applied to religious beliefs, it therefore relegates beliefs to the form of propositions of the sort "I believe that..." with the "that" clause counting as a truth claim. It is, however, a big step from stating that some belief must be true to stating which one it is. Most thoughtful believers and theologians today are aware not only of the plurality of available religious beliefs but also of the next logical possibility: that none of them is exclusively and absolutely true.[32] This is the conclusion of critiques that reduce religion to non-religious motivations or factors.

Another response to relativism takes seriously the incompatibility of various religious positions but finds hope for reconciliation in the evolution of religion and theology. All positions, this response goes, are indeed rooted in personal, social and cultural conditions, and thus should be understood as partial perspectives and attempts at comprehending the one reality there is. That comparative measure is what allows us to judge their relative validity. This is the "critical relativism" of George Rupp in his book *Beyond Existentialism and Zen*. Here the term *relative* implies not yet adequate, and *critical* implies that one religious position can become right or better. For Rupp, that one is the position which uncompromisingly resists evil, is socially committed, and yet allows for unconditional, divine acceptance.[33] Rupp's argument avoids the stricture against contradiction in classical logic and

---

32. RUNZO (1986) defends a form of conceptual relativism which acknowledges this challenge but argues that an absolute commitment of faith is decisive. Rather than examining the relative role and senses of faith in various traditions, however, he weighs his analysis heavily toward the epistemology of theistic beliefs founded ideally on the possibility that we can articulate a single correct schema "such that there is only one set of actual truths" (57).
33. RUPP 1979, 82–3.

finds truth in the process of reconciling opposites toward an ideal. That ideal remains the unitary expression of religion—true to the degree that it grasps "the one reality there is."

Other theologians and philosophers pursue a more classical line of reasoning but resist confining religious truth to logical propositions or positions. They find truth, in some form or another, in all present religions. They see themselves as moving from the pre-Enlightenment posture that one has to be right, and from the Enlightenment posture that all could be wrong, to a postmodern view that all could be right. This move occurs in recent work with two emphases. Some scholars like Huston Smith seek one perennial philosophy in different traditions and argue that the world's great religions are different paths to the same goal.[34] Others such as John Hick celebrate pluralism and see the varieties of religious expressions as different manifestations of the same ultimate reality.[35] Hick more specifically proposes a criterion of the truth of religions, namely, their soteriological effectiveness. To what degree do expressions and practices of the various religions bring about salvation? This would seem a very theological and slippery criterion, since salvation is a concept internal to religions and means different things for different religions. But Hick attempts to generalize the criterion by defining salvation as a transformation from human-centeredness to "Reality-centeredness."[36] The meaning of these terms needs further clarification, but here we may merely note the direction of Hick's response to the problem of relativism. Both he and Huston Smith end up privileging the unity in diversity by their notions of one goal and one ultimate reality. They also apparently ignore non-soteriological religions, such as Shintō and Greco-Roman religion. Perhaps they regard this type as irrelevant to modern humanity, and they could

---

34. H. SMITH 1987.
35. HICK 1989, 373.
36. Ibid., 36–54.

presumably argue that their category of religion is stretched to include this type.[37]

We have been asking who it is that considers the relativism of religious beliefs a problem. We should not overlook the numerous participants in traditional religions who do not see beliefs as the central matter of their religion, and yet who do not espouse relativism. Our second story above mentioned the sixteenth-century Jesuits who insisted on the centrality of doctrine and of the one and only truth. In contrast, the German Jesuit Hugo Enomiya-Lassalle (1898–1990) found no contradiction in pursuing Zen meditation and kōan practice to the point of becoming an acknowledged Zen teacher, a Jesuit Zen master. In New York City, Bernard Tetsugen Glassman (1939–2018) led students in Zen practice as a certified teacher in the Sōtō lineage, and yet continued to observe the Jewish rituals of his ancestors. Teachers such as these do not consider one practice or teaching as good as another, and dabble in whatever suits them. They personally vouch for the traditions they have faith in, and they justify their recommendation of particular religious traditions not by logical argumentation but by an appeal to single-minded practice. Commitment to and responsibility for what one is doing become criteria of truth. Their position is still normative, but no longer a matter of comparison to a measure. Their emphasis on an investigation of experience seems to position them closer to a purely descriptive stance toward religious doctrines.

A purely descriptive account would view religions as neither right nor wrong. That would seem to be the stance of scholars who investigate the structures, functions, or expressions of religions with a view to elucidate them. Is relativism a problem for them? It might be, if they have a philosophical commitment to adjudicate conflicting claims or descriptions. The relevant conflict here is between descriptions that

---

37. Chapter 3 in the present volume reconsiders the category of "world religions" that these scholars presuppose.

the particular religion provides and those that the scholar gives. (The chapters that follow in this section examine how practices alter the descriptive stance.) The scholar can either articulate and attempt to justify criteria, or acquiesce to a basic conflict of interpretations, each of which says that the other misses the point. On the other hand, scholars may see relativism not as a problem to be overcome but as a phenomenon or a feature of the history of religions. This is the response of Frederick Streng in his article on truth in the *Encyclopedia of Religion*.[38] Streng describes a vast variety of meanings of truth and of criteria for validity, with absolutely no mention of the problem of relativism and no attempt to evaluate the various criteria. The problem might also be obviated by recognizing religions as inherently pluralistic. Without mentioning relativism, James Heisig argues that the very existence and persistence of religious diversity is evidence of the human search for completion that has no single proper object but necessarily takes multiple doctrinal and symbolic forms.[39] Insistence on singular expressions of truth would in effect betray our common ground for believing in God or gods, or other forms of transcendence.

Other scholars name relativism as a sign of the vitality of religion in human societies. For some, this view would be plausible to the extent that the relativism did not affect the scholar's methodology. Mircea Eliade seems to have celebrated relativism among religions, but Ninian Smart finds even "the most detached and scholarly" of his writings aimed at an Orthodox Christian redemption from "the exile which deprives us of saving symbols."[40] Still other scholars proclaim the relativity of scholarship itself loudly and clearly.[41] Some call objec-

---

38. STRENG 1987.
39. HEISIG 2019, 77 and 127–8. Heisig's point is not without its own objective. His argument is directed toward a "theological commons" where all participants can recognize the priority of the survival of the earth as the concrete environment that sustains us and all forms of life.
40. SMART 1989, 506.
41. "...contemporary interpretive anthropology is nothing other than relativism, rearmed and strengthened for an era of intellectual ferment...." (MARCUS AND FISCHER

tivity a myth, the myth of objectivism.[42] They find redeeming value in a relativism that inquires into the diversity of modes of representation and can thus be self-critical. They value cultural diversity much as a biologist values diversity in a gene pool for the survival of a species and the well-being of the earth.

Religions provide modes of representation that can be the subject of critique in two senses. First, religions are so pervasive in human cultures that they are bound to influence the questions, concepts, and methodologies of scholarship, even of the scientific study of religion that arose as a critique of it. These influences can and should be investigated comparatively by both scholars and theologians for their respective self-critiques.[43] Secondly, if scholarship recognizes that its methods and modes are relative, it might well allow itself to be relative to religion in a deeper way. That is, it can be open to religion as cultural critique and as a critique of cultural sciences.[44] These approaches may be relative to religion, but the relativity of religions to other factors is not necessarily problematic.

Why religious relativism arises as a problem is illustrated, in a nutshell, in the three stories that began this exercise. The first two stories are examples of encounters that might have generated the problem of religious relativism but did not. Their contrast with the third story reveals the conditions under which that problem arises. Taken together, the stories help us see how the problem of religious relativism

---

1986, 33).

42. JOHNSON 1987, xxiii et passim; LAKOFF 1987, 157 et passim.

43. Ninian Smart's aforementioned critique of Mircea Eliade is an example of the alleged influence of a particular religion on the methodology of the history of religions. SCHOPEN 1997 and his many responses exemplify the controversy about Protestant biases in the study of Buddhism. The essays in LOPEZ 1995 discuss the religion-affiliated influence of colonialism and nationalism on the study of Buddhism.

44. The work of Reinhold Niebuhr is a classic example of how neoliberal religion provides trenchant critiques of contemporary politics and culture. The essays in BYRD 2020 provide examples of how religions have critiqued modernity in interaction with modernity's critique of religion. HART 2020 is a more specific example, where a religious myth, the myth of Lucifer, is brought to bear to critique the politics of nuclear armament.

is relativized. Yet another pathway opens by focusing on the pluralistic nature of practice in religions—how practices mediate religions and the ways we study them. That is the topic of the next chapter.

2
Outsiders and Insiders of Zen, Turned Inside Out

"For the realization of Zen, practice is absolutely necessary."[1] So claimed the Zen philosopher Abe Masao, and he never hesitated to reaffirm this statement. The scholar Ninian Smart, on the other hand, recognized that in Buddhist literature the attainment of nirvana is typically a consequence of meditation, but he certainly did not propose that we need engage in meditation practices in order to understand Buddhist liberation or Buddhist teachings.[2] The contrast between the persuasions of these two teachers epitomizes the issue at hand: one seems to stand within the expansive tradition he interprets and the other outside it. Given the usual platitudes about the scholar's reliance on discursive language and the Zen master's denigration of such language, it may strike us as ironic that here it is the Zen advocate who makes the explicit, propositional claim, and the scholar who intimates but does not assert the necessity of distance and otherness for understanding religions. But the proverbial distinction between insider and outsider stands out clearly enough.

An initial focus on Zen Buddhism brings the general issue into sharper relief, for Zen is a tradition of Buddhism that scholars and

---

1. ABE 1985, 4. The early popularizer of Zen, Alan Watts, proclaimed another version of this point: "To know what Zen is, and especially what it is not, there is no alternative but to practice it...." (WATTS 1957, 15).

2. SMART 1986, 122: "...seeing is a kind of gnosis.... There is an analogy to intellectual discovery in the attainment of nirvana..., [but] typically... nirvana's attainment is not just gnosis. It is also a consequence of meditation...."

Zen literature alike have long associated with the primacy of practice. Indeed, historically *Zen* (*Chan* in Chinese) ostensibly meant meditation practice, and the word often came to define that tradition as the "meditation school" of Chinese Buddhism.[3] Is there any prospect of understanding Zen without engaging in its meditative practices, of understanding it from an objective point of view? This question, once we define it more precisely and extrapolate, will lead us to re-conceptualize the opposition between religious practice and objective, scholarly study—indeed it will lead us to envision differently the tension between thinking and doing.

Zen insiders and outsiders

What is the nature of the difference between Abe's and Smart's claims? Already noted is that in this instance Abe's claim is explicit and Smart's is tacit. Besides that, their terms differ of course: Abe speaks of Zen realization and practice, and Smart of Buddhist nirvana and meditation. But even if we are provisionally able to equate realization with nirvana, and practice with meditation, the difference in what is deemed essential to understanding Buddhist teaching remains. Context makes it clear that Abe's "realization of Zen" means not only the experience of Zen awakening or *satori*, but also a true understanding of Zen teachings and sayings. And "Zen" refers in Abe's text to the same Buddhist tradition as that examined by scholars under the name of Zen or Chan. Both Abe and Smart, then, seem to be offering contrary views about what is necessary for understanding representative Buddhist teachings.

Their status as speakers differs as well. Both statements imply that their speaker is in a position to know, but the truth of Abe's claim

---

3. Like much else in historical studies of Zen, its reliance on a shared set of practices and its identity as "the meditation school" are in fact matters of debate. See GREENE 2021, 23 n.7 and 205–8; and MARALDO 2021, 101.

implies that Abe has attained realization, whereas Smart speaks not as someone who has attained nirvana but as a scholar who can understand texts. (Matters would be different again if their statements were meant ironically, or as merely expedient admonitions, but I read them here to mean what they say.) Smart in fact is no staunch positivist; he later does state explicitly that "a kind of imaginative participation" is required for the understanding of religion. He does not even rule out "active participation," but in considering it a form of *imaginary* participation and in stressing the need for self-understanding, "the understanding of one's own milieu," he is clearly interested in what is required to understand the religion *of another*. Religion, including Buddhist teachings and practice, has for him "both an inward and an outward aspect."[4] Abe's interpretation, on the other hand, would collapse the distinction between self and other, inward and outward. It even suggests that maintaining such distinctions blocks an understanding of Zen Buddhism. Abe and Smart differ about what is required for understanding regarding not only the role of practice but also the stance of the one who understands.

The contrast between these two stances is one that I as the author of this inquiry am turning into a confrontation. As far as I know, Abe and Smart never engaged in direct dialogue or debate with one another, and for the time being at least, I am standing aside from both. But the contrast brings to mind an oft-mentioned dispute between two earlier interpreters of Zen who did address one another directly. Hu Shih insisted on the study of Zen's history for understanding the seemingly irrational teachings of Chan masters. Just as forcefully, D. T. Suzuki insisted that a certain insight or "*prajñā*-intuition" is requisite for understanding the words and actions of Chan masters. They are both interpreting Zen texts, and while Suzuki emphasizes the experience of awakening, in other articles he does not ignore the practice of meditation or *zazen*. While Hu emphasizes historical investigation, he

4. SMART 1986, 198 and 200.

does not dismiss the relevance of one's "ever-widening life-experience."⁵ Their respective stances have provided a model of the insider-outsider distinction for scholars. For example, the scrupulous scholar of Zen, John McRae, characterized Suzuki's reputed authority as "one [that claims] insider access to the profound truths of the tradition."⁶ McRae's critique of Hu Shih, on the other hand, recognized this historian as someone proud to stand outside the Zen tradition, but someone encumbered with his own biases.⁷ The historically correct story nevertheless requires an objective, outside position. McRae divulged his own stance in a comment about the legendary lineage of early Zen masters:

> Here it is useful to make a clear insider/outsider distinction: What is both expected and natural for a religious practitioner operating *within* the Chan episteme, what is necessary in order to achieve membership within the patriarchal lineage, becomes intellectually debilitating for those standing, even if only temporarily, *outside* the realm of Chan as its observers and analysts.⁸

And yet the Zen tradition itself sometimes empties the distinction of its utility, as another scholar suggests:

> "[Song-era] literati texts often deliberately seem to adopt the perspective of an outsider even as the texts themselves, by their very nature, sometimes may become insider accounts.... The distinction between insider and outsider is therefore not always clear-cut...."⁹

---

5. SUZUKI 1953, 26, 32, and 43; HU 1953, 3–4 and 21. See MARALDO 2021, 102 n.6, 103–5, 198 n.34.
6. MCRAE 2003, 74
7. Ibid., 106–7.
8. Ibid., 10. For an explicit critique of McRae's use of the distinction, see HORI 2005, xvi–xix.
9. SCHLÜTTER 2008, 6–7.

Scholarly study versus religious practice, turned inside out

The opposition and tension between objective scholarship and Buddhist practice seems to pose a threat. To put it simply, collapsing critical distance threatens one's objectivity, and maintaining distance ruins one's chances for realization. It may turn out, however, that the differences between Abe Masao and Ninian Smart, or between D. T. Suzuki and Hu Shih, do not stem from any peculiarity in the nature of Buddhist teaching or practice at all. They may derive rather from the relative interests of those who study human activities and texts in general. This is the direction of the present inquiry: to displace the problem from one of threat to one of relevance. And my own argument involves a choice about what is relevant to my purpose. For there are many possible aspects and alternatives to the opposition that I will not explore, as interesting as they might be. I will not discuss the historical occurrence of Buddhist practitioners who are also deemed objective scholars, or historical and cultural variations in the criteria of objectivity, the meaning of scholarship, or the rules of Buddhist practice. Actually, the inquiry need not be confined to the Buddhist tradition at all, for the perceived problem is not essentially linked to that religious tradition. Thus, we need not pursue the narrower question of whether there is anything proper to Buddhist practice or philosophy that requires Buddhology to have unique methods of study, as Ueda Yoshifumi, for example, once claimed.[10] If there is any advantage to Buddhist studies in my argument, it is only the pleasure of company: as a field, Buddhist studies is informed by methods, concepts, and problems shared by other academic disciplines and so keeps company with them.

What are some of these broader issues which define the problem that opposes objective scholarship and Buddhist practice? The desig-

10. Ueda Y. 1977 and 1985.

nation "objective scholar" today carries a number of connotations that form convenient and usually unquestioned oppositions. These oppositions are hierarchic; scholars value one member of the pair over the other, even if occasionally there is debate about which is to be preferred. For purposes of scholarship, it is thought better to be objective than subjective, critical than sympathetic, detached than involved, impartial than biased, outside than inside, etic than emic. And since the ideal for the scholar is the first term in each of these oppositions, the second term is often and mistakenly thought to describe the position of the scholar's sources.[11]

Let us examine the opposition between etic and emic first, since it is more technical and better defined, yet more controversial and hence informative for my analysis. The terms *etic* and *emic* may be out of vogue in their home discipline, cognitive anthropology, but they have sufficiently influenced the study of Buddhist communities and even of Buddhist texts to merit comment.[12] Theoretically, *etic* derives from *phonetic* and denotes universal categories applicable to the study of any culture or, by extension, any text. *Emic* derives from *phonemic* and denotes the particular categories that happen to be used in a particular culture or language. But when translated practically into research methods, an etic approach means that the researcher does not take seriously the claims of informants, ideally does not even listen to their reports of what they do and why, but merely records and analyzes behavior. An emic approach takes into account the reports and claims of the group under study. Obviously, when the object of study is an oral or written text, the researcher cannot avoid what others say about themselves. But she can still suspend belief and question motive,

---

11. Steven Katz is an example of someone who straightforwardly contrasts scholarship and "academic self-consciousness" with confessional and theological pronouncements from within a tradition, i.e., what religions say about themselves. See his reply in KATZ et al., 1988, 756.

12. For current discussions of this opposition, see PIKE AND HARRIS 1990 and MCCUTCHEON 1999.

understand texts as pronouncements within a tradition, compare them to other texts and traditions, and subject them to critique. She can still be etic insofar as she does not take what texts or people say at face value.

As it happens, cognitive anthropologists have subjected the etic/emic distinction to a critique and come to realize that etic categories are themselves relative to cultural contexts, usually those of the scholarly community.[13] *Etic* retains the sense of outside but fails in the claim of being universal and detached. What is more, researchers themselves are subject to the same critique as their target; they may say they conduct etic research but in fact be highly influenced by internal pronouncements. In addition, there is the notoriously difficult problem of how much one can understand without taking into account internal pronouncements. Let us postpone until later a discussion of the problem of understanding without belief and of the relevance of that problem to the study of Zen and other Buddhist practice. The point now is that the pair etic/emic describes *not* the position of the researcher as opposed to that of the group or text under study, but at best two approaches that the scholar can take. *Emic* describes the standpoint of the tradition or text under study no more than *etic* does. Unless that tradition or text recognizes an alternative to what it says about itself, it cannot consider its pronouncements as being within a tradition. If it does entertain views different from its own, it too can relate emically or etically to them. Perhaps the definitive emic situation would be the encounter with a group or textual tradition that was blissfully ignorant of its difference from others, or that naively believed its catego-

---

13. MARCUS AND FISCHER 1986, 180–1. The work of George DeVos on the relation between culture and self in Japan is an example of the continued uncritical use of the distinction. DeVos finds both the etic and emic approaches necessary to understand the meaning of self, but continues to distinguish between etic as objective and externally analytic, and emic as experiential and self-perceptive. The implication is that etic represents the stance of the observer, emic that of the observed. See MARSELLA, DEVOS, AND HSU, 1985, 3 and 141.

ries to be absolute and comprehensive. But in this situation *emic* again refers to the standpoint of a scholar who allows the group or text under investigation to speak to her.

To elucidate this point, consider the pairs inside/outside and native/non-native as they pertain to the scholar's enterprise. As objective scholars, our view of what we study is supposedly from the outside. Sometimes texts are seen as produced from the inside, with the scholar for better or worse stuck on the outside, distanced from the texts by time, culture, language or belief. The scholar today takes great pains to overcome language barriers, but generally is trained to regard differences in time, culture, and especially belief as advantageous to objectivity. Yet the pair outside/inside is obviously a construction of someone who encounters differences. It is not necessarily a description of the scholar's point of view as opposed to the source's, if the source recognizes no outside.

"Going native" is a phrase that describes what happens when an outsider assumes the viewpoint, and participates in the activities, of a foreign people under study. To assume the beliefs of the people is considered particularly a danger to objective scholarship.[14] On the other hand, scholars often remark on how difficult it actually is to go native. One cannot leave behind one's own culture and become completely socialized in another. Nor can one easily attain the understanding required to make one a spokesperson for a group or tradition. What goes unnoticed is that going native, or even being "a native," is a possibility only for one who is aware of differences and who approaches a group or tradition from what she considers the outside. Going native means to adopt a different stance toward the object of one's study, and

---

14. See BITTNER 1973, 109–25. Many anthropologists today dispute the ideal of detached objectivity and propose instead what I would call a stance of reciprocal equivalence, as advocated by VIVEIROS DE CASTRO 2015, 6–8, similar to what TEDLOCK (1992, xiii) calls "observant participation." Paula Arai takes that stance in explaining the ritual life of Zen Buddhist nuns, despite her use of the less accurate description, "participant observation" (ARAI 2008, 186). For clarification, see MARALDO 2021, 283–9.

may mean to cease regarding it as an object, perhaps to stop studying altogether, in any sense of the word. Obviously one can no longer be a scholar if one stops studying, so the perceived danger to the scholar's results is not this abstention. It is rather the view that going native will make one so familiar with one's subject matter that one will no longer discern the differences and discrepancies that are of interest to the world of scholarship. One's subject matter should be sufficiently foreign to that world. The good scholar cannot rely merely on "secondary" literature by people of her own time, culture, and language. (Strictly speaking, it is better to speak of the traditions of scholarship rather than the world of scholarship, so that we can further dispel the notion that a "native" is someone who belongs to a tradition while a scholar is someone who is on the outside of everything. Scholars too have their teachers and are trained in schools and styles of research as well as in languages, texts, history, and culture.)

I suggested that being "native" is a possibility only for an outsider. The following puzzle about the native stereotype will explain my meaning. Natives do not say they are natives. Natives say they are humans, and if they know of others, they may call the others barbarians. But "native versus non-native" does not translate into "human versus barbarian" for the scholar, because both natives and non-natives are humans from today's scholarly perspective. And for the native, who does not consider himself a native, "human versus barbarian" cannot translate into "native versus. non-native." Are we then left with the relativism that to the scholar someone is a native, while to that native the scholar is a barbarian? No, because although the scholar and the native, or the barbarian and the human, may use categories that do not coincide, it is only the scholar's concern to take this fact into account. And when "natives" not only note their difference but seek an account of it, their kinsfolk say they transgress into the realm of scholarship.[15]

15. This depiction is of the "native" versus the "scholar" admittedly plays on stereotypes, but an example of a native's account reproached for taking an outsider's stance is the

Who count as objective scholars in current parlance? A brief answer to this question will support the thesis that the disjunctions discussed above occur within the province of objective scholarship and not between it and other realms. We expect natural scientists to be objective in their research and to produce results that are generic, not dependent upon the personal involvement of the researcher, and so repeatable by other competent scientists. Yet we do not ordinarily use the phrase "objective scholar" to describe natural scientists. It would be unusual, for example, to call physicist Stephen Hawkins an objective scholar. We know that the practice of science requires dedication and commitment, but we suppose that the object of inquiry, the realm of "nature," is sufficiently detachable from the particular practitioner of science so as to allow for one and only one set of true descriptions of nature.[16] We expect philosophers to be objective in their analyses and judgments, by taking into account various viewpoints precisely when it appears that there may be no single set of true descriptions. Yet scholarship is not the usual description of what a philosopher does, in part because the philosopher does not usually produce new empirical knowledge. The work that an artist produces, qua artist, is not considered a piece of objective scholarship because, for one thing, it is too close to its creator.

The term "objective scholar" in current parlance describes an ideal for researchers in fields such as anthropology, sociology, linguistics, and history, that is, in the social sciences and some areas of the humanities. What differentiates these fields from the natural sciences is an interaction with human beings and human products. We need not try to settle the long debates about whether such "human sciences" require methods proper to them and quite distinct from those of the natural sciences. What is crucial here is to recognize that these fields often present to the scholar an object of inquiry that has its own

---

anthropological study of ORTIZ 1972.

16. On the ambiguities of the term *nature*, see MARALDO 2019A, 429–62.

voice, that can speak or has spoken in its own name. This fact permits discrepancies between the scholar's account and that of the source—discrepancies that are quite unlike those which may occur in the natural scientist's questioning of nature. Current usage indicates that the objective scholar is first of all a person who works with the possibility of conflicting criteria, and only secondarily a person who chooses one standpoint over another, objective over subjective, disinterested over involved, outside over inside, or etic over emic. Each of these polarities is a possible stance for the scholar, not for his or her sources insofar as they do not make themselves an object of inquiry. The sources under study may speak or have spoken in their own voice, but it is the scholar, not the sources, who can be subjective, involved, emic, or insider, or who can attempt to "go native."

Understanding versus believing?

Let us next consider the position that pits understanding against believing. Augustine, as we may recall, put these two in a circular relationship whereby each was the condition for the other. Here, however, I want to consider contemporary views, such as Alasdair MacIntyre's, which regard the two as incompatible and suggest that understanding is the stance of the outside skeptic and believing the stance of one inside a religious tradition.[17] For MacIntyre, just as for Ninian Smart, understanding entails knowing what relevant concepts mean, how they are used, and what their social context and consequences are. A problem arises because understanding would seem to be possible only when one could correctly use the concepts in judgments, yet the skeptical scholar, on the one hand and the believer on the other do not agree on the content of relevant judgments. To draw an example from our opening case, Abe claimed that Zen practice is necessary to understand Zen texts, while Smart implied it is not. Per-

17. MacIntyre 1970.

haps the word "understand" would be understood differently by Abe and Smart; perhaps Abe would say, "if you understood what I mean, you would agree with me." But MacIntyre's point is that the one side may not ever really know what the other side means, because the criteria of intelligibility for the skeptical scholar and the believer are different. It is not that the believer necessarily refuses to entertain objections or is never doubt-ridden, but that the believer belongs to a religious tradition, which, to preserve its relevance in a changing world, makes itself invulnerable to radical unbelief and uncriticizable *ab externo*. The believer's doubts can never be the same as the skeptic's unbelief or, we can add, as the scholar's suspension of belief. Nor can the believer's understanding of the relevant concepts be the same as the skeptical scholar's. Or so MacIntyre argues.

In concluding that understanding a religion is incompatible with believing it, however, MacIntyre ends up restricting the word "understanding" to the position of the skeptic and opposing it to the stance of the believer. And in focusing on the incompatibility of *judgments*, he further restricts understanding to the conceptual grasp of propositions. These restrictions in fact eventually displace MacIntyre's initial problem of the incompatibility of judgments, for reasons of which he seems unaware. For the criteria of intelligibility that govern the use of concepts do not necessarily differ for the scholar and the believer. One can quote or mention the judgments of a believer without believing them, and in so doing one is still using the relevant concepts in the judgment as the believer does. Similarly, one can understand a myth without believing in it. The anthropologist can reconstruct the rules for translating the myth as a story in statement form; what is more, she can know how it functions in a given society in a way that the "native" never does. So it may be expedient to restrict understanding to the stance of the skeptical scholar, but this does not mean the scholar and believer must use concepts in judgments in different ways. It more likely means that the uses to which the scholar and the believer put the judgments differ radically. Only the scholar is likely to be concerned with "detecting the standards of intelligibility established in a society" or religion, as MacIntyre would recognize.[18] This suggests further that understanding as the stance of the scholar is not limited to the use of concepts within belief statements, but includes the use or function of statements within a belief system. The crucial issue between a scholar and a believer is not a disagreement about the meaning and truth of judgments, but a difference in what each takes to be relevant.

The question of the function of propositional beliefs occasioned a great many explicit debates and fine-tuned distinctions in various Buddhist schools, but again I will refer to studies completely outside Buddhism in order to challenge MacIntyre's framework and to level the hierarchy of oppositions with which we began. Understanding for MacIntyre is propositional and objective. Recent work in philosophy, linguistics, and cognitive science, however, proposes that objective scholars have often been duped by a myth of their own: objectivism. One feature of objectivism is the assumption that there is a set of objective criteria and methods that allow a description which is independent of the scholar's own beliefs, language, and culture. Mark Johnson and George Lakoff have done detailed analyses exposing the illusion of one set of atemporal criteria that would permit a universally valid reflective stance.[19] In what should be of great interest to Buddhist scholars but is beyond the scope of this chapter, they have shown the connection between this myth and a metaphysics of entities whose identity and existence is independent of mind. More important for our present purposes is their argument against the possibility of a cognitive stance outside of the object of study, from a detached, "God's-eye" point of view. Johnson even demonstrates how categories like "outside" and "inside" derive from non-propositional, embodied, and involved human experiences of containment.[20] My point is not that the objec-

18. Ibid., 71.
19. JOHNSON 1987, xxiii et passim; LAKOFF 1987, 157–9 et passim.
20. JOHNSON 1987, 21–3, 34–5.

tive scholar's study is always relative to her viewpoint and training and therefore less valid. My point is that an objective stance may not at all mean a detached one "outside" the scholar's field of inquiry, but rather one involved with a different set of questions.

Embodied Practice and Disengaged Thought

Even if Johnson and Lakoff are right about all our categories of understanding deriving from non-propositional, embodied, cultural experiences, it would seem that there are relevant differences between propositional assertions and forms of practice in the study of Buddhism. The initial opposition under review here, after all, was between objective study and Buddhist practice. I think that there often is a significant disparity between these two, but it has to do more with the nature of certain kinds of activity in general than with anything particularly Buddhist. Practices such as meditation, chanting, walking, and other rituals, Buddhist or not, are activities that engage the body and mind in a different way than do observation, reading, translating, and analysis. The word practice implies an activity that is geared toward some purpose or objective, so these latter activities too may well be regarded as practices and given soteriological significance in Buddhism and other religions. In general, however, we can distinguish them from forms of practice that engage the body more consciously and disengage discursive thought. I cannot employ such embodied practices as I do concepts or judgments; that is, I cannot engage in them by merely mentioning them, standing back and remaining detached and bodily uncommitted.[21] Such embodied practices engage me and change me physically and mentally in a way that reading, translating, analyzing, and so forth do not.

21. One possible exception is the kind of proposition called a performative utterance. When I say, "I promise," I am engaging in discursive, linguistic activity but I do commit myself and change a situation.

In light of this distinction, there is some force to the truism that one must jump in the water and swim to know what swimming really is. It seems obvious that to engage in bodily activities of all sorts is quite different than to study them without engaging in them. Yet to specify "what swimming really is" is to render a judgment about what is relevant to one's purposes. (We should incidentally not forget that the best swimmers today are usually coached by people who apply scientific research to that activity.) Concomitantly, it is not only perfectly possible to study embodied practices in Buddhism, and to enhance such study with practice and vice versa, but even possible for scholars to do justice to practices without engaging in them—within the confines of what "doing justice" means in the scholarly community. What I think untenable is the position that polarizes and ranks scholarly study and embodied practice, and then claims that only one side or the other can do justice to the matter at hand. Studying without practicing is sometimes compared to looking at a piece of fruit, poking at it, weighing it, analyzing it chemically, and so forth, without ever biting in and tasting it. But fruit is usually eaten for nourishment, not out of curiosity, and someone who is merely curious will be looking for something different than someone who is hungry.

The distinction between embodied practices and more discursive activities by no means precludes an influence of one on the other. Philosophical beliefs can shape meditative techniques, and discursive thought can inform bodily experience, yet we can still distinguish between activities that require bodily commitment and those that do not.[22]

---

22. ARAI 2008 and 2011 are exemplary for illustrating how scholarly study can be informed by embodied practice. The practitioner-philosopher DAVIS (2022, 275–81) offers a lucid account of the interplay between philosophy and Zen practice. Regarding the effect of philosophical beliefs on Buddhist meditative practices, see GRIFFITHS 1986, xiv et passim; and GIMELLO 1983, 76–9. Less studied has been the effect of meditative practices on the formulation of "beliefs," e.g., on the scheme of eight levels of consciousness in Yogācāra Buddhism.

Nor does whatever tension there is between objective study and Buddhist practice reduce to a crucial difference between "dualistic" and "non-dualistic" activities. In the context of Buddhist practice, "non-dualistic" has at least two meanings: no gap between means and end, and no split between subject and object. The medieval Zen master Dōgen, for example, implied that practice (means) and realization (end) are not two.[23] But there are numerous non-Buddhist and non-religious activities in which reaching one's goal is not an activity different in kind from practicing. Running in a marathon and running daily in preparation for the marathon are not different kinds of activity. Likewise, it is not only Buddhist meditation practices which undermine a difference between the subject experiencing and the object experienced. In fact, it is often Buddhist teachers who point out the collapse of this split in ordinary, everyday activities. If they are right, this means that the objective scholar is not necessarily denied access to non-dualistic experience, although she may not have considered her own experiences as relevant to her study. If there is something that the scholar misses by being objective, it has to do first with the difference between bodily commitment and distanced study and only secondarily with the distinction between dualistic and non-dualistic activities.[24]

What then may we conclude with regard to the objective scholar and Buddhist practice? By way of example, I began with a difference in judgment between Abe Masao and Ninian Smart. Abe asserted that practice is necessary for understanding Zen, whereas Smart implied that objective textual study is the requisite to understanding Buddhism. Is there an overarching, outside viewpoint from which to decide whether Abe or Smart is right? And if I say there is not, is there a higher or more comprehensive viewpoint from which to judge the truth of what I say, particularly if it is disputed? The logic I have

---

23. Most explicitly in the *Bendōwa* (辨道話) of 1231; see, for example, its translation as "Negotiating the Way" by Waddell and Abe, DŌGEN 2002, 144.

24. For more detailed analysis, see Chapter 4 in the present volume.

followed in this chapter entails that the search for such an outside or "God's eye" viewpoint would be misplaced. Even if one were to place oneself outside of Abe and Smart and try to determine which of them is right, regardless of what they themselves thought, Abe and Smart (or their advocates) would also need access to the superior judgment for it to make any difference. The difference that religious practice, or disengagement from it, makes for understanding a religion will depend on whether discursive or embodied understanding is the aim. The initial disjunctions between objective and subjective and the like do not necessarily describe the stance of the scholar as opposed to the practitioner; often they represent only a spectrum of choices for the scholar. The domains of relevance that guide the interests and questions of the scholar and the practitioner are not necessarily opposed. There remains, however, a question that is crucial for scholarship. To what extent does our approach to the subject matter of inquiry control our criteria of relevance, and define the relative importance of the questions we ask? The chapter that follows points to an answer by examining the limits of one typical approach in interreligious dialogue.

3
Understanding
An Alternative to the Hermeneutical Model

FRAMING THE ISSUE

For all their achievement in opening religions to one another, participants in interreligious dialogue often encounter an impasse. The first chapter in this section presented one condensed example in the dialogue between the Zen Buddhist philosopher Abe Masao and his Christian and Jewish respondents. "God is not God (for God is love and completely self-emptying); precisely because God is not a self-affirmative God, God is truly a God of love (for through complete self-abnegation God is totally identical with everything including sinful humans)," Abe stated[1]—to which the Catholic theologian David Tracy politely replied, "I am not persuaded that Abe's interpretation of the Christian belief in God is the way for Christians... to think about God."[2]

If I extract from this dialogue an instance of impasse and pass over the complex theological issues involved and the deep resonances experienced, it is not to reduce probing conversations to moments of deadlock.[3] It is rather to illustrate an extraction that such interreligious

---

1. ABE 1990, 16. This application of the Christian idea known as *kenosis* follows Abe's statement, p. 11, that "The Son of God is not the Son of God (for he is essentially and fundamentally self-emptying); precisely because he *is not* the Son of God, he *is* truly the Son of God (for he originally and always works as Christ, the messiah, in his salvational function of self-emptying." See our discussion on page 20 in the present volume.
2. TRACY 1990, 135.
3. The first set of dialogues were continued in a second round, published in IVES 1995.

dialogue itself performs. The sort of phenomenological reduction of religion to what is believed does display an essential form of religious life, but it also reveals a limit of *understanding* in one crucial sense of the word. Beliefs may be essential to religions, but reflecting critically on them and asserting their truth both rest on understanding them in a deeper sense. For the impasse illustrated here does not occur as a conflict between two clearly understood assertions whose truth is in dispute. It occurs when understanding flounders, when an assertion or an expression does not make sense to the other party. (What, for example, might it mean to say that God is God because God is not God?)

In this example, Abe's Buddhist "interpretation of the Christian belief in God" began unsurprisingly with an interpretation of a text, specifically a passage from Paul's Epistle to the Philippians.[4] The interpretation of texts has not only guided much interreligious dialogue; it has continued to govern hermeneutics, the discipline intended to tell us what makes all understanding possible. Interreligious dialogue ostensibly pursues the goal of mutual understanding—as Gadamer describes the original incentive of hermeneutics—but the understanding and the hermeneutics that inform it are, I venture to show, circumscribed by texts and textual language, the language in which doctrines are expressed and elaborated. If dialogue partners sense that something else is relevant and if they pursue something more—something like the embodied understanding proposed in the previous chapter—they will

---

In his review of the second volume, the theologian John B. Cobb, Jr., a participant in the first round, wrote that "whatever limits there may be to this dialogue,... the quality of understanding of Buddhism, especially in its Zen form, has been greatly advanced" (COBB 1998, 438).

4. The passage in *Philippians* 2:7 is the primary reference for the famous *kenosis* doctrine that, in Abe's words, speaks of a Christ who "emptied himself" [ἐκένωσεν] of his divine form and assumed the form of a servant, "becoming obedient even unto death" (ABE 1990, 9). Somewhat ironic for interreligious dialogue that aims at understanding is the later reference in *Philippians* 4:6 to "the peace that surpasses all understanding" (η ειρήνη που ξεπερνά κάθε κατανόηση) alluding to *katanóisi*, intellectual understanding.

need to move beyond text-oriented understanding. Indeed, some religious texts themselves tell us so.

The move to another mode of understanding can, then, begin with texts and textual understanding even if it cannot remain suspended in texts. The following reflections that pursue an alternative understanding are unmistakably a discursive exercise that begins with texts and the kind of understanding they promote. If this chapter concludes with nothing more than a reference to non-discursive and non-textual understanding, it is a referral informed in the meantime by the alternative mode. We may put the point as an inflection of the hermeneutical circle: to understand a text (and tradition) one must practice what it advocates, and to know how to practice one must be informed by the tradition (and text).[5] What is more, in some cases the practice advocated turns out to disillusion initial pursuits, and the reliance on texts begins to obstruct the relevant understanding. This situation highlights the hole in the hermeneutical circle. The deflected circle then says: to understand a text in pursuit of knowing how to put it in practice requires one to forgo pursuits and leave texts behind. What sort of alternative might then move us beyond the standstills that occur in the practice of dialogue as usual?

The strictures of interreligious hermeneutics

In light of impasses encountered in the usual way of understanding another's religion, the support offered by interreligious hermeneutics seems unduly compromised. Its possibilities seem bounded on all sides by assumptions that are as restrictive of its presumed aims (mutual understanding among religions) as they are invisible to its advocates. The assumptions lie behind the very words: *interreligious* and *hermeneutics*. The word *hermeneutics* refers historically to

---

5. For examples, see the hermeneutics of practice I read out of texts by Dōgen and Francis of Assisi, in MARALDO 1981.

a discipline focused on texts, and on language under the guise of texts. The word *interreligious* refers foremost to interaction between so-called world religions. But when religion is confined to the aspects of traditions that are globally represented, when the interaction between them is restricted to linguistic understanding, and when hermeneutics is supposed to guide this understanding of language as it becomes focused in texts, then a lot is left out. There are notable aspects of religion that have nothing to do with texts and little to do with language, and there are religious interactions between people who do not represent world religions or their various sects. If reflection on possible mutual understanding between identifiably different religions is the aim of interreligious hermeneutics, then an alternative sense of understanding is called for.

THE BOUNDS OF RELIGION IN "INTERRELIGIOUS" DIALOGUE

The standard understanding in much interreligious dialogue takes religion to be primarily a matter of teachings and belief in teachings. It presupposes that teachings are formulated and handed down in texts, or at least that they can be so formulated. It often assumes that belief means belief that the teachings are true. Although belief is not necessarily restricted to a set of propositions that can be true or false, it does, in the prevailing assumption, primarily concern linguistic expression. The question of the truth of the teachings vis-à-vis those of another religious tradition, in some sense of truth, is frequently a topic of discussion. To be sure, the mode of believing, often called faith, is also a topic. The standard understanding does not confine religious faith to believing that a set of linguistically expressible teachings is true, and the notion of faith may include trust and *believing in* some reality, as opposed to *believing that* a teaching is true; it may consider faith a mode of belief that is not properly understood epistemologically, in distinction from knowledge. Nevertheless, the usual emphasis is on what adherents of the religion believe, on expressible content. When the standard understanding attends to what adherents do, it more often than not assumes that what is going on is *worship*, the veneration of the object of belief, an expression of faith that arises from religious belief. These assumptions are particularly evident whenever religions are called *faiths* and adherents are called *believers*. The *sacred scriptures* of the believers become a privileged target of investigation.

Many scholars in religious studies today, particularly those who do research from a socio-scientific perspective, consider the traditional focus on teachings and scriptures as limited to the subjective self-understanding of religious people and as oblivious of social, economic, and political factors that enter into the formation and practice of religions. They call into question the validity of the very notions of faith, scripture, and even religion.[6] Many scholars regard the traditional focus as a study of the elite, of the theological expression of literate authorities. They turn their attention to everyday rituals and practices (and sometimes texts) that are describable from a third-person point of view. Their shift has influenced interreligious dialogue and the practice of theology as well, so that theological dialogue now also frequently includes discussion about ritual and practice. Phrases such as "teachings and practices," "beliefs and practices," and "teachings, practices and rituals," are now common paraphrases of religion. Yet the predominant position goes to the first-mentioned, to teachings or beliefs, and a central concern in interreligious dialogue is their truth, even where truth is not explicitly defined in logical or epistemological terms, even when *truth* is left relatively undefined.

---

6. For critical examinations of the category *religion* see FITZGERALD 1997, MCCUTCHEON 2003, and JOSEPHSON 2012. For critical discussions of the notions of *scripture* and *sacred text*, see LEVERING 1988 and TIMM 1992.

The Boundaries of "World Religions" and the Limitation of "Interreligious"

I will not try to define what *religion* is or what makes something *religious*. My call for an alternative sense of understanding would not limit that understanding to specifically religious matters, and it allows for these terms to be used as they commonly are in interreligious dialogue—up to a point. That point is reached when the *inter* of interreligious serves to designate interactions solely between world religions. The focus on world religions carries with it the assumption that adherence to the religion entails some degree of consistent commitment over time, primarily to a set of globalized teachings, even where participants in the dialogue avow the possibility of belonging to more than one religion at the same time. The standard understanding presumes that teachings, if not the only point of interconnection, still play a central role and form a common denominator in different religions. It tends to assume that the teachings of a religion are both what distinguish it from other religions and what explain its geographical spread in the world.

World religions, it is presumed, come in a variety of sects or denominations, which are nevertheless distinguished from those of other world religions by an embracing set of basic beliefs and a history that the sects share. Interactions between sects of the same religion, between Lutherans and Roman Catholics, for example, count more often as "ecumenical" than as interreligious. And standard interreligious dialogue has scarcely if at all included discussions between representatives of a world religion and those of a regional religion, much less a "folk religion," or between representatives of two or more regional religions. To be sure, the interactions within the scope of standard interreligious dialogue typically engage people who represent only one part of a religious tradition. As Catherine Cornille points out, the dialogue occurs for the most part "not between Islam and Christianity, but between Shi'ites and Methodists, or between members of a particular Sufi order and those of an order with the Roman Catholic Church."[7] Standard interreligious dialogue presumes, nevertheless, that the particular sect or order counts as a cross-section of the relevant world religion.

Scholars who would eliminate *religion* as a useful category have taken the category of *world religion* as a specific target of their critiques. They too have stressed the text-orientation of that category. Richard King summarizes the link between textualism and the modern concept of "world religions":

> The universalizing aspects of literacy therefore provide a means of idealizing religions and locating it within the abstract world of the text. It is in this sense that we can understand [Walter] Ong's reference to the "imperialist" tendency of writing. [Jack] Goody argues that it is the development of literature that effectively allows certain religious worldviews to spread beyond their particular and local context and become "world religions".... The "world-religions" approach to the study of religion, which focuses upon a few globalized religious entities as expressive of the religious experience of humankind, shows clear evidence of this texualist bias.... In effect, an exclusive focus upon the so-called "world religions" concentrates attention upon those religious ideologies that remain directly comparable with the universalistic and proselytizing elements of Christian theology, with its emphasis upon universal human salvation.[8]

Insofar as these scholars intend to expose not only the textual bias of the category *world religions*, but also—as they see it—its Christian, theological, and colonialist presuppositions, their intention differs from mine. I do not seek to subvert the discipline of hermeneutics or eliminate the category of religion. The alternative notion of under-

---

7. CORNILLE (2008, 68) notes further that "general religious categories such as 'Christian' or 'Buddhist' have often obscured the reality of internal diversity and dissonance within religions, while at the times setting unnecessary limits on our understanding of 'sameness' and 'difference' across religious traditions."

8. R. KING 1999, 65–7.

standing I seek would serve, among other things, to make interreligious hermeneutics better prepared to guide the interpretation of religious phenomena, and to make it more responsible in representing religions. If standard interreligious hermeneutics takes its clues from examples of interreligious dialogue that represent the norm—text-based dialogue between so-called world religions—then the alternative will need to explore religious interactions that are not focused on understanding texts and not cast as differences (and similarities) between globally represented religions.

THE TEXTUAL BINDING OF HERMENEUTICS
What do I mean by text and textual?

Before documenting the ways that hermeneutics has been bound to texts, even in and after Heidegger, a clarification of the terms *text* and *textual* is in order. By *text* I wish to designate an enclosure of language in sequences of sentences that build up a body of writing presumed to make sense. (The terms I use to define *text* are just as indefinite as that word itself.) Because of its relative unity, a text can be printed on pages that are bound together, or digitally reproduced as a unit with definite boundaries that once again make it possible to reproduce the electronic text in a physical book.[9]

By *textual* I mean linear discourse embodied in sentences, one following after another in a sequence defined by the effort to make sense. Sentences may come in the form of statements, questions, and commands, and also in the form of grammatically incomplete sentences and even single words, but the presumption is that any of these can be transformed into precisely written, punctuated sentences.[10] That kind

---

9. Does the postmodern internet disrupt the relative unity of the text and fragment it into an undefined and unbound intertext? To a degree, perhaps, but my use of the internet in doing research for this article suggests that its fragments easily lend themselves to inclusion into another text.

10. In *Philosophical Investigations*, WITTGENSTEIN (1953, #23) notes that there are

of sentence—even if logically a mere shadow of an atemporal "proposition" cast in one temporary, natural language among others—serves as the primary unit of meaning whose parts are referential words that have their own inter-dependent meanings. (Dictionaries assume they have their own quasi-independent meanings.) The text may serve as the context of the sentences whose meanings emerge in a hermeneutical circle or interplay between part and whole, between "parts of speech" and whole sentence, sentence and whole text. Precisely where hermeneutical theory problematizes the relations between part and whole, word and sentence, sentence and text, text and context, it reaffirms its binding to language as textual. Each of these relations is conceived as an ordering, a sequencing of parts made to make sense. Of course, this sequencing is of a specific kind, not merely temporal but also referential. We makers of sense take these parts to lead us beyond them to their "meanings." The referential character of most language is already familiar to us in the talk of signifier and signified. Something functions properly as a signifier when we see straight through it to what it signifies. The more transparent a sign is, the better it functions. In textual language, however, we look for a whole that does not immediately make sense, and to compensate, we try to capture meanings in the form of sentences. Sentences function as the units of meaning, and all "meanings" come to be transcribable into sentences.

The sentential structure of textual language makes it suitable for expressing religious doctrines, perhaps makes religious doctrines possible in the first place. A doctrine is meant (by an authoritative body if not by an author) to refer to a whole that does not (yet) make sense, that is never completely at our disposal, yet is condensed into a statement. A religious "teaching" is perhaps more ambiguous than a "doc-

---

countless kinds of sentences [*Sätze*], and in #8, #19, and #20 he gives examples of single words functioning as sentences. When the house builder calls out to his assistant, points, and says "Brick" he is using the word to mean "Hand me a brick!" (That is, "hand me a brick" is what we say when we transcribe this particular usage of that word into a complete sentence.) "To understand a sentence means to understand a language" (#199).

trine," but the common presumption is that teachings too can be transcribed into sentences.

I use the word *textual* also to describe the practice of understanding language, that is, using language to render meaning into the form of sentences arranged to refer to a whole that does not make immediate sense. Texts need to be interpreted. Of course, many things besides written texts need to be interpreted. Things like a pet dog's notably non-linguistic response, a person's behavior or utterance or facial expression, the typical patterns of behavior of a group or its entire culture. Human be-ing itself. But when we seek to make sense of these things we often coax them into isolatable units that can theoretically be put in written sentences. They become texts we understand by "reading" them.

The figurative text

A text becomes a figure for any whole that's supposed to make sense. No matter how unbounded and contextual the whole, no matter how indeterminate the whole or limitless the endeavor to make sense of it, the text comes to stand for any phenomenon temporarily taken as a whole that can eventually make sense to a reader. The whole may be truly a comprehensive horizon—the world, so to speak—that along with consciousness allows meaning to take place; the world becomes a text. An author becomes a text, or a collection of texts (This is the way we use the names Heidegger, Gadamer, Ricoeur, etc.) A culture becomes a text. My speech acts and antics in any given situation are read as a text. They are taken to communicate culturally shared meanings that can be interpreted by any competent, acculturated interlocutor or observer. I may misread the meaning of another person's gesture because of cultural difference; the Japanese gesture for "come here" (to put it in sentence form) is easily mistaken by Americans to mean "go away." The figurative uses of text and reading do not disguise the presumption that the understanding of any phenomenon can be articulated in sentential, textual form. This presumption is also at work in the metaphoric uses of "message," "information," and "communication" in computer science and brain research, even where they tend to forget that messages and information require a conscious reader, and communication requires conscious, intersubjective beings.

What is Non-Textual Language?

Not all language use is textual. In actual situations in which focus on language is central, such as a philosophical symposium or meeting of speakers, communication is facilitated by usages of language that are not sentential, not amenable to formulation in sentences building up a text, spoken or written. Communication also flows through gesture, posture, intonation, tone of voice, sighs, the rolling of eyes—all aspects of non-textual language. Much of this is meant to be captured in the expression "body language," but what I wish to point out is not so much the language conveyed by the human body as the body of language.

The body of language encompasses the enormous range of lived language not encoded in grammar or vocabulary, syntax or semantics, that includes non-referential as well as referential elements, and that overlaps with the culture in which one lives.[11] Linguists increasingly recognize that the study of language cannot be confined to analyses of structures and signs but must include the study of situations in which languages are learned and performed.[12] Language in its fully embodied form is learned through personal interaction with others in live

---

11. For a treatment of the overlap between language and culture, see AGAR 1994.

12. Recent social linguistics has elucidated numerous aspects of language not encoded either in its semantics or in its structure. Prosodics, for example, studies the vocal elements of language that are not encoded in grammar or vocabulary. This shift from text-oriented explanations of grammar and vocabulary and from structural analyses of language was anticipated some seventy years ago by the empirical research of Lev Vygotsky. Vygotsky's work suggested that all levels of language learning and all aspects of language (what I call "the body of language") originate as actual, person to person, relationships between individuals, in more or less flexible "zones of proximal development." Infants learn language through interaction with caregivers in their immediate presence. Language is not externalized thought; thought is internalized language that first appeared on a social level, in social interactions.

situations, usually situations in which one is bodily present with others. In fact, to gain communicative competence in a language requires personal interaction well beyond the exchange of linguistic signs. Interaction in person provides a shared context, crucial to language learning and distinct from any form of "distant learning," including learning by listening to audio and video devices. Distant learning or learning via devices takes place by bridging two "places," two or more initially unshared contexts, the learner's situation and the distant source's. There, too, a "fusion of horizons" comes into play. In contrast, the presence of co-speakers opens a horizon of presence that is shared from the beginning, even where the minds of learner and teacher constitute different levels of competence. That horizon may accommodate differences in culture, gender, class, and power; but its initially shared nature makes it singular.

We will return to the implications of this view of language for an alternative sense of understanding. But first let us sketch the ways that hermeneutics has been bound to texts, not only in classical philologists, jurists, and biblical commentators, but more surprisingly in the philosophers known for expanding the scope and deepening the significance of hermeneutics.[13] Contemporary *hermeneutics* names an approach to understanding and explicating a vast range of human endeavors—of virtually everything subject to interpretation. As a research method it applies to phenomena and experiences seemingly far beyond anything that looks like a text. And yet the thinkers who developed its theory explicitly or tacitly took texts to epitomize its object, even where that object was the subject who understands; even where the theory intended to overcome the subject-object distinction. Excursus 1 and 2 at the end of this chapter indicate how understanding written texts served as the model of hermeneutics for the classical

---

13. For a more detailed treatment of philosophical hermeneutics see MARALDO 1974. Here I focus on an aspect of hermeneutics, its text-orientation, that went unnoticed in that dissertation, which itself was an epitome of textuality quite different from the German I was using in everyday life.

theorists Schleiermacher and Dilthey, and how the post-hermeneutical philosophers Derrida and Vattimo remain bound to the textual tradition they criticize. For now we will sketch the horizon of textuality in the twentieth-century paragons, Heidegger, Gadamer, and Ricoeur. Just as a horizon functions as the unnoticed background against which things come into view, textuality serves as a tacit frame for the hermeneutics of those theorists who would go beyond it.

How Heidegger binds understanding to texts

Martin Heidegger is known for definitively releasing hermeneutics from its binding to texts, and for placing understanding at the roots of everyday human comportment in the world. But when the Heidegger of *Being and Time* existentialized understanding, he unintentionally textualized it as well.

Heidegger is after the "meaning of Be-ing" [*Sinn des Seins*].[14] He uses *meaning* here to indicate the intention or projection of what we seek to understand [*das Erfragte*].[15] *Hermeneutics* names the kind of

---

14. I use the hyphenated term *Be-ing* for the German *das Sein*, which is an infinitive form, in order to distinguish it from *being* (*Seiendes*, a gerund).

15. In this context it is important to note what sorts of things are thought to have "meaning." Words do, of course, and discourse (and perhaps, by extension, even life and love). But phenomenology had by this time already expanded meaning far beyond a feature of linguistic entities. Each and every phenomenon is imbued with meaning by virtue of its being intended by acts of consciousness. Husserl's notion of the constitution of phenomena by consciousness refers to the construction of their meanings for consciousness. Heidegger's attribution of meaning to Be-ing itself—to "*the* phenomenon of phenomenology" that is not really a phenomenon at all but more like the very appearing (and concealing) of phenomena—expands the reach of meaning even further. When Heidegger seeks the meaning of Be-ing he is not looking for what the word *Be-ing* (and its Indo-European cognates) means. He is seeking the ways that things (phenomena) have come to be manifest, and these ways are by no means necessarily linguistic. Yet at the same time (it may be said) the attribution of meaning to Be-ing imbues it with a language-like character. In *Being and Time*, the ways things come to be manifest and to be concealed are read out of the texts of the philosophical tradition and the comportment of Dasein. Dasein is both something to be understood and that which understands. "In its familiarity with these [referential] relations, Da-sein 'signifies' to itself. It primordially gives itself to understand

3. Understanding: An Alternative to the Hermeneutical Model | 69

analysis that fulfills this inquiry. Ostensibly *the meaning of Be-ing* is not formulated as a sentence, and *hermeneutics* is not a text that supplies its ultimate meaning. Yet Heidegger's own text exhibits an unmistakable drive to state "the meaning of Be-ing is time" or "is temporality," or (later) "is presencing" [*Anwesenheit*]—however tentative and groping these sentences are. Hermeneutics is a way of reading the meaning of Being wherever it is disclosed, in its being there. Dasein ("being-there") becomes a text that discloses the meaning of Being. But Dasein is also the reader. Dasein reads itself, discloses itself. It (we) can do so because we already always exist as a form of disclosedness—as *understanding* [*Verstehen*]. The main thing (or sentence) that is disclosed is that we exist as beings inseparable from our world. *World* names the context in which we live, that within which we seek and project meanings. The world is structured as a "relational totality of signification," something with significance [*Bedeutsamkeit*]. Usually this referential totality goes unnoticed, but it can show up sometimes when our projections of meaning are interrupted, as when a tool we are using breaks. The tool exists in a whole matrix of relations in which we use this for that, in the same way that we say X to refer to Y within a particular, unarticulated situation. *Understanding* uncovers the "for the sake of which" [*worumwillen*] we inevitably do things; *understanding* is the name for this kind of disclosure.[16] And Heidegger made this *understanding* an "Existential," a fundamental way of being—not a way we sometimes could choose to be at will, but a way we inevitably are.

The alternative sense of practice I will propose undercuts any "for the sake of which," and calls for an alternative sense of understanding.

Heidegger's treatment of *understanding* pretends a fundamental expansion if not reversal of the term, but implicitly betrays a textual model. Heidegger would expand *Verstehen* beyond understanding

---

its being and potentiality-of-being with regard to its being-in-the-world....Da-sein gives itself to understand its being-in-the-world beforehand." HEIDEGGER 1927, trans. 1996, 87. Page numbers given refer to pages in the German edition.

16. HEIDEGGER 1927, 85 and 143.

language, even beyond any thematic cognitive grasp, to mean know-how [*können*]. I understand a hammer when I know how to hammer. Thus, understanding for Heidegger includes (to use my words) bodily interacting with things; it suggests the body's practiced know-how (a suggestion that will feature in our alternative notion). But Heidegger comes to know of this know-how by reading Dasein's comportment with *things* in the world (not primarily with other Dasein, other people, but with things "ready to hand" [*zuhanden*]), and he implicitly treats this know-how as a capacity we gain in the same way we learn to read automatically through words and sentences to their significations. We take a hammer in hand and, paying little heed to it, with our eye on the goal, see through the hammer to what it is for—just as we take a book in hand and see through the print to the meaning of the words. Our engagement with tools is directed away from them toward the goal or purpose of the activity, to its *Worumwillen*, just as our engagement with texts is directed to the matter they discuss. Heidegger's analysis brilliantly elucidates the working of everyday human activities, but it does not take into account activities that have no goal, nor even *the kind of practice whose goal is inseparable from the activity of performing it*. I will suggest how this kind of practice is at the heart of much religious activity, and calls for another sense of understanding.

Heidegger's later work more explicitly challenged that notion that language is a tool, and even in *Being and Time* he anticipates his later emphasis on language as "world disclosure." Later he also framed language as "the house of Being." He began to pay attention to poetic language and other possibilities of "using" language in a way that does not objectify.[17] But by modeling the notion of understanding after the usage and referential system of tools, in *Being and Time* he cast understanding in the framework of textual referentiality, a house constructed of sentences.

17. HEIDEGGER 1927–64, 22–31.

One might think that two of those who followed Heidegger's expansive interpretation most closely, Gadamer and Ricoeur, would have freed hermeneutics from its binding to textuality. They did shift the focus from *texts* in some literal sense, but remained within the same textual horizon.

How Gadamer restricts understanding to language, and language to textualized dialogue

Indications of the implicit textual horizon of Hans-Georg Gadamer's hermeneutics are evident in his model of dialogue or conversation, which itself counts explicitly as the model of understanding. Other indications appear in his broader notion of language.

Gadamer's focus on the back and forth, question and answer dialectic of conversation [*Gespräch*] is rightly celebrated as a major advance in theories of interpretation. What goes unnoticed, however, is the limited kind of conversation he seems to have in mind. Perhaps as a scholar of Plato as well as a hermeneutical philosopher, Gadamer envisions Plato's Socratic dialogues as an ideal, just as Plato in writing these dialogues may have aimed for an ideal form of what he encountered in actual, everyday conversations in the polis. Be that as it may, Gadamer's model of dialogue is a far cry from ordinary, everyday conversations, and betrays a noticeable tendency to the textual guise of language.

Consider Gadamer's sequence of comments on an aspect of hermeneutics that has been lost from sight since Schleiermacher. Gadamer begins with the rather existential statement that "to understand first of all means to understand one another." The desire to come to an understanding [*Verständnis*], that is, to reach agreement [*Einverständnis*], necessarily focuses on some subject matter, some something that has evoked disagreement or misunderstanding and that must be resolved. This matter, at the heart of what one means, is "the path and goal of mutual understanding itself." It might seem that virtually anything could arise as the matter to be resolved, but Gadamer's aim is more specific: It is a matter of *your* meaning or *of the meaning of a text*—"die Meinung des anderen, des Du oder des Textes." The ways taken forward and back to come to an understanding, the paths that make up "the art of conversation—argument, question and answer, objection and refutation... are also undertaken with regard to a text as an inner dialogue of the soul seeking understanding...."[18] If Gadamer here directs hermeneutics at the other person with whom one seeks an understanding, it is nevertheless clear that the model of what is to be understood is the text, whether written or still in formation in the act of conversing.

Gadamer's model is the sort of conversation that takes place in situations like a philosophical symposium. Philosophical conversations are often based on pre-written texts and proceed with participants speaking coherently, in more or less complete and sequential sentences. To be sure, a good deal of back and forth, questioning and responding, enlivens our conversations, but in a style more self-conscious and linguistically aware than the conversations of people on the streets in the workaday world are likely to be. A number of distinct language games may be evident in what goes by the names of dialogue and conversation; certainly, the back and forth of question and answer is not the sole factor. Gadamer's model of dialogue, even in its dialectical structure, depends on sentential semantics and syntax. Non-textual factors that constitute actual conversations, one's tone of voice and gestures, for example, as well as the non-referential aspects of the body of language, go unnoticed in Gadamer's hermeneutics.

A surprising orientation to the text is also indicated in the role assigned to language. For Gadamer language is not first and foremost the object to be understood; it is rather the horizon within which all understanding takes place. The sentence, "*Sein, das verstanden werden*

---

18. GADAMER 1965, 168–9, my emphasis. For a variant translation see the 1984 English version, 158–9.

kann, ist Sprache" ("Being that can be understood is language")[19] means, phenomenologically: if something is to be understood, it must manifest in the form of language. Gadamer explicitly criticizes the theory that takes words as signs and language as a tool. We misunderstand "the life of language," language as it lives in speech, when we reduce it to signs as instruments with more or less univocal designations.[20] As does Heidegger, Gadamer defines (or unbinds) language as *world-disclosure*. What his discussion implies, however, is that the form of language that best reveals its life and discloses world is the dialogical form of an exchange of sentences.

This reading at first sight seems at odds with some of what Gadamer writes: *Authentic language is found first in conversation, not in the statement*, as the early Greeks thought. Making oneself understood is not another matter of acting purposefully, say by producing signs, in order to communicate to others. Communicating is not in need of tools at all; it is a process of living that a community lives out. Language becomes real only in the realization of communication. The statement [*Aussage*] covers up, with the exactness of some method, the horizon of meaning of what there is to say. What is left over is the supposedly "purified" meaning of the stated. This is what goes on record. But meaning reduced to what is stated is always a distorted meaning.[21] What could disqualify more strongly than these statements do a hermeneutics that takes its cues from statements and texts?

Ironically, the limits of Gadamer's understanding of language are apparent in a series of statements that emphasize the power of spoken words to render the totality of being. Gadamer writes:

> to say what one means, to make oneself understood, is to embrace in one meaning both what is said and an infinity of what is not, and in this way to offer what is said for understanding. One who speaks in this

---

19. GADAMER 1965, 451.
20. Ibid., 410, 382.
21. See ibid., 442, 444; my paraphrase.

manner may use only the most ordinary and most commonplace words and yet precisely because of that is able *to put into language* [*zur Sprache zu bringen*] *what is unsaid and to be said.* The one who speaks does so by surmising or speculating, insofar as his words are not copies of things but rather *express a relation to the whole of Being and let it be put into language.* Connected to this is the fact that one who repeats what is said, *just as one who reports statements, need not consciously distort anything at all and yet will change the meaning of what is said.*"[22]

One might ask whether, by reporting Gadamer's statements, I have changed the meaning of what he has written; indeed, whether he himself has changed the meaning of what language can say by putting it into—not just any kind of language but—a series of statements. After all, Gadamer does not present his theory in the form of dialogue, much less of living speech. In the "infinity of what is not [said]" lie features of the body of language that social linguists point out as parts of every embodied instance of language, features that escape not only the semantics and syntax of the statement but the expressive range of the spoken word, that for this reason escape the words that can be rendered in sentences and texts.

More than the terms of his theory, it is Gadamer's hermeneutical practice that veils his pre-disposition toward textual understanding. Gadamer discusses phenomena like living speech that at first sight cannot be equated with textual language, and he reflects on the conditions for the possibility of their appearance (i.e., world, human be-ing, language). But he evidently intends to capture the significance of nontextual language and phenomena, and to describe the disclosive power of language, in the form of sentences building up a text. Gadamer fashions his understanding in the form of a text; and he presumes that textual writing is adequate to disclose this understanding.

22. Ibid., 444–5, my emphasis.

How Ricoeur Textualizes Self and World

The hermeneutical theory of Paul Ricoeur follows the trajectory of expanding classical hermeneutics but ultimately returns it to its *locus classicus* in the text. In the end, it is the meaning and scope of *text* that undergoes expansion—to the point of understanding both self and world in terms of the text. Here we offer only two examples of how this expansion occurs in Ricoeur's work, from the 1960s to the 1980s, when he was explicitly concerned with hermeneutics. He began with a critique of the Romanticist hermeneutics of Schleiermacher and Dilthey that aimed to break the bondage of interpretation theory to the understanding of texts as exemplary forms of dialogue—dialogues between an author with particular intentions in mind and a reader who is the anticipated audience. Ricoeur's critique placed interpretation theory in a broader theory of discourse that recognizes its double role, as self-understanding and as world-disclosure.

This theory harks back to Heidegger, but with a correction. In one essay, Ricoeur writes that "Language itself, as a signifying milieu, must be referred to existence."[23] Because Heidegger's existential analysis or hermeneutic can fall prisoner to language, however, it needs to surpass the linguistic level. For Ricoeur, we need a step that links the understanding of signs to self-understanding. Ricoeur writes:

> In proposing to relate symbolic language to self-understanding, I think I fulfill the deepest wish of hermeneutics. The purpose of all interpretation is to conquer a remoteness, a distance between the past cultural epoch *to which the text belongs* and the interpreter himself. By overcoming this distance, by making himself contemporary with *the text*, the exegete can appropriate its meaning to himself: foreign, he makes it familiar, that is, he makes it his own. It is thus the growth of his own understanding of himself that he pursues through his understanding

23. RICOEUR 1969, English translation 1974, 16.

of the other. Every hermeneutics is thus, explicitly or implicitly, self-understanding by means of understanding others.[24]

Yet, to complete this last thought in line with the previous sentences, we would need to write, "understanding others by means of their texts." Or more precisely, "self-understanding by means of understanding other texts." While self and other are not exactly reduced to text here, the text functions as the means to understanding self via understanding others—as the means to the telos of hermeneutics in its expanded sense. In stressing the disclosive power of the text, Ricoeur not only intentionally grafts hermeneutics onto phenomenology; he unwittingly grafts it onto textual understanding. Again and again he slips from talk of language to talk of text. "Let us in fact reflect upon what the self of self-understanding signifies, whether we appropriate the sense of a psychoanalytic interpretation or that of a textual exegesis."[25] As textual interpretations that take place through language, psychoanalytic interpretation and textual exegesis are evidently equivalent. The language Ricoeur writes of here, furthermore, is not the living *parole* but the abstract *la langue*.

In the conclusion to lectures given in 1973–75, Ricoeur notes the shift that took place in early twentieth-century hermeneutics from historicist to logicist views—from understanding a text as a historical object confined to its time, its author's intentions, and its particular addressees, to explaining a text as a kind of atemporal object that refers to ideal meanings beyond the confines of psychological intention and immediate historical context. Ricoeur's guiding interest here lies not only in maintaining objectivity in interpretation but also in exposing the dialectical nature of relations in the hermeneutical endeavor: the dialectics of understanding and explanation, of alternately distancing and appropriating the object of understanding or explanation, of event and meaning within discourse, and of sense and reference within

---

24. Ibid., 16–7, my emphasis.
25. Ibid., 16–17. The original text is RICOEUR 1969, 20–1.

meaning. (These "dialectical" relations of mutually dependent terms may also be seen as expressions of the hermeneutical circle.) All the while, the consistent referent of Ricoeur's analysis of hermeneutics remains the text as *the* form of fixing discourse. Every general statement about appropriation or distanciation, understanding or explanation, etc., is exemplified in terms of "a text." Exceeding propositional logic, what hermeneutics has to do is to disclose "a possible way of looking at things," a possible world never merely referred to ostensively, but rather disclosed—through the text. Such world disclosure "constitutes the [ultimate] reference of the text."[26] It is the text that opens a possible mode of being in the world, a project of the world. Another dialectic is at work here, but only by implication, an ineluctable dialectic of world and text. Moreover, the ideality of meaning that Ricoeur welcomes as assurance of the objectivity of hermeneutics is traced by him back to Frege's and early Husserl's notion of the ideal meaning—not of a text per se, but of a sentence.

To be sure, if the text is enclosed within sentences that have meanings beyond the intentions of the author and the egoistic reader whose mind is made up, the act of appropriating these meanings requires the opening of the self, indeed the creation of a new self. The last sentences of Ricoeur's lectures on "Interpretation Theory" read:

> Only the interpretation that complies with the injunction of the text, that follows the "arrow" of the sense and that tries to think accordingly, initiates a new self-understanding.... It is the text, with its universal power of world disclosure, which gives a self to the ego [that is, which replaces ego with self]."[27]

26. RICOEUR 1976, 91–5.
27. Ibid., 94–5. Even after his turn to narrativity and storytelling, Ricoeur continued to insist that self-understanding is ineluctably mediated by language in the form of texts—that the text and the (real) world relate dialectically with the text transfiguring the world, and that textual understanding forms the heart of hermeneutics: "Writing tears itself free of the limits of face-to-face dialogue and becomes the condition for discourse itself *becoming-text*." The task of hermeneutics is to explore "the implications of this becoming-text for the work of interpretation." RICOEUR 1983, 191, 193, 194. MOYAERT

In this manner Ricoeur's hermeneutics is clearly fixated on the text; and the text, however disclosive of world and creative of self, is still fixed in sentences.

Perhaps a textual orientation defines hermeneutics only as it appears in "Western" religions and philosophies. An excursus at the end of this chapter puts this conjecture in question.

The ostensible turn of hermeneutics from text to ontology and to the understanding of cultures turns out to be an expansion of its original textual framework. A contrast with the understanding demanded by religions in practice makes this quite evident.

Toward an alternative sense of understanding

If the textual language inscribed in philosophical hermeneutics and often invoked in interreligious dialogue does not reach all there is to be understood in religions, what then is the alternative? In proposing an alternative sense of understanding, I am not suggesting that we have a choice between two or more incompatible approaches. Rather, the alternative I will propose is complementary. Language in textual form does enable understanding and experiencing. But not all of it.[28]

What goes by the name of interreligious dialogue itself provides examples of understanding that is facilitated by non-textual, even extra-linguistic practice. Complementing the textual interpretations and the conversations that exemplify much dialogue between representatives of distinct religions are shared activities such as prayer, meditation, chanting, or participating in other religious rituals.[29] It should

---

2010 indicates how Ricoeur's later philosophy of self and other, while still language-oriented, is no longer bound to textual understanding.

28. I am acutely aware of the ironies of this chapter, itself a sequence of sentences that requires textual understanding, even as it calls for a non-textual hermeneutic.

29. The recent rise of ritual studies as a subfield of religious studies indicates a renewed recognition that religions do not reduce to textually formulated beliefs. But insofar as the scholar of rituals remains an objective or "outside" observer, the practice of this scholarship differs from the engaged practice at the heart of the alternative mode of under-

not be surprising that the Zen Buddhism Abe Masao presented in discursive language is more commonly known to insist on the primary of practice, as Abe himself proclaimed: "for the realization of Zen, practice is absolutely necessary" (meaning primarily *zazen* practice).[30] If Abe engaged in discursive dialogue as a concession to participants who expected a focus on beliefs and teachings, he seemed unconcerned that such dialogue tends to reduce religion to one form and ignore other forms that are relevant to both practitioners and scholars, "insiders" and "outsiders" alike. One master at interreligious dialogue, Jan van Bragt, has awakened us to one consequence:

> When religions are not considered as matters of objective truth, their differences in doctrine lose much of their weight and their boundaries tend to blur: they appear less distinct and mutually opposed. It has often been pointed out that, for the Japanese, religion is, in the first place, a question of ritual and practices, and only very secondarily a question of doctrine (and organization). And when belonging to a religion does not impose any personal obligation, nor involve ethical and social consequences, multiple belonging [the possibility of belonging to more than one] is, of course much less problematic.[31]

Unlike "multiple belonging," dialogue by its very nature assumes the reality and relevance of difference. But the resolution of differences is not necessarily the aim of all dialogue. Recently some interreligious dialogues have combined discursive, text-oriented conversations with forms of shared practice. One ongoing forum has combined academic presentations and discussion with rituals such as the recitation of

---

standing I call for. Anthropologists like Barbara Tedlock try to negotiate this difference in modes of understanding by practicing a kind of observant participation, described in TEDLOCK (1992, xiii). WRIGHT (2008) articulates the limits of the observers' understanding of how rituals function internally for practitioners.

30. See our discussion in Chapter 2, pages 39–41 of the present volume.

31. VAN BRAGT 2002, 9–10. To be sure, Van Bragt also gives examples in Japanese history where religious authorities did emphasize doctrinal difference and exclusive truth, and thus where belonging to a religion has been a matter of explicit avowal. For his own masterful practice of dialogue, see VAN BRAGT 2014.

sutras or prayers and Christian and Zen meditation, without trying to resolve or dissolve differences.[32] Here I want to focus on a more single-minded form of dialogue that better exemplifies the alternative understanding in question.

Intermonastic dialogue

Intermonastic exchange is an exemplary arena for illustrating an approach to non-textual understanding, not because monastics are religiously superior to other people but simply because their lives, on the margins of "world religions," are more focused on religious practices. This exchange has required a suspension of judgment about truth claims formulated or implicit in the texts of the other's religion. Instead of debating truth or interpreting a text, monks learned *how to do* something, an activity that is distinct from believing in or believing that something is the case—distinct from textual matters, in other words.

European Benedictines, for example, have gone to Japan and lived for a week or so in Zen monasteries, and Zen monks have come to Benedictine monasteries in Europe. This exchange takes place between one specific group from one tradition and a specific group of another tradition. Individual Zen monks who practice in Theravada monaster-

32. The "2nd World Encounter, Teresian Mysticism and Interreligious Dialogue: Chan/Zen Buddhism and Carmelite Spirituality" took place in Ávila, Spain, July 26–30, 2022, and followed the First Encounter, on "Theravāda Buddhism and Teresian Mysticism: Meditation and Contemplation Pathways to Peace" in July 2017. The announcement states:

> It is [our] earnest wish... to deepen the mutual understanding of both traditions' beliefs and practices. It must be emphasized that there is absolutely no wish to deny the differences between the two traditions or attempt to reduce them to a common denominator. Instead, the dialogue will be conducted in the spirit of equality, deep respect, openness and wish for cooperation. The aim is to foster genuine engagement, enhance mutual growth, and explore ways of cooperation to approach the pressing social and environmental concerns of today and help improve the welfare of mankind.

<https://www.mistica.es/en/2nd-world-encounter-teresian-mysticism-and-interreligious-dialogue>.

ies are not usually said to be participating in an intermonastic dialogue; nor are, say, individual Catholic priests and nuns, or Jewish rabbis, who undergo training under a Zen master. Unlike interreligious dialogue in general, moreover, the interest of the two groups is to explore commonalities and differences in their devotion to the monastic life, rather than to represent the viewpoint of a "world religion."

We may, then, limit the term *intermonastic dialogue* to the sharing of monastic practices, as distinct from conferences and formal discussions between monks of different religious traditions that occur apart from sharing daily activities.[33] It is significant that these activities are considered a form of dialogue at all. While they may include conversations, formal and informal, the focus is on the everyday practices of the host monks. I think the term *dialogue* properly describes such exchanges, for the participants continue to respect difference while meeting together. But instead of a shared language in which discussion takes place, a shared regimen of practices provides the meeting-ground or commons of dialogue. The guest monks participate in varying degrees in the same activities that the host monks usually practice. Benedictines sit *zazen*, seated meditation, in Japan (although I do not know if they undertake kōan practice and *sanzen* or private interviews with the master), and Japanese Zen monks chant prayers in European Christian monasteries (although they might not receive the Eucharist at mass). Part of the shared practice may include listening to, reading, and attempting to understand texts—listening to the readings during the otherwise silent dinner at Benedictine monasteries, for example, or listening to the Zen master's *teishō*, a verbal demonstration of his understanding of a classical Zen text. While textual understanding forms part of the daily practice, it by no means exhausts the range of

---

33. The web site <http://www.buddhist-christian-studies.org/> gives descriptions of many intermonastic exchanges, as well as of Buddhist-Christian study conferences, in Europe. My account here in no way intends to disparage the value of verbal interreligious dialogue. My point is to differentiate that discursive dialogue from the form of dialogue that focuses on the sharing of traditional practices.

activities that call for another kind of understanding. Indeed, many activities cultivate working and dwelling in silence, a practice that the two traditions share. A statement of Thomas Merton captures this focus: "The deepest level of communication is not communication, but communion. It is wordless. It is beyond words, and it is beyond speech, and it is beyond concept."[34] As wordless as it is, however, I would stress that this communion need not be considered "mystical," if that word designates an extraordinary experience accessible only to the adept. Such communion can simply be being together and doing something together, something quite ordinary in the life of the practitioner.[35]

Just what sort of understanding is occurring between the monks who engage in "intermonastic dialogue"? Descriptions of the exchanges suggest the following features:

The shared activities required mindful, bodily engagement, whether words were involved or not. Consider the practice of chanting. Chanting commonly involves voicing words, and may therefore seem like a textual practice. But chanting words is different from saying them in ordinary conversations and formal discussions, where the focus is on the semantic meaning of the words. Chanting is focused on the quality of the sound, on the vibrations that resonate among the chanters. Both speaking and chanting can be mindful or attentive, but chanting engages one's body more fully than does the usual utterance of words. Singing is similar. Music, even with text, resonates emotionally with performers and listeners and communicates something beyond textual meaning. (Japanese Zen chanting, in comparison with Korean

---

34. Quoted in CORNILLE 2008, 115.
35. Participants in conference-type interreligious dialogue often express a reluctance, as much as a willingness, to share practices, and may go only as far as respectful *observation* will take them. I do not find Merton's *communion* exemplified in such cases. Observing the practices of the other might approximate actual participation in them—to the degree that observing a verbal dialogue from the outside, without participating in it, approximates engagement in actual dialogue. For an example see the *Society for Buddhist-Christian Studies Newsletter* 41 (2008) 3–5.

Zen chanting and certainly with Gregorian chanting, can sound quite monotone and dull; still the intent is to become "one with" the sounds, to experience a kind of communion). All this is not to say that chanting abandons meaning. It functions in a social milieu and carries numerous meanings for the observer; it can function, for example, as a marker of insider identity. What one is understanding through the practice of chanting, however, is a different matter.

The sharing in traditional activities required learning, on the part of the guest participants, how to practice them. The sharing may involve significant differences from the way Zen novices typically learn Zen monastic practices, or the way Benedictine novices learn to be a Benedictine monk; and these differences may have to do with their respective expectations and beliefs, as well as with the (often unwritten) methods of teaching a novice how to be a monk. Nevertheless, when Zen monks engage in Benedictine practices, or when Benedictine monks undergo some Zen training, the methods of teaching the guests typically derive from the same methods that have been in play for training the host monks.

Learning how to do something is distinct from believing in something and from believing that something is the case, from textual matters in other words. The distinction holds despite the relevance of beliefs and doctrines for the particular practices. True, learning to chant scriptures may typically involve, for the host Benedictine monks, background beliefs and commitment to the truths of such scriptures that are not shared by the guest Zen monks. And learning to listen to a Zen master's *teishō* may for the Zen monk be geared toward a kōan practice that is not shared by guest Benedictine monks. But in intermonastic dialogue, strategies of learning often involve a suspension of the beliefs and expectations the guest monk has brought with him, so that he can partake in the practices with a full heart and mind. The practice of listening and of chanting require an openness and a mindful attention that is the same for all.

Sharing in the practices is not focused on a goal separate from the activity itself. If mutual understanding is set as a goal, that goal is achieved in the very process of practicing the activity, be it *zazen* or chanting Christian scriptures. Again, this statement does not preclude the relevance of what seem to be transcendent goals, salvation for the Benedictine monk or awakening for the Zen monk. But in performing the activity the focus is not set on a transcendent goal. Indeed, in the course of the activity, hoping for one's salvation or thinking of enlightenment may be considered a distraction from the practice at hand.

The sharing of activities does not depend on, nor does it confirm, the idea that religious experience is ultimately ineffable and every expression of religious truth, especially every textual expression, is merely relative and inadequate. Such a premise in any case would presuppose an utter disconnect between verbal teachings and experience.

The understanding that takes place in such intermonastic dialogue is first and foremost an understanding of religious life of the other, and this understanding comes about by living that life as fully as possible during the prescribed period of time. It occurs by doing what the other does. The religious life of the other does not function as an object to be grasped intellectually or empathetically. Rather it is appropriated as a daily practice. Practicing is the form that understanding takes here. What is exchanged in this sort of "dialogue" is defined by a set of practices rather than a viewpoint on doctrines. To translate this experience into the domain of language, we could say that in such practice the dialogue partner learns to speak *as his or her own* the words learned from the other. In this context, understanding by way of practices can overlap with textual understanding but shift the role of doctrine. Understanding religious doctrines and dogmas as expressed in sentences and fixed in texts may require enactment rather than cognitive assent. This possibility is explored in recent interpretations of dogma and doctrine inspired by Maurice Blondel's work on action and Henri Bergson's critique of intellectualism.[36]

Intermonastic dialogue does not erase differences between host and guest monks, but it did often set them aside. Differences defined by the respective ordinations, vows, and background beliefs of the two groups, as well as by their language and culture, also became apparent, but usually in "extra-curricular" formal discussions outside the ordinary daily practice of the monks.

In summary, understanding via bodily engagement does not obviate the apparent need for and actuality of textual understanding in the encounter between religions. It offers a complement that, I suggest, forms an indispensable part of interreligious hermeneutics. It would be possible to give many other examples of understanding among religions as it is sought and achieved through mutual practice. All would call us to the hermeneutical task of clarifying further an alternative sense both of understanding and of practice. The following contrasts may serve as pointers.

An Alternative Notion of Religious Practice

Activities such as prayer, meditation, chanting, or participating in other religious rituals engage the body and mind differently than do observation, reading, analyzing, and translating. They engage the body more consciously and disengage discursive thought. We cannot employ such embodied practices as we do concepts or judgments that form beliefs about the world. In the case of concepts and judgments, we may merely mention them while standing back and remaining detached, or we may assent to them and direct our beliefs accordingly while still remaining bodily disengaged. In contrast, practices in the alternative sense require coordinated bodily action and mental attention.

---

36. See MANSINI 1985.

What makes this sense of practice more specifically an alternative to the dominant sense in much philosophical literature is its relation to an objective or end. The word practice predominantly implies an activity that is geared toward an objective or purpose separate from the activity. Religious activities too may well be regarded as practices in the dominant sense and given soteriological significance. They may be aimed ultimately at salvation, for example, or at liberation or enlightenment. Seen in a different light, however, activities, whether explicitly religious or not, can be exercised and experienced as an end in themselves, not as a means to an end different in kind from the activity. Such activities may indeed have an objective, but the objective is not external to the activity that achieves it. The activity embodies the objective in incipient form. To refer to the previous example of intermonastic practice, the intention of Benedictine chanting may ultimately be to glorify God, and that of Zen chanting may be to concentrate the mind and embody the Dharma, but the intention is repeatedly fulfilled in the very act of chanting. If monks engage in a particular activity to partially fulfill the intention of their entire religious life, the performance of each activity in itself can function as an expression of the totality of that life. Chanting, for example, can function as a kind of hologram of the monks' entire religious life when practiced whole-heartedly. The activity expresses a whole that may transcend it.

The chapter to follow elaborates the alternative notion of practice in more detail and expands it beyond its application to religions.

The Alternative Notion of Understanding

Practices in the alternative sense generate a form of understanding distinct from understandings that are merely intellectual, textual, or empathetic. The alternative to textual understanding, however, does not entail an attempt to abandon all language, since not all language use is textual. Language no more than religion can be bound to logos, to worded reasoning. Understanding the non-sentential aspects of the body of language mentioned earlier provided some examples of non-textual understanding. The practice of learning a language offers a related set of examples. And non-linguistic practices provide examples of another sort that are equally relevant to interreligious hermeneutics.

Learning a language is a practice that involves understanding that language, of course, but understanding in this case is not a prerequisite. Rather it is achieved in the process of learning the language. Understanding the language here means the ability to use it, to live in it, rather than to take it as an object of an act of interpretation. Reminiscent of Gadamer, we may say that understanding a language is coming to understand the world through that language. But linguistic understanding is not the only way to an understanding of the world, and it is not confined to textual understanding.

The bond of traditional hermeneutics to textual language actually veils an opening to the alternative notion of understanding—by reminding us of the incompleteness of textual language. When one learns a language, one learns more than what words mean, what their references are, and also more than how they are linked together. Of course, one learns vocabulary and grammar (or, in the view of Cartesian linguists, one activates universal structures of a pre-existent grammar). More significantly, however, one learns how language is used in concrete situations, and that usage involves situationally dependent elements that are not coded in grammar or vocabulary—elements like tone of voice, gesture, and facial expression, as mentioned earlier. Acquiring language and becoming a competent speaker and writer takes practice, and that practice involves more than understanding what words refer to. In particular, learning non-referential aspects of the body of language is different from, perhaps even prior to, studying the semantics and structures of a language.[37] The relevant difference

---

37. The linguist SAVIGNON (1997, 35) writes:
C'est en forgeant que l'on devient forgeron. Just as one learns to be a blacksmith by being a blacksmith, one learns to communicate by communicating. Or, to put it dif-

appears in the stance of the learner: when she is engaged in using the language competently, in living or embodying the language, she makes it her own and ceases to examine it from an outsider's perspective.

It might be thought that the practice of learning a language involves an objective separate from that activity. One learns a language in order to communicate; one usually learns a foreign language for one purpose or another, but not simply as an end in itself. We might look at it differently, however. In practice, the end or goal can be inherent in the very activity of using the language. I may practice Japanese to get better at speaking and reading Japanese, but being good or better at it is still speaking and reading Japanese. I may want to learn Japanese in order to read Japanese Buddhist texts, and to do that in order to pursue a certain line of research; but reading the texts is already an end or goal in the practice of learning. Learning a language by using it exemplifies an alternative kind of understanding.

Non-linguistic practices, that is, practices that do not depend on the employment of language, are particularly exemplary of the alternative sense of understanding. The descriptions of inter-monastic exchange intimate their relevance for the alternative sense, but barely hint at the full range of such practices in the wider domain of religion. A more detailed account must await another occasion.

The alternative form of understanding, I have suggested, is at work in practices done for their own sake or for the sake of a goal inseparable from their very performance. What then is the role of intention in achieving such understanding? The hermeneutical theories of Heidegger and Gadamer stress that no understanding occurs without a pre-understanding, whereby a person has a particular intention in mind, anticipates a particular outcome, or is guided by a pre-formed set of beliefs, however subject to revision they are. The alternative sense

---

ferently, one develops skills by using skills. It is only when we have an incentive to communicate and the experience of communication that structures are acquired. In this sense, then, one might speak of going *from communicative competence to grammatical competence.*

of understanding would seem to call for a total suspension not only of one's own background beliefs but also of any intent to understand the beliefs of the other. I do not think such a double suspension is possible, and doubt that it would be necessary. One is not likely to leap blindly, without anticipation, into the activity practiced by another, although one might be called upon gradually to limit one's intention to imitating the activity of the other or simply following instructions. The crucial point is that the practice can induce a radical alteration of such anticipations, and even of intentional consciousness. There is nothing necessarily mystical or exceptional about such alteration; it occurs regularly in learning and appropriating an initially foreign language. One stumbles in speaking a language when one has to try to speak it; one speaks it competently when the intention of learning it dissolves.

Intentions may also initiate religious practices known for their suspension of intentionality, such as the *zazen* or seated meditation practiced in Zen Buddhism, and the *vipassana* or insight meditation of modern Theravada Buddhism. The practitioner is likely to begin the exercise with a certain goal in mind. She may intend to achieve a peaceful state of "no-mind," an awareness that does not cling to its objects; she may wish to gain insight through mindful breathing, or even to gain enlightenment or have a *satori* experience. Typically, this kind of intention will only get in the way, as would a pianist's conscious focus on her hands while performing a piece. In short, the practice dissolves initial intentions and anticipations; it concentrates one's attention on the performance, until the performance can occur by second nature, by bare attention alone.[38]

Practice not only enhances, but also transforms understanding in the alternative sense. Engaging in practices may not only increase the amount of content understood; it can change the very way that one

---

38. Insofar as this mode of practice begins with embodied attentiveness, the "second nature" it induces essentially differs from that induced by Pierre Bourdieu's sense of *habitus* or interiorized social dispositions and structures.

understands. One can learn anew, often tacitly, *how* to understand.[39] We could in fact call this transformation a kind of conversion—not a switch to another set of beliefs but a turn in the way one does things. Insofar as hermeneutics in a broad sense arises from reflection on how understanding takes place, it necessarily refers back to the experience of understanding (or, as hermeneutical philosophers might put it, to experiencing *as* understanding). In the alternative notion of understanding, this experiencing occurs in the process of practicing. In the context of interreligious hermeneutics, it can occur in the course of practicing what members of the other religion practice, as distinct from coming to believe what others believe. As is the case with the learning of a language, the alternative sense of understanding aims at competence, not at adherence to a set of beliefs. While this kind of learning and practicing may not come easily, may involve frustration or even "lead nowhere," its difficulties are nevertheless distinct from those of teaching the other to understand what seems self-evident to oneself.

Understanding in any sense removes barriers, not distinctions. Distinctions remain, but they can be viewed from two or more sides. Coming to understand a foreign language removes the barrier between one's own tongue and the previously alien tongue, but not the distinction between them. It lets things be seen from the perspective of the other language. Becoming competent in another language does not require that one abandon one's mother tongue or any other acquired language, although at times it may require disengaging them. Similarly, coming to understand the religion of others by engaging in their practices does not eliminate the differences between them. It may call for a temporary disengagement with one's religious beliefs, but it does not require that one abandon them. It dissolves barriers, not differences, and this is one reason the alternative can still be considered a form of

---

39. There are notable similarities between this alternative understanding and Michael Polyani's notion of tacit knowledge, which he developed as the core of an alternative epistemology.

understanding. It lets one experience in a different way, along the way to seeing how others experience the world.

Insofar as religions include non-textual practices, understanding religions requires an approach quite different from the kind of understanding usually conceived in hermeneutics. That approach is through a bodily (re)enactment of the practices rather than a discursive reading of texts and teachings.[40] If "interreligious hermeneutics" is to account for the full range of religious life, it must articulate an alternative notion of understanding that gives access to religious practices as they are lived. This chapter is meant as a step in that direction.

> *Excursus 1*
> How Schleiermacher and Dilthey
> oriented their hermeneutics to texts

The binding of hermeneutics to texts appears to be a matter of course when we consider its beginnings as a formal discipline. Long before the term *hermeneutics* was used, philologists, jurists, and biblical commentators reflected on the methods of interpreting, the problems of translating, and the levels of meaning in texts. In the late eighteenth century philologists like Georg Anton Friedrich Ast and New Testament exegetes like Johann August Ernesti established the term *hermeneutics* more explicitly as a reflection on textual understanding. Friedrich Schleiermacher expanded its usage to apply to spoken language as well, but in the form of conversations that mimic written texts, and of discursive language that not only marked no difference between spoken and written but took both to be outward expressions

---

40. My proposal for an alternative sense of understanding religions via embodied engagement by no means precludes novel extensions of text-based, hermeneutical approaches, as we find in Dickman 2022, a book that employs "confessionally-oriented hermeneutics" in search of questions that decenter us, in the Hebrew Bible, the Christian Gospels, and the Sayings of Zen Master Mazu.

of inner units of thought. "How shall I know a person except from his discourse, specifically, from this text before me?"[41]

Schleiermacher attained the status of the founder of modern hermeneutical theory by absorbing and then transforming what his predecessors had done. He made the phenomenon of understanding questionable rather than taking it as the norm; he expanded the scope of hermeneutics beyond its auxiliary role in interpreting texts, and he narrowed the task of hermeneutics to elucidating a general theory of understanding.[42] Hermeneutics was to be the theory of the *art* of understanding, and commentators have understandably focused on Schleiermacher's proposals for *how* we come to understand—that is, by way of the grammatical and the psychological, artful approaches, and the empathetic and comparative methods.

If we shift the focus to ask *what* is to be understood, according to Schleiermacher, then the text-orientation of his hermeneutics comes clearly into view. Schleiermacher's manuscripts variously designate what is to be understood: a writer or author (*Schriftsteller*), an author's individuality as well as his linguistic sphere, a language, parts of the language such as words and sentences. But what is to be understood is seemingly much more than sentences and texts. In fact, theoretically, there are no bounds to what can become the object of one's endeavor

---

41. SCHLEIERMACHER 1805–33 (1977), 161 (Manuscript 4, written 1826–27). Note that, by shifting *discourse* to *text*, the English translators have specified something with a broader meaning in Schleiermacher's manuscript: "*Denn woher soll ich den Menschen kennen als nur durch seine Rede, zumal in Beziehung auf diese Rede.*" An alternative translation would be: "for how should I know a person except through his discourse, especially in reference to this discourse." But in the following passage, Schleiermacher does imply that understanding aims at something written when he mentions "our knowledge of the *Schriftsteller*" or *writer/author*. His focus here is on the ideal of a "technical interpretation" of the writing in distinction from a "grammatical interpretation" that depends upon a particular language. See SCHLEIERMACHER 1805-33 (1959), 113.

42. For details see MARALDO 1974, 22–9. VEDDER 2000 disagrees with the usual assessment of Schleiermacher's specific contribution to hermeneutics. Indeed, my thesis would extend the title of his book (in English translation): "What Is Hermeneutics: A Way from the Reading of Texts to the Interpretation of Reality"... and back again.

3. Understanding: An Alternative to the Hermeneutical Model | 93

to understand. Yet the language of Schleiermacher's manuscripts is not so inclusive or imprecise. An author is identified and known by his or her texts; a linguistic sphere is defined as the background of written texts; a language is a language as written by authors (and imagined as spoken by them); and the parts of the language we seek to understand appear as sequences of words in sentences building up a text. This holds true equally for the occasional sentence that serves as a text in itself, as Schleiermacher writes is the case with an aphorism (his own *Aphorisms* included). If a child comes to understand only through hermeneutics, as he writes, it is the meaning of words that the child comes to understand, the words in discourse (*Rede*) spoken in a way that is immediately amenable to writing.[43] First he writes that "language is the only presupposition in hermeneutics, and everything that is to be found including the other objective and subjective presuppositions, must be discovered in language."[44] Then he defines his view more precisely: "everything that comes under the task of hermeneutics [can be seen as] part of a sentence."[45]

Schleiermacher's understanding of language is revealed in his wording about it. Each language is a work of art (*Kunstwerk*), a textual production, that doubles as something to be understood and as a means of communication that communicates both its generality and its particularity.[46] The interpreter—literally of anything to be understood—is to take two approaches, both of which are modeled on interpreting a text: "Both [subjective or] artful and grammatical [or objective] interpretation *begin with a general overview of a text*... but in artful interpretation, *the unity of the work*, its theme, is viewed as the

---

43. "Jedes Kind kommt nur durch Hermeneutik zur Wortbedeutung." SCHLEIERMACHER 1805–33, 40.

44. Ibid., 38, English translation 1977, 50.

45. "Alles was Aufgabe der Hermeneutik sein (kann) ist Glied eines Satzes." See Kimmerle's 1959 Einleitung in SCHLEIERMACHER 1805–33, 17.

46. MARALDO (1974, 33–4) presents more detailed documentation and discussion.

dynamic principle impelling the author."⁴⁷ Schleiermacher recognizes varying degrees of unity, the frequent multiplicity of meanings, the loose bounds of a linguistic sphere, and the unending task of interpretation.⁴⁸ When he refers to what is to be understood as "the linguistic sphere of the author," however he delimits its bounds:

> The era in which an author lives, his development, his involvements, his way of speaking—whenever these factors make a difference in a finished text—constitute his "sphere." But this sphere cannot be found *in toto* in every text, for it varies according to the kind of reader the author had in mind.... But determining the sphere common to the author and the readers is only the first step....⁴⁹

The interpreter must also "consciously grasp an author's linguistic sphere" [in a way he himself cannot]; this "implies that we understand the author better than he understood himself."⁵⁰ Later theorists like Gadamer pointed out that "better understanding" can only apply to the subject matter,⁵¹ a matter expressed in texts. It is abundantly evident Schleiermacher knew that learning a language was more than a matter of mastering its grammar and vocabulary. Yet he formulates his theory

---

47. SCHLEIERMACHER 1805–33, English translation 1977, 147, slightly modified. Schleiermacher also writes, "Grammatical interpretation is the objective side; artful [interpretation] the subjective [side]" (English translation 1977, 42, modified). I have changed the standard translation of *technische* as *technical* to *artful*. Although all hermeneutics for Schleiermacher is an "art" [*Kunst*], the artful approach involves the skill and art of the interpreter and not a mechanical application of the specialist. Schleiermacher often used the apposition *Kunstlehre oder Technik*.

48. Ibid., 31, 147, 160.

49. Ibid., English translation 1977, 118, my emphasis. An alternative translation is:
 The region of the author himself is that of his time, his formation, his manner of dealing and speaking, wherever these occur for us as a difference in formed discourse. But the region does not appear in every writing as a whole, but only according to the reader's measure. But how do we experience what kind of readers the author had in mind? Only by way of a general overview of the whole writing.
SCHLEIERMACHER 1805–33, 91.

50. Ibid.

51. GADAMER 1965, 180; English translation 1984, 169–70.

of understanding within the framework of the text. Schleiermacher makes language a veil for textuality.

Wilhelm Dilthey continued this enclosure. The renown biographer of Schleiermacher, Dilthey made hermeneutics foundational for the humanities and social sciences (the *Geisteswissenschaften*), whose proper method was understanding rather than causal explanation. In the reorientation of scientific philosophy called *Lebensphilosophie*, what is to be understood is human life itself and all its expressions. For all its expansiveness, however, Dilthey's hermeneutics tacitly takes the text, in the sense we have developed, as the model of expressivity. A few statements in Dilthey's "The Rise of Hermeneutics" suffice to indicate this orientation in brief. Since hermeneutics is to be a science, Dilthey wants to demonstrate its universal validity:

> Hermeneutical science arose as *the art of interpreting written monuments*. [But] by employing the analysis of understanding to define the possibility of universally valid interpretation, it advanced to solve the more *general problem* we began with: alongside the analysis of inner experience we have the analysis of understanding, and both provide the *Geisteswissenschaften* with evidence of the possibility and limits of their universally valid knowledge, insofar as they are predicated on the way in which the facts of the mind are originally given.[52]

The facts of the mind [*psychische Tatsachen*] are not accessible through some sort of mind reading, nor given by inner reflection in a mirror-mind, but rather evident in the kind of outer signs we find epitomized in written texts and other expressions that, like texts, constitute a unified whole intended to make sense:

> *Understanding* is the name for the process of knowing an inner realm by way of outwardly given sensory signs… the process of knowing the mind from the sensually given signs that express it. This understanding ranges from comprehending children's babbling to *Hamlet* or *The*

---

52. DILTHEY 1900, 320. Frederic Jameson offers a slightly different translation in DILTHEY 1990, 104.

> *Critique of Reason*.... If for example I would understand Leonardo [da Vinci], the interpretations of his actions, paintings, portraits, and writings function together in a single homogenous, unified process.... Such *artful understanding of constant, fixed expressions of life is what we call interpretation.*

Understanding expressions that take forms other than written signs still depends on them:

> Such interpretation of mute works is everywhere reliant on literature for their clarification.... The immeasurable significance of literature for our understanding of history and the life of the spirit lies in the fact that language alone provides the human inner dimension with its complete, creative and objective expression. The art of understanding thus centers on *the interpretation of the remnants of human existence present in written form.*[53]

In an unwritten layer of his writing, then, Dilthey imagined the great expressions of human life that are to be interpreted—laws, literary works, sacred scripture, the lives of individuals, and all the objectifications of life—as textual expressions. The exemplar of an *expression* (*Ausdruck*) is a textual artifact; *expressing* culminates in textual production or printing (*drucken*). When the interpreter puts himself in the place (and time) of the author, this *Sich hineinversetzen* is a transposition of a textualized reader into a textualized author—is a form of intertextuality. When the interpreting self empathizes with the objective other and "re-lives" what she has lived, it is not a magical re-living but the production of a new text. Re-living (*Nacherleben*) is re-formulating a text.

---

53. DILTHEY 1900, 319.

Excursus 2
HOW DERRIDA'S DECONSTRUCTION AND VATTIMO'S "BEYOND INTERPRETATION" REMAIN TEXT-ORIENTED

Deconstruction as presented by Jacques Derrida is allegedly a critique of hermeneutics, and yet it proceeds from a novel kind of immanent critique that still depends upon some principal premises of hermeneutical philosophy. Rather than undermine these premises or show them to be self-erasing, deconstruction exaggerates them. It insists on the primacy of (written) language and the inseparability of experience and language even more than does hermeneutical philosophy. By attempting to demonstrate that writing has transformed natural languages in their entirety and affected/infected the very nature of knowledge, deconstructive grammatology whittles language down not only to its written forms but its form as text, as an ever-receding whole we try to make sense of. The contention that writing rules over all language, thought, and experience ensures that deconstruction in practice is parasitic on texts. However challenging the sentence structure and terminology of Derrida's own writing are, his writing comes in the form of sentences building up texts. "His writing" means, of course, not only the text he is producing, or the work if you will; it means his practice of producing written language, producing sentences and texts. And however pronounced are his attempts at self-erasure, at undermining the determinacy of his own claims, and the closure of his own writing,[54] he apparently does not consider it possible to venture outside writing and see or hear non-textual language, much less to talk about non-linguistic practices. Like Escher's famous "Drawing Hands" that depicts a drawn hand re-drawing itself, Derrida's writing continually draws itself out of one writing after another.

---

54. The translator of *De la grammatologie*, Gayatri Chakravorty Spivak, elucidates the "perpetually deconstructing movement" of deconstruction in her Translator's Preface, in DERRIDA 1976, lxxvii-viii.

Deconstruction begins and ends with texts, is enclosed in texts, is an interpretation of texts that continually re-produce texts. "There is nothing outside the text—*il n'y a pas de hors-texte*"—that could tell us what a textual reference means. We quote this saying out of context but not in a way that deconstruction can disallow.[55] "Jacques Derrida is also this collection of texts [*Writing and Difference, Of Grammatology, Speech and Phenomena*, etc.]," as his translator Gayatri Spivak says,[56] echoing the way we commonly speak of an author as what (s)he has written. I am saying nothing new here.

In another vein of deferring any definitive understanding, Gianni Vattimo's *Beyond Interpretation: The Meaning of Hermeneutics for Philosophy* embraces hermeneutics as a way to recognize the relativity and historical conditioning of all truth. If this slant leads to an apparent nihilism that defies the possibility of establishing itself and anything else as true for all time, it is, in my words, paradoxically a positive nihilism that enjoins us finally to accept the fragile, historical times in which we live. To define hermeneutics, Vattimo does not, can not write "hermeneutics is...." Rather he chooses the way of Heidegger's "hermeneutical as" and writes of hermeneutics "*as* the philosophical theory of the interpretive character of every experience of truth, [a theory that] is lucid about itself as no more than an interpretation"[57]—true for now, as it were. The historical definition of hermeneutics follows the contour the present chapter has outlined: "that philosophy developed along the Heidegger-Gadamer axis." It also leans in the direction our reflections have taken—up to a point. For at first sight it is a gen-

---

55. One context for this saying—can we call it the original one?—is given in DERRIDA 1976, 158. O'LEARY (1996, 37–46) presents another side of Derrida's deconstructive project and gives a sympathetic reading of his critique of determinate meaning and of his alternative, "dissemination." His discussion of the consequences for theological hermeneutics implicitly confirms the text-centrism of "hermeneutics after Derrida" by focusing on the variability of terms and sentences and their contexts.

56. DERRIDA 1976, ix.

57. VATTIMO 1997, 7.

eral *linguisticality* (*Sprachlichkeit*) and not a specific *textuality* that is the linchpin of hermeneutics for Vattimo. Despite Heidegger's later emphasis on language, "interpretation is thought primarily from the point of view of the meaning of Being"—but then we might say in reverse that the meaning of Be-ing is thought primarily from the viewpoint of language as the keeper of all meaning. And despite Gadamer's emphasis on ontology, Vattimo writes, "interpretation is thought primarily from the point of view of language [and not of Being]"[58]—or vice versa, for we could paraphrase Gadamer and say that Being itself is thought from the viewpoint of language. Linguisticality and not ontology thus anchors hermeneutics in Heidegger and Gadamer. But then Vattimo unwittingly goes beyond his own general characterization and implicates the particular textuality of the hermeneutical objective when he pits hermeneutical understanding against the univocal truth of sentences and propositions, or the interpretative character of "the experience of truth" against the verification of statements that compose texts. Textuality remains the context of his oppositions. The iconoclast who would dissolve truth "as incontrovertible and 'objective' clearness" remains bound to the icon.[59]

Excursus 3
The question of "non-Western" hermeneutics

One might be tempted to think that the model of textuality we have displayed is not followed in the hermeneutics applied to "non-Western" religious traditions. After all, theological hermeneutics began in the nineteenth century primarily to resolve questions of how to read the Bible, understood as a singular sacred text. But "religions" outside the Abrahamic traditions do not necessarily call for an understanding of "the Word [of God]" or insist on the exclusive truths of

58. Ibid., 3.
59. Ibid., 5 and 14.

"sacred scriptures." Yet just as scholars of Abrahamic religions retroactively apply the term *hermeneutics* to the ways readers of the past interpreted their sacred text, scholars of "non-Western" religions expansively invoke the term to describe how ancient traditions have been interpreted, for all their differences from "religions of the word." Not surprisingly, studies that invoke *hermeneutics* have taken for granted its textual orientation and present those traditions primarily through their texts. A few examples may suffice to illustrate this orientation and possible deviations.

"For purposes of this volume, hermeneutics will be broadly conceived as concerned with establishing principles for the retrieval of meaning, especially from a text."[60] Thus the editor of *Buddhist Hermeneutics* introduces this exemplary collection of studies by Buddhist scholars who met together in 1984. The conference included the Christian theologian David Tracy, a dialogue partner of Abe Masao quoted in our opening chapter on relativism. As I recall, Tracy and other respondents suggested that the major contribution of Buddhism to the general field of hermeneutics may be its sophisticated if latent theories of application and reference to present-day students of the texts.

"All texts probably contain either explicit or implicit interpretations, but for our present purposes the focus will be on Buddhist texts that attempt to establish rules and methodologies in terms of which scriptures may be explicated."[61] Thus the author of *Hermeneutics and Tradition in the Saṃdhinirmocana-sūtra*, who appeals to "Western hermeneutical theories." Another study seems at first sight to deviate from a textual orientation by pointing to the very inadequacy of language. But then the author of *The Tao and the Logos: Literary Hermeneutics, East and West* writes that the "centerpiece" of his argument is his

60. LOPEZ 1988, 1.
61. POWERS 1993, 83.

"emphasis on silence and the blank as the source of textuality."[62] Perhaps we encounter a genuine alternative in one study included in *Texts in Context: Traditional Hermeneutics in South Asia*, despite the title of this collection. The author notes that "one does not 'understand' the Veda, one enacts it; and ideally one becomes it."[63] At least, in elucidating this tradition, the author, David Carpenter, relies on the text of the fifth-century Vedic scholar Bhartṛhari, whose "hermeneutics" "has little to do with the meaning of canonical texts for a religious community."[64]

If hermeneutics has remained oriented to textuality, ever since Schleiermacher it has not been confined to the study of religious texts, West or East. Nearly a century ago, after sojourns in Europe, two Japanese philosophers introduced the term and the approach in their homeland and, like Heidegger, applied it to the study of human be-ing. They did not follow Heidegger's model that appealed to a text-like referential system, but they, too, came to understand human be-ing via an interpretation of language. Miki Kiyoshi studied under Heidegger alongside Gadamer in Marburg in 1923, and three years later coined the term *kaishakugaku* (解釈学) to translate the *hermeneutics* he employed as his method for studying human be-ing via the texts of Pascal.[65] A decade later, the *Ethics* of Watsuji Tetsurō adapted Heidegger's hermeneutical method to interpret the nature of human be-ing—not by implying a textual model of referential totality, but by explicating the basic words that anchor his theory. Heidegger's interpretation of the German Dasein for the human way of being provided the model for Watsuji's explication of the common word 人間 as humans-in-between.[66] Half a century later, in works like *The Hermeneutics of the Mask*, Sakabe Megumi elucidated transnational cultural phenomena

62. ZHANG 1992, 198.
63. TIMM 1992, 28.
64. Ibid., 5.
65. "The Study of The Human Being in Pascal"; see MIKI 1926 and 1927.
66. MARALDO 2019A, 21–37 demonstrates Watsuji's hermeneutical method.

by exploiting the disclosive power of the Japanese language and texts.[67] The textual and linguistic orientation of hermeneutics has been a matter of course in "the East" as well as in "the West"—terms that themselves conceal the power of texts to frame the world.

Has the wider application of hermeneutics to understanding the cultures of the world—particularly non-literate cultures—released its attachment to textual models? Anthropology is an example of a field outside academic philosophy, religious studies, and theology that also makes use of hermeneutics. George Marcus and Michael Fischer describe *hermeneutics* as one of three theoretical influences in "interpretive anthropology," along with phenomenology and Marxist analysis. Here hermeneutics is a label for close reflection on the way natives decipher and decode their own complex "texts," be they literally texts or other forms of cultural communication such as rituals. This approach seeks to uncover the rules of inference, patterns of association, and logics of implication at work in a particular culture. Hermeneutics also refers to the anthropologist's concern with his own reflexivity (his own text-making) while undertaking cross-cultural interpretation.[68] Anthropological hermeneutics once again models understanding after the interpretation of texts.

---

67. JPSB, 979–92 gives an example.
68. MARCUS AND FISCHER 1986, 30.

Practice

4
Practice
An Alternative Mode

"That might be right in theory, but it won't work in practice." This commonplace word to the wise would guide us to avoid a detrimental course of action, but could also prevent us from "learning the hard way" by actually doing something. Both orientations here, avoidance and performance, pit prior thinking and consequent acting against one another. But if practice were not preemptively opposed to theory—what might *practice* then mean?

This question already holds half an answer: it sets up an expectation of a notion of practice that is not part of the pair, theory and practice. To be sure, the theory versus practice distinction has been a powerful tool both in analyzing philosophical issues and in solving everyday problems. In philosophy, think of Kant's essay *On the Old Saw: That May Be Right in Theory But It Won't Work in Practice*, in which he defends the position that his moral and political philosophy is realistic and useful, but still makes a crucial distinction: practices are of principles of procedure, or theories.[1]

---

1. *Über den Gemeinspruch: Das mag in der Theorie richtig sein taugt aber nicht für die Praxis* is the title of KANT 1773, 201–84. MURPHY (1998, 5–32) suggests that Kant is actually undermining the distinction. Nevertheless, it is clear that Kant is first appealing to the commonplace distinction; moreover, his definition of practice is still aligned with the notion to which I will propose an alternative. As quoted by Murphy (6–7), Kant writes:

> An aggregation of rules, even of practical rules, is called a *theory*, as long as these rules are thought of as principles possessing a certain generality and, consequently, as being abstracted from a multitude of conditions that nonetheless necessarily influence their application. Conversely, not every undertaking [*Hantierung*] is a *practice* [*Praxis*];

In everyday life, we often learn that we must do something by trial and error, because our ideas—no matter how well they fit together—did not work when we tried to apply them. But sometimes the distinction gets in our way in seeing things or doing something better. Sometimes seeing—supposedly the theory part—and doing—the practice part—can't be easily separated. The word *practice* of course has several meanings, and not all of them are opposed to theory. Philosophers and sociologists also write about social practices—what people as members of institutions or societies actually do, for example, even when they have no general view or theory in mind. Still, philosophers and other theorists often see social practices as goal-oriented or "instrumental," and in that respect they are under the influence of the old theory-practice opposition.[2]

In this chapter I draw upon several distinct and sometimes interacting traditions in philosophy to invite us to examine what goes

---

rather, only such ends as are thought of as being brought about in consequence of certain generally conceived [*vorgestellten*] principles of procedure [*Verfahrens*] are designated practices."

Murphy (7) comments that

Kant is here making the very clever suggestion that, at least in the domain of morality, the very distinction between theory and practice—and thus the idea that there could be an important gap between them—is incoherent. An activity or institution is properly called a "practice" (*Praxis*), claims Kant, only if it is viewed as the instantiation of some general principles (i.e., some theory); and a moral theory is adequate only to the degree that it provides a rational reconstruction—in terms of general principles—of those practical judgments that constitute our ordinary moral consciousness. As Dieter HENRICH (1967, 10) puts the point, "[Kant] speaks of the theory as being inherent in moral consciousness and action itself. As such it *eo ipso* is effective in a practical way."

In place of a straightforward opposition here, we seem to have a variant of the hermeneutical circle sketched in Chapter 3 of this volume: a practice instantiates some general theory, but the theory derives from (reconstructs) judgments made in practice.

2. In his 1937 essay, "On Practice" (实践论), Mao Zedong proposes that theory, i.e., perceptual and rational knowledge) and practice reciprocally affect each other in a dialectical movement that nevertheless presupposes the difference and instrumentality of practice.

unquestioned in commonplace ideas about practice. Inspired particularly by my readings in Japanese philosophy and the East Asian traditions that have nurtured it, I sketch a notion of practice that is an alternative to the traditional distinction. I hope to contribute especially to contemporary discussions among Anglo-American and European philosophers who so far have not been much interested in Asian philosophical thought. At the same time, I caution against any strict division between "East" and "West." Even if we are to use these labels heuristically, each of them names such a wide variety of philosophical traditions that the labels soon become useless. The so-called "East" includes philosophers who converse with so-called Western philosophers more than with others in their own historical region. A blanket East-versus-West opposition is a misleading one to begin with. The alternative I sketch deliberately draws upon ancient Greek as well as Sino-Japanese sources, often in fusion with one another. It is this intercultural resource that offers a revealing alternative to the traditional tension between theory and practice.

THE TRADITIONAL OPPOSITION BETWEEN THEORY AND PRACTICE

It is commonplace to take practice as divided from a goal that is the point of an activity or action, the real reason for doing something. Theory, on the other hand, is thought to be removed from reality and—to the extent it is value-free—unable to tell us how things should be. We think of philosophy as a theoretical discipline, one that needs to prove its worth by demonstrating that it is applicable to "real world" problems. Karl Marx famously wrote that "philosophy has only interpreted the world; the point is to change it."[3] Hannah Arendt criticized Marx for neglecting the ancient distinction between labor and work as two distinct modes of the *vita activa*, but she continued to promote

3. Thesis 11 of his "Theses on Feuerbach."

the difference of philosophy as the theoretical life, the *vita contemplativa*.[4] Indeed, the mainstream tradition has long been determined by the Greek distinction between the theoretical or contemplative life on the one hand, and on the other, the life of action concerned with practical matters of everyday living. Although the legacy of Socrates cared about how to live a good life as much as how to think rationally, the predominant tendency even in Socrates was first to think through and test the consistency of one's views, and only then to live accordingly. "Think first, then act," has been the pervading principle. *Know-how*, knowing how to do something, has taken second place to *knowing that* something is the case, because philosophy seeks truth and truth, according to the tradition, is instantiated in propositions, not in actions. Today, of course, we are likely to place the emphasis on the applications of philosophical discourse, especially in relatively new subfields such as applied ethics and practical philosophy. Social and political philosophers increasingly see their work as the application, and not only the analysis, of principles and ideas. Yet there is a fundamental difference between the ideas of applied philosophy and notions that we find in several East-Asian philosophical traditions—notions of knowing by way of practice that let us reinterpret non-Asian philosophies, too. We now turn to this difference.

Toward an alternative

To apply some principle or technique means that we already have a clearly defined principle or theory at our disposal. We might apply the utilitarian principle of the greatest good for the greatest number to a particular way of doing business, for example; or we might apply game theory to particular studies of the kind of choices people make. In these cases, the general theoretical idea comes first, and afterwards it can be developed into a particular practice or way of

---

4. ARENDT 1958, 15 and 72–82.

doing something. Of course, the theoretical idea may be discovered by trial-and-error, or by some activity, but its validity is usually considered independent of its discovery and much more general than the particular process that revealed it. So the first thing to note concerns what practice in the alternative mode is not: *Practicing does not mean applying previously learned knowledge, that is, a prior theory or principle; it is not a matter of application at all.* To define practice more positively, we need to look at some examples.

Let us suppose that you want to know how to act properly in a particular kind of situation. A contrast between Socrates's method and the method of Confucius seems to illustrate two different ways to teach and learn. In Socrates's dialogue with Euthyphro the issue is how to act in a manner that exemplifies *hosion*. *Hosion* is often translated as *piety*, but I think it is very close to what Confucius meant by *li* (禮) or ritual propriety. Socrates questions Euthyphro who thinks it is pious or righteous to prosecute his own father for causing the death of a servant. Socrates tests the consistency of the definitions of *hosion* that Euthyphro offers, and exposes the contradictions and ambiguities in his convictions. This dialogue typifies Socratic *elenchus* or cross-examination in a step-by-step, logical progression. This method does not always lead to a definite conclusion, but we nevertheless consider it valuable for the self-examination it teaches.

The *Analects* of Confucius, on the other hand, contain little discursive, logical progression but much exemplification. Confucius uses language more as indication than as a tool of discursive reasoning. He teaches by pointing out examples of actions that one can emulate, not by leading one through a series of propositions to arrive at the right definition. One example that relates to the dialogue between Socrates and Euthyphro is a story about a community that thinks it upright or righteous (直) to report one's own father to the authorities for having stolen a sheep. Confucius replies that in his part of the country one would act differently, for it is upright to cover for one's father.⁵ The point I want to make has nothing to do with what sounds like ethical relativism ("in our community as opposed to yours"). Nor does my point involve another well-known opposition in classical Chinese thought, that between the filial piety that Confucius advocates and the legalism or legal justification that he rejects. Rather I would like us to notice the relative lack of discourse in this exchange. Confucius does not discursively examine a set of attempted definitions of uprightness to test their validity; he merely points out an example of how one acts rightly. One is to learn proper action by doing, not by testing the consistency of one's thinking and then applying it.

Does the episode in the *Analects* exemplify the alternative kind of practice whereas the Platonic dialogue does not? I think that we can find something of the alternative sense of practice in both texts, though only in part and with priorities that differ from the notion I want to develop. The discursive reasoning that Socrates leads us through actually takes practice, repeated practice, especially for students new to this form of thinking. To be able to think in this way one must do more than read through the dialogue a single time; rather one must enact discursive reasoning in a number of different situations. *How to do that*

---

5. *Analects* 13:18: 葉公語孔子曰:「吾黨有直躬者, 其父攘羊, 而子證之。」孔子曰:「吾黨之直者異於是。父為子隱, 子為父隱, 直在其中矣。」

> The Governor of She in conversation with Confucius said, "In our village there is someone called Upright Person. When his father took a sheep on the sly, he reported him to the authorities." Confucius replied, "Those who are upright in my village conduct themselves differently. A father covers for his son, and a son covers for his father. And being upright or true lies in this."

AMES AND ROSEMONT 1998, 167, translation slightly modified. An alternative translation presupposes the wrongness of the act:

> The Duke of She informed Confucius, saying, "Among us here there are those who may be styled upright in their conduct. If their father has stolen a sheep, they will bear witness to the fact." Confucius said, "Among us, in our part of the country, those who are upright are different from this. The father conceals the misconduct of the son, and the son conceals the misconduct of the father. Uprightness is to be found in this."

Chinese Text Project <http://chinese.dsturgeon.net/text.pl?node=1094andif=en>.

is what Socrates and Plato are trying to teach us: how to think and subsequently how to act accordingly. Here the priority remains: right thinking first, then right action; but right thinking is also a matter of practice. To understand Confucius, on the other hand, one must do more than look at a particular example of upright action in one episode recorded in the *Analects*. One must look rather at the context of many such episodes. Only by seeing what Confucius points out repeatedly can one begin to live the lesson he wants to teach, to become an example oneself. There the priority is: see (that is, understand) over and over again, and right action follows of itself. This "seeing" is akin to the original meaning of the Greek *theorein*. A kind of theory is at work in Confucian examples too, though not a theory that is first articulated in language and then applied to actions. To sum up so far, if Socratic thinking and Confucian seeing both involve practice, this practice arises not after a theory is articulated but rather in the course of a theorizing or seeing, during an exercise in reasoning or in exemplifying. The thinking and seeing themselves are forms of acting or doing.

This reflection offers a step towards a more positive description of the alternative notion of practice. We may note three things so far: *Practice is a matter of training that involves attention and repetition; it is a matter of getting good at something, of performing well; and it presents thinking and seeing as part of doing, of action.*

What about the normative dimension? What about the question of the value, the goodness or the evil, of what one is doing? After all, one might get good at abusing others or at killing them. One might become a proficient axe-murderer. It seems one can practice evil as well as good. To put it this way, however, implies that we have a prior standard of good and evil and then judge a particular practice as more or less good. By putting it this way, we fall back into the same old oppositions—between theory as principle and practice as application, and between normative and descriptive. We will need to return to this serious problem, but for now I want to remind us of the other side: how virtuous behavior entails practice.

Learning by doing is very much at work in Aristotle's notion of virtue or *aretê*. One learns what the virtue of courage is, for example, by practicing courage, by being courageous. When judged by the strictures of logical discourse, this sort of reasoning appears circular. To know what courage is, one has to practice courage. But how does one tell whether it is courage that she is practicing? How could she tell the difference between a courageous action and a cowardly or a rash one? It seems that she must already know what courage is. This impasse is broken, however, when we see the issue from a different perspective. Courage, or any virtue for that matter, is not the sort of thing that can be caught by a general definition that is subsequently applied. Whatever general ideas one has about courage, for example, must be tested by actions, by repeated actions that let one get the hang of the thing and perform it excellently, almost by second nature. For Aristotle, to be sure, there is a measure to tell one is practicing courage rather than cowardice or foolhardiness. But this measure, the "golden mean" between the extremes of excess and deficiency, is again something that must be learned or embodied in concrete situations. The golden mean is not first defined discursively and then applied to particular situations. Rather, one learns the virtue of courage as a particular disposition (*hexis*) by experiencing a range of actions and attitudes and finding the mean.[6]

Contrary to this interpretation one might object that determining the golden mean for Aristotle requires more than learning through practicing different actions; it requires practical reason (*phrónēsis*). Richard Kraut, quoting Aristotle, puts it this way:

> The intermediate point that the good person tries to find is "determined

---

6. The *Nicomachean Ethics* implies two qualifications to this interpretation: first, pleasure plays a role in determining what distinguishes a virtue. "Pleasure in doing virtuous acts is a sign that the virtuous disposition has been acquired"; and second, perception as opposed to reasoning plays a role: "The mean is hard to attain, and is grasped by perception, not by reasoning." ARISTOTLE 1941, 929.

by *logos* (reason, account) and in the way that the person of practical reason would determine it" (1107a1–2). To say that such a person "sees" what to do is simply a way of registering the point that the good person's reasoning does succeed in discovering what is best in each situation. He is "as it were a standard and measure" in the sense that his views should be regarded as authoritative by other members of the community. A standard or measure is something that settles disputes; and because good people are so skilled at discovering the mean in difficult cases, their advice must be sought and heeded.[7]

Yet if determining the mean requires practical reason, we may note that the exercise of practical reason is also a practice, at which the exemplary person excels and thus serves as a standard, a person remarkably similar to the Confucian exemplary person (君人). Aristotle appeals to *logos* not as a prior standard to be applied but as a measure itself learned through practical reasoning: the mean is "determined by logos and in the way that the person of practical reason would determine it." I think that Aristotle's account of the virtues provides an early Greek example of the kind of practice I am talking about. Perhaps I was able to understand it this way only from a perspective I happened to gain from Japanese philosophy.

Often this perspective can help us better understand a mainstream European text or author. Consider the interpretation of Aristotle that says a virtue is a habit that allows one to achieve his or her purpose, and so we need an account of what the human purpose is in order to define human virtues. Suppose we say, following Aristotle, that the purpose or goal (*telos*) of humans is to achieve *eudaimonia*, happiness, and that the moral virtues like courage will help us achieve *eudaimonia*. We would then know more or less what is courageous and what is not by the measure of achieved *eudaimonia*. Yet we still must have an experiential basis for telling whether this *eudaimonia* is present—all the more so if *eudaimonia* means more than a fleeting feeling of happiness. Like the

7. KRAUT 2022.

virtues (*aretês*) themselves, *eudaimonia* cannot be defined propositionally or discursively; it must be lived, and it is lived through practices.

This leads to a fourth characteristic of the alternative notion: *practice defines an activity that is an end in itself, not a means to an end that is different in kind from the activity.* The notions of the practical and the theoretical stance are fairly complex in Plato and Aristotle,[8] but in general, for Plato practice signifies an activity that results in something separate from the activity itself. You might recall that Aristotle, on the other hand, drew a distinction between *poiesis*, the kind of activity that results in a product or *ergon* separate from the activity, and *praxis* that does not result in a separable, made thing. Virtue is the disposition to

---

8. PARRY (2008) details the complexity of the Greek notions of theory and practice in the context of a related distinction: "The relation, then, between *epistêmê* and *technê* in ancient philosophy offers an interesting contrast with our own notions about theory (pure knowledge) and (experience-based) practice." Plato seems more clearly to define the practical side as activities that produce things different from the activity itself. That said, in the *Charmides* (165e), with regard to mathematical calculation, Socrates "suggests the possibility of a *technê* whose goal is not a separate result." Plato implies that "there is a distinction between theoretical and practical *technai*. Practical *technê* brings into existence products separate from the *technê* itself, while theoretical *technê* does not." Parry also notes that in several dialogues, "While the *ergon* of a craft [*technê*] is its goal, the goal is frequently identified with a result separate from the activity of the craft." For Aristotle the issue is more complex. There is a theoretical side to *technê* in that it is based on *logos*: "Aristotle refers to *technê* or craft as itself also *epistêmê* or knowledge because it is a practice grounded in an 'account'—something involving theoretical understanding." Two distinctions are implied: first, that between practical thinking (*praktikê dianoia*), where "we attain truth and falsity with respect to action," and "theoretical thinking (*theôrêtikê dianoia*) [that] attains truth and falsity"; and secondly, especially in the *Nicomachean Ethics*, between two kinds of activity: making something (*poiêton*) or activity that is a means to an end, and action (*praktikon*) that is an end in itself. Parry writes, "Presumably Aristotle means to distinguish between activity, whose end is in itself, and making, whose end is a product separate from the activity of making. When someone plays the flute, e.g., typically there is no further product of playing; playing the flute is an end in itself." Similarly, in the case of virtue, the activity itself is the end; there is no product separate from the virtuous activity. To these distinctions is added one closer to the classical division between theory and practice: In the *Posterior Analytics*, "Scientific [or theoretical] knowledge concerns itself with the world of necessary truths, which stands apart from the world of everyday contingencies, the province of craft [*technê*]."

this latter kind of action. But Aristotle does demand that both *praxis* and *poiesis* be based on a theoretical account, a *logos*, that is separate from the doing or the making and that informs and guides them. We can now say more precisely what we said before: the alternative notion of practice presents thinking and seeing as part of doing, of action, but the thinking or seeing is not a separable part as is usually the case in Aristotle. The scholar of Greek philosophy, Peter Simpson, pointed out the exception in Aristotle: his notion of *prudence* also names a practice in which "the kind of thinking that goes on is internal to the acting and not separable from the acting."[9] In the alternative notion of practice, there is no separate articulated account that is essential to inform or guide the activity. One learns by doing and absorbs the learning, as it were, so that the guidance is internal to the activity. The guiding reason is found not in a separate linguistic account or *logos*; it is found in what in Japanese is called the pattern or right way of doing something, the *dōri* (道理), or the *suji michi* (筋道) of the activity— the thread or pattern that one learns by taking the path. *Practice in the alternative sense is theoretical in that it is a seeing as well as a doing; practice embodies both its knowledge or know how and its goal.* Again, in the alternative view, thinking and seeing themselves approximate forms of practice. The philosopher who for me has best articulated thinking as a practice is Martin Heidegger. His essay, "*Was ist das—die Philosophie?*" (What Is Philosophy?) proceeds to answer the question not with a definition or series of propositions but by leading the reader down a path, the path he describes as thinking.

To be sure, some important questions are left unanswered here. What defines a path or distinguishes one activity from others? How is one to tell the right way from deviant ways? These are questions of criteria, and once again raise the normative issue and the task of demonstrating an alternative to the opposition between normative and

9. Personal communication, December 15, 2008.

descriptive.[10] The alternative notion of practice requires an alteration in our notions of criteria and testing. A criterion usually is an outside, ideally objective measure of the rightness, wrongness or appropriateness of something. The alternative sense of measure would need to be generated on the inside as it were, out of the activity itself. Here I offer only a few pointers.

We might once again find an example in Aristotle's notion of prudence, in which prudent thinking is internal to prudent acting and generated by it. Besides seeking internal criteria, we can point to the role of human exemplars or role models in both Aristotle and Confucius. We take our lead in doing something well from good people, people who are fulfilling their nature in an exemplary way. In Aristotle, the good person points the way because she sees what to do clearly, and she sees what to do clearly because she is good.[11] The serious person is the measure of what is to be done. In China, not long after Confucius, Mencius said something similar with his doctrine of the purity of heart. My actions are to be my own, perspicacious in knowing how things are done rightly. At the same time, I perform my actions in light of what the exemplar or morally serious person does. If we say that such practice assumes that the exemplar fulfills her nature in a way that the nonvirtuous person does not, or in the case of Confucius, that the person acting without propriety cannot, then we appeal to fulfillment and lack rather than to criteria of right and wrong. The medieval scholastics elaborated Aristotle's notion of virtue as a habituality that enables the achievement of something good that makes the doer good in the doing of it. The relevant difference between Aristotle and Confucius here is Aristotle's emphasis on personal balance and Confucius's emphasis on social harmony. But both appeal to the model of practicing what the exemplary person practices.

---

10. Chapter 12 in this book presents an alternative to that distinction.
11. ARISTOTLE 1941: *Nicomachean Ethics* 1114b.

DŌGEN AND NISHIDA: TWO JAPANESE EXAMPLES OF THE ALTERNATIVE NOTION OF PRACTICE

Where do we find the alternative notion of practice in Japanese philosophers? Certainly it is evident in Dōgen's *Shōbōgenzō, A Treasury of the True Dharma Eye* or, as it has been translated, *An Eye for the Truth*.[12] The fascicle "Bendōwa" or "Discerning the Way" defines Dōgen's notion of enlightenment, a word often considered the goal of Zen Buddhist meditation. Dōgen sees it differently. First, he uses a word better translated as *realization*, in the sense of both recognizing and actualizing. Then he speaks of practice, the practice of quiet sitting or *zazen*, for example, as the place—though not the only one—where realization is made manifest. "The Dharma [the truth] is amply present in every person, but without practice, it is not manifested; without realization, it is not attained.... As it is from the first realization in practice, realization is endless. As it is the practice of realization, practice is beginningless."[13] Dōgen's sense of practice as manifestation explicitly subverts the difference between means and end, just as his examples implicitly undermine the classical Western difference between mind and body. On the one hand, practice does not fall into the category of mental activity as opposed to physical behavior, because it takes bodily form, engages the practitioner bodily and disengages discursive thought. On the other hand, practice does not fall onto the opposite side of body in the classical Cartesian sense, because it requires acute attention. Thus, we can add to our list of features of the alternative notion: *practice engages the practitioner bodily as well as mentally; it engages the practitioner as a whole*. Japanese philosophers like Nishitani Keiji and Yuasa Yasuo have expanded upon this aspect of practice.[14] Regarding the necessity of the bodily aspect, however, we might raise a further question.

12. Thomas Kasulis proposes this translation of 正法眼蔵, JPSB, 141.
13. DŌGEN 2002, 8 and 19.
14. YUASA 1993. NISHITANI 1961, trans. 1982, 198–9; the translator has "observance"

Earlier I said the discursive reasoning and right thinking that Socrates would teach us approximate practice in the alternative sense. That is, discursive reasoning takes practice and is meant to be enacted in a number of different situations. That enactment might be considered a purely mental exercise, however, so where is the bodily engagement there? Since Socrates wants us to act *upon* the reasoning, that is, to act *after* it is performed and *in accordance with* it, many people would regard the performance of reasoning as purely mental. Think and see first, then take action. This priority explains why I implied that the exercise of discursive reasoning approximates but does not truly embody the alternative sense of practice. This aspect of practice may also give us a hint as to why discursive reasoning seems lacking in Zen Buddhist texts like Dōgen's. But Dōgen did not just sit around contemplating kōans; he wrote texts and gave lectures as well. There is a "logic" to his texts but they do not exemplify a step-by-step discursive argument. We might see his practice of writing and lecturing as exercises in embodied attention, in contrast to the discursive reasoning that is usually practiced and taught as a disengagement with the body.[15]

A concept coined by Nishida Kitarō also exemplifies practice in the alternative sense. In his middle period, in the 1920s, Nishida pub-

---

for 行, "practice." See also Chapter 6 in the present volume.

15. The analysis of practice in BOURDIEU (1990) offers an interesting contrast both to my alternative and to the standard sense. Bourdieu counters the idea that conscious reflection and rational choice govern our behaviors, and proposes that our actions usually result from habituation, that is, they derive from social structures that become embodied in individuals in the form of a more or less automatic *habitus*. His anti-theoretical theory of the peculiar logic of practice states that the principles governing human action are discovered only by enacting them, not by scientific observation from a third-person point of view. Bourdieu's view converges with my alternative notion of practice at some points: in his view of practice one is unreflectively absorbed in the present, though in pursuit of a result. That view differs from the alternative notion of practice that begins with conscious choices and actions that the actor learns to perform without reflection but in a state of bodily awareness, a mindfulness integrating body and mind. Bourdieu's theory presupposes too strong a divide between body and mind, automaticity and reflection (especially 91–2).

lished a group of essays under the title *From Acting to Seeing* (働くものから見るものへ). Although these essays primarily concern a theory of consciousness, the title suggests that seeing or understanding proceeds from acting. More specifically, there and elsewhere Nishida developed a notion he called *kōiteki chokkan* (行為的直観), which I translate as "enactive intuition" or "performative intuition."[16] Nishida's neologism itself implies the reverse of the usual sequence of "think and understand first, then act." The term *intuition* is used in the sense of direct, non-discursive apprehension. Kant took sensuous intuition or perception as a source of knowledge, and the German Idealists developed the intellectual intuition that Kant had rejected, the mind's supposed direct apprehension of some realities such as the self. Husserl developed the notion of categorial intuition or seeing that something is the case, seeing relationships as well as objects. Nishida's action-oriented intuition proposed a reciprocity between action and intuition, so that we might also call it "intuition-oriented action" or simply "action-intuition." Nishida's term suggests that acting and seeing are not only connected but that seeing or understanding is performative and productive. Seeing is not a passive taking-in of objects, and acting is not acting on things, or merely producing things outside oneself.

It is instructive to contrast this kind of action with Aristotle's *poiesis*. As we have seen, Aristotle distinguishes making something (*poiêton*) from action (*praktikon*). The latter activity, *praxis*, constitutes an end in itself, whereas the end of making "is a product separate from the activity of making."[17] Both virtuous acting and making things well are guided by the proper disposition (*hexis*), and both involve an account or *logos* of the acting or making. Thus, Aristotle, unlike Nishida, also emphasizes the rational side of these forms of acting: practical reasoning is based on the accounts that *technê* or art, and *aretê* or virtue, can

---

16. The essay "Enaction in Cognitive Science and Nishida's Turn of Intuition into Action," in MARALDO 2017 elaborates Nishida's conception but does not develop its relation to our alternative notion of practice.

17. PARRY 2008.

give. Nishida, on the other hand, emphasized the bodily, historical, and "intuitive" nature, that is the seeing/theoretical side of the activity. Often Nishida does not sharply distinguish between *poiesis* and *praxis* in Aristotle's sense, that is, between an activity that produces objects separate from the activity of making them, on the one hand, and an activity that is an end in itself.[18] Nor does Nishida distinguish sharply between the activity itself and an account of it, a *logos* that guides practical reasoning. Both distinctions are undermined, or rather grounded, in a more fundamental attunement, an action-oriented intuition.

One model of this performative intuition is artistic creation, which is of course productive, but we would misunderstand it if we saw the produced work as an end separate from the activity itself. What is "produced," to use that term, is the artist herself, as the embodiment of the activity, as well as the historical world that forms its inseparable context. A twentieth-century master of calligraphy, Morita Shiryū, influenced no doubt by Nishida, actually said that the calligrapher, her brush, and her work create one another, make each be what it actively is in a virtually endless web of relationships called the world.[19] The artist as one who creates art does not pre-exist the work created or the activity of creating. They are co-creative, so to speak, and arise together. This sense of co-creation adds something to the alternative notion of practice, but still exemplifies a practice in which the end is internal to the performance. Even if we say that as an artist you pre-exist the work you "produce," the activity of your production is made visible in the object presented to the world. The end-product is internal to the activity. And in contrast to Aristotle's notion of *poiesis*, the

---

18. Nishida's essay 「ポイエシスとプラクシス (実践哲学序論補説)」 [Poiesis and praxis, Supplement to an introduction to practical philosophy, NKZ 10: 114–76] distinguishes the two only to interrelate them. Haver (2012, 29) notes that here "the relation between poiesis and praxis is transductive; that is, each is the necessary presupposition of the other"—which also subverts their difference from *theōria* as passive contemplation. "Praxis-poiesis becomes not a means to an end but an end in itself...."

19. Morita 1970, 124–5. See also JPSB, 1200–2.

production—or rather the creation—would be misunderstood if we saw it as an application of practical reasoning. Morita as calligrapher in action exemplifies the art called the Way of Writing, *shodō* (書道), which is one of the many arts and martial arts designated by the word *dō* or *dao* in Chinese. Other familiar examples include the Way of Tea, or so-called tea-ceremony, the Way of Flowers or Ikebana, the Gentle Way or *jūdō*, the Way of Harmonizing Energies or *aikidō*. All of these pathways exemplify practice in the alternative sense.[20]

Nishida brings out the epistemological side of these arts or ways in his notion of performative intuition. The kind of knowing or *epistêmê* at work in this intuition is a coming to know by way of interacting with things. What comes to be known is not a world outside oneself. Here Nishida echoes the fifteenth-century Chinese Neo-Confucian Wang Yangming, renown for his notion of the "unity of knowledge and action" (知行合一). Nishida implies that knowledge entails action; it does not proceed merely from a mental activity of forming beliefs about the world and then mentally confirming or disconfirming them, which are basically theoretical activities. In Nishida there is indeed a theory side, the side of seeing called "intuition" (直観), but unlike the usual connotation of the word, this action-oriented intuition is not a grasp that takes in every relevant thing at once.[21] Rather, it is a process and achievement of the embodied self. Using the modern meanings of the words, there is also an "objective" side, or better said, a contra-subjective side to performative intuition: it requires a displacement of the self-centered self or self-conscious self which would act *upon* things rather than interact with them. To use the calligrapher Morita's example, the person gives herself up in the interaction with the brush, ink, paper, and environment. The calligrapher comes to know a world partially of her own making, and

---

20. The "Follow-up" that concludes the present volume elaborates the role of modeling in these "pathways."
21. Cestari (1998, 194) makes this point, referring to nkz 8: 565–6.

comes to know herself as progressively made by that world. If there is a process of reasoning here, it is a give and take, a back and forth, between self and other, rather than an application of an account of the goal. Nishida's performative intuition exemplifies the alternative sense of practice in which neither the goal nor the accounting is a separate thing from the activity itself.

We would limit the field too much, however, if we were to look for the alternative notion of practice only in Buddhist writers or Japanese philosophers inspired by Buddhism. Confucian thinkers both in China and in Japan also exhibited this notion of practice, in at least some of its features. One example from Japan is the thought of the Confucian Ogyū Sorai. John A. Tucker explains that

> Sorai emphasized practice as a way to learn, one that was more effective than book learning and the study of texts. In effect, what he advocated was learning how to do something rather than learning how to understand. Or, more positively, he believed that understanding was physical, with the ability to practice something as evidence of one's understanding of it.[22]

This seems to go beyond even Sorai's model, the Chinese Neo-Confucian Zhuxi, who "affirmed the value of theoretical study through book learning, but ultimately thought this had to be expressed in the practical world."[23] An example from China is the thought of Wang Yangming, the founder of the other major school of Neo-Confucianism. It would be worthwhile to explore Wang Yangming's idea of "forming one body with the universe and all things," as well as his idea of unifying knowledge and action, as sources for presenting practice in an alternative sense.[24]

---

22. Personal communication, 10 October 2008. See also TUCKER 2018, 156–9.
23. Personal communication, 10 October 2008.
24. LEDER 1990, 156–9.

THE ALTERNATIVE DEFINITION OF PRACTICE AND THE SENSE OF ALTERNATIVES

A brief account of two dominant models of reasoning in Greco-European philosophy provides a foil to clarify the alternative sense of practice sketched in this chapter:

> The logical model of reasoning is most at home close to its origins in codifying *theoretical* inference, the way beliefs can provide reasons for other beliefs. The instrumental model of [means-end] reasoning begins with *practical* inference—in particular, the way desires or preferences, together with beliefs, can provide reasons for *action*.... What one has reason to do, on this model, is what provides a means to an endorsed end.[25]

This apt account by Robert Brandom eventually finds reason to subsume the logical model, "as a special case," under the instrumental model.[26] But his summary works by contrasting *theoretical* with *practical* and by placing both under the aegis of (mental) *reasoning* as opposed to (bodily) *acting*. And it limits *action* to acting as a means to an end.

In contrast, *practice in the alternative sense means action done over and over again, performed for its own sake but with a learning curve toward improvement, with the whole person engaged, "body and soul," that is, with attentive seeing or know-how built into the action*. I use the word action instead of activity because action implies bodily activity. I have found this sense of practice most pronounced and best articulated in Sino-Japanese philosophies, although by no means is it totally absent in traditional European philosophy. Indeed, as indicated earlier, in classical Greek philosophy we can also find an alternative to the theory-practice opposition that shares some features of the alternative notion. Again, however, the Greek alternative usually insists on a rational account separable from the practice and so differs from the internal

---

25. BRANDOM 2002, 3.
26. Ibid.

feedback, as it were, of the Sino-Japanese alternative. The alternative notion of practice has the potential to heal the divide between theory and practice and make philosophy, traditionally a very theoretical discipline, more relevant to everyday life in society. If that is an unending goal, it is one to be pursued within the practice of philosophizing together.

The next chapter displays another way to contrast the alternative mode with the standard model. Some texts of Martin Heidegger, a philosopher who rooted his philosophy—indeed all "philosophy"—in Greek discourse, bring the difference to light.

5
Four Things and Two Practices
Taking Heidegger Farther East

> A German friend of Heidegger told me that one day when he visited Heidegger he found him reading one of [D. T.] Suzuki's books. "If I understand this man correctly," Heidegger remarked, "this is what I have been *trying to say* in all my writings." ...There is much in [Heidegger] that is not in Zen, but also very much more in Zen that is not in Heidegger; and yet....
> — William Barrett, 1956[1]

> In Heidegger's case there was *nothing tangible* on which his fame [in the early 1920s] could have been based, nothing written... but the name traveled all over Germany like the rumor of the hidden king.
> — Hannah Arendt, 1969[2]

If the rumor of Martin Heidegger's teaching spread all over Germany well before he published his seminal *Sein und Zeit*, the rumor of Heidegger's self-proclaimed affinity to Zen (the Zen of D. T. Suzuki) spread well beyond the confines of German philosophy to capture the curiosity of way-seekers worldwide. As rumors go, the earlier case may well have been a deserved reputation, and the later case less reliable hearsay. As massive as Heidegger's published work now is (more than 100 volumes in the *Gesamtausgabe*), Arendt's remark reminds us that it was first of all Heidegger's live presence and ques-

---

1. BARRETT 1956, xii, my emphasis.
2. ARENDT 1971, my emphasis.

tioning in the lecture hall that entranced scores of students. And Barrett's story reminds us that facile comparisons based on cursory readings should be taken with a grain of salt. Heidegger's own spoken words cautioned against using Zen and East Asian thought as a resource. In 1966, he told a *Spiegel* magazine interviewer that "a conversion (*Umkehr*) [of the modern technical world] cannot happen by adopting Zen-Buddhism or other Eastern experiences of the world."[3] The end of our reflections here will return to the critical question of the future of the world. In the meantime, we will see reasons to question Heidegger's rejection of alternatives from "the East." And yet the depth of the connections between Heidegger and East Asian traditions, and the perceived distance between them, have motivated a considerable amount of literature that both documents historical contacts and probes convergent themes.[4]

3. HEIDEGGER (1966, 216–7, trans. 1981, 62, slightly modified) continues, "For this conversion of thought we need the help of the European tradition and a new appropriation of it. Thought will be transformed only through thought that has the same origin and determination." A few moments earlier, Heidegger said, "the last 30 years have made it clearer that the planet-wide movement of modern technicity [*Technik*] is a power whose magnitude in determining [our] history can hardly be overestimated" (53).

4. Several recent articles by Bret W. Davis, such as DAVIS 2019, elucidate themes common to Heidegger, Zen, and other East Asian traditions. Although in need of updating, MA 2008 is the most detailed and trenchant investigation of Heidegger's connections to East Asian thought and recent literature about them. She draws attention to the full statement by William Barrett in 1956, but does not mention D. T. Suzuki's short visit with Heidegger on July 8, 1953, described by Suzuki in a Japanese diary entry translated in BUCHNER 1989, 169–72. (According to Suzuki's English-language diary, Karlfried Graf Dürckheim helped arrange this meeting—and another with Jaspers—and acted as interpreter. See SUZUKI 1952–53, 71.) Ma (13–15) notes that the Japanese Zen philosopher Tsujimura Kōichi studied with Heidegger in Freiburg a bit later, from 1956 to 1958. On May 18, 1958, Heidegger and Tsujimura's teacher, the lay Zen master Hisamatsu Shin'ichi, held a public colloquium on "Art and Thinking." Another teacher of Tsujimura, the Zen philosopher Nishitani Keiji, had studied with Heidegger from 1938 to 1940. I surmise that Nishitani, Hisamatsu, and Tsujimura were also sources of what little Heidegger knew of Zen. Ma (218 n. 23) notes that Tsujimura once spoke of "a deep chasm (*tiefe Kluft*) between Heidegger's thought and Zen Buddhism." Yet there was also bi-directional influence: TSUJIMURA (1963) translated Heidegger's *Gelassenheit* with the Buddhist term 放下, "release from worldly attachments." In a letter to Heidegger in 1965, Tsujimura wrote:

5. Four Things and Two Practices: Taking Heidegger Farther East | 127

My approach here will be different: I will dwell on a difference that Heidegger seems often to forget and that Zen Buddhism seems to think nothing of. More pervasive than what we read in Heideggerian and Zen literature alike, this difference crosses everyday experience and marks two distinct if interacting ways to conceive things in practical terms. Reflection on two practices will disclose the difference by shifting attention from things to the activity behind them.

To begin with Heidegger...

We find an entry into this difference in early Heidegger's thoughts on our relation to things—useful things, that is, the things he calls *Zeuge*. I will propose that there are two different but interacting modes of practice in our dealings with such things: instrumental, goal-oriented practice and the alternative practice of attention that guides instrumental practice. Examples of this interaction and difference will bring precision to the alternative notion of practice sketched in the preceding chapter. Instrumental practice is at the root of technological use, and the practice of attention is central to artistic creation. Both are crucial in human interactions with the environment, as well as in our relations with one another. We are familiar with instrumental practice from Heidegger's treatment of useful objects and the mode of being called *Zuhandenheit* in *Being and Time*, and we will be reminded of the practice of attention in his conversation on *Gelassenheit*. But Heidegger does not go far enough. I will attempt to cast some light from an East Asian perspective on Heidegger's treatment of the thing, in

---

It is a strange phenomenon, though a natural one for us Japanese, that the young students who in some way are serious about your thinking almost without exception practice Zen Buddhism. I think at least one reason for this lies in your relationship with language, or in your language itself.

Denker et al. 2013, 23, my translation. As is well documented in Ma 2008, Parkes 1987, May 1989, and Denker et al. 2013, Heidegger conversed with numerous students and visitors from China and Japan from 1921 on.

other words, to re-think our dealing with things *ex oriente lux*.[5] By re-orienting Heidegger's thinking we will be able to recast his famous question concerning technology and ask: just what kind of practice among us humans does the problem of technology—the problem of relentless will to discover and control—call for?

The Hammer

The carpenter's hammer is an example of the useful thing that Heidegger discusses in *Being and Time*. A hammer exists, comes to be, only because of what it is for. A hammer is for pounding and for nailing, for prying and levering. A hammer lets us pound one thing into another, pound a measuring stake into the ground, for example; and lets us nail or attach one thing to another, say, a supporting stud into a beam. The claw of the hammer lets us remove bent nails and pry attached pieces apart. The hammer also lets us repair the things we have built. We may use the hammer for building a house for our shelter, our survival, work, and enjoyment, for living together with family. The hammer exists as something inherently related to the other things it needs and uses to function—stakes and nails and boards, for example. It works as a piece in a chain of intentions leading to an objective we have in mind, such as the construction or the repair of the house. When hammering goes well we need not pay heed to the hammer; it is inconspicuous and our sight is directed to the thing to be hammered, the stake or the nail, and to the wall and the house we are building for our use and our enjoyment. When, in the course of building something, the handle of the hammer breaks off or loosens, the hammer becomes dysfunctional and the task at hand is disrupted; the chain of intentions is broken. Or when the hammer we need is missing, out of sight, the work again is interrupted. On these occasions the dysfunc-

---

5. May 1927 reads Heidegger *ex oriente lux*, in light of his engagement with East Asian thought.

tional or missing hammer captures our attention, as it were; it now becomes a separate thing no longer useful to us, no longer there for our task. If it is truly unusable, the hammer becomes a piece of junk, *ein altes Zeug*. These occasions bring to light the fact that, all along, we have been presupposing and projecting a context for the way we relate to the hammer and to all useful things, a context that Heidegger calls the world. The world has always been there, of course, but withdrawn as a kind of hidden background; now it is disclosed as the referential totality that it is. The world, a horizon that usually allows things to be brought into relief, is now itself brought into relief. The way that the "phenomenon of the world" can show itself, when a useful thing like a hammer breaks, is one of Heidegger's significant contributions to phenomenology.

Another contribution is his presentation of useful things as the way we most commonly relate to things in the world. The things of the world are not there first of all as objects in nature that we discover and subsequently put to use. What we call nature and natural things are discovered only after a disengagement with our usual way of relating to the world. For first of all we relate to things as things-there-for [our use], things there-in order-to [accomplish some objective or task]. And *we* are that for the sake of which they exist, at least in our initial take on them. "The forest is a forest of timber," Heidegger writes, "the mountain is a quarry of rock, the river is water power, the wind is wind 'in the sails.'"[6] The analysis of how we most commonly relate to things in the world is not limited to "man-made" objects, in other words. Moreover, the useful things we encounter are what they are precisely in their being utilized or put to work. The hammer is what it is when it is hammering, when we are hammering something with it. And we come to know what a hammer is by hammering, not by a disengaged and detached observation of an object called a hammer just lying there.

6. HEIDEGGER 1927, translation 1996, 70. Page numbers given refer to pages in the German edition.

Heidegger suggests that knowledge usually comes about through engagements that develop into pre-reflective practices, rather than through reflective, more or less explicit beliefs about the world that are then confirmed or disconfirmed.[7] That insight is one of his early contributions to theories of knowledge. We come to know "nature" or the "natural world" by interacting with it, not by distancing ourselves, theoretically observing it, and then testing our beliefs. Before there is "knowledge about," there is "know-how."[8]

Let us follow this clue and focus for a moment on this know-how. That is, let us reflect on the activity of using a useful thing, rather than on its being a kind of thing, and focus on hammering rather than the hammer. I will call the kind of activity involved in hammering *instrumental practice*, to denote the activity of using something to accomplish some goal or objective. In *instrumental* practice, the goal or objective is different in kind from the activity we engage in to achieve that objective. Using a hammer we nail supporting studs to a beam, for example, and when the frame of the wall is built and the house is finished, we have reached an objective that is different in kind from the activity of hammering. When we accomplish what we intend by hammering, we are no longer hammering. Indeed, the "end" of hammering is a different "activity," a mode of being. In our example, the end or objective of hammering is the activity and mode of being of living together in a sheltering house. Heidegger's analysis implies this seemingly obvious "fact" when it presents the hammer-thing, for example, as *there for the sake of* something else, for the sake of building and shel-

---

7. Compare Henri Bergson's insight, made as early as 1908, that perception is first in the service of action, not of theoretical knowledge. BERGSON 1988, 31.

8. This insight is reflected in a tentative proposal that appears in the conversation on *Gelassenheit* (HEIDEGGER 1995, 6): technology is not applied science; rather—in a reversal beyond merely opposing the terms—science can be considered as applied technology. Unless otherwise noted, all translations of Heidegger are my own. For putting the words of this conversation into English, I am also indebted to the translation of Bret W. Davis, HEIDEGGER 2010. Chapter 2 in the present volume clarifies the contrast between a disengaged, "objective" stance and a bodily engaged attunement.

5. Four Things and Two Practices: Taking Heidegger Farther East | 131

tering us. But Heidegger's reformulation of the traditional relation between means and end presupposes that our usual practice, in relating to things if not other people, is the kind of activity that is directed at a goal *different in kind from the activity itself.* Heidegger assumes instrumental practice as the norm. To be sure, Heidegger finds a theoretical side in this practice; that is, a kind of seeing is involved in our practical dealings with things. Taking things as useful objects is itself a mode of seeing; it is seeing something as there *for* something else, a circumspection Heidegger calls *Umsicht*, that is, a view to a goal in sight [*eine Sicht um zu...*]. So Heidegger's instrumental practice is not simply an applied *praxis* as opposed to a prior detached beholding or theory. Heidegger's instrumental practice is not simply acting without seeing, in other words.[9]

Heidegger is not concerned with how hammers are made, with their production and manufacture. Rather, he is concerned with their mode of being once they are here, and with their way of bringing to light the phenomenon of the world when they break down. We may follow Heidegger's limitation and for the moment ignore the activity

---

9. Both theory and praxis, moreover, are active stances; both are forms of comportment or behavior:

> Das "praktische" Verhalten ist nicht "atheoretisch" im Sinne der Sichtlosigkeit, und sein Unterschied gegen das theoretische Verhalten liegt nicht nur darin, daß hier betrachtet und dort gehandelt wird, und daß das Handeln, um nicht blind zu bleiben, theoretisches Erkennen anwendet, sondern das Betrachten ist so ursprünglich ein Besorgen, wie das Handeln seine Sicht hat. Das theoretische Verhalten ist unumsichtiges Nur-hinsehen. Das Hinsehen ist, weil unumsichtig, nicht regellos, seinen Kanon bildet es sich in der Methode.

HEIDEGGER 1953, 69. My translation:

> "Practical" behavior is not "atheoretical" in the sense of a lack of seeing, and its difference from theoretical behavior is not only that the one involves observation and the other action, and that action applies theoretical knowing so as not to remain blind. Rather, observation is as originally a kind of being concerned as action has *its* kind of seeing. Theoretical behavior is only looking at, without looking to [get something done]. Since it does not look to, this looking at has its rules; *method* forms its canon [of rules].

of making useful things like hammers, except to note that such activity also exemplifies instrumental practice. But again, let us focus more closely on the activity of using a hammer.

We learn what a hammer is by hammering, but hammering is not merely an instrumental practice. Ordinarily we must learn to work with a hammer and practice until hammering becomes second nature. Becoming adept at hammering may in fact be a practice done *for its own sake*, at least initially, as a first step. One may practice hammering simply to learn to hammer and get better at it, with no further objective in mind. Or—even if one learns to hammer well by practicing hammering "on the job," in the course of accomplishing an objective external to the activity of hammering—one temporarily loses sight of the objective precisely in order to hammer well, to hammer better. Hammering, temporarily at least, is done for its own sake. Such non-instrumental practice entails *the practice of attention*.

Certainly as a beginning step, and later as well, the practice of attention is essential to the later competent use of the hammer.[10] In adept hammering, one must pay attention to the movement of the hammer, to the object being hammered, and to other things in the immediate environment; that is, to the several things that make any one useful thing what it properly is.[11] In fact, inattention or inadequate attention can bring about the disruption of the activity and the interruption of the sequence of hammering "in order to...." Inattention to the condi-

---

10. In Zen practice, some teachers suggest that one must always remain a beginner; the Zen mind embodies the beginner's mind.

11. Does this apply to Heidegger's other examples of the use-thing or *Zeug*: things to write with [*Schreibzeug*], to sew with [*Nähzeug*], to work with [*Werkzeug*], to drive [*Fahrzeug*], to measure with [*Meßzeug*]; a plane, a needle, a shoe, a clock? See HEIDEGGER 1927, 68–9. Do we "practice" something seemingly so simple as wearing shoes? It would seem that putting on and wearing shoes is soon easily learned while we are still very young children. Wearing shoes now seems so natural, and so easy, indeed that for many people it seems unnatural *not* to wear shoes (at least outdoors). But this fact should not distract us from the realization that wearing shoes once did require "getting used to." And perhaps one still needs to practice how best to utilize high-tech shoes, specialized sports shoes, for example.

5. Four Things and Two Practices: Taking Heidegger Farther East | 133

tion of the tool can lead to its breaking or becoming dysfunctional. The proper use of tools and equipment, their proper way of being we might say, requires attention and care-taking.[12] It does not happen simply in the inconspicuous use of the functional tool.[13] Indeed, the lack of attention to equipment can have disastrous consequences, as we saw in the oil spill in the Gulf of Mexico in 2010, and in the failure of nuclear power reactors near Fukushima, Japan the following year.

The practice of attention in the proper care of useful things might alter Heidegger's later critique of technology. Heidegger later analyzes the instrumental practices of technology as a way of presenting (and concealing) things—as a way of truth in other words—but a way that seeks complete control and disclosure without remainder. Technology is a practice that would conceal its own inability to reveal everything without remainder.[14] In the conversation on *Gelassenheit*, Heidegger

---

12. In lectures given in 1951–52 Heidegger comes closer to this thought. Interpreting a saying from Parmenides, Heidegger says:

χράω, χράομαι means: I handle or wield and so keep in my hand, I use, I need the use of.... Needing the use of [*Brauchen*] does not mean mere utilizing, using up and exploiting. Utilizing is only the degenerate form of needing to use that gets out of hand. When for example we handle a thing, our hands must conform to the thing. Needing to use is a matter of a fitting response.... Letting what is so needed and used stay in its essential be-ing by no means implies some lax carelessness or negligence.... Needing to use something is letting us enter into its essential be-ing, is preserving the truth of its essential be-ing.

We should note, however, that Heidegger seems to devalue the need for the human care of things, by leaving the meaning of *Brauchen* out of human hands: "this use-oriented needfulness is in no way performed and consumed by humans" (HEIDEGGER 1961, 114).

13. In his work on the phenomenology of attention, B. WALDENFELS (2004, 29) cites as the only examples of attention in Heidegger's analysis here the three modes that make the tool an object of attention when our work with it is disrupted: we notice its conspicuousness [*Auffälligkeit*] when it breaks, its obtrusiveness [*Aufdringlichkeit*] when it is missing, and its obstinacy [*Aufsässigkeit*] when it proves inappropriate and gets in the way of doing the job. It is noteworthy that these three terms refer to a perceived quality of the thing, not first of all to a kind of attention. Moreover, as Waldenfels mentions, these three modes of attention [*Aufmeksamkeit*] are exercised in a narrow pragmatic framework where they function in a manner that merely detects and is not productive.

14. On technology not as a human product but as the form of untruth that would

suggests that technological thinking threatens to annihilate not only the environment but the very essence of being human.[15] In other words (not Heidegger's words), technology seeks total world-wielding, but in the course of technological practices it is we humans who come to be wielded and used up. Is it possible that another mode of practice might circumvent this danger—the practice of attention performed for its own sake, caring for things simply to care for them, caring for the surrounding world simply to care for it? This question must remain open here, but an answer is intimated in our second example of a thing.

The cleaver

The butcher's or cook's cleaver, the large knife used to carve an animal carcass and to cut meat, is the topic of a conversation in the ancient Chinese text known by the name of its legendary author, Zhuangzi (Chuang Tzu). Heidegger was familiar with this text at least at early as 1930 if not before, from a rendition done by Martin Buber in 1910, and it is likely that the text had some influence on his later thinking of *Gelassenheit* and non-willing, although he explicitly mentions the *Zhuangzi* only in seminars and lectures.[16] The story is often cited

---

exhaustively reveal the nature of all things and bring them under control, see MARALDO 1976 and MARALDO 2017, 413–35.

15. HEIDEGGER 1995, 18–19.

16. PÖGGLER (1987, 52) reports that Heidegger invoked Zhuangzi's story of the happy fish (see WATSON 1968, 188–90) as a mode of *Mitsein,* Being-with, in a 1930 lecture in Bremen about the essence of truth, and (in 1960?) Heidegger recalled Zhuangzi's story of the bell-stand; in Pöggler's words, "through long fasting and through concentration and meditation the woodworker becomes able to find in the forest that one tree which is already the bell-stand yet to be made, in such a way that matter and form in this consummate work of art can be completely one" (56). That reading finds the finished product in the original matter and contrasts with Heidegger's comment in a 1962 lecture that mentions another story by Zhuangzi about the *"useless* tree"; see MA 2008, 122 and WATSON 1968, 63–5. MAY (1989, 16 and 64) and HEUBEL (2022) document Heidegger's familiarity with Zhuangzi. On a probable influence, see also the complementary essay by Graham Parkes in MAY 1996. For current explorations of "Daoist resonances in Heidegger," see CHAI 2022. DAVIS 2020 offers an insightful reading of Heidegger's "unnecessary being"

as an illustration of the Daoist notion of *wu-wei*, "effortless action" or action unimpeded by the will. Here I will focus on the kind of practice that the story implies. Indeed, the story seems ambiguously to suggest both an instrumental practice, doing something in order to attain a goal, and the alternative practice of attention for its own sake.

First, let us listen to the story in one abridged version:

> Cook Ding was carving an ox for the Ruler, Wenhui. Wherever his hand touched, wherever his shoulder leaned, wherever his foot stepped, wherever his knee pushed—with a zip and a whoosh, the blade sang and he never missed a beat. The Ruler, Wenhui, exclaimed, "What a joy! It is good, is it not, that such a simple craft can be so elevated?" Cook Ding laid aside his cleaver. "All I care about is *dao*," he said, "It is just that I find it in my craft. When I started carving oxen, I saw nothing but oxen. After three years, I no longer saw a complete ox. These days, spirit carries me through and my eyes are no longer used to see. 'Reflective awareness' has ceased and 'spirit-like impulses' come into play.... Even so, there are always difficult places, and when the going gets rough, I take care, my gaze settles, my movements slow, and I move the cleaver ever so slightly. Then, poof!—it all crumbles apart like a clod of earth. I stand there, cleaver in hand, and behold my work with satisfaction. I then wipe off my cleaver and put it away." On hearing this, the Ruler, Wenhui, replied, "How wonderful! I have learned how to nurture life in the teachings of Cook Ding!"[17]

This story seems at first sight to illustrate instrumental practice in the usual sense. The cook uses the cleaver in order to accomplish a series of goals: to carve the ox and make it suitable for cooking its meat, to produce a fine meal for the Ruler, to give the Ruler sustenance and well-being (and perhaps to provide himself with the same, sustenance and well-being, since his own well-being is subject to the Ruler's). We

---

in terms of Zhuangzi's uselessness, and HUNTINGTON 2020 suggests how Heidegger and Zhuangzi transform the phenomenological reduction.

17. This is the translation, slightly modified, of BEHUNIAK 2010, 161–2. His incisive article examines this story and other passages in the *Zhuangzi* for their relevance for moral theory and an alternative to the means-end relationship.

can imagine, along the lines of Heidegger's analysis, that if the cook's cleaver were to break, or to become so dull as to be unusable, then the task would be interrupted, the useless cleaver would become the object of attention, and upon reflection the entire referential context of the ox-carving would come to light. But all that is avoided in this story and the ox-carving proceeds smoothly, though without the capacity to highlight the true nature of the instrument. In this reading, the proclamation by the Ruler Wenhui would mean, "I have learned how to nurture life, by a skillful use of things to attain my goals."

Yet this interpretation is contradicted by the cook's statement, "all I care about is *dao*.... It is just that I find it in my craft." The cook disavows interest in a goal, even interest in the ruler's and his own nurturance and well-being. He seems to collapse the chain of intentions into attention to present details, the movement of the cleaver that conforms to the openings it finds in the contours of the ox. To use an image not in the *Zhuangzi*, it is as if he were walking through a very narrow canyon where his body must fit through the crevices. In carving the ox he exists in the space of the bones. When he encounters difficulties, what is called for is more attention and care, slower work, rather than struggle and force. The practice of the cook requires careful attention to the activity immediately at hand, and this immediate attention takes long years of practicing the carving of oxen—until reflective thought is no longer needed, willful control is relinquished, the spirit moves of itself and the object of carving is forgotten. The practice of the cook also requires care of the instrument, and this instrumental care to keep the cleaver sharp is exercised for years—until it is rendered unnecessary by attention to the activity at hand. For the first few years of practice, the cleaver requires continual sharpening, an action done to it separately from the action of carving. But as the practice progresses, as the cook learns to conform to the contours of the ox and find the openings, the care of the cleaver shifts and all that is required is to pay attention while it is being used, and to wipe it off afterwards. The cook remarks,

A good cook changes his knife once a year—because he cuts. A mediocre cook changes his knife once a month—because he hacks. I've had this knife of mine for nineteen years and I've cut up thousands of oxen with it, and yet the blade is as good as though it had just come from the grindstone. There are spaces between the joints, and the blade of the knife has really no thickness. If you insert what has no thickness into such spaces, then there's plenty of room—more than enough for the blade to play about in. That's why after nineteen years the blade of my knife is still as good as when it first came from the grindstone.[18]

I suggest that the cook's practice is not instrumental in the end, is not the use of a thing as a means to achieve an objective external to the activity. In the translation I cited, the cook finds the *dao* (道) *in* his craft, not outside it, external to it. Other translations render this passage slightly differently: the *dao* [or way] goes *beyond* technique, method, or skill; and one translation has the cook speaking of the *dao* that "is *in advance of* any art."[19] But whether we find the *dao* "in the craft, " beyond mere technique, or in advance of technique, it is clear that the *dao* is not an end or objective apart from one's present actions. The practice of the cook is ultimately not an instrumental practice (nor is the practice of nourishing life). It is rather an example of how instrumental, goal-oriented practice is transformed into the practice of

---

18. This passage, elided in Behuniak's translation, is taken from the translation in WATSON 1968, 51.

19. Wayne Yokoyama (personal communication, October 2022) offers an alternative translation that notices the symmetry between Ruler Wenhui's remark 「技盖至此乎」 "That your art should have become so perfect!" and the Cook Ding's incisive response about his art: 「臣之所好者道也，進乎技矣。」 "What I care about is the Way—that's how I've advanced to the level where my art has become so perfect!" WATSON (1968, 51) has Cook Ding saying, "What I care about is the Way, which goes beyond skill." Behuniak (personal communication, July 14, 2010) notes that "進 *jin* in Chinese means both 'to advance beyond' and 'to enter into' so it could mean that Dao is found 'beyond' the skill, or 'in' the skill." The translation by LEGGE (1962) has: "What your servant loves is the method of the Dao, something in advance of any art" (<http://oaks.nvg.org/zhuangzi1-.html#3>). The German rendition of Martin Buber that Heidegger most likely read is not available to me, but the English translation of Buber's text reads, "Your servant has surrendered to the Tao. This is better than skillfulness" (HERMAN 1996, 21).

attention for its own sake.[20] Is the cook's practice with the cleaver akin to Heidegger's practice of *Gelassenheit*, if *Gelassenheit* can be considered a form of practice at all?

The Jug

The jug or pitcher (*der Krug* in Heidegger's essays) serves to hold something for us to drink, for our enjoyment and our nourishment. What we call the jug here may be a fine cup that we buy in a marketplace or at a crafts-fair, or it may be an exquisite work of art on display in a gallery. As a jug, however, it is most often simply a useful thing [*Zeug*] whose everyday use exemplifies the instrumental practice we are familiar with. The treatment of this kind of thing shifts in Heidegger's later writing on *Gelassenheit*, where its usefulness takes an oriental turn. In Heidegger's imagined conversation between a scientist, a philosopher-scholar, and a thinker, on their walk along a country path one evening, the jug serves as an example of a thing that can be thought of in two different ways: by way of representational thinking [*vorstellendes Denken*] and by way of an alternative thinking called *Gelassenheit*.

Gelassenheit is Heidegger's word for the way to experience the essential be-ing [*das Wesen*] of humans and of things. With regard to things, *Gelassenheit* is a fundamental shift from the kind of seeing and apprehending that the Heidegger of *Being and Time* elucidates as our most common way of treating the things we encounter in the world. Instead of using things in expectation of reaching a goal or objective, *Gelassenheit* calls for a waiting quite different from expecting, a wait-

---

20. The French commentator BILLETER (2002, 67–9) suggests that another level of critical reflection is at work in the cook's activity, operating at "a certain distance from the activity of the body, taking the attitude of an ironical spectator... toward what happens inside ourselves ... [and acting as a] limited control, as simple supervision" of incorporated actions. But I find no hint of that critical stance in Zhuangzi's description of the accomplished art of the cook.

5. Four Things and Two Practices: Taking Heidegger Farther East | 139

ing that has no specific object already in mind, that leaves open that upon which we wait.[21] Instead of looking with a view to a goal in sight [*Umsicht, eine Sicht um zu...*] that is at work in our usual comportment with things, waiting is staying with whatever might open itself to us. Instead of looking to see, when a thing becomes dysfunctional, how the world is disclosed as the horizon of representational thinking, *gelassenes Denken*—the thinking that lets go of representations and expectations—simply lets things be. *Gelassenheit* promises to open a way to experience our essential nature.[22] The three participants come

---

21. HEIDEGGER 1995, 115–6. This notion of *Gelassenheit* has been the subject of illuminating treatments by Ōhashi Ryōsuke, Ueda Shizuteru, Graham Parkes, David Michael Levin, and Bret W. Davis, among others, from whom I have learned much. My treatment here focuses not on *Gelassenheit* as a form of meditative non-willing, but rather as a form of action and practice. This practice resonates with the Linji's imperative to "accord with all things," cited in Chapter 9, "Personal Autonomy: An Alternative View," in the present volume. Here I confine my discussion for the most part to the conversation composed and posthumously published as "Ein Gespräch selbstdritt auf einem Feldweg" in HEIDEGGER 1995.

22. Graham Parkes's chapter, "Thoughts on the Way: Being and Time via Lao-Chuang" (in PARKES 1987, 119), has suggested that the contrast between early Heidegger's accounts of instrumentality and of *Gelassenheit* is not as pronounced as one might think. Both accounts appeal to a letting-be, a freeing or release: In the account of *Being and Time*, we can let ourselves be involved [*bewendenlassen*, ordinarily meaning "letting well enough alone"] with things that are there in-order-to [*Zuhandene*] and we can free them to be what they already are and what they can be [*Zuhandenes so und so sein lassen*]. This, Parkes remarks, is not an imposition of our will on things, but anticipates the kind of releasement expressed later as *Gelassenheit*:

> Through the prior freeing of a being for being to-hand we help it come into its own. This is not a one-sided operation in which we unilaterally impose our will on things, but rather a reciprocal interaction. In forging a piece of metal into a knife, for example, the metalworker realizes a certain potential of that metal for sharpness, a potential it could never realize on its own. But the success of the work depends in advance on certain properties of the metal itself—since no amount or working on wood could ever achieve such sharpness.

POLT (1999, 58) also reads the "letting something be involved [or relevant]" as foreshadowing the notion of *Gelassenheit*. On this point, DAVIS (2007, 315 n.12) comments, and I agree: "And yet, without denying an element of such foreshadowing, it is hard to deny that a long shadow of the will still distinctly looms over the idea of disclosing things as first of all tools in an environment structured by Dasein's projection of a *Worum-willen* [that is,

upon the thought of the jug in trying to express the essence of thinking as to what is essential to human be-ing.

Let us stay with the thought of the jug for a while. The thinking of the natural sciences tends to represent the jug in causal terms. Although the sciences have long ago abandoned analysis in terms of the four classical kinds of cause, these terms are still helpful to express the representational thinking of something like a jug. Scientific, representational thinking may be said to determine the jug in terms of its material cause—the material, say the clay, of which it consists; its formal cause—the sides, rim, bottom, and handle that give the jug its shape; its efficient cause—the activity of the potter who makes the jug; and its final cause—the purpose of the jug. (Heidegger's conversation appeals explicitly only to the formal and the efficient causes, albeit without using these classical terms.) Thinking of the final cause—the purpose or use of the jug—invites an alternative way of thinking the essence of the jug, a way that is closer to everyday experience, to the way of seeing previously called circumspection [*Umsicht*], and farther from the scientific view of the jug. The jug is a container and exists to contain drinkable liquids. But it can be a container, Heidegger suggests, only by virtue of its emptiness.[23] In the guise of all three participants in the conversation, Heidegger says that the essential be-ing of a thing like a jug opens itself to the thinker only when the thinker waits upon this essence and lets himself be released into the free expanse, the *Gegnet*, that frees the thing to be what it is.[24] Here it looks as if the self-determination of the jug essentially as an emptiness has come

---

a 'for-the-sake-of which']." Davis interprets the German expression "*um* (*jemandes* oder *einer Sache*) *willen*" as a manifestation of the will. Ordinarily the expression translates into English simply as "for the sake of (something or someone)." For example, *um Gottes willen* means "for God's sake" or "for heaven's sake"; it does not mean "for the will of God." The German *willen* in this expression indicates rather a giving over to and benefitting someone or something. Of course, Heidegger's *Worum-willen*, that for the sake of which Dasein engages in projects, is ultimately Dasein itself.

23. HEIDEGGER 1995, 130.
24. Ibid.

about only because of the thinkers' association[25] of its final cause—its purpose as a container—with the emptiness that makes it possible to contain drinkable liquids. In other words, the final cause of the thing appears to be the determining factor in establishing its essence.

Of course, Heidegger would object to this sort of description: waiting is not establishing a final cause, and the freeing on the part of the free expanse is not determining a purpose or use.[26] If we allow his interpretation a bit freer reign, we must concede that the purpose of the jug is, after all, not emptiness. Yet emptiness is not all there is to it. What makes a jug a jug rather than another kind of container is presumably more than its emptiness, its cavity. All containers contain—hold in—an emptiness, in order to contain or hold something else, such as drinkable liquid. But not all containers are jugs, even in the broad sense of the word. A jug [*Krug*] is not a barrel [*Barrel*], a vat [*Bottich*], a canister [*Büchse*], or a watering can [*Gießkanne*]—yet all these things are containers with cavities or empty spaces. Apparently, the essence of the jug is not confined to its emptiness. And even if Heidegger would object to this description, the emptiness that frees this thing to be a jug is discovered only in retrospect of the jug's utility.

This is precisely the point of the original text that most probably gave Heidegger the clue about emptiness: chapter 11 of the *Dao de ching*.[27] There the legendary author Laozi acknowledges the utility of this emptiness rather than supposing that the jug has an essence that

---

25. Indeed, the entire course of the conversation proceeds by what psychologists commonly call associative thinking, letting the mind freely associate and move from one topic or word to another. Would it conversely be possible to re-think associative thinking in terms of *Gelassenheit*? We might also note the roots of the German word *Ding* and the English *thing* mean an assembly of people. Heidegger plays on the word *Ding* as a gathering, a *Versammlung*, though not of people.

26. Here I interpret Heidegger's verb *vergegnen*, translated by Davis with *enregioning*, as freeing into its own; and I translate that which does the freeing, *die Gegnet* (Davis's *open-region*) as the free expanse. HEIDEGGER (1995, 114) also parses *die Gegnet* as *die freie Weite*.

27. See MAY 1996, 30, for documentation. Heidegger similarly determines the essence of the container-thing as emptiness.

transcends its utility. Laozi says, "Clay is fired to make a pot. The pot's use comes from emptiness."[28] Or, in a different translation: "We throw clay to shape a pot, but the utility of the clay pot is a function of the nothingness (*wu*) inside it."[29] The Daoist text recognizes the instrumentality of the action: we throw and fire the clay in order to make a pot (in order to drink, to survive, or simply to enjoy a drink).

Laozi would of course agree with Heidegger that the emptiness of the pot is not something manufactured by humans.[30] But Laozi highlights the relevant contrast between something "substantial" like clay and something ungraspable [*unfaßlich*], like the cavity or emptiness of the pot, precisely to let us see what is needed for utility—not what is needed for an essence of the thing.

Heidegger sets the essential be-ing [*das Wesen*] of the jug in a series of things that belong together: the essence of the jug is its emptiness, this emptiness resides in the emptiness—that is, the absence—of a drink, and a drink resides in all that goes into drinking: the gathering of what gives itself as drinkable to be drunk—in the case of wine for example, the gathering of grapes that reside in the grapevine which in turn resides in the earth and the gifts of the sky, and so in an open expanse.[31] This series ostensibly replaces the series involved in instrumental practice, where we use the jug for drinking, which is for enjoyment or sustenance, ultimately for human well-being. The gifts provided by the open sky ostensibly replace the willful doing of humans in making a jug or pot. And the gathering that is in the nature of such a thing, the gathering—to allude to Heidegger's fourfold—of earth, sky, mortals, and gods,[32] contrasts with the disclosing of the

---

28. ADDISS AND LOMBARDO 1993, 11.
29. AMES AND HALL 2003, 91. Laozi makes the same point about the utility of a wheel and a room, likewise dependent on their emptiness or nothingness (無).
30. HEIDEGGER 1995, 130.
31. Ibid., 134–5
32. In other essays, Heidegger frames this series in terms of the *Geviert*, the fourfold that brings together earth, sky, mortals, and divinities. See, for example, HEIDEGGER 1954.

5. Four Things and Two Practices: Taking Heidegger Farther East | 143

world as our referential totality when a useful thing breaks down. This is a contrast between early and latter Heidegger that deserves further attention. Here we may merely notice a feature shared by the two sides of the contrast: the series ending in the expanse of the open sky also begins with the thought of what the jug is for, its purpose or final cause.[33] Here we see the latent instrumentality of Heidegger's thinking that would let go of human purposes.

All the same, we cannot say that *Gelassenheit* names an instrumental practice. *Gelassenheit* leads us to think of the jug from out of an opening to the expanse that allows us to be (an open-ing that Heidegger calls *Vergegnis*), and to the conditions that allow the thing to be (which Heidegger calls *Bedingnis*). Here we may simply pose the question: Does this sort of open-ing need the practice of attention?

There are two thoughts to consider here. First, the open-ing [*Vergegnen*] is an active doing on the part of the free expanse itself and removes the agency from the humans who otherwise would manifest and determine things.[34] How then would it be in need of any practice on our part? And secondly, how might *Gelassenheit* be considered a practice? Heidegger offers a clear answer to the first question: the free expanse needs releasing (needs *Gelassenheit*) for its open-ing; truth as manifestation (and concealment)—precisely to be independent of the human—needs the essential be-ing of humans.[35] This answer can be rephrased: when we let the world show itself not as the horizon of our projections but "as itself," in its own active be-ing or "worlding," and when we let things show themselves not as things we represent as there for our sake, but as gatherings within the world, then we come to

---

33. The "open sky" might recall the Buddhist conception of *śūnyatā* or emptiness, rendered in Chinese with the character for empty sky, 空. But that "emptiness" pertains to the lack of everything's independent, separate existence.

34. In phenomenology this agency could be called the agency of manifestation. I read Heidegger's notions of *Vergegnis* and *Bedingnis* as an alternative to the Husserlian notions of eidetic intuition and constitution. An attempt to demonstrate this connection must await another occasion.

35. HEIDEGGER 1995, 147.

see that the world in its worlding needs the human for its gathering of everything and letting all things rest in themselves.[36]

But in what sense is *Gelassenheit* an active practice? The word itself, in ordinary usage, connotes sedateness, placidity or simply serenity. True, Heidegger distances himself from the conventional sense of the word and appeals to Meister Eckhart's sense of *Gelassenheit* as a letting go of one's will, although he does not appeal to Eckhart's invitation to submit to the greater will of God. Furthermore, Heidegger invokes the notions of rest and resting or repose [*Ruhe, ruhen*] in describing the way that we are to arrive at the essence of something.[37] Yet the conversation makes clear that rest does not mean doing nothing. It can mean letting things rest in, or be based on, their proper essence. If the proper thinking differs from actively working on things, it can also be a mastering and overcoming of inactivity [*Meisterung und Überwindung der Untätigkeit*].[38] Although it cannot be willed and is not an exercise of the will, *Gelassenheit* is far from passive impotence.[39] Indeed, the thinking called *Gelassenheit* is Heidegger's alternative to the opposition between activity and passivity.[40] *Gelassenheit* is an active waiting, if not a doing on our part.[41]

The notion that *Gelassenheit* is something that must be practiced never becomes a theme of the conversation. Yet its course along the country path clearly shows that the three participants are slowly learning to let go—to release their habits of representational thinking and willing. Over and over again they must keep from going astray, keep to the bearing [*Verhalten*] of waiting, and they let themselves be engaged

36. See HEIDEGGER 1995, 149.
37. Ibid., 69–71; 149.
38. Ibid., 70.
39. Ibid., 62, 108.
40. Yet this alternative is not merely another opposite: "by positing the opposite we just entangle ourselves yet further in a dependence on that from which we want to free ourselves" (ibid., 154). Heidegger wants to avoid "the thicket of dialectical discussions" (59).
41. Ibid., 109–110.

5. Four Things and Two Practices: Taking Heidegger Farther East | 145

in [*sich einlassen in*] the matter in question. They must persistently attend to the question of the thinking that properly defines human beings, and find themselves returning over and over again to this question[42]—just as the practitioner of Zen meditation, *zazen*, returns over and over again to his breath and continually lets go of thinking. Although *zazen* practice seems to go farther than *Gelassenheit* as a kind of meditative thinking, many have found a deep resonance between them.[43] Here I would like to divert from Heidegger's path and consider another possible mode of *Gelassenheit*, by returning to the matter of the jug.

Heidegger's thoughts on the jug explicitly disregard the making or fabrication of such a thing and consider the jug only as already there: "We can now disregard the making or fabrication [*Verfertigung*] [of the jug], since only the already fabricated jug standing there is the jug-thing."[44]

In this respect, the conversation follows the treatment in *Being and Time* of things as already there, if not merely there-for our use. It is remarkable that Heidegger, despite his interpretation of *things* as *gatherings* and of an artwork as the working of truth, implies here a certain fixation on the finished thing in contrast to its making and functioning. Indeed, his 1958 conversations with Hisamatsu on art

---

42. In his 1955 address in Meßkirch on *Gelassenheit*, Heidegger says, "die Gelassenheit zu den Dingen und die Offenheit für das Geheimnis fallen uns niemals von selber zu. Sie sind nichts Zu-fälliges. Beide gedeihen nur aus einem unablässigen herzhaften Denken." That is, "letting things be and remaining open to the mystery [of the meaning of the world of technology] never just happen to occur to us. They are nothing coincidental. Both blossom only by way of unremitting mindful thought" (HEIDEGGER 1959, 25).

43. The practice of *zazen* also offers a hint as to how a paradox that haunts Heidegger's conversation is resolved: the paradox of willing non-willing. In *zazen* one willingly assumes a posture, both mental and physical, that lets one let go of thoughts—similar to the way one assumes the posture of sleep when wanting to fall asleep. Trying to sleep, willing sleep, is counter-effective. There is much more to be said here. Heidegger's *Gelassenheit* might be contrasted with the "letting go of thoughts" of which the Zen teacher UCHIYAMA (1993, 64–5) speaks. UEDA S. (1994) explicitly compares Zen practice and *Gelassenheit*.

44. HEIDEGGER 1995, 130.

display the same tendency to fix a phenomenon (an art object or language/*Sprache* itself) in its nominal and objective form and disregard its active or verbal being.[45]

Let us instead consider the making of a jug as a possible form of practice. We may take as our example the kind of making that Heidegger himself would most likely prefer: hand-making a jug of clay rather than mass-producing it. And we may focus on the formation of the jug or pot on the potter's wheel, and for the moment leave aside the practice that goes into the firing and glazing of the pot. A potter I know described it this way: making a pot is a matter of ever adjusting one's control over the clay, of both actively shaping and releasing control in response to the clay, the spin of the potter's wheel, and the factors of the environment. "Throwing a pot" is a matter of feeling one's way with the formation of the jug.

The clay must be moist enough to shape easily, but dry enough to hold its shape. A ball of clay is thrown onto the wheel head and has to stick. Hands press down on the rounded top of the now rotating ball to make a disk broader than it is tall, and then thumbs and fingers move down the center, let a hole form in the middle, and then make a base. The clay is opened up; there's an inside and an outside. The thick walls of the jug are pinched between fingers that ride up the sides, inside and out, making a ridge that spirals up and gradually thins as the fingers release pressure, until the thickness of the walls is balanced. Then the handle is formed and attached.

Throwing a pot takes a practiced hand and a practiced body as well as attention, but it can be "perfected" until it becomes "second-nature" and can be done without reflective thought. Even when the potter is practiced enough to let her thoughts drift while shaping the jug on the wheel, her body naturally attends to the shaping, and subtly adjusts to it when more pressure or less pressure is needed. Even if the potter has a particular shape in mind, she must often give in to the way the

---

45. See the summary in MA 2008, 157–9.

jug is taking shape. She attends or waits upon the formed thing that comes to be in an interaction between the potter, the wheel, and the clay. In foresight, to make a particular jug means to willfully carry out a particular intention, and in hindsight the jug is made for a particular purpose. A made jug is the result of instrumental practice. The act of making the jug, on the other hand, is a matter of practicing attention for its own sake. To be sure, the potter is aware that the container she is making must be trustworthy: the user places his trust in the jug that its handle will not break and spill the drink, or scald the user with hot liquid. The jug is made to contain, so the user has to trust it to contain the drink and to pour it. Building trust is a crucial part of forming the jug.[46] The emptiness, after all, is for filling, not for its own sake. Yet to fulfill that intention, it and all other intentions must be concentrated in attention to what is happening then and there. Even the potter's intention gives way to the moment-by-moment attending. If *Gelassenheit* can name this practice, it is a more bodily, though equally thoughtful and attentive, *Gelassenheit*.

THE BRUSH

The calligrapher's brush, like the carpenter's hammer, the cook's cleaver, and the potter's jug, appears as a thing useful for a purpose that its maker and its user have in mind; it appears as a thing there in order to accomplish a goal. The brush is for writing or drawing (the Sino-Japanese character 書, pronounced *sho* means both).[47] *Sho* is Japanese word for the art of writing or brushing Chinese characters or Japanese phonetic script in sumi ink on paper. Chinese, Korean, and Japanese cultures revere beautifully executed writing or calligraphy as a high form of art, so the calligrapher's brush appears to be a tool for

---

46. I am grateful to Julia Livingston for these insights and this description of throwing a pot. See also her blog, < www.100cupsblog.blogspot.com >.

47. The "Follow-up" that concludes the present volume explains how the pathway art called *shodō* (書道) is traditionally taught and learned.

the production of this art. The twentieth-century calligrapher Morita Shiryū saw it differently, however. Let us listen to what he says in an essay called "What Is a Brush?"[48]

> At birth I am thrust into a world of things and words without willing it myself, without being able to choose a place with no things and no words. Once born, I cannot but live, here and now, in connection to things and words. I derive my life, my very being, from things, and things derive their being from me. The very fact that I am alive means that I am fundamentally and essentially this kind of being.
>
> If I now live by picking up a brush to compose a work, this brush is not simply a brush. From the start, it is a thing from which my life and my being emerge. The brush is a brush by being a thing that lets me be, here and now; without it I would not be. Nowhere is there simply an I, a self by itself; there is only this self here and now, living by way of the brush. The brush likewise exists here and now only as a brush from which I derive my life. Because there is no self by itself and no brush by itself, no relationship comes about between some prior "me" and some prior "brush." Rather, we must say that what exists is a whole we may call "I and my brush." The one, inseparable whole lives here and now, and that is the very substance of my being a calligrapher here and now....
>
> Only in the moment I and the brush truly become one, does it really happen that "I do calligraphy".... I and the brush are one. I am the brush, the brush is me. I am not something restricted by the brush. I am not I (but rather this totality here and now), and therefore I am I. The brush is not a brush (but rather this totality here and now), and therefore it is a brush. As a calligrapher I transcend myself and am released from myself; this liberation continues to work within me. I am no longer restricted by my self. This is where I can truly become myself.... To say that without the brush there is no self means that without it I have no freedom. Without this brush I cannot truly become myself.

48. "What is Brush?' appeared as an English translation of part of a longer essay, 「書と抽象絵画」 [Calligraphy and Abstract Painting], in MORITA 1970. Here I use my own translation, which appears in JPSB, 1200–2. The Japanese book also included a German translation of the excerpt by Irmtraud Schaarschmidt-Richter, "Was Ist der Pinsel? Ein Instrument als Ort zur Freiheit." A somewhat longer extract in English appears as "Sho as Creative Transformation of Self," in *Chanoyu Quarterly* 10 (1974): 17–24.

Here and now the brush is the "I" that (as activity here and now) I am not. This way of seeing takes the brush is not something outside me, not something confined to an external tool. Rather, it lets me see myself in the brush and lets it live therein. This matter is no mere desire on my part.

It must point to the fact that "I and my brush" exist here and now, that here and now I am alive.

Morita's words are truly surprising. First of all, he suggests not only that a thing like a brush does not exist as a separate being—Heidegger too says as much of the useful things or *Zeuge*. But Morita suggests that the creative artist as well exists only as part of a whole; calligrapher and brush live by way of one another.

Neither pre-exists the act of doing calligraphy. And to this surprising proposal Morita adds that the act of doing calligraphy occurs only when I and the brush become one; when "I am the brush" and "the brush is me." Then, to top off that proposal, he expresses the nearly inconceivable thought: I am not I, and therefore I am I; the brush is not a brush and therefore it is a brush.

This last mentioned, nearly inconceivable thought derives from the Buddhism that Morita drew from the writings of Kyoto School philosophers Nishida Kitarō, Morita's teacher Hisamatsu Shin'ichi, and perhaps Nishitani Keiji.[49] To illustrate this thought, Nishitani uses the examples of the seeing eye and of a sword. The eye is the organ that sees and lets us see; the eye does not see itself and therefore it can see (other things). A cleaver is something that cuts, but cannot cut itself; therefore it can cut (other things). And we might add, the hammer cannot hammer itself, and therefore it can hammer (other things). For Morita we could say the brush cannot brush itself, and therefore it

---

49. NKZ 11: 399, cites the classical formulation of the Diamond Sutra that can be found in a Japanese translation of section 8 of Kumārajīva's Chinese version of the *Vajracchedikā-prajñāpāramitā-sūtra*: "The Buddha is not the Buddha, therefore the Buddha is the Buddha." See NISHITANI 1961, trans. 1982, 125 and 116–18 for other instantiations, and Chapter 1 of the present volume, page 20.

can brush Chinese characters or sinographs. These examples shift the emphasis from the concrete thing (the eye, the cleaver, the brush) to the activity the thing allows to happen, or rather, that allows the thing to be what is is. The thing is *not* the thing that is lying there objectively before us, but is a thing hammering, a thing cutting, a thing writing or drawing—and therefore it is a hammer, a cleaver, or a brush.

From what point of view is it possible to make such pronouncements? From an objective, third-person perspective, it seems obvious that the calligrapher and the brush exist before the act of writing with the brush begins. The calligrapher prepares the paper and the sumi ink, dips the brush in the ink, and touches the paper with the brush, moving it on the paper and occasionally lifting it, in a few deft gestures, until the completed Chinese characters appear. From a pre-reflective, first-person perspective, however, while the act of writing is taking place, in that moment, my body and the brush become the ONE that is writing. When I (that is, the calligrapher) have practiced writing over and over again, there is no need to consciously recall the number of strokes and the stroke order of a sinograph. Each time is an occasion of attending to the activity. On each occasion my body becomes more adept at subtly but swiftly adjusting to the flow of the ink and the surface of the paper. At last the writing seems to unfold without a body or a brush—what is present is solely flowing ink and following its flow. In the retrospect that isolates my self, I seem to be following the brush rather than leading it—just as the cook follows his cleaver rather than coercing it, or the potter follows the shape as much as she steers it.[50] To be sure, there may be unanticipated surprises along the way, as when in using a brush as big as my arm some ink happens to splatter on the paper. But "never mind": just follow the surprise. This then is the perspective that comes with practicing attention for its sake, the purpose of the writing forgotten.

50. A rough analogy is with white-water rafting, where a constant interplay takes place between guiding the raft or canoe and following the current.

The practice of attention here may indeed be attendant upon goal-oriented instrumental practice: the act of writing sinographs may be geared toward producing a work that can be hung in a *tokonoma* alcove or in an art gallery. Yet even then the finished work shows traces of the activity of the writing, of the path the brush took along the paper. The practiced eye of a viewer looks for these traces and reveres the work all the more for letting them be seen, for letting the work in action be seen.

IN CONCLUSION

The practice of attention may gratuitously bring to light something that has escaped the notice of Heidegger in his thoughts on instrumental practice and the practice of *Gelassenheit*. Heidegger elucidates how instrumental practice, when disrupted, lets the world show up as the normally withdrawn context of that practice. Later he intimates how the practice of waiting and letting go can let our benefactors—earth and open sky—come to light through the emptiness of the jug. (In other texts he names the fourfold interplay of earth, sky, mortals, and the gods, that comes to light in a thing.) It seems Heidegger has forgotten the self in these practices, that is to say, he has forgotten how self is forgotten and how self as forgotten comes to be noticed. In the attentive, adept practice of hammering, carving, throwing pots, and writing sinographs, one may in a sense lose oneself in the activity at hand. That is, one may lose the self that intends (where the word intend is used in its ordinary volitional sense rather than the broader phenomenological sense of directed consciousness) and may actually become aware that this intending self is left behind. In the practiced writing with brush and ink, for example, there is a sense that the brush is moving of itself as the artist watches the brush move, the sinographs unfold. A similar sensation can arise in throwing a pot or using a cleaver, perhaps even in wielding a hammer. Intending is no longer needed; an other awareness opens up, a self-awareness to be sure, but one from which the intentional self has withdrawn. The practice of attention brings to light the awareness that the self of intentions, the self that pursues its projects in the world, can and must sometimes be left behind. I have come to think of this instance of attention as attentive absorption. A beautiful example is found in the novel *The Elegance of the Hedgehog*, by Muriel Barbery, in a scene of a man who lets go of his exhausting attempts to mow wheat fields by hand and instead lets himself be absorbed into an effortless and much more fruitful activity. For the scene we are transported to the wheat fields of Russia where the character Levin, in Tolstoy's *Anna Karenina*, struggles to help the peasants mow the fields by hand, using their scythes. After first exerting himself prodigiously, Levin begins to learn with his body:

> with each successive pause and start, his awkward, painful gestures become more fluid.... Gradually, his movements are freed from the shackles of his will, and he goes into a light trance which gives his gestures the perfection of conscious, automatic motion, without thought or calculation, and the scythe seems to move of its own accord. Levin delights in the forgetfulness that movement brings, where the pleasure of doing is marvelously foreign to the striving of the will.[51]

This passage in the novel illustrates the particular kind of attention at work in practices we may call self-less.

But even where the attention is intentional throughout, I hope to have shown that the calligrapher's brush, the potter's jug, the cook's cleaver, and the carpenter's hammer are four things that illustrate the instrumental practice and the practice of attention that let these things do their work—that lets them be what they are. We are now able to recast Heidegger's question concerning technology in a way that must remain open here: can the practice of attention performed for its own sake—caring for things simply to care for them, caring for the surrounding world simply to care for it—help salvage not only the environment but the very essence of being human?

51. BARBERY 2008, 123.

6
Practice, *Samādhi*, Realization
Three Innovative Interpretations by Nishitani Keiji

Most of us, I think, connect Nishitani Keiji to Zen. Before I had any experience with Zen, I envisioned it as a way to connect everyday bodily existence with philosophical reflection. My vision soon proved to be short of reality. My first experience with Zen practice, during a seven-day *sesshin*, shrank the entire world to a body of intense pain and left no room for philosophical thinking. On the other hand, my first readings of "Zen philosophy" were either baffling old Chinese anecdotes (kōans) or abstruse, highly abstract speculation (Nishida philosophy), both far removed from my everyday life. Later I tried to make the connection by spending days struggling to read an essay, "The Standpoint of Zen,"[1] at a time when I could read it only once removed, by translating it. When I first met the author of that essay, Professor Nishitani Keiji, at his home at the foot of Yoshidayama in Kyoto in 1978, I began to understand that the connection between everyday existence and philosophical reflection cannot be contrived, but must be lived. Nishitani Sensei showed me this indirectly, by directing attention from his life to the matter of his thought.

1. NISHITANI 1974.

Practice

The connection between philosophical reflection and everyday activity is traditionally signified by the word *practice*. As Chapter 4 of this book has shown, this term has a complex history in Western philosophy but often a simple connotation. Practice is the application of a principle or theory to a concrete activity. By practice we apply what we think to what we do. And what we do usually has a certain intent or goal. Through practice we become "good at" something; and something is practical if it is "good for" something else. In common usage, then, practice takes its meaning from something outside of practice: the theory or principle to be applied; the objective or goal to be attained. What is more, practice is understood as a kind of activity that only human beings can engage in, insofar as only humans are capable of willful intention.

Taking this understanding of practice for granted, I was immediately baffled when I read in an essay by Nishitani that clouds moving across the sky, water flowing, leaves falling, and blossoms scattering are all forms of practice. They are, more exactly, "forms of non-form," that is, of selflessness. To practice is to adopt the form of non-form as the form of the self.[2] Nishitani's text, *Religion and Nothingness* in English translation, formulates the point carefully. It does not present these examples of practice as an analogy, as if to say that when we truly practice, we are in flux "like" moving clouds, flowing water, falling leaves, scattering blossoms. Such an analogy would compare human activities and natural occurrences, but at the same time differentiate between them. Rather, Nishitani suggests that their form and our form are in practice the same "form of non-form." Here again, the text does not simply repeat the Buddhist teaching that such natural phenomena in themselves are empty, devoid of *svabhāva* or self-subsistent being, nor does it say that by practicing *we* come to see the emptiness of things.

2. Nishitani 1961, 220; trans. 1982, 200.

True to the point he is making, Nishitani's language here makes no distinction between us and them; it posits no forms as things outside the self. It does use verbal parts of speech and focuses on activities in its examples: clouds moving, water flowing. In this respect it would seem to make some connection with the ordinary notion of practice, which after all is a kind of activity. But the activities in Nishitani's examples neither arise from a willful self nor are they directed toward something else, and so they run counter to the usual instrumental understanding of what practice is. Clouds moving and water flowing are themselves without will and intent, and are not aimed at any goal.

Perhaps the discrepancy arises because we are trying to convey two different meanings with the same word, *practice*. In his discussion, Nishitani is clarifying a passage by Hakuin, who in turn uses the cited examples in a comment about the occurrence of the word *practice* in the Heart Sutra: Avalokiteśvara Bodhisattva is engaged in the practice of deep *prajñāpāramitā*. The relevant word is 行 (J. *gyō*, C. *hsing*), a term literally meaning "going" that is often translated as practice in Sino-Japanese Buddhist texts. The opening passage of the Heart Sutra speaks of Avalokiteśvara "moving in the deep course of the Wisdom which has gone beyond," as Edward Conze literally translates the Sanskrit text.[3] Conze equates this practicing with contemplating emptiness or nirvana. To be sure, the Bodhisattva is compassionate and does not enter final nirvana, but Conze's reading suggests that to be engaged in the practice of this wisdom is already to realize nirvana. Although Nishitani refers neither to the Sanskrit text nor to Conze's interpretation, he too suggests a sense of practice that includes realization. Hence in his interpretation of the opening of the Heart Sutra he can cite passages by Dōgen that play upon the convergence of practice and realization (*shushō* 修證). (The compound 修行 is another common word for practice, where 修 has the connotation of cultivation or study.) It would appear that Nishitani's notion of 行 here is confined to

---

3. Conze 1958, 77.

some very particular instances and hardly represents the kinds of practice that are applications of a theory or are directed toward a goal.

In fact, many Buddhist texts use the term 行 to denote a practical activity or exercise engaged in by a person (or personified being) in order to gain something other than the activity itself. Hence, many traditional occurrences of the word seem to have the instrumental sense of the English word *practice* that is conveyed by the modern Japanese term *jissen* (実践). Nishitani himself initiates the discussion of the standpoint of practice earlier in his book by using the terms 実践 and 行 interchangeably.[4] His language there at first suggests a method to "get directly in touch with the reality of things." He raises the question of how such a method or practice could be possible as long as it involves a [willful] subject trying to reach an objective world, or as long as its theory reduces both of these to merely material or merely ideal existence. He then presents the possibility of non-instrumental practice, an "action of non-action," that opens "a field where things would become manifest in their suchness." But Nishitani is not contrasting different kinds of practices and determining which of them affords access to the reality of things. Rather he proposes that there is a "field" (*ba* 場) wherein all things *and* practices become manifest as they are, and this he calls the "field of emptiness." He implies that tacit metaphysical presuppositions such as the subjectivity, objectivity, materialism or idealism of self and things are what determines our understanding of activity or practice, even social praxis. Hence, it seems to me, Nishitani is talking not about two different kinds of practice but about various understandings of practice, one of which presents (but does not represent) religious exercises and clouds moving—or water flowing—in the same light.[5]

---

4. NISHITANI 1961, 137–8; trans. 1982, 120–2. Jan Van Bragt's revised translation usually renders 行 as "observance," to distinguish it from 実践, "praxis"; see his glossary, p. 300. On page 121 of the translation, however, where Nishitani's text shifts from 実践 to 行, Van Bragt retains "praxis" for both.

5. Chapter 4 of the present volume elaborates the non-representational and non-

Nishitani's interpretation of religious practice has a precedent not only in Hakuin's comment but also in statements by Dōgen that Nishitani does not mention. In the *Mountains and Rivers Sutra* fascicle of *Shōbōgenzō*, for example, Dōgen writes that "because water is practicing-confirming itself as water, we exhaustively examine the way water is expressing itself as water (水の水に修證するがゆゑに、水の水を道著する參究あり). In this passage, Dōgen's word for practice is 修, the first half of his often used compound 修證, "practice-confirm/authenticate/realize," and so it already indicates an understanding of practice that does not posit a separate goal. Confirmation/realization is already incorporated in practice. Indeed, this notion of nondual cultivation can be traced back to early Chan texts in China, alongside texts that clearly retain a goal-oriented sense of religious practices.[6] Yet it is still startling to read in Dōgen of water practicing-confirming itself, for water is usually represented as a substance incapable of self-cultivation. It is incapable of anything except being water, by virtue of all other things—and perhaps that is Dōgen's point. Similarly, Nishitani may be using Hakuin's examples of the formless forms of practice to give our expectations a jolt. With these precedents in mind, we see that there is nothing original in Nishitani's extension of practice to forms not ordinarily covered by this concept. What is innovative in Nishitani's exposition is the view that the different senses of practice must be clarified in terms of the respective fields in which they emerge, and that the standpoint of emptiness provides the field wherein all others, and all senses of practice, become manifest for what they are.

Nishitani's exposition can throw light on many questions of practice that he does not expressly consider. Indeed, his mention of both Hakuin and Dōgen in the same context clarifies a basis common to two Zen figures whose views of practice are usually contrasted with

---

instrumental view of practice.

6. BIELEFELDT 1988, 161–3, offers a penetrating analysis of Dōgen's conceptual heritage and of problems concerning the description of the nondual Chan Dharma that transcends the distinction between theory and cultivation.

one another. In the usual interpretation, Hakuin reviles mere sitting in *zazen* and insists on the breakthrough of *kenshō*, seeing one's true nature by way of kōan practice; whereas Dōgen is the champion of *shikantaza*, just sitting, with no mind or intention to gain enlightenment.[7] Which, one may ask, is the true practice of Zen? Nishitani's text displaces this question by pointing out the quality of practice common to both Hakuin and Dōgen, the quality we might call non-contrivance. For neither teacher is practice (行) to be taken as a form contrived by the self. Stepping beyond the boundaries of the Zen tradition, I wonder whether one might revisit the meaning of Shinran's denial of practice in light of Nishitani's emphasis. Shinran denies the efficacy of any practice that is self-motivated, and so raises questions about what sort of practice the recitation of the *nenbutsu* is, if it can be called practice at all. For Shinran, only the enlightened mind of the Buddha has saving power; one practices to no avail. In general, the Pure Land Buddhist way of "other power" (*tariki* 他力) is sharply contrasted with Zen's way of "self-power" (*jiriki* 自力). Notwithstanding the historical consequences of this perceived difference, the quality of non-contrivance suggested by Nishitani's interpretation would seem to provide a common ground for understanding both ways, specifically both Shinran's denial and Dōgen's or Hakuin's advocacy of practice. I think this would be an "ecumenical" avenue worth exploring. The question to be asked of both sides is: who practices? Who recites the *nenbutsu*? Who practices *zazen*? Nishitani's interpretation again displaces this question by implying that self is not foremost the practitioner but rather what is practiced.

Practice involves the question not only of who practices and what is practiced, but also of the place of practice. Here Nishitani's language directs our attention from the physical location of practice to its place

---

7. The meaning of *shikantaza* (只管打坐), "just sitting," is itself controversial. FOULK (2012 and 2015) argues that Dōgen uses that very term as a kōan to challenge his disciples. Be that as it may, it is indisputable that Dōgen often has recourse to kōans in his writings and even compiled a collection of kōans himself. See HEINE 1994.

in the scheme of things. This ontological place he also calls the place of "self-joyous *samādhi*," invoking Dōgen's use of a Yogācāra term. Nishitani's understanding of *samādhi* is another example of his innovative thinking.

SAMĀDHI

Samādhi is a practice central to Buddhism. The term actually applies to a large number of different exercises that have to do with mental concentration. It is common to think of all the various forms of *samādhi* as states of mind, sometimes as trance states. Traditional descriptions in the literature of Buddhism and pre-Buddhist Yoga support this understanding. The Buddha sitting under the Bodhi tree is said to have progressed through four such states (or *dhyānas*), immediately before his enlightenment, and numerous arhats, bodhisattvas, and masters are depicted as entering one *samādhi* or another.

It is true that many descriptions make it difficult to think of someone, some self, as being in a particular state. In the third *dhyāna* of the Buddha's progression, for example, both self-consciousness and concentration on external objects have disappeared; and in the fourth *dhyāna* there is said to be no trace of self at all. The fourth state is thus aptly called the body of the Tathāgata, but it is also considered a state of equanimity, which in some sense still implies a mental state. If there is no self in such states, the implication is that at least there is some mind involved. Philosophically, that assumption also turns out to be problematic in some literature, for the disappearance of any consciousness directed to self or things would seem to rule out speaking of a mind. There is even a state of "cessation," whose attainment (*nirodha-samāpatti*) in an eighth and final *dhyāna* eliminates all mental functions.[8] Some texts depict the Buddha attaining this state before his

---

8. For an analysis of problems related to the "attainment of cessation," see the aptly titled book of GRIFFITHS 1986, *On Being Mindless*. That this thorough study remains

parinirvāna, although they question the value of this and other trance states for the attainment of liberation. Notwithstanding these difficulties, the traditional descriptions, particularly when read in contemporary translations, overwhelmingly give the impression that the central practice of *samādhi* in its various forms refers to someone entering a mental state of concentration, meditation, or trance. This impression is not diminished by the Buddhist schemes that place *samādhi* as the eighth part of the eightfold path to liberation, or as the fifth *pāramitā* or perfection. There, too, *samādhi* seems to refer primarily to a state of mind, enjoyed by beings with the mental capacity to attain it.

It is therefore somewhat startling to read in Nishitani's *Religion and Nothingness* of burning fire being in its fire-*samādhi*, or of a falling leaf, flying bird, or swimming fish, as manifestations of "*samādhi*-being" (定在, where 在 suggests a living location).[9] *Samādhi* is not ordinarily attributed to beings like fire, birds, and fish, and we would better see Nishitani's point by hyphenating *be-ing* to express its active character. His text further softens the surprise a bit by playing on the traditional Sino-Japanese character for *samādhi*, 定. The Japanese verbal compound 定まる (*sadamaru*) has the meaning of being settled in a position. For Nishitani this meaning naturally suggests being gathered together or concentrated, as the mind would be in a state of *samādhi*. The meanings associated with the character 定 thus allow Nishitani to interpret a state of mind as a state of being. *Samādhi*-be-ing is the mode of being or form of something as it is, determining it as the definite (定まった) thing it uniquely is. Accordingly, it designates the "sheer definition (定義) of the selfness of a thing."[10]

There are three points to notice regarding Nishitani's notion of *samādhi*-be-ing. First is the active character of his examples: a fire burning, a leaf falling, a fish swimming, a bird flying, all exemplify

uncritically bound to a language of "altered states of consciousness" is an indication of how radical and revealing Nishitani's reformulation of *samādhi* is.
 9. NISHITANI 1961, 145 and 157; trans. 1982, 128 and 139.
 10. Ibid., 146; trans. 1982, 129.

things in activity. A thing's "being settled in its own position" paradoxically takes the form of the distinctive *activity* of the thing; it "is" itself by "do*ing*" something. Secondly, what a definite thing does, it does not do to itself, and thus it can be itself. Fire does not burn fire and therefore it can burn other things and be fire. This formulation alludes to the logic of *soku-hi* (即非) made famous by D. T. Suzuki, and would seem to apply only to activities that are expressed by transitive verbs such as burn.[11] This is a grammatical delimitation that neither Suzuki nor Nishitani take into account; their point here is a thing can be itself only in interdependence with other things, and can be defined only in reference to other things. What is more, such interdependence is interactive: things in flux are designated grammatically as forms of verbs, the English gerund *burning*, for example. Nishitani's examples suggest therefore that a thing in its *samādhi*-be-ing, its "own home-ground," is neither settled in a static position nor does it exist independently "in-itself." This second point connects Nishitani's notion to *samādhi* as the concentrated state in which ego or self is forgotten, although he emphasizes that *samādhi* is an ontological concept and not simply a psychological one.[12] Thirdly, this active state of being can define the true (formless) form of things because it includes the full range of their manifestations. Thus, for example, the psychological self is not always concentrated, but "no matter how dispersed the conscious self is, its self as it is in itself is ever in *samādhi*," or more precisely, "that dispersed mode of being, such as it is, is *samādhi*."[13] Hence Nishitani thinks of *samādhi* not as a state of mind that one enters into, as if from the outside, but as the state of be-ing that allows all psychological states of mind to manifest themselves. One cannot "enter" that within which one already is. On the other hand, many Zen texts and sermons suggest that the self actually emerges from a state of *samādhi*, or that one breaks

11. See MARALDO 2017, 406–7, for further explanation of this idea.
12. I use the term "ontological" guardedly; it covers not only Nishitani's "field of beings" but also the fields of nihility and of emptiness.
13. NISHITANI 1961, 185; trans. 1982, 165.

"out of" *samādhi*. Nishitani's language seems to say that both "entering into" and "breaking out of" occur within one's *samādhi*-be-ing. Are there precedents to Nishitani's notion of *samādhi*-be-ing within Buddhist literature? D. T. Suzuki cites a legendary example that could be taken to illustrate the third point above. According to this legend, around 723 CE, Master Dai Yong visits Master Zhihuang who is renowned for his ability to enter into a state of *samādhi*. Yong questions Huang:

> "At the time of such entrances, is it supposed that your consciousness still continues, or that you are in a state of unconsciousness? If your consciousness still continues, all sentient beings are endowed with consciousness and can enter into a *samādhi* like yourself. If, on the other hand, you are in a state of unconsciousness, plants and rocks can enter into a *samādhi*."
>
> Huang replies: "When I enter into a *samādhi*, I am not conscious of either condition."
>
> Yong says: "If you are not conscious of either condition, this is abiding in eternal *samādhi*, and there can be neither entering into a *samādhi* nor rising out of it."[14]

---

14. SUZUKI 1969, 34–5, names updated to Pinyin. Suzuki cites the *Platform Sutra of the Sixth Patriarch* as the source, but RED PINE (2006, 277) clarifies that it is the Zongbao edition of 1290, and not the Dunhuang edition of 780, which relates this story. Red Pine's (Bill Porter's) translation reads:
> Once, when the Master's [Huineng's] disciple Xuance, was traveling north of the Yellow River, he heard about Zhihuang. When he finally arrived at his hut, he asked, "What do you do here?" Zhihuang said, "Enter *samādhi*." Xuance said, "When you say you 'enter *samādhi*,' is there a mind that enters? Or is there no mind that enters? If no mind enters, then any lifeless thing, like a tile or a rock or a stick or a piece of straw, should be capable of *samādhi*. And if the mind enters, then any living thing that possesses consciousness should also be capable of *samādhi*." Zhihuang said, "The moment I enter *samādhi*, I don't see if there is a mind that exists or not." Xuance said, "If you don't see if there's a mind that exists or not, then you would always be in *samādhi*. So how could you leave to enter? And if you can leave or enter, then it isn't true *samādhi*."

McRAE (2000, 69) translates the relevant passage as:
> Xuance said, "When you say 'enter into *samādhi*,' does the mind of being enter or does the mind of nonbeing enter? If it is the mind of nonbeing that enters, then

This passage continues to speak of buddha-nature as all-inclusive, and Suzuki himself emphasizes the legendary Sixth Patriarch's point that meditation must be understood as nondual, in other words, not a means to the goal of emancipation. This point ties in with the non-instrumental view of practice mentioned above, but I think this dialogue also undermines the prevalent notion of *samādhi* as a state of mind that one can enter and exit. To be sure, the term 入定, "entering *samādhi*," does occur in Buddhist texts, yet there are other usages of 入 that might better be rendered "to be enlightened to," such as 入法界, to be enlightened to the *dharmadhātu*, where this last term indicates the whole universe in which we already are.[15] This sort of example might therefore serve as textual evidence for the third part of Nishitani's interpretation of *samādhi*. There is nothing new in the second point concerning the interdependence and selflessness of things, or the first point defining things in terms of activities; both of these points are amply illustrated in Zen dialogues and kōan, among other Buddhist texts. What is new, to my knowledge, is the designation "*samādhi*-being" and the ontological shift it occasions.

Nishitani's neologism is more than a metaphoric extension of a state of mental concentration in which self is forgotten and the practitioner is "like" a fire burning, a fish swimming, a leaf falling. Presumably, whenever we talk about *samādhi*, we are still referring to a state or states of mind cultivated by people (or personifications). Nishitani's innovative term "*samādhi*-be-ing" challenges this

---

all the insentient plants and rocks would be able to attain *samādhi*. If it is the mind of being that enters, then all the sentient beings who have consciousness would also be able to attain *samādhi*." Zhihuang said, "When I have entered into *samādhi*, I am unaware of the existence of the minds of being and nonbeing." Xuance said, "If you are unaware of the minds of being and nonbeing, then this is permanent *samādhi*. How can you enter it or come out of it? If there is entering and coming out, then this is not the great *samādhi*."

15. An example of a shift from the meaning of "enter" to that of "be enlightened to" in the context of *samādhi* can be found in a Northern Chan School document translated in McRae 1986, 186–7.

presumption by exposing the metaphysical priority that underlies it. We naturally presume that first of all there exist people, or representations of people, who subsequently achieve a certain state of mind. That transitory state might then be compared to things that we experience—a fire burning, a leaf falling, etc. Nishitani would consider this sort of description an objectification, a kind of representational thinking from a particular and limited standpoint. There is no reason not to presume instead that a *samādhi* is a (formless form of) being and that people and other things are manifestations of that be-ing. Nishitani's "*samādhi*-be-ing" or "position" is meant to represent, in his own words, "the non-objectifiable mode of being of a thing as it is in itself."[16] In effect, his terms represent this by *not* representing things as self-sufficient identities, that is, by unsettling beings from their place in a substantialist metaphysics, and by unsettling our expectation that *samādhi* is foremost a psychological state. Fire too is "in" *samādhi* by burning, but not burning itself, that is, by not being fire.

Nishitani applies his ontological understanding of *samādhi* particularly to passages from various fascicles of Dōgen's *Shōbōgenzō*. He identifies Dōgen's "Samādhi that is the King of Samādhis" with *samādhi*-be-ing, and again implies that this King Samādhi refers not primarily to a mental state cultivated by sitting practice but rather to the activity of the actual world. Dōgen himself expressly identifies the "King of Samādhis" as sitting crosslegged. It is easy to read his text simply as an exhortation to practice single-minded "crosslegged sitting" to the exclusion of all else. The impression that even Dōgen considers this King of Samādhis a state of mind is strengthened when he writes that at the very time of sitting you should exhaustively examine (参究すべし) various matters, and that "if you wish to realize *samādhi*, if you wish to enter *samādhi*, put all your wandering thoughts and various discords and disorders to rest. Practice in this way and you enter

---

16. NISHITANI 1961, 210; trans. 1982, 189.

into realization of the King of Samādhis Samādhi."[17] It is true that this impression is challenged by other statements in the text—that there is a difference between mind sitting, body sitting, and sitting with body and mind cast off, for example. And Dōgen implies an ontological understanding in his statements that this crosslegged sitting is a total realm (hence not a particular psychological state), and is the body of suchness, the mind of suchness, the buddhas and patriarchs in their suchness, etc. (直身, 直心, 直佛祖). But Nishitani undermines the psychological interpretation more clearly in his mention of "crosslegging the King Samādhi" in which there is "neither mind nor thing nor Buddha."[18] To support his reading further, he might also have referred to Dōgen's "Ocean Reflection Samādhi," whose opening statement might be translated: "All the buddhas and patriarchs, just as they are, are without fail the ocean-reflection-*samādhi*."[19] There clearly are precedents to Nishitani's ontological interpretation of a Buddhist practice often taken to be simply a matter of mental concentration. Nishitani's neologism "*samādhi*-be-ing" articulates this interpretation in modern terms and presses us to examine our own psychologistic assumptions in translating certain texts. It would be fruitful for scholars to explore further whether and where the ontological understanding of *samādhi* helps to clarify Buddhist texts and practices.

REALIZATION

Consonant with Nishitani's interpretations of practice and *samādhi* is his view of realization. In the context of discussions of Buddhist practice, we often take *realization* to mean the awakening of the

---

17. *Shōbōgenzō Sammai Ō Sammai*, translated as "The King of Samādhis Samādhi," by Norman Waddell and Abe Masao, DŌGEN 2002, 99 and 102.

18. NISHITANI 1961, 211; trans. 1982, 189.

19. Hee-Jin Kim emphasizes the ontological dimension even more in his translation: "The manner in which buddhas and ancestors exist is necessarily ocean-reflection *samādhi*." He notes that "*samādhi* in Dōgen's thought is preeminently ontological and soteriological, not psychological." See KIM 1985, 167 and 171.

practitioner, an achievement of the individual or at least something that happens to someone. Nishitani subverts this usual impression in the first chapter of his book. There he is concerned with explaining his approach to understanding religion, an approach in terms of the "self-awareness of reality" (実存の自覚). By this he means "both our becoming aware of reality and, at the same time, the reality realizing itself in our awareness."[20] Writing in Japanese, he draws upon the dual meaning of the English "realize" (to actualize and to understand), in order to clarify his point. When we understand something in Nishitani's sense, we appropriate it such that it realizes (actualizes) itself in us. On the other hand, Nishitani would not say that we who appropriate are prior and privileged subjects on whom reality is dependent. He is not advocating philosophical idealism. Quite the contrary: subjectivity is realized in one way through the realization of its nihility. The term for *realization* here, 自覚, primarily connotes awakening and recognition. But Nishitani adds the second sense when he writes that "realization of the self itself" (自己自身の自覚) involves *becoming* that nihility, "and in so doing becom[ing] aware of itself from the limits of self-existence."[21] Subjectivity is actualized in this kind of radical questioning. Such existential (実存的) questions return to reality our attempt to understand religion, from Nishitani's perspective.[22]

Nishitani takes up the theme of the self-realization of reality again when he speaks of *samādhi*-be-ing and practice. Things are "manifest in their suchness," and "realize themselves non-objectively" in their *samādhi*-be-ing.[23] It is not that they are manifest to a subjective self, for Nishitani could as easily say that self is manifest to things. Later he

20. NISHITANI 1961, 8–9; trans. 1982, 5.
21. NISHITANI 1961, 22–3; trans. 1982, 16–17.
22. Despite his existential interests, Nishitani does not locate the essence of religion in "the individual's experience," as his critic Paul GRIFFITHS (1986B, 155) would have it. On the contrary, Nishitani's view of realization suggests a critique of subjectivistic and experiential reductions of religion. If we are to follow Griffiths's agenda and test the truth of Nishitani's propositions, we need first to pay heed to the meaning of their terms.
23. NISHITANI 1961, 183; trans. 1982, 163.

quotes Dōgen's famous line from the *Genjōkōan* : "To forget one's self is to be confirmed by all dharmas."[24] In an ontology where "all things come forward, and practice and confirm (修證) the self," neither the subjective self nor objective reality are recognized. Nishitani also calls this place the point where the "world worlds," alluding to Heidegger's phrase that undermines any idealism or realism. He might also have mentioned Dōgen's water that practices-realizes (修證) (itself as) water. And doubtlessly, his talk of the self-awareness (or self-realization) of reality reflects the philosophy of his teacher, Nishida, who wrote of a self-aware (自覚的) place and world. Nishitani's view once again has precedents. His interpretation is distinctive for its power to expose subjectivist assumptions about the meaning of religious realization. In its own way, his philosophy contains parallels to contemporary western critiques of psychologism and subjectivity. Yet, unlike them, he holds that existential concerns, not conceptual dead-ends, give rise to the philosophically important questions. Only then can these questions can be returned to the reality of pressing personal issues.

24. NISHITANI 1961, 219; trans. 1982, 199.

Self and Others and In-Between

7
Writing the Self
The Autobiographic Practices of Rousseau, Hakuseki, and Hakuin

Exhaustive inquiry into the self is at the heart of Zen Buddhist practice in the eyes of Nishitani Keiji. Nishitani presented Zen's way of investigating the matter of the self (己事究明) in a series of contrasts. Zen investigation assumes a standpoint freed from both subjective inquiry—reflecting on the self as it is conscious of itself—and objective inquiry—reflecting on the self from a removed or a third-person, scientific perspective. (The distinction of Zen self-inquiry will engage our attention further in Chapters 8 and 13.) It is remarkable that Nishitani sees an affinity between scientific inquiry into the nature of the self, on the one hand, and the stance of the modern novel, on the other. For the modern novel, in particular the "I-novel" written from the first-person point of view,

> includes its author's self-reflection... [whereby] the author peers into the consciousness of his characters as if through psychological analysis, probes and exposes the lurking motivations in their actions and life that they themselves are barely aware of or unconsciously try to keep from their own eyes.[1]

If modern confessional literature exemplified by Rousseau's *Confessions* seems most conspicuously to display an author's self-reflection, this is

> not confession in its original sense, as moral or religious confession,

1. NISHITANI 1974 (1984), 4.

which involves the completely solitary self and concentrates on the self as an individual. Rather, the consciousness of the self revealed in such literature and psychology is inevitably displayed in such a way that its contents appear capable of being universalized at any time. In effect, the self that sees itself and the self that is seen by itself, although actually one and the same, are split in two.[2]

Where Nishitani finds a split in the self-reflection of modern novelists, contemporary literary critics, as we shall see, tend to locate the pretense that an author can truthfully present his or her life experience. Typically leaving the objectivity of their own stance unquestioned, critics would expose the ruse of truthful autobiography and presumptions of individuality. In contrast, the following exercise examines the ways that specific autobiographic practices produce divergent senses of "self" and so diversify the entire notion of "autobiography."

NOVELIST TŌSON'S SELF-DISCOVERY AND THE PROBLEM OF PARADIGMS OF SELF.

> ...as I was reading it enthusiastically, I had the feeling that my self, an entity of which I had been unaware up to that time, was being drawn out.[3]

These remarkable words of Meiji novelist Shimazaki Tōson provide the starting point for our inquiry. Written in 1909 in an essay entitled "The Self I Discovered in Rousseau's *Confessions*," Tōson's statement is all the more perceptive for being uttered not by a philosopher seeking an articulated concept of the self, but by a novelist spontaneously expressing a new-found way to write in fiction of the truths of life and nature. Is it possible that Tōson had no model available to him, within Japanese culture, of what it is to be a self? And what is this

---

2. Ibid., 5.
3.「私はその頃…熱心に読んで行くうちに、今迄意識せずに居た自分というものを引出されるような気がした。」TŌSON 1978, 10. Shimazaki Tōson (島崎藤村) lived from 1872 to 1943.

"self" that Tōson discovers? In her work on the ideal of individuality in the Meiji novel, Janet Walker suggests that Tōson was "jolted into an awareness of his own self that existed, like Rousseau's, in the past and in the present, in the form of experiences, memories, and reflections." "The Japanese writers who created the first modern literature in the Meiji period," she claims, "discovered themselves as individuals through their reading of Western literature."[4]

In today's era of cultivated individualism, it is difficult to imagine that someone could be unaware of being a self-contained individual, existing "in the past, and in the present, in the form of experiences, memories and reflections." In the following I want to show that this apparent lack of awareness is best interpreted as a confrontation with certain European paradigms of self that were undeveloped, or at least underdeveloped, in Japan. A survey of all possible models of self within Japanese and Anglo-European culture is beyond the scope of this chapter; but a more modest sketch of self-identities is selected Buddhist, Confucian and popular literature, juxtaposed against the heritage of Rousseau, will serve our purpose. Following Thomas Kuhn's clue that a paradigm governs a group of practitioners who have training in common,[5] I will suggest that different methods of investigation were crucial to the formation of different paradigms of self. At the same time, our sketch will expose some of the difficulties of uniting "paradigm" and "self" in one prepositional phrase, for a paradigm by definition functions to unify and identify a set of objects under investigation, but self-unity and self-identity are seen precisely as problems in modern Anglo-European thought, and much of Japanese philosophy understands self as something that cannot be objectified at all.

---

4. WALKER 1979, 144–5. For further details about Tōson and the autobiographical novel, see MCCLELLAN 1971A.
5. KUHN 2012, 176–80.

ROUSSEAU'S SELF-CONSCIOUS SELF.

I have resolved on an enterprise which has no precedent... to display to my kind a portrait in every way true to nature, and the man I shall portray will be myself. Simply myself [*moi seul*].[6]

These words that open Jean-Jacques Rousseau's *Confessions* express his awareness of what we now call a paradigm shift—ostensibly, a shift not only in literary genre, but at bottom a shift that established a newly emergent concept of self. In *The Modern Self in Rousseau's Confessions*, Ann Hartle argues that the solitary, self-centered individual actually depicted by Rousseau, more than the man he would portray true to nature, signals the modern understanding of human nature as mutable convention rather than invariable essence.[7] Here we will not attempt to descend into and describe the inner sanctum of the self that Rousseau exposes, but rather to point out the character and assumptions of the method he attempts.

At the beginning of *The Confessions*, Rousseau states his intent "to present myself before my Sovereign Judge... [to bare] my secret soul as Thou thyself hast seen it, Eternal Being!" Rousseau's assumption that he commands an omniscient purview of himself was taken by Tōson as an admirable attitude of objectivity missing in Japanese literature—one that, Janet Walker surmises, was associated with the introduction of Anglo-European scientific methods into Japan about 1900.[8] "I know my own heart," Rousseau writes, and proposes to display himself as "vile and despicable, when my behavior was such, and good, generous, and noble when I was so." The implication of self-omniscience is qualified by some "defects of memory," but never by a lapse in sincerity or honesty: "I have never put down as true what I know to be false." At the end Rousseau proclaims, "I have told the truth. If anyone knows anything contrary to what I have here recorded, though he

---

6. ROUSSEAU 1953, 17. Rousseau lived from 1712 to 1778.
7. HARTLE 1983.
8. WALKER 1979, 96.

prove it a thousand times, his knowledge is a lie and an imposture...."[9] Notwithstanding the self-righteous and rather defensive tone of this remark, it is hard not to hear it as a disclosure of belief in Cartesian self-certainty: "I cannot go wrong about what I have felt, or about what my feelings have led me to do."[10]

It is important to realize that Rousseau's claim to be telling the truth about himself, however questionable it may be, is distinct from a claim to be representing facts or events as they are ascertained by others. Rousseau seems to believe that only he can truthfully depict his inner or true self regardless of how factual or fictive his self-portrait is. Although there is a fascinating controversy about the extent to which Rousseau understood his work to be fictional, and his portrayed self to be his own creation,[11] we can separate this issue from that of the incorrigibility of self-knowledge. Rousseau's portrait can be an imaginative construct and still purport to present his true feelings and thoughts, all the more so when they include how he imagines himself to be. Rousseau's remarks show that he imagines a self that can know itself without error.

9. ROUSSEAU 1953, 605. For a deconstruction of Rousseau's disingenuous prose, see DE MAN 1979, 278–301. NISHITANI (1990, 149) reminds us of the "difference between the 'truth' sought by Rousseau and by Dostoevsky [in his *Notes from Underground*], between one who sees 'nature' and health as normal, and the retort-made man who considers it normal to say that 'all consciousness is a disease.'"

10. ROUSSEAU 1953, 262.

11. STAROBINSKI (1988, 186–8) argues that Rousseau not only believes his account of himself is true because it comes from the inside, but also sets it up for others as a model of self-knowledge. For GUÉHENNO (1966, vol. 2, 240), both Rousseau's attempt at self-knowledge, and the reading of his work in order to know the truth about him, are misguided. HARTLE (1983) presents the most nuanced account and tries to overcome the problem of Rousseau's self-knowledge by emphasizing the nature of the work rather than Rousseau's private person. She argues that Rousseau did not intend his work as factual biography and was aware of its fictional character; *The Confessions* bear witness to the nature of every man as private, inner self. GUTMAN (1988, 112) also points out Rousseau's references to the fictive quality of his work, but argues that he eventually undermines his strategy to individuate the self.

In similar remarks proclaiming his absolutely unique individuality, Rousseau betrays a commitment to Cartesian privileged access: my inner self is invisible to others save by my voluntary confessions. "[My] readers... cannot have helped seeing, throughout the course of my life [that is, my *Confessions*], countless inner emotions of mine utterly unlike their own."[12] Yet Rousseau's method of disclosing the truth about himself is confirmation not of an inviolable Cartesian substance but of a Lockean self bounded by self-consciousness and memory. "I know nothing of myself till I was five or six," Rousseau confesses.[13] He reconstructs his life for us by remembering, recollecting, all the experiences he can (or will). "I trace my nature back in this way to its earliest manifestations...."[14]

To be sure, his *Confessions* are not those of a mind simply spilling out its memories into a stream-of-consciousness by free association, but rather are self-consciously reflective and selective descriptions of himself and the others he encounters. Still, Rousseau's primary practice is remembrance; and in writing his *Confessions* it is a life *as remembered* that he presents for others to see as he confesses to see it. When Shimazaki Tōson writes his recollection, fifteen years afterwards, of his own experience of reading Rousseau and discovering his self, he is in fact already practicing writing according to the paradigm of a self constituted by its inner experiences, memories, and reflections. He is thus in a position to see Rousseau's life as the epitome of moral "self-discipline," as he calls it. For Tōson, Rousseau's self-scrutiny is totally modern and admirable.[15] Yet if there is something novel about Rousseau's willingness, and satisfaction, in exposing himself—vileness, virtue, and all—to the public eye,[16] a scrutinized and recollected self is not without precedent.

12. ROUSSEAU 1953, 595.
13. Ibid., 19.
14. Ibid., 28.
15. WALKER 1979, 146.
16. The suggestion of exhibitionism is not accidental. Rousseau confesses that he was

THE HERITAGE OF ROUSSEAU'S SELF: LOCKE.

For it is by the consciousness it has of present thoughts and actions, that it is *self to itself* now, and so will be the same self, as far as the same consciousness can extend.[17]

John Locke (1632–1704), in his *Essay Concerning Human Understanding*, concludes that it is consciousness and memory, as opposed to spiritual or material substance, that constitutes the self. He is, as we know, contradicting Descartes, but in the steps of his argument we find evident if unvoiced assumptions about the nature of self which both he and Descartes share. Locke argues that one could be the soul of Socrates, but unless one had Socrates's thoughts and memories, he would not be "the same person with Socrates."[18] To be a person here means to be unified by consciousness of a strictly personal, that is, individual sort. Reciprocally, consciousness signifies here a capacity to recollect a sameness throughout the various moments of its activity. For Locke, my identity is not jeopardized by interruptions of consciousness, lapses of memory, or absence of thought—these would only challenge a self consisting of a thinking substance, although we might wonder if psychological disorders such as multiple personality or ego-disintegration would not challenge Locke's thesis. (Although he might relieve those suffering from such disorders of personal moral responsibility, it is questionable that he would claim there is one person for each and every fractured personality, or, respectively, no person there at all.) But if Locke disputes substance as the identifying factor, just what notion does he share with Descartes?

For as far as any intelligent being can repeat the idea of any past action

---

given to such behavior at the age of sixteen, and one wonders whether the whole of *The Confessions* is not a kind of vicarious outlet: "I haunted dark alleys and lonely spots where I could expose myself to women from afar off... what they saw was nothing obscene. I was far from thinking of that; it was ridiculous" (ROUSSEAU 1953, 90).

17. LOCKE, 1924, 189.
18. Ibid., 192.

with the same consciousness it had of it at first, and with the same consciousness it has of any present action; so far it is the same personal self.[19]

Locke's rather awkward formulation here stipulates that identity is constituted by what is repeatable throughout my experiences; and what is repeatable is not, of course, an action as I once uniquely experienced it, but rather the felt sense of its being, both originally and upon recollection, my action. The formulation is awkward, and suspiciously circular, only because Locke (unconsciously?) struggles to express a felt sense of something seemingly so self-evident that it nearly defies expression: There, behind every moment of consciousness, I am, always recallable by an act of reflection. Consciousness, and with it, self-identity, are inherently egological. The problem Locke addresses is that of "personal identity"; but the paradigm he adopts is that of an "I" (eye) whose scope of vision defines the bounds of the self. That this paradigm is not universally self-evident is recognized easily enough in Tōson's remark at the beginning of this paper. And if it were universally self-evident, it would not be recognizable as an historically conditioned and perhaps culture-bound paradigm at all. (It is unlikely that Socrates, or any ancient Greek philosopher, lacking as they did a distinct concept of consciousness, would have understood Locke's views.) On the other hand, the fact that Locke took this recollective awareness of oneself for granted (it is just "plain experience" in his words), indicates the influence of a sweeping if unarticulated paradigm, whose cultural reign we cannot gauge here. What I do wish to point out, however, is the sort of method employed by Locke, the practice that is both governed by and creative of the paradigm.

> The understanding, like the eye, whilst it makes us see and perceive all other things, takes no notice of itself; and it requires art and pains to set it at a distance and make it its own object.[20]

19. Ibid., 189.
20. Ibid., 9.

Locke's statement, from the opening passage of his *Essay*, reveals clearly enough his intent to distance himself from, to objectify, what is immeasurably near: "the understanding, that sets man above the rest of sensible beings," and consequently, the self, which sets one man apart from all others. The "art and pains" Locke engages in are a prototype of what we today call philosophical analysis: critical reflection at a distance from the immediate data of consciousness. To see remembered self-awareness as the identifying factor of the self, Locke cannot merely practice remembering his experiences, as Rousseau did, much less present his awareness in a stream of consciousness mode. Although the paradigm of a self-conscious self made Rousseau's and James Joyce's genres possible, neither of them could have articulated the paradigm, because neither puts sufficient distance between the writing and the writer. Locke isolates memory and awareness from their natural linkage to particular experiences and then reflects in detachment on the outcome. For this reason, Rousseau's work seems much more personal than Locke's; reading his *Confessions* makes us feel we know the heart of Rousseau—whereas the person John Locke, we feel, remains forever hidden behind his *Essay*. Locke is practicing a kind of reflection that may be said to be as creative of the paradigm of a self-conscious self as it is ruled by it. Once again, however, his detachment and isolation of this self are not without example and exaggeration. It was René Descartes (1596–1650) who meditated in his oven-room, who methodically detached himself from every worldly stimulus and discovered the thinking "I" (*ego cogitans*) at the root of a suspiciously solipsistic self that became the European paradigm, despite its controversial substantiality. That story, however, is beyond the confines of the present chapter.

ARAI HAKUSEKI AND THE CONFUCIAN SELF.

In the old days, when people had anything to say, they said it without unnecessary additions, expressing their meaning fully in as few words as possible. My parents were like that.[21]

And so, too, is the author of these words like that. Arai Hakuseki (新井白石, 1657–1725), great Confucian scholar and government reformer who advised the sixth and seventh Tokugawa shoguns, is more than reticent about the personal affairs he would consider unnecessary additions to the work which opens with the quoted passage. Composed in 1716, his *Oritaku shiba no ki* (translated as *Told Round A Brushwood Fire*) is considered, for better or worse, the first proper Japanese autobiography and is often, if controversially, compared to Rousseau's *Confessions*.[22] The comparison would seem to be warranted. Both authors base their works upon recollection, and both aspire to the honest truth. Both are driven by a felt need to justify their lives in the eyes of others. Rousseau writes to show himself "as he actually was,

---

21. ACKROYD 1979, 35. The original text can be found in ARAI Hakuseki 1964, 149.
22. ACKROYD 1979, 17. In a review of this translation, HAROOTUNIAN (1985) warns us of comparisons and translations that overlook the various ways narratives are constructed to support varying ideologies. He is critical of Ackroyd for virtually rewriting the *Oritaku* into a monologic narrative authorizing a single voice, in a confessional autobiography reporting the author's conversations and confrontations with others. Although I have relied almost solely on the translation, my analysis will suggest how far Hakuseki's work is from being confessional autobiography. Ironically—absent is any reference to a legendary Zen or Neo-Confucian no-self—Harootunian's reading would make Hakuseki's authorial self disappear altogether into a Barthean "proairetic code... which is the subject and author of the story" (177). Even Rousseau's *Confessions* appear to scholars like Hartle to be other than autobiography. In contrast, I will suggest how the term must be used pluralistically. The preeminent scholar of Japanese autobiography, Saeki Shōichi, juxtaposes Rousseau and Hakuseki to place the writing of Futabatei Shimei, an older contemporary of Tōson, in Japanese literature; see the chapter 「ルソーと白石の間」 [Between Rousseau and Hakuseki], in SAEKI 1981, 232–57. BESEMERES (2002) investigates the effects of translation, both cultural and linguistic, on the portrayal of oneself via autobiography, although her study focuses on contemporary bilingual autobiographers.

and not as his unjust enemies unremittingly endeavored to paint him." Hakuseki writes to

> set down past events just as they occurred to me, with no thought-out plan.... I am the only man alive who knows the full story, so it would be inexcusable if, unworthy though I am, I did not set it down.[23]

The full story Hakuseki will tell, however, is not a confession of his inner life, but the story of the "details that concern His late Highness [the Shogun Ienobu]"[24] and that present Hakuseki as an exemplary public figure loyal to his lord and adept at right conduct. He writes so that his sons and grandsons "will not swerve from the path of loyalty and filial piety when they remember the laborious rise of their father and grandfather...."[25] It is not surprising, then, that Confucian Hakuseki begins his autobiography with a mention of his parents and a long account of his father and grandfather. When the author continues with a report of his own life, it is solely a life of external events, political consultations and public administration that he presents.[26] Though he hesitates not, he says, "to write... of delicate matters," the reader searches in vain for a glimpse of the secrets of the soul which Rousseau so readily reveals.

The few passages of unconscious revelation in Hakuseki's work are recognizable, for the translator at least, more by their tone than their content.[27] Even if the "vehemence of Hakuseki's expression bears out

---

23. ACKROYD 1979, 35f.
24. Ibid., 36.
25. Ibid.
26. NAKAI (1988, xvi) notes that this work,
   reflecting both Hakuseki's tendentious disposition and the intrinsic nature of the autobiographical form of literature, does not offer a disinterested view of the events and human relations it depicts... [the work] was intended to provide an account of his aims and actions for "the day one hundred years hence when history shall pass impartial judgment."
27. ACKROYD (1979, 30) comments that
   so clearly does... his [irascible] personality emerge throughout his autobiography, that his style sometimes erupts into bitter invective and sometimes has an overtone of hys-

the disturbed state of his feelings as he wrote," Hani Gorō's remark that his autobiography "represents an awakening of individual awareness"[28] seems a gross exaggeration when *Told Round A Brushwood Fire* is placed beside *The Confessions*. Hakuseki leaves but a trace of self-consciousness or awareness of himself, either as the author or as the subject matter of his autobiography. "I shall now set down what I have seen myself since I reached years of discretion,"[29] he writes, and proceeds to describe not himself, but once again, his father—"not a man who showed his feelings." Hakuseki is equally Confucian in betraying no hint of his own feeling toward his father's reticence. The few instances where he permits himself some introspection function as moral example, not as the confession of a hidden self:

> I was born quick-tempered, so my anger was harder to control than anything else. However, this also, as I have made my way through life's difficulties, is declining as my years increase, and now, perhaps, I am not as I used to be. I most earnestly desire that those who come after me should regard this [that it is necessary to learn to endure in everything, as my father taught] as an ancestral precept, and take it to heart above everything.[30]

Personal incidents where we today might expect an outpouring of elation or grief—or at least some expression of personal concern— deserve only a perfunctory, newscast-like report in Hakuseki's work. His marriage is not mentioned at all; and the first of three mentions of his wife occurs in a totally impersonal sentence: "Although I was attached to an unsatisfactory service and had barely enough to support a wife and family...."[31] The death of his first child and illness of

---

teria. Except at these points [which appear very seldom to this reader], it is dignified and grave as befitted a Confucian scholar.
28. Hani Gorō, *Arai Hakuseki and Fukuzawa Yukichi* (1936), cited in ACKROYD 1979, 22.
29. ACKROYD 1979, 46.
30. Ibid., 57.
31. Ibid., 70.

his son are recorded as interruptions in his plans to teach his lord the Confucian classics: "At that time [1694] my eldest daughter caught smallpox and died.... Akinori also caught it. On account of these events, I did not begin lectures on the *Shih Ching* until the 8th of March."[32] The death of one child and birth of another, which occurred twice within a one-year period, go unmentioned.

When I focus on what Hakuseki does not write of, and contrast that silence with our modern sensibilities, I do not mean to imply that the Confucian author was cold-hearted or discompassionate. He is simply not writing in order to break the seal on the private confines of his heart; but rather in order that "my posterity should understand the conditions of society."[33] And it is not that he chooses to conceal his inner self, but that he does not recognize any such individual domain worthy of expression. As Joyce Ackroyd, the translator of Hakuseki's autobiography says, traditions such as the Reformation which led to the exaltation of the individual's inner life [and] bore fruit in such writings as Rousseau's had no counterpart in Japan. "On the contrary, in that age in which the theoretic basis was Neo-Confucian ethics, the spiritual and material aspirations of the individual were schooled to subordination to social obligations." And even after Rousseau's type of self was discovered by people like Tōson in the Meiji era, "the auto-

---

32. Ibid., 74. Contrast Hakuseki's reticence with Tōson's emotional depiction of the deaths of his daughters in his autobiographical novel *Ie*, written 1910–11 and translated as *The Family* (see TŌSON 1976). This contrast in what is deemed fit for literary disclosure, however, should not mislead us to think that the family was of primary value for Tōson whereas for Hakuseki it was not. Cecilia Segawa Seigle, the translator of *Ie*, suggests that Tōson regarded the deaths of his daughters as sacrifices enabling him to work on his first novel (TŌSON 1976, xi). Tōson has a character in a later novel, *Haru* (Spring), rationalize leaving a job: "My family is of course important. But it is still more important that I find a way of life that is right for me. This is what all of us must do. What is the point of being a good son and brother when one does not even know the purpose of one's own existence?" (quoted in McCLELLAN 1971B, 100). Tōson's works emerge out of a subtle revolt against family-centeredness; in that sense, his own newly found individualism is strongly related to the traditional value placed upon the extended family.

33. ACKROYD 1979, 88.

biographical genre attracted little attention. Unless self-revelation was transmuted into an experience of universal validity by art, the prejudice against enlarging on personal affairs was too strong."[34]

This assessment, however, makes an assumption that undermines the entire identification of the genre.[35] For if the self-revelation proper to the autobiographical genre is essentially a revelation of personal affairs, then Hakuseki's work can hardly be called autobiography. If, on the other hand, the self that is disclosed (or hidden) in the Confucian work is not to be located essentially in personal and intimate matters, then it will be necessary to question accepted assumptions about what an autobiography, and a self, can be.

Hakuseki clearly did not live in a milieu where personal affairs could be experienced as the essence of self, but this does not mean that he lacked a notion of self. It suggests rather that a constant practice of allegiance to one's ancestors and principles, and service to one's lord and nation (identical when the lord was the shogun), will create a different sense of self-identity and self-worth. The personal life that is recollected in this Confucian autobiography may not even look personal to someone nurtured on the model of a Rousseauean self. It may indeed appear to be a "selfless" life, an expression that certainly did not go unused in later Confucian literature. Within a century after Hakuseki's work, the ideal of "no-self" [無我] was extolled in ethical *shingaku* (心学) manuals written for the populace. One such work, *Kyūō's Moral Discourses, Continued* (鳩翁道話続), written in 1835, asserts that,

> if one had no selfish motives but only the supreme virtues, there would be no self.... If he serves selflessly, he does not know what service is [does

---

34. Ibid., 19–20.
35. That premodern literature in Japan included types of autobiography is amply demonstrated by SCHAMONI 2016, which presents a wide-ranging study of autobiographical writing in seventeenth century Japan; and by SAEKI 1985, which illustrates such writing in medieval diaries.

not recognize it as service]. If he knows what service is, he has a self....
[To think] only of parents but not of yourself... is what I call no self.³⁶

This concept of no self, as the psychologist Minami Hiroshi notes, "is identical with the spirit of service above self, where every spontaneous impulse is rejected as selfishness."³⁷ Even today, among the older, more traditional generation in Japan, the anthropologist Thomas Rohlen finds that "*ga* [我, ego-self]... is definitely related to *kokoro* [心] development.... In the training of children and adults, overcoming and controlling *ga* is an important goal.... Training ('to kill *ga*') and age... both serve to reduce the hold of *ga* on persons."³⁸ The Confucian scholar Ishida Baigan had founded the *shingaku* (mind-discipline) movement, later popularized by people like Shibata Kyūō thirteen years after Hakuseki's work. But his ideal of training did not stand unchallenged within Confucianism. Robert Bellah suggests that Baigan chose the expression *shingaku* in reaction to a contemporary of Hakuseki who had criticized such "mind discipline" as profoundly self-contradictory. Sorai's criticism sounds suspiciously Zen Buddhist: "The mind is without form. It cannot be controlled by itself.... To use one's own mind [我心/わがこころ] to control one's own mind is like a lunatic controlling himself by means of his own lunacy."³⁹ Sorai's aim, however, is not an enlightenment of no-mind or no-self, but a way to ethical action. Slightly before Sorai and Hakuseki wrote, Kumazawa Banzan (熊沢蕃山) clearly pointed to the public sphere external to the self as the training ground for one who would investigate nature, regulate family and state, and live according to principle.⁴⁰ Such differences

36. Quoted in MINAMI 1971, 11.
37. Ibid.
38. Cited in BELLAH 1978, 150. Recent nationwide surveys on the life philosophy of the Japanese people, however, suggest that the younger generation no longer holds such values, but rather is most interested in living "one's own life according to one's own tastes, without much regard for money or fame." See MINAMI 1971, x.
39. BELLAH 1978, 145.
40. See MCMULLEN, 1979, 354–5. Kumazawa Banzan (熊沢蕃山) lived from 1619 to 1691, Ogyū Sorai (荻生徂徠) from 1666 to 1728, and Shibata Kyūō (柴田鳩翁) from 1783

teach us that Hakuseki's absence of self-description is perhaps a clearer expression of the Confucian paradigm than is the phrase "no self."

Equally controversial is the issue of consciousness of individuality in the Confucian paradigm we have delineated. Hakuseki's father and grandfather were *rōnin*, masterless samurai, and Hakuseki himself remained a samurai when he served his lord not as a warrior but as an educator. Various arguments have been advanced as to whether *bushidō*, the way of the warrior formed by the Confucian values of loyalty and submission to one's lord, actually killed a sense of individual self. The teachings of Yamamoto Tsunetomo, recorded the same year as Hakuseki's autobiography in the popular volumes known as *Hagakure* (Hidden Leaves), are often cited as evidence of an affirmative answer. Inatomi Eijirō recently blamed the lack of a clear sense of individual self among the Japanese on the long-reigning feudal system and quotes the *Hagakure* as expressive of the tradition:

> Whenever one is taken into service to a lord, he should serve the lord without any consideration of his own self. Even if one... is ordered to commit *harakiri*, one should accept [it].[41]

This quotation, as well as those above that admonish selfishness, imply that one naturally does have a sense of self—but only of an egoistic self. But Uchimura Kanzō, a Meiji contemporary of novelist Tōson, a Christian and advocate of individualism, argued that the samurai obviously exhibited the kind of self-respect, self-assertion, and independence that formed the core of modern individualism.[42] These qualities still find expression in such sayings as *jibun ga aru*: "I am someone."

Whether Hakuseki would have denied his self to the point of committing *harakiri* (which was by his time outlawed) or not, his self-portrayal fits both Inatomi's and Uchimura's descriptions. More than

---

to 1839.

41. Cited in FURUKAWA 1967, 236. Yamamoto Tsunetomo (山本常朝) lived from 1659 to 1719.

42. Ibid., 237. Uchimura Kanzō (内村鑑三), lived from 1861 to 1930.

7. Writing the Self | 187

once Hakuseki demanded enormous sacrifices, in body and purse, of himself and his family by remaining for a time in the service of a dispossessed lord. Equally often he sought out opportunities to realize his own lofty ambitions.[43] Hakuseki, in other words, was not clearly committed to either selflessness or self-assertion; nor are these values necessarily opposed.[44] What seems to be decisive is that a widely-shared paradigm of individual consciousness was not operative in Japanese Confucianism before Meiji times, and so could not serve as a source of inspiration for novelist Tōson.

Eighteen years before Tōson made his self-discovery, Fukuzawa Yukichi, the great educator and advocate of a new individuality, himself of samurai stock, had proclaimed that "Japanese warriors did not have any individuality."[45] Four years after Tōson read *The Confessions*, and probably uninfluenced by Rousseau, Fukuzawa serially published his own autobiography, which later was compared to *The Confessions* for its "freedom, directness, and simplicity."[46] It may seem curious, then, that Fukuzawa's autobiography did not also inspire Tōson to discover his personal self and write from its perspective. Fukuzawa freely reports of his virtues and vices; he writes that he is neither afraid of blame nor solicitous of praise, and is ashamed of his drinking habits, for example. Yet these occasional revelations are generalizations quite different in style from Rousseau's detailed self-exposé. Indeed

---

43. ACKROYD 1982, ix–xv.

44. Instead of selfless service versus self-assurance, the relevant issue in the controversy about the "individualism" of samurai may be the sense of individuality as separate self. George DE VOS (1985, 179) makes the apt generalization that the "Japanese sense of self is directed toward immediate social purposes, not toward a process of separating out and keeping the self somehow distinct, somehow truly individual, as remains the Western ideal."

45. MINAMI 1971, 17. Fukuzawa Yukichi (福澤諭吉) lived from 1835 to 1901.

46. Koizumi Shinzō's Introduction to FUKUZAWA 1960, viii. Koizumi notes (xiii) that Ishikawa Kanmei's preface to the 1899 edition reports that the *Fukuo Jiden* was dictated at the request of a certain foreigner to share reminiscences of the period of the Meiji Restoration and was based on notes of memories recollected at random: "more an informal talk than an autobiography."

Fukuzawa, as if telling the reader what to expect, admits that "my sociability did not go to the extent of opening myself completely to the confidences of others, or to share with them the inner thoughts of my heart."[47] If Fukuzawa's autobiography had nowhere near the impact of Rousseau's *Confessions* (and the naturalism of Émile Zola) on Japanese writers like Tōson, it was perhaps because Rousseau had given them not merely a verdict about individuality but a whole new paradigm to emulate in their writing.[48]

Hakuin's No-self

> Anyone who wants to achieve the Way of enlightenment must drive forward the wheel of the four great vows.[49]

The opening words to Zen master Hakuin's *Itsumadegusa* (Wild Ivy) announce the driving force of his own life as well as his intention in recounting it. But they hardly foretell the intensely personal nature of his account. Hakuin's "spiritual autobiography," as translator Norman Waddell calls it, is not entirely without precedent in Japanese Zen literature. But compared to Dōgen's autobiographical remarks in the *Hōkyōki* of 1227 or Bankei Yōtaku's memoranda recorded shortly before Hakuin,[50] *Wild Ivy* reaches a new height of style and self-revela-

---

47. Ibid., 290, 327.
48. This does not mean that Rousseau's paradigm actually began to govern the methods of their writing, which some critics see as a continuation more than revolution of traditional Japanese literary forms. See MIYOSHI 1974, 72, and FOWLER, 1988, 53. WALKER (1979, 62) sees a strong connection between Rousseau and Tōson, Western naturalism and early Japanese "novels," and suggests another reason that Fukuzawa did not inspire the new literary movement as did Rousseau and Zola at that time: Fukuzawa "considered the Western liberal ideal of individualism in a samurai context of ethical service to the state."
49. WADDELL 1982–3. An edition of the original wood-block text can be found in 『白隠和尚全集』 [Complete Works of Preceptor Hakuin] vol. 1 (Tokyo: Ryūginsha, 1934). Hakuin Ekaku (白隠慧鶴) lived from 1686 to 1769.
50. Strictly speaking, the *Hōkyōki* (寳慶記) is a work about and conceivably authored by Tiantang Rujìng (天童如淨, 1163–1228), Dōgen's teacher in China. Dōgen kept it secret

tion. Written in 1765, Hakuin's work in seven-character Chinese verses was perhaps styled after the "mad poetry" (狂歌) popular in his day; but read according to colloquial Japanese syntax, as it must be to make sense,[51] it does not fail to engage the readers constant attention.

Though his personal account is prefaced by a sermon on true versus false Zen, Hakuin quickly immerses the reader in what European sentiment would call the passions of the soul. He begins by vividly describing his childhood fear of ending up in hell. Hearing a Nichiren priest detail the torments of the eight Buddhist hells, his "whole body shook with mortal terror. When I went to bed that night, even in the security of my mother's bosom my mind was in a terrible turmoil. I lay awake sobbing miserably all night, my eyes choked with tears." He is terrified at the sight of flames heating bathwater, overjoyed at his mother's promise to resolve his anxiety, and intensely preoccupied with the problem of escaping the fires of hell.

The author's childhood obsession forms a textual occasion for revealing his innermost feelings as well as the actions that set him on his spiritual path. The text is replete with psychological self-descriptions, no matter what the event, although the recollection may be fanciful in part. "I sweated and squirmed in distress," he writes of some childish mischief. "I can't possibly return to lay life. I'd be too ashamed.... I am at the end of my rope.... Brooding, pondering my future over and over, cudgeling my brain for an answer...," he writes of his discovery that becoming a monk did not exempt him from the fires of hell. "I was struck by an indescribable joy" at finding a stack of books that might hold the answer. Engaging in meditation practice "I entered a cave of pitch darkness—when I walked, I didn't even know that I was walking." When *satori* first dawned, "my body and mind dropped completely away.... Beside myself with joy, I cried out

---

throughout his life (BODIFORD 2012, 20). Bankei Yōtaku (盤珪永琢, 1622–1693) did not leave behind any writings at all, but his disciples recorded his Dharma talks and wrote records of his life; see WADDELL 1984, ix and 3.

51. WADDELL 1982, 72.

at the top of my lungs.... Afterward, I was possessed by a feeling of enormous pride." And when rejected by Master Shōju, "I was totally disheartened and frustrated. I sat red-eyed and miserable. My cheeks burned from the constant tears." To such descriptions of extreme elation and depression, we could add countless recorded memories of quiet sadness and burning desire, all of which form a pattern in Hakuin's account of his relentless search. The vehemence of his frequent condemnations of "silent illumination Zen" (默照禅), a Zen of undriven quietude, equally reveals Hakuin's personality, as does the self-deprecation with which he ends the chapters of *Wild Ivy*: "I have constantly held up the ugliness of my house for others to see.... Call it filthy verbal refuse"; and "Any wise man who claps eyes on [my writings] will fling them to the ground in disgust, and spew them contemptuously with spit."[52]

Yet the "ugliness" held up for others to see, and all the psychological self-descriptions, serve a quite different purpose from Rousseau's, which were written just three years later but in an entirely different world. Hakuin is writing not for personal display or self-justification, but to recollect a spiritual journey that might serve as an example to others. In this regard, his work parallels Augustine's *Confessions* and St. Teresa's *Life of Herself*, the two great European autobiographies before Rousseau. Hakuin wanted to demonstrate the necessity of an intense search, unrelenting struggle, and constant practice. He describes how he regretfully gave up his desire to live alone in the mountains and settled in his home temple, Shōinji, at the age of thirty-two. At the time of writing *Wild Ivy*, he had some three hundred monks practicing under his guidance, and had written scores of letters and made numerous trips to impart the Dharma. Other writings, in particular the *Orategama*, show us that his works were often directed to lay commoners and nobility, and sometimes read like Confucian epistles, advocat-

---

52. Ibid., 81, 85, 87–9, 93, 95, 98. 109, and WADDELL 1983, 138.

ing "a humane government and the proper treatment of the farmers."[53] Even so, the intended audience of *Wild Ivy* is primarily Zen monastics, perhaps even limited, the author admits, to "a single superior seeker who has broken through the barrier.... I humbly and respectfully pass this work along to that patrician of the secret depths."[54]

Whatever the range of its audience, the intent of *Wild Ivy* and its presentation of self cannot be adequately discerned in a survey of psychological self-descriptions, explicit accounts of *satori* experience, or references to true practice. Despite its frequent interpolations of Zen stories and attacks on false teachings, Hakuin's work has a definite storyline which advances the author from a fear-obsessed child to a fearless teacher, and this storyline in general reveals the nature of his quest for something he never names and never finishes attaining. His years of wandering are not stopped by *satori* experiences but by circumstances compelling him to settle at Shōinji, and finally by a resolve "to devote my energies to the countless suffering sentient beings of the world." Clearly his task will never be finished, although the words that close *Wild Ivy*, depicting a visit one day by a monk, would aptly portray his life: "He pressed his hands together, bowed deeply, and then he was gone."[55]

What can be said of the self in Hakuin's work? The language of *Wild Ivy* is intensely personal and concrete, devoid of abstract or metaphysical terms like "no-self," (except for the mention of "Dharma" and of the "Unborn," the false doctrine "that life ends with death"). But if the conceptual language itself is missing, the underlying theme of rebirth in *Wild Ivy* provides a clue to an inchoate concept, which becomes clearer when we look at his other works. Hakuin's childhood preoccupation with the thought of being reborn in hell is countered, at the age of fifteen, with a vow described in a supplement to an ear-

53. YAMPOLSKY 1971, 17.
54. WADDELL 1982, 109.
55. WADDELL 1983, 136 and 138.

lier work: "Even if I should die, I will not cease my efforts to gain the power of one whom fire will not burn and water will not drown."[56] The same work recalls the first resolution of the problem, if not the final fulfillment of the vow, in details missing from the *Wild Ivy* account: "There is no cycle of birth and death through which one must pass."[57] Hakuin says he uttered these words upon his first *satori* experience, after grappling with the *Mu* kōan.[58] (*Wild Ivy* fails to mention the kōan also.[59]) Later Hakuin presents his experience to Master Shōju, who asks, "What about the dog and the buddha-nature?" When Hakuin spontaneously replies, "There's no way at all for hand or foot to touch it," Shōju grabs his nose and twists it sharply. "How's that for a firm touch!" he declares. In *Wild Ivy*, Hakuin records his response as, "I was incapable of moving forward. I couldn't retreat. I couldn't spit out a single syllable."[60]

Hakuin's reference to something untouchable and the master's attack on his body clearly indicate that the issue here is the self beyond birth and death. The kōan that Shōju gives Hakuin after this rebuke is another case on rebirth: "What happened to Nansen after he passed away?" After a period of intense concentration, Hakuin resolves this kōan, and others, upon being beaten senseless by a village woman. This time Hakuin gains the approval of master Shōju, who encourages him to engage in "after *satori* practice" and to strive

56. YAMPOLSKY 1971, 116.
57. Ibid., 118. But in "Wild Ivy," Hakuin reports that he cried out, "Old Gantō is alive and well!" (WADDELL, 1982, 95). Gantō Zenkatsu (C. Yantou Quanhuo, 828–887) survived Emperor Wu's persecution of Buddhism, taught the Dharma as a layman, and was eventually killed by bandits. Young Hakuin wrote of the torment he experienced when thinking about the fate of this great monk and his own vulnerability.
58. The *Mu* kōan, case 1 of the *Gateless Barrier* (無門関) is in essence Zhaozhou's (J. Jōshū's) answer "*Mu!*" to the question, "Does a dog have buddha-nature or not?"
59. Hakuin does mention his struggle with the *Mu* Kōan in autobiographical remarks in letter known as the *Yabukōji*, translated by YAMPOLSKY (1971), 163.
60. Waddell, "WILD IVY," 98. But the translation of the earlier account in the "Supplement to *Orategama* III" in YAMPOLSKY (1971, 118) has Hakuin remaining "nonplussed" at Master Shōju's attack.

every minute... to revolve the great Dharma, pledging yourself to benefit and save all sentient beings, while having nothing—*nothing*—to do with fame or self-profit in any shape or form... then you will be a true and legitimate descendant of the Buddha-patriarchs..., an even greater reward than being born as a man or a deva.[61]

Shōju's injunction expresses the ideal of self and the form of practice to which Hakuin was to devote his life. Once again, however, only other writings provide a more conceptual description. *Orategama IV*, written fifteen years earlier, advocates the practice of concentrating on "one's true self, which is no-self, that original nature may come to self-awareness [*kenshō*]."[62] Hakuin clarifies:

> there are two kinds of no-self [*muga* 無我]. Thus one person, having always been weak of body, timid in spirit, and fearful of other persons, kills his feelings and yields to all external conditions. Even when abused he does not become angry, and does not become upset even though he is beaten. This habitual fool and dull-wit who [really] experiences nothing... believes thus: ... As for me, I have fully attained this No-Self.... If one wishes to achieve accord with the true and genuine no-self in its purity, he must necessarily let go his hold on the steep precipice and then, after dying, come to life again. Only then will he directly experience the true and real self....[63]

The description of the first type of no-self may be heard in part as a criticism of the Confucian ideal that we have mentioned. The typology itself, although it expresses a model of the true self, seems not as satisfying as the concrete story of *Wild Ivy* precisely because of its more abstract and metaphorical terminology. "Letting go one's hold on the steep precipice" is further explained by way of analogy: finding oneself on "the steep face of a cliff, covered with slippery moss," where one "can neither advance nor go back."[64] Because of its personal context,

61. WADDELL 1982, 101.
62. W. KING et al., 1972, 82.
63. Ibid., 97.
64. Ibid., 98.

the description in *Wild Ivy*, where Hakuin was incapable of moving forward, retreating, or spitting out a single syllable, seems more illustrative of the self-imposed barrier between one and one's "true self." At this precipice, *Orategama* continues, "only one thing remains: death. To break through the barrier of death of mind and will is the 'way of self-awakening.'"

> Brought to life again, suddenly one experiences a great joy like that of drinking water and knowing in his own self its coldness or its warmth.... We call [this] *kenshō*, original nature come to self-awareness.[65]

Imagine, for a moment, novelist Tōson reading these words. Would they, or *Wild Ivy*, have struck him as forcefully as Rousseau's *Confessions*? I think his reaction, at least after reading Rousseau, would have been similar to Paul Tillich's in a conversation with Hisamatsu Shinichi in 1957:

> Hisamatsu: The Self is the true Formless Self only when it awakens to itself.... It is always at once one's own and not one's own... The Formless Self includes, insofar as it is Self, Self-awareness. But by this Formless Self (or Self-awareness) I mean the Formless-Myself, which... expresses—or presents—Itself in its activities.... The True Awakening—or Formless Self—in Itself has neither a beginning, an ending, a special place, nor a special time.
>
> Tillich: Then it cannot happen to a human being.
>
> Hisamatsu: ... with this Self-awakening... one is no longer an ordinary human being.
>
> Tillich (later): Even so, you can't eliminate the "my."... Is it that there is no centered self, no self-related self, which would be a hindrance?
>
> DeMartino (translator for Hisamatsu): The barrier is created by the reflectively self-conscious ego —or "I" which discriminates itself dualistically from "not itself"—or "not-I." *Muge*, "no hindrance," [is] the overcoming of this barrier.

65. Ibid., 98.

Tillich: By the removal of individuality?
DeMartino: No, by the fulfillment of individuality.
Tillich: What is the difference...?[66]

This conversation may be ironically called a paradigm of the incommensurability of paradigms. Tillich's question is never answered to his satisfaction. At the end, Hisamatsu's translator intimates that the conversation reached an impasse because the theologian is pursuing an analytic approach, while the Zen teacher is attempting to express something ungraspable by this approach but did not resort to methods appropriate to the expression of Formless Self. Tillich had admitted earlier in effect that even the kind of meditation he practiced was analytic: a reflection on problems, on the "contents of the universe." For Hisamatsu, on the other hand, "that which concentrates is that which is concentrated upon."[67] The two practices are quite distinct. The result is that Tillich is not only not "converted" to a different paradigm; he does not even understand it. How could such an unconditioned Formless Self be grasped as an historical paradigm at all?[68] One can trace the development of the concept and locate it in history, but its meaning negates any specific location.

Tōson might surely have discovered something from Hakuin (or Hisamatsu), but it would not have been the individual "I" with an inner life (内部生命) of its own that was depicted in his novels. The awakening to true selfhood (自我の目覚め) in Tōson's novel *Hakai* (Breaking the Commandment) occurs when protagonist Ushimatsu reads the Confessions of fellow *eta* (outcaste), Inoko Rentarō. Ushimatsu becomes aware for the first time in his adult life of who

---

66. I select these quotations, with many ellipses, from the conversation published in three parts (noted here as I, II, and III), in TILLICH AND HISAMATSU 1972–3, in this page order: 98 and 101 (I), 107 and 124 (II), and 94–7 (III).
67. Ibid., 96 (I).
68. Hisamatsu's words shortly before his death express the point poignantly: "I tell my family I do not die. I say that I am the formless Self. Therefore, I do not die. In fact, death never even crosses my mind. I have some work to do." Quoted in MERRILL 1981, 129.

he is, and resolves to reveal his socially despised origins which he has hitherto concealed and forgotten. "What Ushimatsu awakens to," Janet Walker writes, "is not the need for social freedom [the right to vote or to an education] but the need for a sense of self that he can be proud of and that he can show to others without fear."[69] Seeking this "spiritual freedom of the inner *kokoro*,"[70] Ushimatsu's (and Tōson's) self is perhaps like Hakuin's. In desiring moral justification it is perhaps like Hakuseki's self, and as a voice of conscience and critic of the abuses of society it is Rousseau's self—and yet it is not. It is a paradigm unto itself.

WRITING ONESELF INTO LIFE

> A paradigm is what the members of a... community share.... A paradigm governs, in the first instance, not a subject matter but rather a group of practitioners. — Thomas Kuhn[71]

Our sketch of three "autobiographers" has been a study in contrast. The "autobiographies" of Rousseau, Hakuseki, and Hakuin, and the words of Tōson as a foil to all three, differ not only in emphasis, theme, and cultural assumptions, the methods of their writings as ways to narrate a self are different as well. Indeed, their narrative practices seem sufficiently different to challenge comprehensive concepts both of self and of autobiography.[72] What autobiography is becomes as questionable as what a self is.[73] We noted that specialists have, for different reasons, disassociated Rousseau's *Confessions* and Hakuseki's *Told Round*

---

69. WALKER 1979, 176. See TŌSON 1974.
70. WALKER 1979, 177.
71. KUHN 2012, 179.
72. The investigation of twentieth-century autobiographic writing by EAKIN (1985) concludes that the self at the center of such writing is necessarily fictive.
73. Recent cross-cultural studies have explored cultural assumptions in the constructions of self and autobiography; see for example STANTON 1987 and GRANOFF AND SHINOHARA 1994. Deconstructions of what has been taken as a single genre explore its gendered assumptions as well; see GILMORE 1994, KOSTA 1994, and KASZA 2022.

A Brushwood Fire from the autobiographical genre—the first for being fiction rather than biography, the second for not being confessional.[74] And surely it would easy to locate Hakuin's *Wild Ivy* in another genre. Tōson's autobiographical novels, for their part, have been said to abandon both fiction and descriptive biography.[75] All the same, the lesson to be learned is that autobiography no more constitutes a single literary genre than "self" names a univocal entity. I use the same name, *autobiographia* (a writing of the life of oneself), for the three works simply because their authors purport to write of themselves. We might better say that each literally writes his self into life. The theme of investigation in each of these three "autobiographies" is not so much a unique self to be discovered as it is as a manner or method of writing, constructing from a singular perspective a model life for others.

These lifelike models necessarily vary, of course, with authorial innovation, cultural convention, and philosophical presupposition. Such conditions of life allow certain generalizations: we read of a European intellectual, a Japanese Confucian reformer, a Japanese Zen monk. At the same time, we might look for the unique person in each author: Rousseau, Hakuseki, Hakuin. But these are our identifications, not the perspectives of the authors, whether concealed or explicit. Each of them, however differently, constructs a model of how others beyond the bounds of such identifications might live their lives. These conditioned and self-constructing authors, seeking

---

74. See note 22 above.

75. MIYOSHI (1974, 73) suggests that the writer of the so-called Japanese "I-novel" [*shishōsetsu*] sets himself up not to invent, nor to report life, but to "live the very substance of his work." In a later essay, MIYOSHI (1991, 17–27) challenges the entire classification of *shōsetsu* as novels; as opposed to the art of the novel, the predominance of the first person in *shōsetsu* functions to conceal the narrator and to mark the continued suppression of the individual self. The analysis of modern Japanese literature in FOWLER (1988) confirms the difference between the genres of novel and *shōsetsu*, and traces the development of *shishōsetsu* not from the Western "I-novel" but from Japanese genres. Critical of Walker's *The Japanese Novel*, Fowler (75–6) argues that early *shōsetsu* were anything but a celebration of individualism; Tōson's *Hakai* (Broken Commandment) in particular is better seen as a "non-expression" of the so-called modern self [近代自我].

their own perspectives in writing, are each setting up a self that others could be. Their selves thus display the paradox of the paradigm, the model that is meant to describe something universal, but whose manner of describing is ineluctably particularized by conditions. Like a paradigm, moreover, the self emerges from social practices. The autobiographical self arises from narrative practices. The self that Tōson "discovers," for example, is not so much one already there as one he can now cultivate, or continue to cover up, through his writing. A self abstracted from lived practices is no less questionable than the grammatical use of "self" as an independent substantive capable of being the subject of a verb.[76] Apart from such practices, the written "self" makes no sense at all.

Annie Ernaux: a timely paradigm

The writing of Annie Ernaux, the French novelist and 2022 Nobel Laureate in Literature, confirms an observation that began this chapter. What is more, it offers insight into an author's own recognition of distances from and within herself. Ernaux confirms Nishitani's observation that the self depicted in modern literature is typically generalizable if not universal. She writes "speaking from my condition as a woman." She is praised for connecting "individual memory to collective experience, particularly for women and for members of the working class"; her memoir *The Years* has been called "a collective autobiography." At the same time, she is keenly aware of writing at a distance. Of her memoir *Shame* she said, "I shall carry out an ethnological study of myself." She is equally aware of "the roots, estrangements and collective restraints of personal memory," and has "examined and re-examined the same events in her life from different angles."[77] Annie Erneux's

---

76. On the grammatical "self" see Bernard MAYO 1952, 93–4; and RICOEUR 1992, 1–3.
77. "A French Writer Who Unflinchingly Cut Into Personal Memory," *New York Times* (October 7, 2022), 8.

writing practice displays a paradigm for knowing how selves are written into existence both as subjects and as authors.

The chapter to follow considers an alternative model for a direct "knowing of self" that does not go by that name and is not self-referential at all.

8
Finding the Self in Mountains
Zen Landscapes of the Mindful Heart

> Because mountains and waters are the self
> before such words arise, they are a liberating presence.
> — Dōgen, *Mountains and Waters Sutra*[1]

For many years I have been fascinated with Zen verses that seem to speak of the self in terms of the environment. We may call these texts simply landscapes of the mindful heart (心), for 心 is taken to be the core of the self. This chapter takes us on a tour of some of these poetic expressions and offers a few views of them. They range from descriptions of a scene around someone, to a metaphoric transposition of oneself and one's surroundings, to one's full identification with the environment. These expressions add dimension to those presented in Chapter 9 about autonomy—about Zen master Linji's exhortation to "accord with all environing things," and Nishitani Keiji's enjoinder to respect the reciprocity between self and other.

Our selective tour here will straddle differences among languages—medieval Chinese and Japanese and modern English—as well as between poetic language and philosophical analysis. I will refer to the *heart-mind*, an expression often used to convey the overlap that

---

1. My rendition of「而今の山水は... 朕兆未萠の自己なるがゆゑに、現成の透脱」from the opening lines of the "Mountains and Waters Sutra" (正法眼蔵山水経). Carl Bielefeldt translates: "These mountains and waters of the present... because they are the self 'before the germination of any subtle sign,' they are liberated in their actual occurrence." DŌGEN 2001, 11.

the Sino-Japanese 心 covers, and sometimes I will rest content with the ambiguity of *mind*. But I will also speak of the *mindful heart* to better convey the connotations of 心 in Zen poetics. Like that sinograph, this English expression suggests a centered or attentive sensitivity, an embodied rather than detached mind. To view some landscapes of the mindful heart is to view some ways in which embodied self and environment divide, comingle, move together and apart, and sometimes lose their separate identities. These verses have something to teach us about current philosophical views of mind—what such views distinguish mind from and what they take for granted.[2] An identification of self and environment is not a feature exclusive to the Chan or Zen tradition, however. We find resonances of this identification among Native Americans of the Southwest and among Australian aboriginals, for example. The embodied, enheartened landscape is not the exclusive property of any one people.

To raise the question of the relationship between poet and natural environment, I begin with a story about founder of the Fayan School of Chan Buddhism, Fayan Wenyi had heard a story about Jiashan Shanhui, who was named after the mountain (夾山) where he lived. Someone once asked Jiashan, "How are things with Jiashan," and he replied: "Monkeys retreat behind the blue ridge, holding their young in their arms; birds dive in front of the blue cliff, holding flowers in their beaks."[3] Later Fayan made a remark about this description: "For thirty years I mistook this to be a picture of the world around Jiashan." Then Fayan wrote his own verse:

> With reason exhausted, feelings and deliberations are forgotten.
> How can it be likened to anything!
> Right here this frosty night's moon

---

2. Chapter 13 takes up this theme in more detail.
3. My rendition of Jiashan's and Fayan's Chinese verses is indebted to the translation of Thomas and J. C. CLEARY 1978, 214–5) and to Nishitani Keiji's reading of the *kanbun*, in NISHITANI 1974, 26. Fayan Wenyi (J. Hōgen Bun'eki) lived from 885 to 958, and Jiashan Shanhui (J: Kassan Zenne) from 805 to 881.

> Sinks serenely into the river valley ahead.
> Ripened fruit hang heavy with monkeys.
> The mountains deepen as if to lead astray.
> Raising my head, there's still some light—
> Originally to the west of my abode.

This verse is included in Case 34 of the *Blue Cliff Record*, a famous collection of kōans. Nishitani Keiji says that, in Fayan's verse, the moon setting in the river valley on a frosty night, the monkeys coming to pick the fruit, and so forth, all depict features of Fayan's daily mountain life. Nishitani goes on:

> All this, however, is no other than "perfected real nature"[4].... It is, as it is, the mind of Fayan, a man of Zen. We must not understand the features expressed in this verse as a description of a landscape.... The features of Fayan's mountain life in the verse... are not just a description of the world around a quiet, secluded place in the mountains.[5]

Nishitani's comments immediately elicit a question: if such descriptions of the natural environment are not—or not always simply—a picture of the surrounding world outside oneself, just what do they refer to?

There are several possible answers to this question, depending upon the particular poet or verse. Sometimes a verse or passage may indeed primarily be a description of a scene around the poet, and often in this context a clear view of the world-around is said to require a calm mind. Sometimes poets may be describing their own state of mind, but using words that can refer to features of a natural environment rather than using language we would recognize as psychological. And sometimes the poet (I use that word in a very broad sense) seems to identify directly with the environment. Let me present a few examples of each

---

4. Fayan's verse was his comment on "completely perfected true nature" (*parinispanna svabhāva*), an allusion to Yogācāra Buddhism that denotes the mind freed of self-attachments and discrimination.

5. NISHITANI 1974, trans. 1984, 23–4.

of these possibilities. All of them, even the description "merely" of a landscape, have as their theme an intimate relation between poet and natural environment.

This theme is noticed by several scholars of Chan and Zen literature. Richard John Lynn translates into our language the view of the influential eleventh-century poet, painter, and statesman Su Shi (1037–1101): "the poet... should, indeed must, tap into the well-spring of Nature itself, and the primordial creative force to which he gives himself over should take hold of him, and the poetry which results should be a 'natural event.'"[6] This view is shared by scores of other poets through the centuries, in both China and Japan. Joseph Parker examines the connection between Sino-Japanese poetics and painting and finds numerous instances of the heart-mind as their central theme. For example, Parker notes Su Shi's interest "in what the [painting] revealed about the heart-mind and the innermost thought and character of the painter," and he quotes Su Shi's verse that was inscribed on a landscape painting by Song Di (ca.1015–1080):

> How expansive is your heart,
> Hills and rivers cool themselves inside....
> A river village with few houses,
> A misty hamlet with clusters of old trees.
> I know you [Song Di] have hidden thoughts.
> I examine closely to find them.[7]

And David Pollack notes that between 1200 and 1500 the Zen poems of the Five Mountains in Japan were sometimes written merely for aesthetic gratification, but he finds their epitome in poems that "reveal to the trained eye the Zen state of mind of the poet."[8] There is an expanse between verses about nature that reveal a state of mind, and verses that

---

6. LYNN 1987, 385.
7. PARKER 1999, 37–8, quoting a translation by R. Egan; see 227 n. 63.
8. POLLACK 1985, 5.

dissolve the embodied mind into the natural environment. Let me cite some examples along the way.

First, here are two examples of what we may at first take to be purely aesthetic descriptions of a landscape, with little or no reference to the mind or self:

> A branch of bamboo stretched over the wall
> Rises and falls unpredictably in the wind.
> While sparrows, trying to perch for the evening, with
>   unsettled hearts
> Flutter up to it and then away again.[9]

This verse, by the Five Mountains (*Gozan*) poet Kisei Reigen, describes not a scene that Reigen is viewing outside, but a painting on a fan. A verse by the Gozan poet Mugan Soō may likewise describe a painted scene. The translator, David Pollack, titles this verse "Walking in the Mountains":

> Tiring to the feet but refreshing to the eyes,
> This wandering with a cane through mist and fog;
> Hard to tell if it's real or a painting—
> Against a pale wash of cold woods, the dark ink of crows.[10]

Is the poet seeing a real scene or a painted one? I read his indecision as a sign of his absorption into the scene. If there is a difference between the "real" landscape and the landscape depicted in a painting, we may take it as suggestive of the difference between the landscape—whether real or painted—and the mindful heart of the poet. And where there is a blur between "real" and "painted," we can, I think, see an initial step toward the identification, or better, the nonduality, of inner and outer, mindful heart and environment.

On the way to this expression of nonduality we may stop at another overlook, where poets and painters seem to follow the practice of

9. Ibid., 90.
10. Ibid., 129.

calming the mind to see clearly the world around them, but with a turn to a mutual transformation. The linked-verse poet Nijō Yoshimoto (1320–1388) writes, "Facing the flowers of spring and composing poems beneath the autumn moon, clear your mind, dim your nature [性]"—and Nijō immediately follows this with a promise of self-realization: "and you will spontaneously attain enlightenment."[11] With mind (心) cleared and one's own nature (性) withdrawn, one identifies fully with flowers and moon. The abbot of Tōfukuji in 1410, Kiyō Hōshū connects the art of landscape painting to self-realization in a slightly different way. He is commenting on the expression "Manifesting the Mountain" that was the byname of Shogun Yoshimochi. The Shogun wanted to know what it meant for him to manifest the mountain, and Hōshu wrote, "'Manifesting' is 'luminosity' and 'mountain' is the image of 'bringing to rest'.... inwardly illumine the mind and outwardly bring the objective world to rest.... When the mind and its objects are united into one, then luminosity and bringing to rest will be merged."[12] The translator notes that the couplet "illumining" (明) and "bringing to rest" (止) derives from the opening of the classical Chinese *Great Learning* 大學. But notice that Hōshū's advice to the Shogun reverses the order we might expect in Zen landscape painting: calm the mind and illumine the environment. Hōshū writes instead of illumining the mind and calming the world. This reversal signals another step toward nonduality.

Yet another step is the exhortation to internalize the scene to be depicted in a poem or painting. Su Shi writes:

> In painting bamboo one must first attain the completed bamboo inside the breast. Then when one grasps the brush and gazes intently, one will see what one wants to paint and rise quickly to follow it.... If one knows

---

11. Parker 1999, 128.
12. Ibid., 124. The usual reading of the artist's name, 岐陽方秀, is Giyō Hōshū, who lived from 1363 to 1424.

the way things should be and cannot do it, inner and outer are not one and mind and hand are not in accord."[13]

The Five Mountains figure Taihaku Shingen (1357–1415) takes it a step further, and exhorts the painter or poet to "attain [the landscape] in the mind and forget external things."[14] "Attaining the landscape" is a turn on the more usual Zen phrase "attaining the mind" that alludes to attaining enlightenment. The Japanese Kitayama Five Mountain poets followed Su Shi in seeking to bring the mindful heart (心) into accord with things in the environment (境 C. *jing*), or even further, seeking to achieve the nonduality of inner and outer.[15]

This aspiration echoes the statements of the influential Chan master Huangbo Xiyun (d. 849) that "mind and things are one" and "mind and things are both extinguished."[16] It is also possible to glimpse a Buddhist Yogācāra philosophy in the background of these descriptions. The term for "objects" or "things in the environment" in both Huangbo and the Japanese Five Mountain poets is 境 (C. *jing*, J. *kyō*), a translation of the Sanskrit *visaya*, the realm created by deluded ego-consciousness that divides the world from mind and takes it as external object. In Yogācāra philosophy, as later in Huangbo, inner and outer are constructions of the ego-mind. The Zen monks of the Five Mountains were schooled in this philosophy and most likely incorporated it in their poetics.

Let us turn now to instances where at first sight a poet is depicting a landscape that may be viewed as a description of her own mindful heart. Such instances might appear to be merely a variation on the use of metaphor: comparing the inner world of the mindful heart with the visible, external world. We find a rather obvious example in the similes of the nineteenth-century English poet Christina Rossetti's verse:

13. Ibid., 140.
14. Ibid., 118.
15. Ibid., 140.
16. Ibid., 139–40.

> My heart is like a singing bird
> Whose nest is in a water'd shoot;
> My heart is like an apple-tree
> Whose boughs are bent with thickset fruit;
> My heart is like a rainbow shell
> That paddles in a halcyon sea;
> My heart is gladder than all these
> Because my love has come to me.[17]

Of course, we would need to supply some extra steps to read the Chinese and Japanese poems this way. For example, the verse I cited previously by Su Shi, "How expansive is your heart/Hills and rivers cool themselves inside..." could be read as saying "your heart is expansive enough to take in the hills and rivers, river villages and misty hamlets" or further, "your heart is as expansive as hills and rivers...." Here we would read the poet's mindful heart in words about the landscape.

Translators often interpolate personal pronouns into Chinese poems so as to make explicit a reference to one's inner feelings in verses about travel or landscape. Beata Grant translates a poem, "Expressing My Emotions," by the Buddhist nun Xingche (行徹, 1606-?):

> The road through rugged terrain, at times easy, at times obstructed,
> In leisure I observe the affairs of the world like a river flowing east.
> I gaze toward the end of the sky, empty of past and present,
> I walk among the clouds, freely coming and going.
> I often sit together with a master of stream and boulder
> And occasionally travel with a wayfarer of the pine flower.
> At times I manage to come up with a phrase, and whistle as I ride the void,
> Better even than exchanging poems with the fisherman and woodcutter.[18]

17. ROSSETTI 1870, 37.
18. GRANT 2003, 99.

The word "I" and references to the self are the translator's interpolations, no doubt justified by the context and grammar of the poem, but nonetheless one choice among other possible translations. For example, the opening lines might be more ambiguously rendered this way:

> The road through rugged terrain, at times easy, at times obstructed,
> Observing leisurely the affairs of the world like a river flowing east.
> Gazing toward the end of the sky, empty of past and present,
> Walking among the clouds, freely coming and going.

...and so forth.

Indeed, poems do often seem to reveal the poet's mood or mind directly, and not always a particularly nonattached mind, as in this verse by Gidō Shūshin (1325–1388):

> Miserably cold, the temple before dawn,
> Still and lonely, few monks to be seen:
> The temple is old, with soot-blackened walls,
> The pond overgrown, its surface like folds in a robe;
> Incense before the Buddha has burned, gone out, turned cold,
> The sermon over, blossoms fly in the rain;
> I've reached the point of doing away with happiness and sadness—
> A white board door swinging to and fro in the breeze.[19]

Beyond metaphor, the poem seems to swing to and fro between a description of a landscape and a description of the poet's mood in viewing it, on the way to something beyond happiness and sadness.

A similar verse, the second of two called "Living in the Mountains" by Gozan poet Tesshū Tokusai (d. 1366), captures the poet's landscape this way:

> Old cedars and ancient cypresses impale rosy mists,
> Through huge boulders and hanging vines a small path winds;

---

19. POLLACK 1985, 47.

Even monkeys and cranes won't come to a mountain *this* desolate—
Only the wind-borne cassia pods that fill my thatched hut.[20]

If we read the poet's mindful heart in these lines about a landscape, I think we apply a hermeneutics different from the romanticist hermeneutics that would look for the author's intention or try to relive the poet's experience. Romanticist hermeneutics was formulated on the assumption that the author's mind was an interior realm describable in psychological terms, and when words about nature stood in for psychological terms they were considered straightforward metaphors. In contrast, the assumption of the Chinese and Japanese poets and landscape painters was that the seen and depicted world could directly express the artist's mindful heart when it was clear and open enough to accommodate its environs or to identify with them—in some cases, for the mindful heart, that is, the embodied self—to extend to its environs, to become them. So when the literati official Ouyang Xiu (歐陽修, 1007–1072), who was no friend of Buddhism, said in effect that "the reading and writing of poetry centers on the author's idea [or intention 意] in the literary work as it expressed 心,"[21] his language implied that the work could express the poet's environs and mindful heart at once.

The contrast between these two assumptions exposes other interesting aspects we tend to take for granted when we describe the mindful heart and its states of being. In philosophical, scientific, and popular accounts, we today tend to describe the landscape of the mind in psychological or physiological terms. *Satori* or enlightenment, for example, is an experience of liberation, an altered state, a peak experience, or—in the popular book by the physician and Zen practitioner James H. Austin—a process in the brain.[22] The Japanese *satoru*, on the other hand, is merely a matter of opening the eyes and realizing or com-

20. Ibid., 57.
21. PARKER 1999, 33, slightly modified.
22. See, for example, AUSTIN 1998.

ing to understand something. The notion of intentionality in the phenomenological tradition comes closer because it shifts the focus to the objects of perception and away from an enclosed, inner state of mind. Yet Buddhist philosophies also claim that there is a non-intentional consciousness where the mind is fully aware but not directed to anything at all. Such an experience—to use that overrated word—is the philosophical basis of descriptions that refer to what looks like features of a landscape but refer equally well to the mind. Under the Buddhist assumption, today's psychological terminology and brain-language are not any more realistic as descriptions of the mindful heart. Indeed, if Sino-Japanese poetics often renders the human heart or mind in terms of nature, it also depicts natural objects in terms of 心—of their *kokoro* (to use the Japanese word) or their *xin* (in Chinese transliteration) and even of their "sincerity" (J. *makoto* 誠). Nishitani titled one of his books *Kaze no kokoro*, "heart of the wind." The philosopher of aesthetics Izutsu Toyoko has argued that classical uses of *kokoro* do not necessarily indicate a subjective state or entity at all. Only after the thirteenth century did *kokoro* designate a subjectivity that transcends the transience of experienced phenomena.[23]

23. MARRA (2011, 1168–9) summarizes Izutsu's contention:
Kokoro... is variously translated as either "heart" or "mind." In [Ki no] Tsurayuki's [868?–945?] version of *kokoro* a variety of subjective events take place, such as the thinking of thoughts and the feeling of emotions. However, these thoughts and emotions do not find verbal articulation unless they are "entrusted to what a person sees and what a person hears." In other words, only metaphors can provide the inner self with an exit into the world—metaphors which in the *Kokinshū* are mainly drawn from nature ("the voice of the warbler singing among the blossoms, and the voice of the frog dwelling inside the water"). As readers of the *Kokinshū* immediately realize, were it not for the scanty information we have about the poems included in the collection, it would be impossible to trace the object of poetic expression back to any specific subjectivity. The poet's calculated attempt to defer expression to a background that is fore-grounded in natural images (scattering cherry blossoms and falling maple leaves) has led Izutsu Toyoko to deny that Tsurayuki ever used the word *kokoro* to indicate any particular state of subjectivity. She argues that only in the poetry of the Shinkokin period (1205), and especially in Fujiwara no Teika (1162–1241), *kokoro* became genuine subjectivity transcending the transience of phenomenal experiences.

According to an old verse ascribed to the legendary figure Bodhidharma, enlightenment opens one's eyes to see one's true nature and become buddha (見性成仏), to see as a buddha sees. In Chinese Buddhist extensions of "buddha" there is no essential difference between buddha and the world as it truly is. What we call the environs around us are another perspective of ourselves. This of course is why a depiction of landscape can be a depiction of the mindful heart, and why the features of the natural world and its sounds can be said to be the body and the words of buddha.[24] In 1240, Dōgen composed a commentary on Su Shi's enlightenment verse that begins:

> The sounds of the valley streams are his long, broad tongue;
> The forms of the mountains are his pure body.[25]

Nine years later, Dōgen echoed this verse in a Dharma talk to his monks: "the great earth, mountains, and rivers are still the pure body."[26] Another poem by Dōgen reads:

The color of the mountain peaks	Mine no iro	峰の色
The echo of the valleys	Tani no hibiki mo	谷の響きも
All flowing together:	Mina nagara	皆ながら

This transformation in the notion of *kokoro* followed the impact that the philosophy of Tendai Buddhism, especially the concept of the "experience of self-illumination," had on the construction of the subject in medieval Japan. Thus, *kokoro* became a "state of mind." By stressing the unindividualized state of mind which he called "no-mind," Teika argued that the products of the *kokoro* originate spontaneously without ever being controlled by any conscious endeavor. Consequently, Teika considered a poetic masterpiece to be the result of a process of spontaneity in which the *omoi* spontaneously arises from the *kokoro* and spontaneously flows into words (*kotoba*). Teika drew many of these insights from his father Fujiwara no Shunzei (1114–1204), whose poetic treatise of 1197, *Poetic Styles Past and Present*, was deeply infused with ideas coming from the philosophy of Zhiyi's (538–597) *The Great Calm-and-Contemplation*.

24. And the buddha-mind, unexcelled, pure and clear, can be said to be mountains, rivers, and the great sea. In saying this, DŌGEN (1971B, 9), in his recorded talks with monks, alludes to the Chinese Buddhist text, *The Awakening of Faith in the Mahāyāna*.

25. From the *Shōbōgenzō Keisei Sanshoku*, translation by COOK 1999, 69.

26. 「大地山河清浄身」, Dharma hall discourse 328, trans. by LEIGHTON AND OKUMURA 2010, 300.

> Our Shakyamuni's   *Waga Shakamuni no*   吾が釈迦牟尼の
> Voice and form.   *Koe to sugata to*   声と姿と²⁷

In another discourse of 1240 called the *Mountains and Waters Sutra*, Dōgen brings us back to the themes of travel and the embodied mind, but goes further than a metaphoric identification of self and environs.²⁸ Keep in mind that the expression "mountains and waters," *sansui* 山水 in Japanese, is a term for landscape or scenery. Dōgen writes of verdant mountains walking, quoting a verse by the Chan master Furong Daokai (1043–1118) or "Preceptor Kai" as he is called. The Preceptor tells his assembly at Mount Dayung: "The green mountains are constantly walking." Let us take a few steps back to consider this strange view.

In an essay on this saying, the American poet Gary Snyder reminds us that Dōgen walked miles and miles both on Mount Hiei above Kyoto, Japan, when he was a young monk in training there, and later through the mountains in southern China when he sought an authentic teacher.²⁹ When we speak of travel today, we tend to think of riding trains, taking planes, or driving cars. But for millennia the most common mode of travel was walking. And as Gary Snyder reminds us, walking follows the pace of the human body and provided the scale some countries still use for distance, no matter how we travel (a mile is an old Roman measure of a thousand paces). We tend to think of a landscape as the vista we view when we stop our travel and gaze out, from a stationary point or perhaps from a car or a train window.

Consider a change in perspective. You may have had this experience: you are sitting in a train that slowly begins to move; you feel the

---

27. My translation; see also HEINE (1997, 97–8) and Shohaku Okumura (Dōgen Zenji's Chinese Poems, <https://dogeninstitute.wordpress.com/2014/12/02/nothing-other/> who translate 「皆ながら」 as "one in all, all in one" and "all of them as they are" respectively.
28. There are numerous English translations of this fascicle of Dōgen's *Shōbōgenzō*. Bielefeldt offers an accurate one with scholarly notes; in DŌGEN 2001.
29. SNYDER 1990, 9.

momentum as this enormous train-body takes up speed, and then you suddenly see that it is the train on the track next to yours that is moving, not the train on which you are actually riding. Or, in a change of scene, you are standing on a bridge over a rapidly flowing river and peer down into the water rushing by, and all of a sudden you feel yourself and the bridge moving instead of the water. Now think of riding a bicycle. Nishitani Sensei once encouraged me to experience myself on the bicycle as not moving at all, but instead to sense the ground moving beneath me. Gary Snyder does not mention the change in perspective when he makes the connection between Dōgen's practice of walking and his talk of green mountains walking, but we may imagine Dōgen sensing the mountains moving beneath his feet, the whole earth moving as a treadmill moves when you walk on it but remain stationary. Dōgen walked and walked and walked and walked until the mountains were walking under his feet.

Ordinarily, when I walk through a landscape I look out at it, and the things and the horizon I see shift as my head turns and I walk along. In my vision, my surroundings are ever changing with respect to me, to the placement of my body. My body, that is, I myself, am walking and moving, and my awareness stays with my moving body. If "I" am always with my body, if I am my body, then "I" do not move with respect to this body. As embodied, I am the unmoving reference point for all else. All else moves with respect to me. This is an ordinary way of seeing things. A slight shift produces another, somewhat out of the ordinary but not uncommon perception: I move my legs but they go nowhere, the mountains are walking by me, the earth turns under my feet. Yet Dōgen is not talking only about such a shift in perspective. He writes: "Because [the mountains] have been the self since before forms arose.... If you doubt mountains walking you do not know your own walking." The poet-translator Gary Snyder comments: "they are what we are and we are what they are." Dōgen says: "Blue mountains are neither sentient nor insentient. You are neither sentient nor insentient. At this moment, you cannot doubt the blue mountains walking."[30] The mountains not only metaphorically stand (in) for us, for the self. The self moves into mountains.

Strangely enough, the shift Dōgen enacts seems to be not a change in perspective but a loss of perspective—the perspective that takes oneself as the center of the world.[31] It is as if Dōgen answers the question: what would happen if I thoroughly identified with my environs, say, of surrounding mountains? Then mountains could walk. And that is the ways mountains practice to be mountains. Dōgen sees it this way: "A mountain always practices [參學] in every place.[32]

I think it important not to fall into the deep hole where such views look like dark, impenetrable mysticism that has nothing to do with everyday life in our workaday, politically troubled world. I have hinted at the relevance of Dōgen's view for ecology and political life elsewhere, and others have explored that relevance in much more detail.[33] Many of Gary Snyder's essays and poems apply the sight of living mountains to bioregionalism, which shifts our view of vast geopolitical territories to sustainable, decentralized areas with natural boundaries and features. To be sure, this natural world may include

---

30. Ibid., 105.
31. DAVIS 2011 further elucidates Dōgen's "egoless perspectivism."
32. Ibid. With the reminder that many Chan figures were named after mountains (think of the poet Hanshan, Cold Mountain, or the masters Kueishan, Yangshan, or Tungshan), translator Hubert NEARMAN (2007, 141) reads Dōgen's words as straightforward metaphors, where mountains mean accomplished Zen masters, blue or green means alive and ever renewing, and so forth:

> In this discourse in particular, "mountain" is most often used as a descriptive epithet for one who is sitting in meditation, as still as a mountain among mountains (that is, one who is training among other members of the Buddhist Sangha), as well as for a wise and saintly person whose path has led him or her to seek a spiritual abode in a mountain, in both a literal and a figurative sense. Hence, the Chinese Zen Masters are referred to as 'mountains', and because their training never comes to an end but is ever green, they are referred to as "verdant mountains." And because they are not rigid or static in their practice, they are sometimes referred to as "flowing mountains."

33. MARALDO 2019, 452–4; WIRTH 2017.

human abodes and activities as well. Another Japanese poem by Dōgen leaves us with a question:

Attaining the heart	*Kono kyō no*	此の経の
Of the sutra,	*Kokoro o uru wa*	心を得るは
Are not even the sounds	*Yo no naki ni*	世の中に
Of the bustling marketplace	*Urikau koe mo*	売り買う声も
The preaching of the Dharma?	*Nori o toku kana*[34]	法を説くかな

Dōgen concludes his presentation of mountains and waters with this reminder: "When you investigate mountains thoroughly, this is the work of the mountains. Such mountains and waters of themselves become wise persons and sages." Gary Snyder adds: "become sidewalk vendors and noodle-cooks, become marmots, ravens, graylings, carp, rattlesnakes, mosquitos. *All* beings are 'said' by the mountains and waters—even the clanking tread of a Caterpillar tractor, the gleam of the keys of a clarinet.[35] The bioregional landscape includes the human world but humans are not its center.

Let me end this tour with some words that show it is not only the Chan or Zen tradition that has identified self and environment. Out of another era and another place on earth, we find resonances of such identification among Apache peoples in the American Southwest. Seventy-seven-year old Annie Peaches puts it this way: "The land is always stalking people. The land makes people live right. The land looks after us. The land looks after people."[36] The anthropologist who recorded this observation, Keith Basso, comments:

> For Indian men and women, the past lies embedded in features of the earth—in canyons and lakes, mountains and arroyos, rocks and

---

34. Translation by HEINE (1997, 92–3), who remarks on two versions of this poem and finds in the quoted version here a suggestion of doubt in the final question. Okumura (DŌGEN 2022, 282) translates the later, more assertive version: "Grasping the heart/of this sutra/even the voices of buying and selling/in the world/expound the Dharma."
35. SNYDER 1990, 114–5.
36. BASSO 1996, 39.

vacant fields—which together endow their lands with multiple forms of significance that reach into their lives and shape the ways they think. Knowledge of places is therefore closely linked to knowledge of the self, to grasping one's position in the larger scheme of things... and to securing a confident sense of who one is as a person.[37]

Basso cites the Kiowa author, N. Scott Momaday: "The sense of place is paramount. Only in reference to the earth can [the Indian] persist in his identity."[38] I would take the link between place and self-identity among the Apaches and other Native Americans a step further. Such self-identification can occur only because one does not understand oneself as separate from one's environment. The Pueblo writer Leslie Marmon Silko suggests as much when she invokes a sense of place that is not apart from self. She notes that language can be misleading if it misses this connection. The English word "landscape," for example, does not capture the sense of place as it is lived by her people; indeed it does not correctly describe the relationship between the human being and his or her surroundings:

> ["Landscape"] assumes the viewer is somehow *outside* or *separate from* the territory he or she surveys. Viewers are as much a part of the landscape as the boulders they stand on. There is no high mesa edge or mountain peak where one can stand and not immediately be part of all that surrounds. Human identity is linked with all the elements of Creation....[39]

I conclude with a word from an Australian aboriginal woman that expresses more explicitly the nonduality of place and self that is intimated among the Native American aborigines: "With your vision you see me sitting on a rock, but I am sitting on the body of my ancestor. The earth, his body and my body are identical."[40] This woman does

37. Ibid., 34.
38. Ibid., 35 and 105.
39. SILKO 1999, 32.
40. LAWLOR 1991, 42.

not envision the earth as a tremendous landscape she can imagine from the outside, but as the place of a continual creation. Ancestors created specific places by living on them, or perhaps better said, by living or enlivening them—in a primordial time called Dreamtime that bridges past and present. People re-create a place when they visit it and live on it—even if only for an overnight camp.

There is more to be said about such places as landscapes of the mindful heart, and I have said more about the Apache and Aboriginal views in another essay.[41] For now let me conclude with this poem by Gary Snyder:

> Green mountain walls in blowing cloud
> White dots on far slopes, constellations,
> Slowly changing, not stars, not rocks
> "by the midnight breezes strewn"
> cloud tatters, lavender arctic light
> on sedate wild sheep grazing
> tundra greens, held in the web of clan
> and kin by bleats and smells to the slow
> rotation of their Order living
> half in the sky—damp wind up from the
> whole North Slope and a taste of the icepack,
> the primus roaring now,
>   here, have some tea.[42]

41. MARALDO 2001.
42. SNYDER 1990, 108.

9

Personal Autonomy
An Alternative View

> Treat humanity, whether in your own person or in the person of another, Always at the same time as an end and never simply as a mean.... What else, then, can freedom of the will be but autonomy, i.e., the property that the will has of being a law to itself?
> — Immanuel Kant[1]

> The autonomy, or "being one's own master," that comes about with becoming a "thing" and a means for all other things, is a matter of a dimension altogether different from that of the autonomy of the moral subject. Here the absolute self-negation that sees the *telos* of the self not in the self but in all things, and the absolute self-affirmation that sees the original selfness of the self in all things, are one.
> — Nishitani Keiji[2]

The evident contrast between Kant's and Nishitani's statements quoted above epitomizes in condensed form the radical difference I wish to exhibit. My entry into that difference will be by way of a "background check," a disclosure of the prevalent assumptions of Kantian autonomy, followed by a sketch of the alternative they obscure. Although the concept of autonomy at first sight seems foreign to the East Asian traditions I draw from, the modern trans-lation of the existentialist conception of *subjectivity* as *shutaisei* (主体性) and its asso-

---

1. KANT 1785, *Groundwork* 429 and 447.
2. NISHITANI 1961, 276–7; NKC 10: 303.

ciation with freedom and self-determination have already provided a bridge. Examples of such self-determination in Zen and Confucian terms, and their implication of interdependence, will convey the alternative.

THE STANDARD NOTION OF AUTONOMY

The word *autonomy* comes from the Greek *auto nomos* and means being a law unto oneself, self-governance, or having authority over one's own actions. The modern Japanese translation of *autonomy* as 自律 connotes self-regulating; and the Chinese translation 自主 suggests ownership and independence as well. But the modern Asian translations fail to convey the broader Kantian sense of responsibility, which implies a relation with others. The relational aspect of Kant's concept may be dim, but its elucidation by way of contrasts allows us to see a related but alternative conception.[3]

Kant's appeal to autonomy in his ethical theory makes it clear that being a law unto oneself means the condition in which one's will is free and determined internally, by its own nature; it does not mean that people may simply follow any arbitrary rules they make for themselves. Personal autonomy, then, means the capacity for self-governance that makes accountability possible. It is linked to self-integration and authenticity, as opposed to alienation and being at war with oneself. This link is evident in some antonyms of *autonomy*: dependency, loss of self-control, brainwashing, compulsion, submission to authority, slavery. It is important to note that *personal autonomy* differs from *group autonomy* or *political autonomy*: personal autonomy assumes

---

3. The alternative developed here contrasts not only with Kantian autonomy but also with Japanese adaptations of the Kantian idea, such as Kimura Rihito's notion of "relational autonomy" in which one makes independent, autonomous decisions but within a relationship that strives for harmony (JPSB, 1233–4). Another exercise independent of East Asian sources explicates a "relational autonomy" implicit in Spinoza's relational sense of freedom (AGUILAR 2022).

an inseparable relationship between the actor or agent and her own authority to act, which she as a person has but a group does not.[4]

What determines one's autonomy? According to the standard notion, I am autonomous when I can exercise the power to act of my own will or on my own intentions. When others have power over me, I am autonomous when I authorize that power. Thus I remain an agent, a person who acts on his or her own. Personal autonomy entails that one's self alone is entitled to initiate one's actions. As Sarah Buss and Andrea Westlund write,

> an agent is one who acts. In order to act, one must initiate one's action. And one cannot initiate one's action without exercising one's power to do so. Since nothing and no one has the power to act except the agent herself, she alone is entitled to exercise this power, if she is entitled to act. This means that insofar as someone is an agent, i.e., insofar as she is one who acts—she is correct to regard her own commitments to acting, her own judgments and decisions about how she should act, as authoritative.[5]

Why is the idea of personal autonomy appealing? Why do we want autonomy? If I am autonomous, I can and do act on my own, following my own desires and intentions. I am the source of my actions, hence both commendable for them and accountable for them. What I do will not be forced upon me; I will do it of my own volition. Whatever outside influences there may be on me, they are such that I will accept or authorize them, and so I count as the author of my actions. I am often willing to follow the orders of others or comply with their wishes, but I never want their will forced on me, for that would deny me a most intimate and essential part of myself; it would in effect negate me. I cannot truly *be* without being a person who acts for him(or her)self, by him(or her)self. When I act for others, for their benefit, I do so of

---

4. I take this point, and much else in my presentation of the standard idea, from the excellent article by BUSS AND WESTLUND, 2018.
5. Ibid.

my own accord. If I "sacrifice myself" for others it means I have chosen to do so. If others compel me to make a choice I do not want to make, it is really their choice, not mine. If I am autonomous, I am myself, free, self-ruled, self-governed, expressive of myself, able to fulfill a fundamental impetus of my being.

Of course, I (or anyone) can also be weak-willed. I can "know better" but not do what I should do. Or I can be ignorant of what I should do. I can be of a divided mind and have conflicting desires and act arbitrarily on one rather than another. I can probably, in some sense, deceive myself about what I want or about how much I am in control to act as I want. I can be oblivious of the strength of influences on my desires and my actions. Or I can sometimes tire of wanting and desiring and choosing and acting on my own, and want to let circumstances determine what happens, or let the will of others prevail. But these deficient modes of self-determination partially confirm, as well as challenge, the idea of autonomy. If I am weak-willed I myself have the power to know better. If I am ignorant of what I should do, what I do do is still taken as my own action. If I am ignorant of the causes of my actions, I still have the power to think of them as my own. If I am of a conflicted mind and act arbitrarily, I myself know of choices I did not make. If I tire of having to decide and would rather rest in resignation, that is still what I myself want. And even if "I myself" turns out to be an idea built on shifting sands, everyday experiences confirm its elusive solidity.

There are significant internal challenges to my personal autonomy: personal subjugation, compulsions, obsessions, addictions. In Sarah Buss and Andrea Westlund's explanation, I am autonomous in face of these challenges when I can distance myself from mental states that move me to act and can be responsive to reasons. Presumably, to be self-integrated, I would have either to unify my motives to act or discard some of them.

The external challenges to my personal autonomy are oppression and subjugation by others such as oppressive governments or dominating persons. Explanations of autonomy often do not address how to remain autonomous in face of such challenges; rather they call for a change in the oppressor. Explanations also do not address the question of how one might deal with factors that are necessarily, by nature, beyond one's control. Autonomy is human-oriented or, more precisely, self-oriented.

Within the differing accounts of autonomy are disagreements about the scope of autonomy and the conditions under which it is preserved. Although the authors of these accounts may differ, they generally acknowledge that behind the idea of personal autonomy lies a metaphysical conception of the person or the self. I will not try to explain this metaphysics here, but instead will conduct a background check, as it were, that reveals some practical assumptions in the standard idea.

Presuppositions of the standard notion.

What are the assumptions behind the standard idea of autonomy? In brief, the idea assumes that

1. I am a self-contained subject who has, or should have, the power to act on its own.
2. There can be a gap between me or my potential power and what actually happens, the action. And if what happens does not issue from me or my decisions, then we cannot properly call it my action at all.
3. Actions (and intentions) not under my control but issuing from me are detriments to me, my well-being, my autonomy, my freedom; they must be the result of external forces or forces not authorized by me—or they must be of the nature of compulsions, impulsive behavior, brainwashing, or additions. If not willed and authorized by me then not mine, they are not autonomous, therefore forced.

And hence, the assumption that

4. we can speak of the causes of actions as forces, where the forces could be my own—my acting as a force—or not my own but endorsed by me, or forced upon me. Autonomy is connected to agency and then to force. The opposite, loss of autonomy, is connected to dependency, compulsion, loss of self-control.

Toward an alternative notion of personal autonomy

If a metaphysical conception of the person underlies the standard idea of personal autonomy, as many philosophers assert, then an alternative metaphysics of the person (or the self) might provide an alternative idea of autonomy—and of action and agency. Here I will not propose an alternative metaphysics, however, but will start with examples that intimate an alternative idea of autonomy. In fact, my examples come from disparate but related traditions that themselves imply somewhat different conceptions of person and self. (While the word *autonomy* translates roughly as self-law or self-governance, it is much older than the stand-alone noun *self* in English, which dates only as far back as the time of John Locke.) My textual examples moreover serve only as imperfect intimations of the notion I will propose, not as instantiations of a new abstract idea of autonomy. Each example points to some but not all features of the alternative notion, and we can learn from what each example lacks as well as what it articulates. I follow the common practice of many commentarial traditions by taking these examples out of their original historical context and using them for my own purposes. I follow here my contention that philosophy grows by way of the "trans-lation" of texts, by incorporating and transforming their questions and responses. The thinking of any era is nourished by such trans-lation.[6]

---

6. I develop this idea in the Prologues to Maraldo 2017, 11–14, and Maraldo 2019a, 1–14.

A SENSE OF AUTONOMY IN THE ZEN *RECORD OF LINJI*

A perhaps surprising example that intimates an alternative notion of autonomy is found in Discourse XVI of the *Record of Linji* in the Chan or Zen tradition:

> this very person of the Way, dependent upon nothing, comes forth availing himself of every circumstance.... Followers of the Way, if you want to accord with Dharma, just be persons of great resolve. But if you are indecisive and easily led, you will never get it, just as a cracked jug is unfit to hold ghee. One who would be a great vessel must not be led astray by others. Make yourself master, take charge wherever you are, and wherever you stand will be a true place.[7]

There are several significant links to the standard idea of autonomy in this example, indicated by translations like *free of dependency... availing [oneself] of every circumstance, making yourself master, being of great resolve*, and by implication, being self-determined, seeing the truth yourself rather than submitting to the views of others or going along indecisively. The relatively ambiguous grammar of the Chinese allows a translation in terms of verbal imperatives: "*be* a person of great resolve," "*make yourself* master, *take charge*." Notice the intimations of authenticity, too: don't be spineless, be of great resolve, don't be led astray by others; find out for yourself.

There are also significant alterations of the standard idea: be a *follower* of the Way, not governing it, nor governing oneself. Become a great *vessel*,[8] a container that accepts and holds the Dharma, the manifest truth or law, rather than trying to define the truth for oneself. In the alternative notion we will develop, to be autonomous is not to

---

7. 「還是這箇無依道人、乘境出來... 道流、爾若欲得如法、直須是大丈夫兒始得。若萎萎隨隨地。則不得也。夫如嗄之器、不堪貯醍醐。如大器者、直要不受人惑。隨處作主、處皆眞。」The English translation here modifies SASAKI 1975, 17 and SASAKI AND KIRCHNER 2009, 16, with suggestions from Richard John Lynn.

8. 大器, "great vessel," is a term borrowed from the *Daodejing* and the *Analects* of Confucius.

be self-governing in the sense of being a law unto oneself, but rather to understand controlling circumstances so well that one is not overwhelmed or subjugated by them.

With respect to a fully developed alternative notion of autonomy, however, this example seems to lack a crucial element: an explicit reference to the social relationships that are implied by the idea of autonomy. Social relationships are relations between oneself and others. Although *autonomy* in the standard sense means *self*-governing, it necessarily bears a relation to others that one interacts with, be it other people or forces understood as extrinsic to oneself. One is autonomous only over-against others and their power. Even where the force or controlling influence seems internal to oneself, as in the case of a compulsion or addiction, insofar as it threatens one's autonomy it may be taken as opposed to one's will or intention, to one's natural way of being or one's core self. The ideas of *availing oneself of every circumstance, making oneself master*, and *taking charge wherever one finds oneself* do not by themselves intimate the dimension of social, interpersonal relationships. Where is the Other in the alternative sense of autonomy?

A seventeenth-century gloss on the expression "the place you stand" in Linji's discourse makes an explicit connection to the interdependence of self and all else. Ban'an Eishu trans-lates *the place you stand* as *pratītya samutpāda*「立処者縁起」, and writes, "The *place* of dependently originated dharmas is called 'the *place* you stand.'"[9] This interpretation carries the "freedom of dependency" of our earlier translation into the freedom of standing within the world of codependent origination rather than the deluded pretense of standing outside it.

To elaborate on the place that reciprocity with others holds in the alternative sense of autonomy would require an inquiry into a related alternative—one that undoes standard ideas of self as opposed to other and restores the relational side of self.[10] For now I would stress that

---

9. Broughton and Watanabe 2013, 176.
10. That alternative is sketched in the Chapters 8 and 10 of the present volume.

the sense of mastery in alternative autonomy differs from that at work in the popularized version of the master-slave dialectic of Hegel. The master subjugates the other and enslaves him, to the point of relying on and becoming dependent on him. In Robert Brandon's perceptive interpretation of the dialectic, the master has authority with no admitted responsibility; the slave has responsibility but no recognized authority.[11] Hegel recognized the need for the kind of reciprocity that I think the idea of autonomy requires, but it is at work only when his kind of unstable and ultimately non-autonomous mastery is dissolved, or in Hegel's terms, is sublated (*aufgehoben*). We will return later to the important issue of reciprocity and domination by others.

To extrapolate a bit from the example in the *Record of Linji*, we find there a hint of a sense of self-mastery linked with others. Linji's "master" is one who is autonomous in the sense of availing himself of circumstances with no need to take control over others. He is resolute and decides himself rather than simply submitting to the views of others. Yet he has no need to subjugate others in order to free himself, nor to dominate his surrounding environment to exert his own will. Finally, and most significantly, he *accords with* reality (in Linji's words, with the Dharma or the Way).

"According with reality" suggests another nuance of the phrase translated as "availing [oneself] of every circumstance" ("this very person on the way, free of dependency, comes forth availing himself of every circumstance"). It echoes Nishitani's stance of the "pure practice" of according with all things. The revised edition of Ruth Fuller Sasaki's translation puts it more forcefully: "…this very person of the Way… comes forth *in control of every circumstance*."[12] The Chinese expression 乗境 is amenable to a variety of translations, from a milder *perfectly in step with circumstances* to a stronger *master of circumstances* or *master*

---

11. In a videotaped interview, Robert Brandon stated further that Hegel's argument means "unless authority and responsibility are commensurate and reciprocal, no actual normative statuses are instituted" <https://www.youtube.com/watch?v=WdIPuERVjko>.

12. Sasaki and Kirchner 2009, 208.

of the environment. Since the issue of control is central to notions of autonomy, let us clarify that metaphor in a little more detail.

How can anyone (except perhaps God) actually be "in control of every circumstance"? Who might possess this God-like power? Consider for a moment the predominant notion of control. The usual notion denotes an exertion of power over something in order to direct it, restrict it, or stop it from acting. To practice self-control by controlling one's desires, for example, is to stop oneself from "automatically" acting on those desires. This notion of control is close to the idea of governing implicit in the literal meaning of personal autonomy as self-governing. The idea behind governing oneself in the question of autonomy is, as we have noted, to prevent or disallow others from controlling oneself; but to govern oneself is also to control oneself and not give in to inner impulses that would restrict one's power to act of one's own will. Similarly, to govern others is to direct and restrict them in some measure. To govern or control one's circumstances would be to bend them somehow to one's will, so that they accorded with what one wanted or intended. Self-control and control of other people or things, in the usual sense of these phrases, denote restricting oneself or restricting others, so that they conform to the will of the one in control. They must accord with the one in control; the one in control need not accord with them. The alternative sense of autonomy requires a shift in this thinking: it encourages being in accord with something both within and beyond one's control.

How can one who is "in control of all circumstances" still be in accord with reality, with every circumstance? When one accords with circumstances, particularly those deemed "beyond one's control," one willingly yields to them so as not to be overwhelmed by them or unwillingly controlled or dominated by them. One is in a position to "freely use circumstances," which is yet another rendition of the relevant phrase 乗境.[13] If I may be allowed a very free translation, the sino-

13. The translation into Japanese as 境を使いこなす (deftly handle circumstances or

graph 乗, translated here as *availing oneself of* and alternatively as *in control*, can in other contexts mean *ride* or *operate*, as when one rides a horse or a bicycle (it can also grammatically indicate the active voice[14]). In riding a horse one must be in control but let oneself be carried by the horse; one must allow the horse to move of *its* own power. In riding a bicycle, one must balance oneself continuously and remain in control of the direction; but balancing oneself requires the practice of harmonizing one's own weight with the weight of the bicycle, not resisting but going along with the pull of gravity. The bicycle rider is autonomous when her activity conforms with the force of gravity. To use an English idiom, the master who is autonomous in the alternative sense *rides along with the environment without riding roughshod over others*.

NISHITANI KEIJI'S "ELEMENTAL AUTONOMY"

Nishitani Keiji's Zen Buddhist critique of Kantian autonomy, as expressed in our epigraph, would extend Linji's metaphor to the possibility of according with *all* things, indeed, of identifying with all things. That extension also expands the degree of reciprocity between self and all others. If Linji's mastery of circumstances is also a mastery of self by *according with* environing things, Nishitani self-mastery calls for acting for the sake of things. And Kant's imperative that forbids the use of persons as instrumental things takes a radical turn:

> the standpoint, where the self returns to the home-ground of all other beings and finds its "destination" in them, has to be opened up as a complete negation of any standpoint of subject or autonomy... even in its authentic ethical sense.... The self, such as it is in its totality, has to become a "thing" for the sake of all other beings.... Absolute subordination and absolute autonomy come about in unison.... The standpoint on which one is able to lay oneself beneath all things is no different from

---

environing things 境) is found in YANAGIDA 1972, 120; AKIZUKI 1972, 76; and IRIYA 1989, 69.

14. BROUGHTON AND WATANABE 2013, 16.

the standpoint where one is "master of all things".... This autonomy or
"'being one's own master" [自主] comes about with becoming a "thing"
and a means for all other things.¹⁵

Nishitani recognizes that Kant's ethics also require self-negation—the
negation of those selfish desires that could not be pursued universally
by all other persons—just as his sense of autonomy and self-sufficiency
positively implicates other persons—by completing my being an end-
in-itself in a universal "commonwealth of ends." But the reciprocity
that Nishitani calls for is farther reaching than Kant's strictly human
universal. A "thorough-going reciprocity" of self and all other beings—
not only rational persons—matches the reciprocity of self-mastery
and self-servitude, being master of oneself by being subservient to all
things. Therein is found the "elemental autonomy of the self." This positive sense of autonomy [自主] in an alternative sense is consistent with
Nishitani's positive sense of subject and subjectivity.¹⁶ Lest one think
that Nishitani's critique of Kantian ethics abandons the moral dimension of action, notice his reference to Christian and Buddhist religious
ethics. The self of love (*agape*) or compassion (*karuna*) negates the
autotelic, self-directed mode of being but completes itself—affirms

15. NISHITANI 1961, trans. 1982, 275–7.
16. Nishitani refers to this sense in his Preface (ibid., xlviii; NKC 10: 4), where he clarifies that "the quest is for the 'home-ground' [もと] of religion, where religion emerges from
the human being as a subject [主体], as a self living in the present." His account in this
work, *Religion and Nothingness* of 1961, clarifies remarks first published in 1936, which
may be paraphrased:
> Our standpoint that contrasts with egoic will does not eliminate its moral or ethical
> character. Rather the elemental autonomy [主体性] of selflessness displays non-dis-
> crimination; it breaks through the concept of a substantive, existent self and liberates
> the natural life that had become a mere expression of basic desires.... It is a stand-
> point of the *pure practice* of subjectivity or autonomy that runs through all the vari-
> ous stages of life and accords with all things by de-transforming and restoring them.

NKC 1: 88–9, see also MORI 1997, 15–16. It may have been Nishitani's *senpai* Miki Kiyoshi
who first used the term *shutaiteki* (主体的) for *subjektiv* (that is, "sensual human activity,
praxis") in his 1930 translation of Marx's *Theses on Feuerbach*, or perhaps it was Nishitani
who introduced 主体性 to translate Kierkegaard's term.

itself and achieves true self-mastery—by becoming subservient to all things, where it can see its *telos* in all others.[17] In place of "subservience," Nishitani might also have referred to the Franciscan notion of *obedience*, conceived as a form of freedom from stubbornness, selfishness, and self-centeredness, and harking back to the root meaning of *ob-audire*, "listening to." That this listening is directed to *all beings* is implied in Francis's invocation to "Brother Fire" (which Nishitani does mention[18]) and to Brother Sun, Sister Moon, Brother Wind, Sister Water, and Mother Earth in the famous Canticle. We note, too, that Nishitani's "subservience to *all* others" precludes another sense of subservience and self-power—the subordination to anyone who claims dominion over others, the autocrat.

Confucian examples that link with social relationships

Confucian traditions may not imply such an expansion to all beings, but they clearly return us to aspects of autonomy that center on social relationships and interactions with other people. Examples of Confucian notions of *ren* (仁) offer a starting point. Usually, *ren* is not connected to autonomy at all, and scholars like Roger Ames and Henry Rosemont note that there is no corresponding idea in classical Chinese thought.[19] Nevertheless I think we can find a straightforward connection with autonomy.

Classical notions of *ren* (仁) imply both the reference to oneself and a reference to others that the notion of personal autonomy requires. The two parts of the sinograph 仁, the 人 and the 二, reflect this double reference: "one cannot become a person by oneself," as Ames and Rosemont put it.[20] Further, although the metaphysics of the

17. Nishitani 1961, trans. 1982, 274–5, 280.
18. Ibid., 283.
19. Ames and Rosemont 1998, 54.
20. Ibid., 48.

person implied in classical Chinese thought may differ from that in the modern notion of autonomy, the person of *ren* and the autonomous person are both considered achievements; one achieves *ren* and one accomplishes autonomy. At the same time, to connect the notion of autonomy with ideas in Confucian traditions requires that we alter the standard notion in some significant ways.

As noted earlier, autonomy in the standard sense means to be one's own person. In contrast, *ren* requires that one *not* be motivated by selfishness. The seventeenth-century Japanese scholar of the Ancient Learning School, Yamaga Sokō, quotes Confucius in this regard: "'Humaneness' (仁) makes people truly human. One becomes humane by 'overcoming selfishness and returning to propriety.'"[21] Autonomy in the standard sense implies that one acts out one's own will, but *ren* (仁) requires subduing that will when it is directed primarily by one's own desires. Yamaga's contemporary, the Neo-Confucian scholar Kaibara Ekken, also quotes from the same passage in the *Analects*, which in another translation reads: "If for one day a person can *subdue himself* and return to propriety, all under heaven, the whole world, will return to humaneness." Kaibara continues,

> One day means for a sustained period. It refers to an ongoing period of moral practice. "Disciplining oneself and returning to propriety" is an extremely difficult thing. Sustained effort toward that must be made over a long period of time.[22]

Elsewhere Kaibara writes, "people must practice *self-control*" regarding their own happiness at the expense of others' happiness.[23] Even the standard notion of personal autonomy calls for disciplining oneself, at least to free oneself from internal forces in governing oneself. The Confucian examples suggest another aspect as well: the

---

21. 「克己復禮為仁」, *Analects* 12.1」, trans. John A. Tucker, in JPSB, 340.
22. 「一日克己復禮 天下歸仁焉」, trans. Mary Evelyn Tucker, in JPSB, 369–70, my emphasis.
23. Trans. John A. Tucker, in JPSB, 372, my emphasis.

reciprocity of autonomy, that is, if my autonomy and that of others go hand in hand, then one who acts only selfishly is not truly autonomous insofar as he jeopardizes the autonomy of others. Confucius puts it in a positive way: When Fan Chi asked him about *ren* (仁), his reply was "love others."[24]

What about the part of personal autonomy that is concerned with freedom from domination by others? This brings us to the second connection that alters the standard idea of autonomy. The standard notion stresses the importance of self-authorship and authority. In contrast, Confucian notions of *ren* seem again to undermine self-authority and stress submission to social custom. Summarizing the standard idea of personal autonomy, Buss and Westlund write that

> every agent has an authority over herself that is grounded, not in her political or social role, nor in any law or custom, but in the simple fact that she alone can initiate her actions.... In order to form an intention to do one thing rather than another, an agent must regard her own judgment about how to act as authoritative—even if it is only the judgment that she should follow the command or advice of someone else.[25]

In contrast, Confucius and his Japanese interpreters want one to submit to *li* (禮) or ritual propriety.[26] Ames and Rosemont's translations of terms in the *Analects*, however, reveal another side to what seems like one-sided submission. They translate *ren* (仁) as "authoritative conduct," "to act authoritatively," or "authoritative person." The person of *ren* is authoritative in the sense that she acts as the authoritative model of proper conduct in a community, as well as in the sense of "'authoring' the culture for one's own place and time."[27] The passage in the *Analects* cited above by both Yamaga and Kaibara, in this translation, continues: "Becoming authoritative in one's conduct is self-orig-

---

24. 「愛人」 *Analects* 12.22.
25. BUSS AND WESTLUND 2018.
26. YU (2021), writing about the relational autonomy implied by the sense of freedom in Confucius and Mencius, argues that *ren* and *li* are mutually constitutive.
27. AMES AND ROSEMONT 1998, 50.

inating—how could it originate with others?" Ames and Rosemont translate *Analects* 4.3 as "The authoritative person alone has the wherewithal to properly discriminate the good person from the bad" (唯仁者能好人能惡人).²⁸

What is more, *ren* (仁) conveys some of the sense of reciprocity that the alternative sense of autonomy calls for:

> Authoritative persons establish others in seeking to establish themselves and promote others in seeking to get there themselves. Correlating one's conduct with those near at hand can be said to be the method of becoming an authoritative person.²⁹

Reciprocity (恕) is the key to the Confucian version of the golden rule: "Zigong asked, 'Is there one expression that can be acted upon until the end of one's days?' The Master replied, 'There is *shu* 恕: do not impose on others what you yourself do not want.'"³⁰

Freedom from domination by others also requires a benevolent government as a social institution. What is the early Confucian model of government? Numerous passages in the *Analects* reflect the reciprocity of ideal governing. One example is *Analects* 2.3:

> "Lead the people with administrative injunctions (*zheng* 政) and keep them orderly with penal law (*xing* 刑), and they will avoid punishments but will be without a sense of shame. Lead them with excellence (*de* 德) and keep them orderly through observing ritual propriety (*li* 禮) and they will develop a sense of shame, and moreover, will order themselves."³¹

---

28. Ibid., 89; see also *Analects* 12.1, 152. The translators point out an alternative etymology of *ren* 仁 suggested by oracle bone inscriptions where 二 does not refer to two but is an early form of 上, *above*, that was also written 二 (Introduction, p. 48).

29. *Analects* 6.30: 「夫仁者、己欲立而立人、己欲達而達人。能近取譬、可謂仁之方也已」, ibid., 110.

30. *Analects* 15.24, ibid., 189.

31. 「道之以政、齊之以刑、民免而無恥；道之以德、齊之以禮、有恥且格」, ibid., 76.

Ames and Rosemont refer to proper governing (政) as "noncoercive governing," where "authority is authoritative rather than authoritarian." We may recall that autonomy is opposed to force, and coercion is the exercise of force; thus noncoercive governing means government that does not force others or need to enforce laws. They also see in this idea an analog to the Daoist *wu-wei* 無爲 or "nonassertive action."³²

The notion that autonomy must be reciprocal, already intimated by Hegel, has a surprising corollary when considered in the context of the Confucian examples we have cited. The reciprocity of autonomy means that people are autonomous in relationships of mutual respect, of course, but it also entails that individuals are most autonomous when they do not dominate others. Reciprocity sets a more severe limitation on the alternative notion of autonomy: not only is freedom from domination its apparent precondition, but the practice of respect for others is also entailed. (This condition would turn Kant's ideal of reciprocity into a necessary condition for true autonomy.³³) Not dominating, as well as not being dominated, are equally aspects of the true achievement of autonomy. The corollary would mean that despots, slave holders, and concentration camp guards are not being authentic human beings who exercise self-governance. Individuals who attempt to control others may be authoritarian but they are not authoritative human beings who display autonomy. Does this mean that they are immune from responsibility, since autonomy is consid-

---

32. Ibid., 231–2, n. 23, 21. The notions of governing in Japanese Confucians need further investigation in this regard. Many wrote in support of harsh domination by a central government, the Tokugawa *bakufu*.

33. Reciprocity plays a role in Kant's conception primarily with regard to the relation between free will and self-legislation, and only indirectly between oneself and others: "Freedom and self-legislation of the will are both autonomy and are hence reciprocal concepts" (KANT 1785, G450). The translator (vi) describes Kant's ideal whereby "each member [of a community] would act as a law unto himself (and hence autonomously) but yet would cooperate harmoniously with every other member." The "reciprocity" commanded by Kant is better conceived as the capacity to universalize the autonomous individual's will, that is, the capacity to legislate moral laws that are valid for all rational beings.

ered its precondition? In lieu of an alternative account of responsibility I have given elsewhere,[34] here I would only suggest that the logic of preconditions or requisites does not do justice to the Confucian idea of reciprocity and autonomy in the alternative sense. In contrast somewhat to Nishitani's Zen-inflected "elemental autonomy," Confucian reciprocity is better conceived in terms of the exercise of autonomy than as a requisite for it. Similarly, autonomy is part of the exercise of responsibility, not simply a precondition for it. Those who are not exercising autonomy, in the alternative sense of the word, are not taking responsibility. And that is why we hold them morally accountable.

FEATURES OF THE ALTERNATIVE SENSE OF AUTONOMY

What can we conclude from this preliminary inquiry? What alternative notion of autonomy do the examples point to? If we list the elements of such a notion, we now have an alternative autonomy that entails

– Self-mastery that negates mastery over others.
– A method of self- mastery or self-governing by which one accords with something that transcends self—that accords with the Dharma, follows the Way, serves all others, or practices propriety. (That with which one accords is transcendent in the sense that it is not merely a matter of human conventions or institutions like governments. It is not transcendent in the sense of being above and beyond this world, as is a God who is the source of the moral law.)
– An ongoing practice and continual achievement.

---

34. MARALDO (2019, 91–5, 109–13) discusses the ambiguity of personal autonomy in Watsuji Tetsurō's *Ethics*, followed by a proposal for a positive sense of relational dignity. "The Question of Responsibility in Tanabe's Metanoetics," in the same volume, especially 190–94, presents Tanabe's "metanoetics" as an alternative to the responsibility that is based primarily on the classical sense of autonomy. See also Chapter 11 in the present volume.

- A power by which one accords with natural conditions necessarily beyond one's control, by acting within them or internalizing them, making them one's own—where "according with" does not mean acquiescing, giving in to, or giving up.
- Reciprocity of self and other: becoming an authentic self by respecting or serving others.
- On a social level, a way of governing others by letting others govern themselves, as Laozi tells us, or by showing others how to govern themselves by being an exemplary model (a 仁者 or a 君子), as Confucius would say.

The presupposition of the alternative notion is a recognition of interdependence, as opposed to strict independence. Insofar as the alternative implies some notion of selfhood, it is a sense of self where one must interact respectfully with others in order to be oneself.

Let us conclude with a tentative formulation of the alternative notion. Autonomy is the practice of self-mastery or self-control that enables one to act in accordance with one's true nature, hence one's authentic desires and intentions, which are at one with the natural universe and respectful of others. Autonomy is reciprocal: it is exercised fully only when it allows the freedom of others. That means that human institutions like government, social laws, marriage, etc., ideally act as mediators of personal autonomy, allowing and promoting mutual autonomy. Governments that so act are themselves autonomous in an alternative sense of political autonomy.

We will pursue the question of the moral or ethical character of this practice in Chapter 12.

10
Alternative Configurations of Alterity in Dialogue with Ueda Shizuteru

Alterity, the difference that being-other makes, is not an overt theme in the writing of Ueda Shizuteru, and yet by bringing alterity to the fore we are able to connect and examine several themes that Ueda does engage explicitly. It will turn out that several models of alterity are discernible in Ueda's philosophy, and their common ground opens a mode of being-other that offers an alternative to dominant models of alterity.

ALTERITY AS A TWO-FACED PROBLEM

In modern and postmodern cultural theory, alterity as a political conception is a two-edged sword. On the one hand, representations of other peoples as alien traditionally supported a stance of self-superiority and a justification of domination, oppression, and exclusion. Imposed otherness subjugates. The familiar term *orientalism* is a name for one manifestation of this negative edge. Critics argue that constructions of an alien Other that privilege the side of the self must be deconstructed. On the other hand, in opposition to certain streams of German idealism that subsume the Other into the self, the irreducible difference of individuals must be maintained. And on a social scale, the recognition of irreducible difference and otherness serves as the requisite for exposing and overcoming exclusion and the injustice of oppression. Recognized alterity empowers. The denial of alterity is thought to underlie forms of discourse that are hegemonic and do not allow others to speak for themselves. Linked to the social and political issue of alterity is the twofold problem in modern philosophy: how to give an account of the Other that does not reduce it to the self or the same as self, yet that permits the self to relate to an irreducibly different other.

The problem of alterity and irreducible difference is further complicated by critiques of the very notion of the Other. Recent treatises that theorize alterity have shown it to be a protean conception. The title of one incisive interpretation, Mark C. Taylor's *Altarity*, alters its spelling to indicate its tendency to compound and confound definition rather than delimit one meaning in difference to another.[1] One prominent critical thinker that Taylor does not discuss is Luce Irigaray, who has criticized both the historical configurations that oppress others, and the constructions that celebrate the Other. Irigaray argues that the very designation of "women" or "the feminine sex" as the Other is a masculine construction that substantializes an absence and monopolizes a discourse that would misrepresent as monolithic what is actually multiple.[2] Irigaray thus undermines the whole notion of the One or the Other. Her book, *This Sex Which is Not One*, could alternately be called *This Other Which is Not One*, that is, not single, not the same as self, and not an entity at all. Her later poetic essay titled *To Be Two* proposes instead that for one to be oneself, one autonomous self, there must be two, including a you who is never reducible to oneself. The critic Judith Butler, on the other hand, is reluctant to substitute any positive proposal for the bereft notion of the Other. Alterity for her seems dangerously to signify something that ultimately cannot be represented. Trinh T. Minh-ha avoids the term alterity altogether in her direct presentations of "the inappropriate/d other."[3]

1. See M. TAYLOR (1987, xxviii) on the author's play on the word *alterity*.
2. BUTLER (1990, 9–10) gives this summary of points that Irigaray makes.
3. MINH-HA (1989, 76) writes that "trying to find the other by defining otherness or by explaining the other through laws and generalizations is, as Zen says, like beating the moon with a pole or scratching an itching foot from the outside of a shoe."

Parts of these critiques seem to parallel the kind of Buddhist discourse that aims more to undermine than to construct. Expressions like "neither the same nor different" and "not one not two" undermine assumptions of both fixed identity and immutable otherness.[4] It is clear that the Buddhist expressions undercut irreducible difference. As a self-avowed Zen Buddhist philosopher, Ueda roots many of his investigations in this double negation, even when he does not refer to it, as we shall see. Note that neither difference by itself, nor distinction-making which recognizes difference, is enough to converge with notions of alterity, protean as they are. Senses of alterity arise when difference and distinctions generate social and political consequences; alterity has to do with effective differentiation among humans—with human relations, human others. (Rarely included are animal others, or nonhuman animals as the Other.) It may at first seem that Ueda's alternatives sometimes exceed alterity's usual social context that is confined to human relations, human others—the context of "I and You (and they)." But it will become evident that his configurations relate the social context back to the three fundamental types of alterity widely recognized in philosophical literature since Levinas: the alterities of nonself (world), oneself as Other, and Other self.[5]

One initial question, then, is just how Ueda implicitly configures alterity differently. A consequent question asks what place is left for the otherness of others. I will attempt to answer these questions in dialogue with Ueda and with the texts he interprets, rather than by way of a straightforward exposition of his writings.[6] As a partner

---

4. For the context of these expressions in Zen Buddhism, see NAGATOMO 2020.
5. See ZAHAVI 1999, 195.
6. Much of the content of this article derives from papers presented at sessions of the American Academy of Religion and other meetings in the early 1990s, some of which included actual dialogues with Ueda as a participant. Other conversations with him in the process of translating his work likewise inspired my responses to his writing. Ueda often repeated or closely paraphrased parts of his work in various published articles, and my presentation here will draw arbitrarily from some rather than others. It goes without saying that the themes of Ueda's vast corpus exceed the selection chosen here.

in dialogue, I place myself at once over-against him, challenged and changed by what he has said, in the hope that my appropriation may inspire continuing conversations by others. Four models will focus my inquiry; all have to do with language. The series I place them in reflects my responses and not any sequence proposed by Ueda himself.

LANGUAGE AS NOTHING OTHER THAN PURE EXPERIENCE

A conventional mark of alterity is language difference, often experienced as the barrier of a foreign tongue. A seemingly unrelated model of alterity presents language as the Other to a selfsame, pre-linguistic, and unmediated "pure consciousness" or "pure experience."[7] Ueda's interpretation of Nishida Kitarō's early philosophy of pure experience undermines both barrier and immediacy by laying a common ground for both language and the experience of otherness.

As I read Nishida's first and perhaps most influential work, *An Inquiry into the Good*, "pure experience" is originary knowing that precedes the division between who knows and what is known. But the moment of pure or pre-experience has its own momentum and develops of itself into thinking, willing, intuiting, and other modes of consciousness that form the individual on the one hand, and that develops into the full spectrum of objective reality on the other. Language is not named as a moment or a mode generated from pure experience. Indeed, Nishida's text seems utterly silent about language, except for the single comment that one's language shared with others figures only as an "abstract shell" and not a transmitter of true reality.[8] Other comments clearly point to language usage. But Ueda

---

7. FORMAN (1990) and S. KING (1998) are representative of the vast literature on the lively debate between proponents and critics of the notions of pure consciousness or pure experience. Note that the entire debate implicitly confines language and experience to human beings.

8. NISHIDA 1990, 51–2; NKZ 1: 63.

10. Alternative Configurations of Alterity | 241

expresses the movement of pure experience in three successive steps, each of which directly entails language.⁹ The expression "pure experience" itself is a primordial or proto-word (*Urwort*, Ueda sometimes writes in German), that gives way to the proposition, "pure experience is the sole reality," which in turn leads to the sentence that expresses Nishida's intent: "to try to explain everything on the basis of pure experience as the sole reality."¹⁰

We might contradict Nishida's and Ueda's statement that pure experience is the only reality (that allows one to explain all things) from several angles. It would seem that if pure experience really were the sole reality, then we would not need to say so; indeed, we could not say so, for we would not have a concept of pure experience, any more than we would have a concept of green if everything were green and only green. To say that pure experience is the sole reality implies that we can somehow stand outside this reality and give it a particular name, qualify it. And yet the content of this statement also implies that we, and our saying of it, belong to this reality, belong inside it. Our statement both is part of this reality and is other than it. As other than the sole reality, the statement makes it possible for us to recognize this reality for what it is. We are aware of it as such, but that means we are aware of ourselves as part of it, the sole reality, so we are really saying that it is (through us) aware of itself. At the same time, this self-awareness implies a distancing and difference that would seem to abrogate the claim that something is the sole reality, by naming it pure experience. Not only is the name "pure experience" antithetical to pure experience, since it names the ineffable, but any name is antithetical to whatever is called the "sole reality," since any name is other than that which it designates.

Several responses to this situation would seem possible. One might say that the proposition, "pure experience is the sole reality," is

---

9. For example, in Ueda S. 1982c, 181–7; 1991, 101–18, and 1993, 69–71.
10. NKZ 1: 4; Nishida 1990, xxx.

obviously not true, since it posits something other than this reality, that is, its name. Another response might read the proposition as a kind of incoherent self-referential statement, like the famous paradox, "This statement is false," in which "this statement" refers to that very sentence. Or "sole reality" and "pure experience" are names that would have to include themselves in what is named and thus, like the notorious set of all sets, would entail Russell's paradox. In this case, Nishida's proposition would not be false, but simply meaningless. Indeed, the proposition would predicate something of its subject, which is a "fact" that has no meaning: "the fact of pure experience [has] no meaning whatsoever." It anticipates but does not possess a meaning, a connection between present and past consciousness.[11]

A consideration of the sequence of parts in *An Inquiry* seems to mitigate this difficulty. If we look at the table of contents of Nishida's book, we find that it is divided into four parts. We read in Nishida's own preface that he wrote part two before part one, and that those reading the book for the first time "should leave [part one] for later."[12] We do not read that the order of sections and their titles were decided by Kihira Tadayoshi (1874–1949), at the time an editor of the journal *Tetsugaku Zasshi* (Journal of Philosophy) in which various parts had previously appeared. We notice, too, that there is no distinctive change in style between parts one and two, although there is some change in themes. But Ueda would read the second part as a reflection upon the first part. Does he simply mean that the first thirty pages or so of the text, titled "Pure Experience," actually express pre-reflective language, and that the pages in the part two, titled "Reality," change to a language of reflection? Does Nishida indicate such a shift when he says, in his Preface, that part one is "the foundation of [his] thought," and that in part two he "sets forth [his] philosophical thought"? We might, then, reconsider the two parts to refer not simply to discrete sections

11. NISHIDA 1990, 15 and 9.
12. Ibid., xxix.

of the book but to different moments (*keiki* 契機) or stages of analysis. One moment may predominate a certain section of the text, but both may occur throughout. One moment lays the foundation; the other moment carries reflection forward; it "sets forth philosophical thought." It is not really a sequel to the first; it carries on the first but in more detail. Or so it might appear.

But Ueda's reading is more performative. Part two, he tells us, is written from the standpoint of reflective self-consciousness in a manner that aims at retrieving the theme of part one, which is pre-reflective pure experience. How can reflection retrieve the pre-reflective? Only by disrupting itself, Ueda suggests, by being broken up. Part two is represented by the statement that pure experience is the sole reality, and this statement breaks down when analyzed as above. Is the aim thus achieved? Do we arrive at pre-reflective pure experience in this way? Not if we are left only with incoherent logical fragments, I think. And probably not simply by returning to part one, whose starting point is the primitive fact of pure experience, and then reading it in the usual manner. Ueda's response to the text suggests rather a different reading, which does not take part one as philosophical reflection, and which would therefore preclude reading this part as a series of seemingly abrupt and unfounded propositions or claims about something called pure experience. The "proposition" of part two, stating that pure experience is the sole reality, is in effect a generative sentence that brings us to the brink of the possibility of reflection. We are already in the process of thinking about pure experience, and when thought through, it stops thinking in its tracks and issues into silence. The statement emerges from an act of reflection, but what it names as the object to be reflected upon is actually, in this case, the end of reflection. It intimates, in other words, an Other to reflection and to the articulate language that composes philosophical reflection—yet an Other that is a One which generates difference from itself.[13]

---

13. This tentative formulation is reminiscent of Fichte's philosophy of an absolute self-

Let us approach Ueda's interpretation from another angle. What kind of text or language could disrupt reflection? We are, after all, dealing with a philosophical text, not an inscrutable poem by Étienne Mallarmé or Paul Celan. If texts do not exist apart from readings, what kind of reading could disrupt? Simply posing this question suggests that Nishida's text can be read as a kind of performance or reenactment, perhaps, of the primitive fact, the primordial state, and the standpoint, of pure experience. We have seen an example of Nishida's and Ueda's reenactment of the primordial state in their retrieval of "pure experience as the sole reality"; we have attempted to reenact this state of affairs for ourselves by showing how this statement cannot state what it means. It turns out to be a proposition that cannot be taken as a founded philosophical claim. It is like an axiom that founds a whole mathematical system, that cannot be proven but must simply be accepted; but it is an axiom that, once accepted, "breaks down and destroys propositionality," as Ueda once said.[14] It is a principle, a *Grundsatz* or founding sentence, that cannot be traced back any further—precisely because this principle disrupts reflection in its midst. Ueda's reading suggests, then, that the founding proposition can function only by "unfounding" itself, as it were. It cannot refer to any thesis more basic, but it must give rise to (all) other theses. If it cannot rest upon any other thesis, it cannot found itself or corroborate itself by referring to the referent of any other sentence. Nishida's particular *Grundsatz* refers *prima facie* to "all things" in terms of "pure experi-

---

consciousness or will that gives rise to both self and other. Nishida wrestled with Fichte's philosophy in works that followed *An Inquiry*, such as *Intuition and Reflection in Self-Consciousness*, and continued (with many discontinuities) the idea of a unitary source in developing his signature philosophy of place, the dialectical universal, and the world of historical reality. For example, his notion of "contradictory self-identity" suggests a unity that preserves difference rather than sublating it in, say, a synthesis of thesis and antithesis. For Nishida's own outline, see the third preface in NISHIDA 1990, xxxi–iii; for a précis of this development, see MARALDO 2019B.

14. In his presentation to the Seminar on Process Thought and Nishida Philosophy, American Academy of Religion, New Orleans, November 18, 1990.

ence," but its tacit referent is: nothingness. It has no referent. Yet it is (or becomes) meaningful somehow; it gains its meaning from the whole (the text) that unfolds from it. Reading Nishida through Ueda, it appears that the phenomenon of language emerges as the articulation or (dis)jointing of pure experience, which refers to nothing outside itself.[15] It is in this sense that language is "nothing other than" pure experience. It would be a further task to examine whether any philosophical first principle functions in like manner.

The task for the present discussion, however, is to suggest how pure experience is a unity that founds what appears other to it, including propositional language. So far, we have shown principally how it confounds language. Nishida writes that the sentence "the horse is running" is based upon the immediate experience of [perceiving] a running horse.[16] He suggests that all judgments like this unfold out of pure experience. What about propositions of a more general sort, such as "pure experience is the sole reality"? Is there any pure experience that gives rise to this *Grundsatz*? I do not think we could identify any. Pure experience could be said to give rise to this general principle only in retrospect and only by way of a negation, a reversal, of any further thesis-making or judgment. It seems more cogent, therefore, to reverse the order and say that the principle evokes the state of pure experience, by bringing us to the limits of the sayable. But it would not give rise to the fact of pure experience unless it then broke through these limits. Before we move on to the possibility of language that overcomes these limits, however, some retrospection is called for.

Two factors appear to constrain the foregoing interpretation of language as a fully sketched configuration of alterity. To be sure, the generation of language, meaning, and articulation out of pure experi-

---

15. The connection with *nothingness* is my own proposal in light of Ueda's and Nishida's developed philosophy. Unlike Nishida's later philosophy, in *An Inquiry* the term *nothingness* rarely occurs, where it has a privative meaning and designates a stop to consciousness (NISHIDA, 1990, 46) or a lack of qualities (46, 55, 165).

16. Ibid., 1990, 11.

ence is a creation of significant differences. Signitive language, language that exists in the form of signs, inherently depends on otherness, for a sign is something that signifies something other than the sign itself. But alterity, we may recall, is not simply differentiation; it is the difference that being-other makes. For one thing, the developing difference between (pure) experience and language, as discussed so far, has proceeded on a level so abstract that differences among individuals and groups of individuals seem discounted. In *An Inquiry*, Nishida writes that (pure, unitary) experience underlies and precedes individual being; as it undergoes development, it is what gives rise to individuals as subjects of experience, rather than the other way around.[17] Language as the common ground of a group of individuals, or as a factor in the construction of self-identity, is neglected. Languages as the differentiating factor between groups of people seems likewise discounted. Nishida's articulation of pure experience, and Ueda's reflection on it, do not reach the alterity of language differentiation on a social level. Then again, within the development of Nishida's later philosophy, the explicit notion of pure experience is left behind and the creative agency implicit in it eventually shifts to the entire world. Nishida describes this world as a font of "expressivity" (表現性). He writes of human learning by interacting with things (and with others) as a manifestation of the world's "expressive activity."[18] Human language counts as a development of this expressivity, although it supersedes the phenomenon of language and includes the arising of individual beings as well as the creating of meaning.[19] Inherent in the world's expressivity is

---

17. More exactly, the Preface states "it is not that there is an individual person who then has experiences, but that there is experience and then there are individuals." NKZ 1: 4; see also NISHIDA 1990, xxx and 16, 19, 28, 50.

18. The three volumes of 『哲学的論文集』 [*Philosophical Essays*], composed from 1935 to 1943, develop the concepts of expressive activity and learning-by-way-of-acting (行為的直観, enactive intuition). William Haver translates three of these essays in NISHIDA 2012.

19. If Nishida's term 表現, translated as *expression*, seems out of place, note that 表現型 translates the biological concept of the *phenotype* as the way a genetically inherited general trait gets expressed or embodied differently because of interactions with the environment.

10. Alternative Configurations of Alterity | 247

the plurality of expressive forms and expressive individuals that might plausibly account for an alterity of social language difference. (That is a topic for another occasion.)

For now, we may note that Nishida himself develops his conception of language beyond the implicit treatment we find in *An Inquiry*, but Ueda does not reflect here on the notion of expressivity in later Nishida.[20] Instead he reconsiders the possibility of specific expressions that might be said to break through the limits of the sayable and thereby to evoke the sublinguistic roots of language. The question will be whether such expressions sufficiently express otherness.

LANGUAGE AS THE OTHERING OF SILENCE

Whether and how this breakthrough occurs becomes clearer if we shift from propositional language to poetic expression. So far, our discussion has focused on the emergence of propositional language. In attempting to make sense of Nishida's propositions, I attempted a reading that returns them to their experiential ground by undermining them. Ueda, on the other hand, frequently evokes the more basic level by recalling the language of the poem that Rainer Maria Rilke chose as the epitaph for his gravestone:

| Rose, oh reiner Widerspruch, Lust, niemandes Schlaf zu sein unter soviel Lidern. | Rose, oh pure contradiction, yearning to be no one's sleep under so many eyelids. |

The related idea that language is a form of expression of reality is found in writings of several medieval Japanese Buddhist teachers such as Dōgen, Shinran, and Nichiren; see MARALDO 2019C, 58–9.

20. Ueda's reflections here also omit reference to Nishida's 1932 essay "I and Thou" that directly treats the problem of alterity. For a detailed elucidation of Nishida's essay, see DAVIS 2011B.

Interpreters have noted that rose petals symbolize eyelids (or vice versa), that sleep alludes to death, life's Other, or that "no one's sleep" may suggest loss of self, that *Lust* can mean both desire and delight, that *Lider* (eyelids) is homophonous with *Lieder* (songs or poems), and that "*reiner Widerspruch*/pure contradiction" is itself a puzzling apposition. Rather than elaborating on its symbolic meanings, however, Ueda focuses directly on the exclamation "oh."[21] This "oh" is not a word that refers to any object, nor does it really signify anything, not even the pure presence of things as they are. Rather, it evokes an experience, calls the experience forth into language, and then itself fades into the background, hardly noticed among the descriptive phrases of the verse. When uttered, the "oh" takes away words, then gives them back, robbing one, as it were, of one's being a rational, linguistic being... and then giving one back to the world. Fully exclaimed, it takes one's breath away, leaving an empty space ready to be filled again. As pure experience, this "oh" is a rose bud that blossoms into a perceiving subject, an "I," and an object perceived, a rose. The "oh" articulates the experience that comes to be expressed in the entire epitaph of Rilke.

Apparent are parallels with Ueda's elucidation of the movement in Nishida from pure experience to discriminatory thought and judgment, meaning and propositional language. There, reading Nishida, Ueda suggested that language does not function as the autonomous Other of a pure experience that remains ineffable. Nor is all experience infused with language from the very beginning, as some hermeneutical philosophers and current empiricists maintain. Rather, pure experience expresses itself in and as a proto-word that occasions articulation—into subject experiencing and object experienced, and into words differentiated from other words and from the things they designate. Here, interpreting Rilke's poem, Ueda writes of the articulation of the "oh" as the self-unfolding of pure experience. It opens a chasm between what has been articulated and what has not. Hence it

21. See UEDA S. 1982A, 30–34; 2001, 4: 186–95.

10. Alternative Configurations of Alterity | 249

is appropriate that Rilke follows the "oh" with "pure contradiction," a *Widerspruch* or warning "against saying" anything that would pretend to capture the experience, the rose, which is not so much an object experienced by someone as an emotion motivating the "sleep of no one." An elaborated translation of the first line might read, "Rose, oh how you speak silently against us" when you move us toward eternal sleep. "Oh" is the proto-word, the exclamation that takes away words then gives them back again, the eruption out of silence, which founds and evokes language.

Silence is the tacit but unmistakable referent of Rilke's "oh" for Ueda. In fact, Ueda's interpretation of Rilke's poem usually appears in essays that thematize the roles of silence and language in Zen Buddhism.[22] Ueda makes the case that Zen awakening is a language event, dynamic and twofold. From the standpoint of our everyday preoccupied lives, it is a movement out of language into silence, and then, refreshed, back into language. Like the metaphor of awakening, it suggests a movement from one state or condition to another (and back again). Ueda's interpretation of the bidirectional movement between silence and language in the context of Zen has been amply elucidated and critiqued elsewhere.[23]

But Ueda does not confine his interpretation to Zen experience. Playing on Heidegger's use of *Ereignis* as appropriating event, Ueda speaks of the *Worterignis* or "word-event" that names the coming about or coming into its own (*er-eignen*) of language. His interpretation is meant to elucidate the place of language (and silence) in all experience from a Zen perspective. Language, Ueda notes, is two-edged. It not only binds us and inhibits new experiences (leaving us in "the prison house of language," to use Nietzsche's epithet); it can also open a world to us, presencing things for the first time. How then can language fulfill its creative task without turning into a mere cage?

---

22. See, for example, UEDA S. 1995 and 1982B.
23. See, for example, DAVIS 2019B; DAVIS 2022, chapter 20; and MÜLLER 2015.

That is, how can we be released from the danger of language so that language speaks through us creatively, openly, opening the world? Through a movement from language back to language, Ueda suggests. A Zen perspective sharpens the question: is an extreme kind of movement possible, taking us entirely out of the world of language and from that point, creating a world anew, taking us back into language? Ueda answers with a resounding YES. One must break through language to silence, and then this silence must be broken through to become language anew.

Ueda's answer contrasts with the premise of much current continental philosophy and challenges cultural connotations of silence as language's unspeakable Other. Culturally, silence can indicate a lack, a loss of ability, a withdrawal or even alienation. In modern drama, silence portrays "the experience of inadequacy, incompleteness, impermanence," as well as the ineffable and inexplicable.[24] *Out of Silence* is the story of an autistic boy "trapped in silence, struggling to regain language."[25] Voices that "break the silence" reveal what has been oppressed or repressed, shamed or shunned, deliberately hidden because unspeakably horrid. In philosophical reflection, silence often remains a sign of inability. George Steiner writes that philosophical insight can move toward an "ever deepening silence. The highest, purest reach of the contemplative act is that which has learned to leave language behind it. The ineffable lies beyond the frontiers of the word."[26] Heidegger, whose voice we often hear in Ueda's interpretation, mentions silence as a counterpart to logos—more precisely, the sigetic (from *sigan*, Greek for keeping silent) as a counterpart to logic. We need this "telling silence" to consider appropriately the event of being (*das Sein*) in difference to beings presentable by logic.

24. KANE 1984, 2.
25. Book description of MARTIN 1994.
26. STEINER 1967, 12.

One interpreter reads Heidegger's silence as an inability: "At the heart of [Heidegger's] language there is silence. This is not a refusal to say something that could be said but an *inability* of which he is keenly aware.... [The] theme—be-ing itself—is intrinsically mysterious...."[27] Yet, as another interpreter has pointed out, for Heidegger silence also functions as enablement. We need silence to make us aware and to articulate how language unfolds; silence "attunes us to the concealed dimension of be-ing," and thus enables the disclosure of be-ing via language. Language is needed to preserve silence and yet ordinarily covers it over. Silence is needed and yet is generally betrayed by the spoken.[28]

Ueda goes still deeper into silence. First, in contrast to many cultural connotations, silence names much more than a lull between words or an absence behind them. It is the realm utterly without words and concepts, but as such it is a liberating possibility for humans bound by language. Silence enables and initiates appropriate language. This much is intimated by Heidegger, but Ueda goes beyond a mere appreciation of silence as both depending on and originating language. Silence is an actual practice and not only a preserve; our linguistic creativity blossoms when we return to the practice of silence. Heidegger famously wrote that we live in language as the "house of be-ing." Ueda proclaims that we must exit this "house" and only then return to it, that is, let it re-create revelatory language. Rilke's poem, emerging from the silence that inspires the proto-word "oh," is a paradigm of this movement.

What may we gather from these reflections on pure experience and on silence as altered Others to language? The sign of pure experience for Ueda is not that it is unmediated, unconditioned by language, history, culture, and so forth, but that it is unitary. In it, subject and object are undifferentiated; silence and language are nondual. All experience, including the experience of thinking, and all language, includ-

27. POLT 2013, 128–9.
28. DAVIS 2016B, 146–7; DAVIS 2020, 173–4.

ing propositions and textual explanations, are (for Ueda) founded in the proto-word of "pure experience" which presents itself to thought as an abyss. Accordingly, if we take pure experience as the abyssal foundation of all else, would we not re-duce/lead back both self and other to this unitary source, this abrupt chasm or *Abgrund*? Ueda perhaps intends his mention of a chasm to recall the "absolute nothingness" that re-places unitary pure experience in Nishida's later philosophy and will reconfigure the place of self and other.[29] But in Nishida's first work and Ueda's elucidation of it, individuals and difference are not primary; they unfold out of a single source. Here Ueda's model of the proto-word and Nishida's text of pure experience prioritize unity and render difference derivative. This model undermines a place for absolute or ultimate difference.

Ueda's interpretation of Rilke's poem re-presents the movement from wholeness to difference as a movement from silence to language. This, too, would seem to prioritize unity, but then Ueda emphasizes that the movement is bidirectional, from language to silence and back again, renewed. The interplay of silence and language betokens a twofold experience in which the two inspire one another. Ueda's interplay of silent wholeness without difference and differentiation by way of language clearly contrasts with the findings of current linguistics. In linguistic studies of language, difference functions as the sole root of language, as it were. Structural semiotics shows how language exists only when there is difference among words and difference between the word and the thing, the sign and the signified. Pragmatics adds that language as a social phenomenon further requires a plurality of speakers, a difference among users of language. But Ueda's paradigm and linguistic models may also be complementary rather than absolutely

---

29. In some essays, Ueda speaks of the *Abgrund*, the abyss, in others, of the *Un-grund* underlying grounds or reasons (see, for example UEDA S. 1989, 3; UEDA S. 2011, 40). In still other essays, he writes of the *Kluft* or chasm that opens after language is evoked and articulated in a proto-word like "oh" that expresses unity. See, for example, UEDA S. 2011, 32.

different. Ueda's model broadens linguistic perspectives by incorporating the experience of silence as language's nutritive other. Linguistic analysis, pragmatics in particular, recalls the necessity of difference-in-action. In the practice of speaking, that difference manifests in the form we call dialogue. So far, our presentation of Ueda's interpretations has remained silent about dialogue. To catch sight of the movement from silence to dialogue, we turn now to the third model in our inquiry.

The Other as emerging through the selflessness of the self

Ueda's writings frequently make use of Zen encounter dialogues, and some essays thematize the dialogue form as exemplary of the creative potential of language. Dialogue has the potential to transform its interlocutors, free them of self-centeredness, and manifest the selfless self.[30] To illustrate the creative power of dialogue, Ueda frequently comments on the famed Oxherding Pictures, which other interpreters more often see as illustrating stages on the path to self-enlightenment. Ueda's interpretation contextualizes this popular Zen parable differently. His reading reveals the pictures as an extreme example of the philosophy of "neither the same nor different." Implicitly, he places the pictures among the texts and practices that advocate the negation of self. Rather than allowing a straightforward recognition of the Other, his reading advocates the nonduality of self and other. This seems simply to undermine ultimate difference, as did the models of unitary pure experience and silence. And yet, this time, difference precedes and supersedes unity.

[30]. See UEDA S. 2011, 19 and 1982A, 20. We find an interpretation of the dialogue form in general in, for example, in 「対話と禅問答」 [Dialogue and Zen mondō] in UEDA 2001, 261–319. For more on Ueda's philosophy of dialogue, see DAVIS 2022B.

254 | Self and Others and In-Between

Recently some Western language books have used the Oxherding Pictures to portray the Mahāyāna path in general.³¹ Traditionally, however, the pictures are found in literature associated with Zen and function in effect to define the distinctness of Zen in difference from other schools of Buddhism. Of several extant versions of the Oxherding Pictures, the series of ten images attributed to the twelfth-century Zen master Kuoan Shiyuan (J. Kakuan Shion) have been the predominant version in Japan since the Muromachi Period (1336 to 1573) and probably the most published version in Europe and North America.³² We may focus principally on this version as it is illustrated by the paintings by the fifteenth-century artist Tenshō Shūbun that are housed in Shōkokuji, a Rinzai Zen temple in Kyoto. The pictures are accompanied by verses, but we may bypass these to catch sight of Ueda's reading of alterity into what is depicted.³³

1. Looking for the ox   2. Seeing the tracks

31. See, for example, TRAINOR 2001, 79. Not surprisingly, there are now also Christian and comparative versions; see for example, CLASPER (n.d.), and all sorts of contemporary adaptations, such as the garish version by SAVITA 1987. There has also been a mime performance of the pictures by Yoneyama Mamako, performed in Kyoto in 1983.

32. For accounts of the various versions, see SUZUKI (1960, 127–9) and Yanagida Seizan's bibliographical introduction in his co-authored book with Ueda (UEDA AND YANAGIDA 1982, 243-86).

33. See DAVIS 2022A, 320–38, for an explication of the Pictures in general, and on Ueda's interpretation, see DÖLL 2020, 493–6.

3. Seeing the ox

4. Catching the ox

5. Taming the ox

6. Returning home riding the ox

7. Ox forgotten, person stays

8. Person and ox both forgotten

9. Back to the origin, returning to the source

10. Entering the market with open hands

Let us first briefly review the sequence of the ten pictures with their standard labels. Picture 1, "looking for the ox," depicts a person alone with a searching gaze. Next he is "seeing the tracks"; then, "seeing the ox," he runs after it as it disappears behind brush and cliffs. Fourth, he "catches the ox," tying a tether around it, then "herds (or tames) the ox," leading it on the tether, and "returns home riding the ox." In the seventh picture, "the ox is forgotten, the person stays," gazing at the full moon. The eighth picture, of nothing but an empty circle, depicts "person and ox both forgotten." To pause a moment at this picture, we may note that it both evokes the wholesome silence described earlier and widens one's vision from a focus on the moon to the whole world. Some versions of the Oxherding Pictures actually ended with an empty circle, but Kuoan's version includes two more scenes: "back to the origin, returning to the source," in which we see a scene of a tree in blossom beside a stream, and finally "entering the market with open hands," where we see a young traveler meeting an older, rotund figure (sometimes identified as the legendary monk or "Laughing Buddha" Budai (J. Hotei).

In most widespread interpretations in contemporary literature, the Oxherding Pictures depict the journey of one roused to the aspiration for enlightenment. The ox symbolizes one's own heart-mind or other equivalent names for the "true self": original nature, true nature, buddha-nature, original face, or no-mind. Implicit in the standard interpretation is the expectation that we, the readers, put ourselves in the place of the oxherd. The oxherd represents the self who begins as deluded and ends as a bodhisattva, enlightened and back in the world. Embarking upon the path, one—any one of us—searches for the true self, taking it to be outside, an object apart. First one sights the tracks or traces of one's true self; then one finds it, catches and disciplines it, and comes home, ultimately realizing that it is not different from oneself, not a separate identity, not objectifiable, not identifiable at all, and certainly not visible from the outside. The realized self has forgotten its search and eventually forgets itself—dissolved in an empty circle, followed by a selfless world appearing just as it is. Finally, the new self, without separation and self-assertion, unobtrusively enters the world of society with helping hands.

We are likely to gather something different from the pictures when they are viewed not so much as a parable of self-awakening but rather as a slant on alterity. After all, the very starting point of the pictures, in the standard interpretation, is that the oxherd is none other than any one of us. The pictures work insofar as we identify with the oxherd, which initially means not identifying with the ox, who is other. This other is no stranger, however, but is intimately known by the oxherd, who is what he is only by virtue of his relationship with the ox. The unruly ox eventually comes under his control. Their relationship dissolves when the ox is completely re-appropriated; the Other has disappeared from the picture. And when the oxherd too disappears, with the dissolution of self in the empty circle, any remnant of a relationship between us and the oxherd also dissolves, for we no longer function as disparate viewers.

These two stages (pictures 7 and 8)—first the dissolution of other into self and then the dissolution of self—seem to epitomize exactly what champions of alterity most sharply criticize. That is, the other is taken as a version of the self, is reduced to self or to the terms in which the self constructs its other. This objection holds both for the ox appropriated by the oxherd and for us; we can no longer act as others, as viewers, when in the empty circle there is nothing left to see. This erasure of the Other is not altered if we reverse the roles that the ox and oxherd play in the standard interpretation.[34] We could just as easily see the oxherd, rather than the ox, as the true self. In some ways this reversal makes more sense: it is the activity of the true self that seeks to recover the lost, deluded self that has gone astray, thinking it is other,

---

34. Bae Yong-kyun's 1989 film *Why Has Bodhi-Dharma Left for the East?* similarly reverses the roles: the oxherding boy is lost when the ox finds him and leads him out of the forest to his home temple. At the end, the boy, able now to take care of himself, is leading the ox.

and that needs to be tamed or disciplined. Either reading leads to the disappearance first of any other and then of any self who could construct its others. The ninth picture, of a flowering tree on the bank of a stream, reconfirms a world without othering or selfing.

At this point, the Oxherding Pictures seem to leave no ground for alterity. Buddhist readers might well object that the pictures were never intended to depict alterity, much less irreducible difference. Rather, they are a story of the realization of the true self, a realization that self and other are "not one and not two." In this absence of ultimate difference, it is irrelevant whether relationships based on the premise of irreducible difference are erased. The only point Buddhists and alterists seem to have in common is the conviction that self-partiality is a root of the problem.[35] In fact, Buddhists might argue, the conviction that self and other are "not one and not two" better promotes the very kind of equality that alterists desire. This is not "the 'conceit' of equality between real selves" but rather true impartiality. As an ideal, it has a long history in Buddhism and harks back to the impartiality of "neither the same nor different," an impartiality achieved only by not making the distinction "this is another being." Steven Collins, in his analysis of these crucial phrases in early Buddhism, notes that they give self and other the same epistemological and soteriological status.[36]

Yet the Oxherding Pictures seem to go beyond the practice, mentioned by Collins, of "breaking down the barrier" between self and others and seeing the equality of all beings to oneself. Both others and self are ultimately dissolved in the empty circle, and if this picture is meant

---

35. APP (n.d.) cites the diagnosis of the Japanese Zen master Bankei: "Your self-partiality is at the root of all our illusions. There aren't any illusions when you don't have this preference for yourself."

36. COLLINS 1982, 190-91. Although the phrase "neither the same nor different" conventionally describes the relationship between the one who acts and the one who is reborn to experience the consequences, the implication is that one's past and future selves are no closer than contemporaneous other selves (see 180 and 190). I take this Theravadin position, which Collins places in opposition to the Personalists or Puggalavadins, to be definitive for Mahāyāna thought as well, and thus applicable to the Oxherding Pictures.

to recall ultimate as opposed to conventional truth, then it seems all the more to undermine any place alterity could stand. Perhaps the last picture reintroduces the reality of otherness—at least in Zide's version of 6 pictures and Kuoan's version of 10 that do not end with the empty circle (as do Jingju's version of 5 and Puming's of 10).[37]

Ueda in fact interprets Kuoan's final picture as the real emergence of self and other. The artist Shūbun's depiction of picture 10 shows one person, staff and gourd in hand, facing another person who looks much like a very rotund Budai. Ueda sees the two figures as greeting each other in dialogue and, through this communicative act, mutually giving rise to one another. In Ueda's interpretation, both the self and the Other are born out of the experience of self-negation, out of the practice of selflessness. "Split open by absolute nothingness the self spreads out and unfolds itself selflessly into the *between* where the Other in its otherness belongs to the selflessness of the self."[38] The inference usually drawn from this kind of description is simply that, to be oneself, one's true self, one must become selfless. Taken alone that would miss Ueda's implication: to allow another to be fully other, to be himself or herself, one becomes selfless. The other appears through the selflessness of the self. Self and other appear, as in the dialogue imagined in the picture, in a reciprocal relationship of selflessness and autonomy (*Selbstlosigkeit* and *Selbständigkeit*, Ueda writes in German). One recognizes "selflessly *one's other self* in the encounter with *an other.*"[39] In this sense, self and other are neither two nor one.

How does this picture of nonduality fare as an alternative to the positions regarding alterity sketched at the beginning of this inquiry? Insofar as he depicts the self as a relationship, Ueda resonates with some

---

37. For an overview of various versions, see the "Oxherding Pictures Index" on the Terebess Asia Online web site < https://terebess.hu/english/oxindex.html>.

38. UEDA S. 1982A, 34.

39. UEDA S. 1989, 2, my emphasis. Ueda develops this interpretation further in UEDA AND YANAGIDA 1982, 15-153.

contemporary feminist perspectives.[40] Perhaps in difference to them, however, his view of the self is even more de-substantialized. Certainly, he negates irreducible difference, but then such difference is usually not asserted for its own sake. It is meant principally to assure that the Other is not taken as a version of the self, that others are empowered to speak in their own voices—and that there remains someone to whom they can speak. Paul Ricoeur focused on this dialectical and dialogical structure in writing the book *Oneself as Another*, a statement that selfhood requires difference, even if not ultimate and irreducible. To be a self, he writes, is possible only in relationship to others. "The selfhood of oneself implies otherness to such an intimate degree that one cannot be thought of without the Other, that instead one passes into the Other, as we might say in Hegelian terms... [being] oneself inasmuch as being other."[41] The Oxherding Pictures in Ueda's view go so far as to suggest that, in authentic conversation with others, the self passes through silent oblivion; the position of self goes through dissolution. In Ueda's terms, we might then speak of a circling of self and other. Recalling Irigaray's "this sex which is not one," we might speak of this self which is not one, not a fixed entity. With Ueda's reading as a starting point, theorists of alterity would have much to reconsider.[42]

---

40. McCarthy (2010), in developing an ethics of nondual self in relationship, brings contemporary feminist thinkers such as Irigaray into dialogue with Japanese philosophers.

41. Ricoeur 1992, 2–3. The title of the Japanese translation is resonant with Buddhist connotations: 他者としての自我 (Ego-Self as the Other). Ricoeur takes pains to distinguish between the sense of self defined in terms of an unchanging core of the person—what he calls *idem* identity or the sameness preserved when we make comparisons—and self defined in terms of selfhood, or *ipse* identity.

42. We find a remarkable parallel to Ueda in Minh-ha (1989, 76), who writes:

> The other is never to be known unless one arrives at a *suspension* of language, where the reign of codes yields to a state of constant non-knowledge, always understanding that in Buddha's country... one arrives without having taken a single step; unless one realizes what in Zen is called the Mind Seal or the continuous reality of awakening... a process of constantly unsettling the identity of meaning and speaking/writing subject, a process never allowing I to fare without non-I.

To identify or to deconstruct the contested Other, they would need to take into account much more thoroughly how *self* is construed, how selves are constructed. They might look much more closely at philosophies of self that are latent in the discourse regarding the Other or others. The Oxherding Pictures might be especially relevant to such reappraisal because the figure of the Other appears quite obviously in the pictures, in contrast to much Buddhist discourse about the self.[43]

There is a problem with Ueda's view, however. As obvious as the two figures are in Shūbun's final Oxherding Picture, Ueda has imagined a conversation occurring between them. It is certainly not far-fetched to picture a conversation, but neither the title nor Kuoan's verse indicate any exchange of words. In fact, aside from the implicit reference to the "marketplace" in the title of picture 10, the verses attached to Kuoan's pictures do not even allude to the presence of another person.[44] In one crucial respect, Ueda's imagined dialogue in the tenth picture is no different from the classical philosophical dialogues of Hume, Berkeley, and Plato: there is but a single author behind a depicted plurality of voices. Typical philosophical dialogues as an author's invention of a conversation differ from a dialogue with a live partner who can surprise one and even undermine one's entire manner of engagement. Ueda's dialogical reading of this text seems to flow into a dialogue within oneself. Are there better examples of a kind of dialogue where selves and others emerge through self-negation? Ueda also uses

---

43. For another way to recognize alterity from a Buddhist perspective see the insightful book, KLEIN 1995, especially the chapter "Gain or Drain? Compassion and the Self-Other Boundary."

44. The only "other" that the verses explicitly present is the figure of the ox, which is a manifestation of the self. In the translation of Victor Sōgen Hori, the verse to the twelfth picture reads: "With bare chest and unshod feet, he walks into the market, daubed with dirt and smeared with ashes, laughter fills his face. Without using mystic arts or divine powers he makes withered trees at once burst into flower." In that site, in stark contrast to Ueda, the contemporary Zen master Harada Shōdō reads the last picture as relating the Zen teaching "to know how to be truly alone, how to be one with one's solitude in a full way."

traditional Zen encounter dialogues to illustrate the interplay between self and other, but critical historians have demonstrated that these dialogues are more likely legendary constructions or reconstructions than actual exchanges between historical people. What is more, such examples can tend to become dialogues within oneself when they serve as cases for an individual to understand.[45] The non-dual alternative to alterity then faces the same old problem of letting others speak for themselves.

Interplay and Interlude in *Renku* as Moments of Creative Alterity

Genuine dialogue must reflect and respect difference. Unlike Rilke's monological poem, or conversations that are merely imagined, according to prevalent models of alterity authentic dialogue should cultivate difference by preserving a polyvocal space between speakers. The poetic form of *renku or* linked verse, in Ueda's reading, not only opens such a space but intimates how it helps create a world in common. Japanese *renku* is the source of the better-known *haiku*, which was originally taken from the opening verse (*hokku*) of a series of thirty-six (more or less) verses.[46]

In *renku* several poets take turns composing verses, one at a time. The first three verses of the poem "At Imashinmei Shrine" exemplify this style:

---

45. One text that uses Zen *mondō* to exemplify an event of the free exchange of self and other is UEDA S. 1989, 35–6. DAVIS (2022A, 121-2) explains how Ueda's examples of Zen dialogues call on each interlocuter to be other-centered rather than self-centered. Deserving further attention is the power of live dialogue to challenge self and other that is evident in the Rinzai Zen practice of *sanzen* or interviews with a teacher. MARALDO (2021) examines the limits of critical studies of encounter dialogues and historical construction in Zen in general.

46. *Renku* (連句) are also called *renga* (連歌): *ku* (句) suggests the line or verse; *ga* (歌) refers to the entire poem. The Buddhist background of *renku* poetry is explored by EBERSOLE 1983.

Resenting the early summer rains,
Smoke rises in faint trails
From the brine-boiler's hut on the coast.

Dimly, far away,
The pine has faded into dusk.

When was it that I waited
By myself 'til morning,
In the vain hope you would come?[47]

Notice that while each verse stands on its own, themes and scenes (and sometimes seasons, too) change from one verse to the next, and yet a play of the imagination easily establishes a link or connective theme between any two verses. With the first two verses, for example, I may picture myself as an observer who shifts his view from smoke rising from a solitary cabin on the seacoast to an inland forest seen in declining light. Between the second and third verses, I might imagine another temporal shift and vaguely recall a time when I waited alone, pining after someone who never came. Ueda notes that in writing *renku* each of the three or four poets is in turn challenged (1) to listen to the verses composed up to then, (2) to find a link between the two immediately preceding verses, and (3) to write an autonomous verse that creates a new world between it and the verse before it. It is as if one poet challenges the next in line: "Can you reinterpret my verse so that you can escape my world and disclose a new world of your own? If you are not able to do so, you will remain only a part of my world; you will not be yourself." "On the other hand," Ueda writes,

> this means that the [challenging] poet quite selflessly places his verse at the disposal of the [next] poet, allowing her any interpretation she would give it.... He is prepared to accept any interpretation, even the

---

47. Different from the *renga* chosen by Ueda, I choose an example translated by BARNILL 2010, 2. See HARE 1979 for the history of the linked verses at Imashinmei Shrine, which the poet Sōgi compiled from previous *renga* masters in 1476.

most surprising, in the hope that in an unfamiliar reading he will discover himself anew.

In this way, "both correspondence and autonomous creation are essential" in composing linked verse.[48]

There is, moreover, a moment in the movement of *renku* that so far has gone unnoticed. It seems to me that, in the course of this poetic exchange, we can hear an unspoken moment that recalls Ueda's model of the alterity of silence. The link/gap that connects/separates verses that could stand on their own is unvoiced and unwritten, yet perceived by practiced poets who each take their turn; it is an utterly silent link/gap. And each poet's release of their words to the discretion of others emerges, I suggest, from an interlude of interior silence that frees one to allow alteration and creation by others. The silent interludes between speakers and within each of them are as essential to the composition of linked verse, and to the model of alterity it provides, as are reinterpretation and release.

Renku models the language of alterity better than do the propositions ensuing from pure experience, the epitaph of Rilke that voices a silence, or the imagined dialogue in an Oxherding picture. The point of departure from a unitary foundation, or from a solitary silence or individual awakening that empties difference, gives way here to an interplay of difference from the start. In Ueda's reading, *renku* arises from an authentic interplay between oneself and another that creates an open space for the Other fully to emerge and express herself. Complementing that interplay are the interludes of silence that let one discover oneself anew. Arising as it does from interplay and interlude, this poetic form also serves as an aesthetic model for the creative potential of language. Echoing in part the philosophy of Hans-Georg Gadamer, Ueda presents dialogical language as a power that discloses a world in common. Re-composing this philosophy, Ueda stresses

---

48. UEDA S. 1989, 29–30.

that to speak means to listen to the voices of others, to voice words we have learned and learn to express as our own. I hear in his voice the imperative that one must then listen anew—listen out of an interlude of internal silence that lets one truly hear the Other. The obligation to be openly receptive to the voice of others already meets the normative demand of allowing otherness to make a difference, as standard models of alterity enjoin. But Ueda's interpretation adds a link that suggests an alternative model. As in the practice of *renku*, we are not only to be receptive to what others say and to respond sincerely, but also to be willing to let go of a grip on what we say and allow others the freedom to recompose it. I may stand by what I say while releasing it from its standing as the "last word." And released moments of silence then open a space to realign selves and others. The receptivity and release enabled by silence are what empowers language to create a world in common.[49] And the unvoiced links in the linked verse of *renku* serve as a model for understanding how discrete beings help create such a world.

49. For an elaboration of Gadamer's and Ueda's approaches to language via a longer poem by Rilke, see MARALDO 2019, 6–13.

11
History from a Buddhist Perspective
Nishitani's Account and Accountability

> So long as history does not radically mean that something absolutely new is being created at each moment in time, it is deprived of its true meaning.[1]

THE PROBLEM

In an age of international scholarship exploring the history of Buddhism, indeed in the entire span of that history, Nishitani Keiji stands as one of the very few thinkers who have offered a Buddhist philosophy of history.[2] His project, to throw light on Western, particularly Christian-influenced conceptions of history and to present an alternative from a Buddhist perspective, commands close attention. His alternative also presents challenges to the most basic assumptions of modern secular historians who have long abandoned the Christian and Enlightenment conceptions of history. Even the array of postmodernist notions of history that Nishitani did not anticipate will be called into question by his proposal. This chapter presents my own struggle to come to terms with Nishitani's Buddhist conception of history, with a particular question in mind: the possibility of experiencing the world as a sequence of events and of rendering judgments about those events.

---

1. My paraphrase of a statement in NKC 10: 238. See NISHITANI 1961, trans. 1982, 212, for a more literal translation.

2. MARALDO 2021, 13–22, sketches the various meanings of history for Buddhist traditions.

We may begin by paraphrasing a point that Nishitani made as early as 1954, in essays that would later become chapters in his book *Shūkyō to wa nanika*, translated as *Religion and Nothingness*. Writing about the fulfillment of time in history, Nishitani states that historicity is able to realize itself radically only on the standpoint of emptiness (*śūnyatā*), the standpoint of the bottomlessness of each moment. Each individual moment of unending time possesses the very same solemnity that is thought in Christianity to be possessed by the special moments of the creation, fall, redemption, and second coming. "In bottomlessly embracing the endless past and endless future, we bring time to the fullness of time at each and every moment of time."[3] Whether one believes in the events of Christian salvation history or not, Nishitani's point here undermines the most basic assumptions concerning the experience of an historical world—assumptions about temporal sequence and the relative importance of different events. Does the equivalence of moments proposed by Nishitani allow for any discrimination of value? Can such equivalence account for the experience of temporal events? What do equivalence, and the emptiness underlying it, have to do with history? These are the primary questions that this chapter will engage.

Our first task is to clarify the way that Nishitani connects history with the Buddhist conception of emptiness. In particular, we will need to reconstruct Nishitani's argument that historicity is able to realize itself radically only on the standpoint of emptiness. Nishitani's reasoning is rarely explicit, and the nearly incessant excursions into various topics make the connections less than obvious. Our exposition will require several steps to clarify the primary question he poses and its answer. That question appears to be a more generalized version of the question regarding the possibility of value judgments. In effect, Nishitani asks: what is the contemporary crisis of religion and culture

---

3. Points made in NKC 10: 238, 299–300; NISHITANI 1961, trans. 1982, 217, 272. The quotation is from p. 181.

and how might Buddhist conceptions resolve the crisis? The first step, then, will be to define the crisis or problem and describe its nature. That will involve some explanation of the problem as an historical phenomenon. Then we will need to show how emptiness might resolve the problem. These steps will require a connection between the conceptions of emptiness, time, and history. We will give the explanation in Nishitani's own terms, rather than subject the terms themselves to a critique. In many cases we will need to make connections and supply reasoning that are at best implicit in Nishitani's writing. After we have reconstructed Nishitani's problem and solution, we will be in a position to examine my questions more directly. This part will offer a critique and will review some related critical treatments of Nishitani's work. The critique in this chapter attempts not only to point out a shortcoming in Nishitani's account of historicity, but also to identify the basic conditions that I think are necessary for historical consciousness to emerge. It is only on the supposition of these conditions that Nishitani's account appears to be deficient; but in fact it was my struggle with his account that helped me better identify them as essential to historicity. Thus, my statement of the elements of historical consciousness comes at the conclusion of my essay and thanks to Nishitani's penetrating thought. Finally, my critique is meant to leave open some crucial questions for further exploration.[4]

---

4. The remaining questions should be explored not only in general investigations of Buddhist conceptions of history, but especially in Nishitani's essays written after the publication of *Shūkyō to wa nanika* in 1961. The articles by HASE 1997 and by VAN BRAGT 1998 provide hints at Nishitani's later thought, although their aim is not directly to examine the question of history. Whatever new developments there are in his later essays, Nishitani did not alter the fundamental standpoint in *Shūkyō to wa nanika* when he assisted with and added to its English and German translations as late as 1980.

NISHITANI'S ACCOUNT OF HISTORY, RECONSTRUCTED

What has emptiness (*śūnyatā*) to do with history? As every student of Buddhism knows, emptiness pertains to the nature of things: there is no inherent, lasting nature in anything. Many Buddhist schools regard the personal realization of this insight as part, if not the whole, of a liberation that today counts as religious, as opposed to social or political. It may come as a surprise, then, to hear that the notion of emptiness has something to do with conceptions of history, other than that *śūnyatā* is an "idea" or result of analysis that occurred in the history of Buddhism.

Nishitani's project is not so much to explicate the Buddhist philosophy of emptiness, as to address "the problem of religion and science."[5] In his view, this is the most fundamental problem facing us today, and requires for its solution an appropriation of the notion of emptiness. The problem itself is both an historical one, resulting from particular developments in the course of world history, and a personal one, resulting from a crisis in the individual. The name for this problem is "nihilism," which is also the theme of a previous series of lectures resulting in a book Nishitani published in 1949.[6]

Nishitani's thought on the topic was obviously influenced by Nietzsche and Heidegger.[7] Like these philosophers, Nishitani sees

---

5. NISHITANI 1961, trans. 1982, 46. Paul Swanson shows that Nishitani's interpretation of emptiness or absolute nothingness is orthodox Buddhism in its avoidance of the extremes of nihility and substantial being. Like Zhiyi's threefold truth, *Religion and Nothingness* offers a middle way. The recognition of the "middle," according to SWANSON (1996, 107), "allows for the positive manifestation and even affirmation of the conventional, for the actual living out of compassion." This recognition would seem to provide a "metaphysical" or better, meta-ontological basis for the import of history, which after all has to do with the course of living in the conventional world. As we shall see, however, Nishitani's account exceeds a basis for living in the conventional world.

6. NKC 8; NISHITANI 1990.

7. MARALDO (2019, 348–51) differentiates Nishitani's equivalence from Nietzsche's notion of the "suprahistorical," the dimension of "eternally the same meaning" (not to be confused with a transcendent source of history), as Nietzsche presents in his essay, *Vom Nützen und Nachteil der Historie für das Leben*.

nihilism as an event occurring in history. Modernity brought about the loss of meaning and values that give human existence hope, spiritual sustenance, and the promise that human efforts are not ultimately in vain. Such values and meaning, once supported by the notion of something transhistorical or supernatural, were eventually undermined by the scientific worldview that depicts nature as wholly indifferent to human concerns. Ironically it urges, rather than obviates, the personal quest for a meaningful life that even the scientist seeks in the face of his or her own death. Modern science and technology exacerbate rather than alleviate our fundamental need to know our life is not in vain. Nishitani's references reveal that he has predominantly Christianity in mind for religion, and the European (if now globalized) worldview for the scientific one. His previous book on nihilism suggested that modernized Japan fell under the sway of nihilism because of its absorption of Western values and loss of tradition. Hidden behind his earlier treatment of nihilism and the crisis of personal identity and values, then, we can discover the problem of Japanese national self-identity and values. The problem of nihilism, as Nishitani understands it, clearly has its political side, although it encompasses more than his own political crisis or that of his country. Examining the political side will help us determine how both nihilism and its solution are historical.

In the context of Nishitani's career, this problem might appear to be one urged upon him by the ravages of war, after the devastation and defeat of his country. During the war Nishitani participated in dialogues in which he proposed that Japan's mission was to awaken the world to a global, non-Eurocentric standpoint. Whether and to what extent Nishitani failed to recognize just how Japan-centered his vision was, is a question I and others have explored elsewhere.[8] In any case, Nishitani did not appear to be deeply disillusioned with his claim that it is necessary to awaken humankind to an Asian ("Eastern") way of

---

8. See MARALDO 2019, 337–56 and 357–95. See also the discussions by MINAMOTO 1995 and VAN BRAGT 1995, and the critical review of related literature by PARKES 1997.

addressing and solving the most fundamental problem. It is mistaken to see Nishitani as creating an apolitical philosophy of religion after he abandoned political writing.[9] He did eventually abandon explicitly political writing, but his concern with the problem of religion and science both preceded and outlived his explicitly political essays from the late 1930s intermittently to the early 1950s. This concern was evident even in his remarks in July 1942, during the famous discussions on "Overcoming Modernity" (by which was meant "overcoming European modernity"). On that occasion Nishitani introduced a topic alien to most of the participants, and seemingly remote from the problem of the Eurocentric worldview, when he asked:

> What kind of religiosity will it take to give culture, history, ethics and so forth, all of which entail a complete affirmation of the human, the freedom to pursue their own standpoint, while at the same time insuring equal freedom of activity for the sciences, whose standpoint is one of indifference to the human, and then to unify the two standpoints?[10]

Although Nishitani would eventually alter his goal of unifying religion and science, he continued to pursue a solution to the global problem of the disparity between ethics, religion, and science—a problem that for him was deeper and broader than the political task facing Japan. At the time, in 1942, Nishitani thought the answer to the deeper problem might lay in recognizing the nothingness of the subject or "the standpoint of subjective nothingness," a notion later expressed as the "field of emptiness." At that time, he suggested to his Japanese audience that when they respond to the deeper problem through self-negation, both at the individual and the national levels, they begin to meet the political task facing the nation of Japan, the "establishment

---

9. HAVER (1992, 630) for example, mentions a "continuity between Nishitani's wartime writings and his postwar exercises in an apolitical and thereby 'innocent' philosophy of religion."

10. *Kindai no chōkoku* [Overcoming Modernity] (Tokyo: Fuzanbō, 1979), 23; cited in MINAMOTO 1995, 218.

of a new world order," a just and truly global, non-Eurocentric, order.[11] One might wonder if Nishitani contrived this link between the deeper religious problem and the immediate political one, but the point is that for him there is a connection between the religious and the political-historical.

Just as there is a religious undercurrent to his explicitly political thought, there is a political dimension to his philosophy of religion from early on, and even, it will turn out, to his appropriation of the doctrine of emptiness. One example occurs on the last page of *Religion and Nothingness*, where Nishitani writes that "true equality is not simply a matter of an equality of human rights and the ownership of property," which, he says, reflect the "self-centered mode of being human" that lead to discord and strife. Rather, true equality takes place "only on the field of emptiness." Nishitani's lack of elaboration leaves it mostly to the reader to surmise just how emptiness ensures any political sense of equality, and we need not second guess him at this point. Similar statements about freedom are slightly more perspicuous and suggest that liberalism likewise reflects only subjective freedom and the self-centered mode of being, whereas true freedom is "an absolute autonomy on the field of emptiness, where 'there is nothing to rely on'" and where one makes oneself "into a nothingness in the service of all things."[12]

In the context of the modern problem of nihilism, such statements assume that modernity is characterized by an increasingly widespread assertion of subjectivity, of individual subjects defined by their own wills. This problem is brought about historically in a particular age of history; it does not merely reflect for Nishitani the relevance of the Buddha's insights for all historical ages equally. And if the problem is historical, so must the solution be. It is not my intent here to show how

11. MINAMOTO 1995, 219.
12. NISHITANI 1961, trans. 1982, 285. Chapter 9 on alternative autonomy in the present volume elaborates the sense of this "service to all things."

a philosophy of emptiness might provide a basis for a political philosophy, but some explanation is in order for how the conception of emptiness could provide an historical answer to the problem of nihilism.

The problem Nishitani sees is that humans on a social and a global scale in the modern era are consciously threatened with the meaninglessness of their existence. Nishitani recounts some historical ways in which various philosophies try to "save" history from being ultimately meaningless. Christianity offered divine providence and the eschatological fulfillment of history at its end, the time of the second coming, when the transhistorical breaks into and ends the dimension of time and history. The European Enlightenment proposed an increasing reliance on reason or an historical growth of rationality. Nietzsche imagined a principle of absolute becoming called the Will to Power, his substitute for God, that explained why life is the way it is but rendered our values meaningful only if we totally affirm the eternal recurrence into which that non-human Will empties.

For Nishitani, these and other philosophies fail to ensure the meaningfulness of historical existence. They offered either a transhistorical guarantor or a prosthetic god in history, while science and technology undermined belief in any transhistorical reality such as God's providence. The course of history itself—the ceaseless history of wars, for example—undermined the Enlightenment belief in cumulative rationality. And Nietzsche's eternal recurrence does not allow for something absolutely new to be created in time. Although it is the closest of these philosophies to the Buddhist standpoint of *śūnyatā*, it does not undermine time enough to reach this standpoint of "time originating as truly bottomless time."[13] If we can no longer go above history and human time to establish meaningfulness, we must go beneath them, as it were, and undermine them even more. Time and history, in Nishitani's words, require emptiness for their realization.

---

13. Ibid., 216. Pages 211–16 discuss the various ways philosophies try to "save" history from being ultimately meaningless.

Nishitani's reasoning is less than evident, and the following attempt is no more than a tentative reconstruction of a possible argument. In order for history to have meaning, it must be possible to create something absolutely new in time,[14] and only the emptiness of temporal moments can ensure that newness. That is because, ordinarily, the temporal moment we call the present is conceived to be constantly slipping away into the past, which is given and unchangeable. The future is at least partially determined by the present, as the present is by the past, but the future is not yet real. In ordinary conceptions, then, the impermanence of the present moment, the insubstantiality of the future, and the conditioning of both by what happens prior to them, all seem relatively obvious.

The difficulty lies more in the conception of the past. If the past is completely fixed in its nature and if it determines the present, then only a transtemporal factor, something outside of time, could bring anything new into the present. But there is no such transtemporal factor—at least not one recognized in a nihilistic, scientific age. If, however, the past is equally impermanent and insubstantial—that is, if *all* temporal moments are "empty" of a fixed nature—then there is no substantial difference among these temporal moments, and further, there is no hindrance to incessant becoming, the coming to be of something new. No moment of time can be "contained" or definitively defined. I take this to be what Nishitani's means in saying that "time originates as truly bottomless time" or that time "only comes about" by virtue of the "infinite openness" underlying it.[15]

There is also an argument by metaphoric association implied in Nishitani's text. It proceeds from his tacit Buddhist presupposition: In a world that emerges in terms of co-dependent origination (*pratītya samutpāda*), there is no first cause and no final cause. Hence all things—not only things in time but also time as distinct if inseparable

14. Ibid., 212.
15. Ibid., 222.

from beings—have no single cause or ground from which they can be derived or from which they originate. They are ultimately "groundless" (though they can still be caused or conditioned in multiple ways). On this assumption Nishitani can say metaphorically that there is an infinite openness at the "bottom" of time, in other words, that time has no bottom or ground. He can affirm mythological phrases such as "from the beginningless past" and can say more philosophically that "time must be conceived of without beginning or end." He can reason that each and every present time or "now" is novel, since it has nothing that completely determines it, and is impermanent, since there is nothing that sustains it. The emptiness of time entails "newness without ceasing."[16] The crux of this argument is the association of terms like "bottomless" and "infinite openness" with the idea of no ultimate "ground" or cause.

It would be a further task to draw out other implications of the claim that the past is no more a fixed reality than the present or future—or more precisely, the claim that we *should* not view the past in this manner if we are to let time originate and to ensure our existence of meaning. (Nishitani's writing frequently slides back and forth between descriptive and normative statements, a style that assumes the alternative notion of normativity in much of Zen that Chapter 8 presented. The stress, I think, is on the normative side, that is, on an implied exhortation to *make* existence meaningful, whether by re- or de-conceptualizing or by the practice of *zazen* to which he alludes.) We may note for now that the claim would seem difficult to square with the idea of karma, which Nishitani treats at length. The idea of karma, he writes, "expresses an awareness of existence that sees being and time as infinite burdens for us." The sense of inextricable necessity is the negative face of time, whose positive face is "one of creation, freedom, and infinite possibility."[17] In this respect, the meaning of the

---

16. Ibid., 219, 221.
17. Both quotations are from ibid., 221.

newness of time is ambiguous: it evokes both negative images of things vanishing like dewdrops, and positive images of moving forward unhindered as birds do through the air. Basically, Nishitani describes karma as an existential plight and not as objective causality. He also alludes to a realization that cuts through karma, and to the "field of emptiness" as transcending the "field of karma."[18]

The denial of any objective reality in karma may remind one of Nāgārjuna's analysis, but the existentialist interpretation is clearly different. Nishitani and Nāgārjuna differ "substantially."[19] Nāgārjuna's analysis dismantles any real referent to the parts of time: past, present, future.[20] It challenges our way of conceptualizing time and reality and ultimately loosens our hold on such conceptions. Nishitani's discussion is also a challenge to our conceptuality, primarily by being so difficult to understand. He presupposes the interdependent nature of the parts of time but undermines not so much our concept of time as our sense—or our hope—that something outside time, particularly outside the present, will redeem the meaning of the present moment, will give it lasting meaning. Time and karma have to do with the way we live our lives; they are not merely mental constructions to be deconstructed. Nishitani takes time more seriously, and as someone with an acute, modern historical consciousness, he takes the notion of history seriously.

Why does history need emptiness? More precisely, why is it that "historicity is able to realize itself radically" [only] "on the standpoint

---

18. Ibid., 263.
19. A point of convergence, however, may be found in Nāgārjuna's answer to an objection, in which he affirms rather than denies the connection between emptiness and origination: "By virtue of emptiness everything is able to arise, but without emptiness nothing whatsoever can arise." *Mūlamādhyamakakārikā* 24/14, quoted at the end of *The Self-Overcoming of Nihilism*, NISHITANI 1990, 180.
20. See *Mūlamādhyamakakārikā* 19 in STRENG 1967, 205. Nāgārjuna deconstructs time by showing that one cannot take the past and the future as separate; rather they must be taken as simultaneity.

of *śūnyatā*"?[21] Nishitani once emphasized to me that he is talking not about history as a course of events but rather about "historicity" (*Geschichtlichkeit*). He has in mind historicity not in the sense of historical factuality (as in "the historicity of the Buddha") but in the sense of the condition for the possibility of history, a sense that includes awareness of historical conditioning. He explicitly refers to historicity "as historical consciousness and as history become conscious."[22]

While we may need a Hegelian imagination to understand what it means for history to become conscious, the notion of historical consciousness is consonant with the Buddhist idea of the conditionality of all things, that is, with *pratītya samutpāda* understood as a correlate to emptiness. It follows that a recognition of emptiness could strengthen a sense of historical conditioning and vice versa. This recognition is a sort of subjective prerequisite for the realization of historicity. More than historical conditioning, however, Nishitani stresses the newness needed if time and history are to be "actual." This emphasis points to another kind of prerequisite, one we might call ontological. It is the same as that for time. Time needs to be empty; each moment needs to be "bottomless" or without a supporting ground, in order to move on; history needs to be free of predetermination in order to allow "new, once-and-for-all" events. In the end, Nishitani combines the two kinds of prerequisite in the way he speaks of realization, meaning both recognition and actualization.

The sense of recognition suggests how the "realization of emptiness" overcomes nihilism: it gives meaning to each moment of time, while not privileging particular moments or epochs. (We will return to this point later.) The sense of actualization implies that Nishitani's notion of emptiness is normative, and not merely descriptive of (the lack of) the nature of things. We tend to think of the doctrine of emptiness as descriptive of reality, even if it entails a description that emp-

21. Ibid., 217.
22. Ibid., 211.

ties things of lasting reality. Empty (of independent, substantial being) is the way "things" (conventional designations) *are*. On the other hand, we acknowledge that, according to Buddhist teachings, release from suffering requires that such emptiness be recognized, even if this eventually entails a recognition that there is nothing to be released. Emptiness is an insight that we, whatever reality we have, *should* attain. A normative dimension is implied in the notion that one should undergo Nāgārjuna's analysis, for example, as well as in the notion of the path (*marga*) in general. Nishitani's "logic" suggests that something truly new can come about, can be actualized, "when" we recognize emptiness.[23] From the standpoint of people acting in history, then, "realizing reality" is an ideal—an ideal that, in religious terms, contrasts with a goal of *personal* salvation.

Nishitani's connection of traditional Buddhist conceptions to modern historical consciousness appears particularly innovative when we contrast it with other contemporary Zen views. His statement that "historicity is able to realize itself radically only on the standpoint of *śūnyatā*" contrasts sharply with what D. T. Suzuki once wrote: "Zen does not affirm or negate temporal actuality. Actuality has historicity, with which the ultimacy of Zen has no dealings."[24]

---

23. Nishitani does not elaborate on what it means to actualize reality, much less to realize emptiness, but he does give an example of the kind of realization he has in mind in his discussion of humans realizing the laws of nature. We not only discover and recognize such laws; we also utilize them in technology to bring about new things. We are both bound by them and freed by them, i.e., freed through technology from certain imposed conditions. We actualize the laws of nature by making use of them while being bound to them. The mistake is to suppose that we humans stand outside the laws of nature and can simply manipulate them to our own ends, or in general to imagine ourselves (or even "enlightenment") as outside of *pratītya samutpāda* (ibid., 79–88). I once asked a Shinshū priest what the Buddhist sense of sin was, and he replied, "acting as if one stood outside *engi* (*pratītya samutpāda*)."

24. The source of the quotation is *Suzuki Daisetsu Zenshū* 15 (Tokyo: Iwanami Shoten, 2000), 219, as cited in Ives 2009, 67, and quoted by Ichikawa Hakugen, the critic of Zen's involvement in the Pacific War, from his *Zen hyakudai* [One Hundred Zen Topics].

QUESTIONS OF ACCOUNTING AND ACCOUNTABILITY

Our reconstruction suggests that Nishitani's philosophy of history will call into question the experience of the world as a sequence of events and the framing of value judgments about those events. It will call into question not only the task of giving an account of historical events, but also the demand for accountability or ethical responsibility.

We in turn can question whether the kind of historicity that Nishitani affirms can salvage the sense of history and accountability that is demanded by contemporary (modern and postmodern) historical consciousness. Today, after all, historians and philosophers do not seek any teleology in history or any transhistorical ground of history. Nor do they worry about meaninglessness if humans bear the responsibility for historical events and for evaluating them. What historians and philosophers so often require is an account of how humans order the world temporally and find value in it. They simply take for granted that human beings do find a temporal order in the world, even if it is of their own making, and that human beings do expect to judge, if not to be judged. Nishitani implicitly asks whether we must, and whether we should, conceive our life and live it according to these assumptions. But what happens to history in his conclusions?

Let us first reflect on the question of judging importance in temporal order. According to Nishitani, historicity realized would give meaning to each moment of time, while not privileging any particular moments or epochs. It seems, however, that the human reckoning of history does in fact necessitate that we select and privilege certain times and events, ordering them in sequence, often in causal continuity. Nishitani amply appreciates the sense of continuity, in both its negative aspect of burden and positive aspect of freedom. His discussion of causality is less developed. He does speak of "historical, causally conditioned being-at-doing [*saṃskṛta*]" and he fully recognizes nihilism, for example, as an event brought about historically, with causal factors giving rise to it. (Nishitani also recognizes non-karmic action, which he calls "unconditioned non-doing."[25]) Even if we jettison strict notions of causality in history, as both historicism and postmodernist views of history do, it seems we give up most if not all notions of history when we eliminate the privileging of particular moments or epochs.[26]

Postmodern resonances and differences

Superficially, Nishitani's position seems to bear resemblance to some postmodern theories of history and historicity. According to these theories, the meaning of events past and present is objectively indeterminate; they are inevitably reconstructed *post eventum* according to prevailing assumptions and linguistic practices. Privileging certain moments or epochs is arbitrary insofar as the assignment of significance and of moral valence is contingent and inconstant. In an article on Nishitani's Zen philosophy of history, Steven Heine noted that postmodernist theories problematize assumptions of linear, teleological time evident in efforts to define the origins or causes of things in the past and to seek progress in the future. Such theories contend that events are not objective, substantive entities in the world (which parallels Nishitani's view) but rather constructions of certain discursive practices (which exceeds his view). In conclusion, Heine suggests that because such theories offer an explanation of the structure of historical discourse, they could account for the historicity evident in Zen narratives better than Nishitani's theory.[27] I have found that the senses of history displayed in traditional Zen narratives mingle with quasi-historical legends as well as myths, and thus diverge considerably from

---

25. NISHITANI 1961, trans. 1982, 271 et passim.
26. Interestingly enough, Nietzsche's eternal recurrence of the same can be understood as a great principle of selection and discrimination. Graham Parkes pointed out to me that if Nietzsche enjoins us to act now as if our actions were to recur eternally, then we need to select our acts with great care. Nishitani seems to overlook this possibility and criticizes Nietzsche's idea for precluding the newness of each moment that is requisite for true historicity.
27. HEINE 1994, 255, 262–3.

a sense of historicity as factuality. For their part, contemporary Chan and Zen historians commonly presuppose modern, naturalist views of what happened and why.[28] Only a few, Heine among them, engage in discourse analysis. Nishitani's account of Western conceptions of history does not include postmodernist views, and I presume he would not be interested in discourse analysis, since he is not composing or invoking a narrative history of Zen or Buddhism. The relevant passages he cites from Zen literature function as expressions of the equivalence and equal appreciation of all moments rather than episodes in a narrative history.[29]

The question for us here is whether Nishitani could accommodate even a postmodernist notion of history that does not assume linear time, teleology, or historical causation. Postmodernist critiques urge the non-objectivity of events and the relativity of privileging particular moments or epochs, but they do not offer an alternative history of totally equivalent moments. As Heine notes, postmodernist theories reveal that the "primary structure of historical discourse is narration, *which describes events selectively*...."[30] If events are narrative constructions and not objective realities, then the human discrimination among moments and the need for reflective evaluation are all the more necessary. Postmodernist theories, instead of eliminating the elements of history that Nishitani does, require them all the more.

---

28. See MARALDO 2021. One insightful postmodernist approach to Zen history and the ethical issues it raises is found in PARK 2008. For examples, see MARALDO 2021, 132 n. 49, and, in the present volume, page 310 in Chapter 12.

29. Some examples: Yunmen's "Every day is a good day" (NISHITANI 1961, trans. 1982, 182); Dōgen's "Every morning the sun ascends in the east, every night the moon descends in the west. Clouds retreat, the mountain bones are bared, rain passes, the surrounding hills are low.... We meet a leap year one in four. Cocks crow at four in the morning" (188); and Hakuin's verse: "Yesterday at dawn I swept the soot of the old year away. Tonight I grind and knead flour for the New Year's sweets. There is a pine tree with its roots and an orange with its leaves. Then I don new clothes and await the coming guests" (217). To this last verse, Nishitani comments, "Hakuin's words are enough to give us a glimpse of how radically *actual* time is in Buddhism...."

30. HEINE 1994, 262, my emphasis.

Resonances and differences with Kierkegaard

The problem of the *equivalence* of moments is also laid bare in an account presented by Kierkegaard, who sought to overcome nihilism in his own way, and who anticipated the postmodern problem of arbitrary significance.[31] Kierkegaard's account is tentative and the situation it describes will itself be overcome; the problem appears as a stage on the way to a truly religious mode of existence. Commentators Hubert Dreyfus and Jane Rubin summarize the relevant problem as overcoming the *leveling* the self faces when it realizes that

> if nothing has any immediate significance, everything can have the significance I choose to give it.... [But] when choice is world-defining, it is impossible to have any standards for making particular choices, since these standards, too, must be objects of choice. Once it is up to me to give everything significance, the significance I give is completely arbitrary.... Only once I give up trying to become a self can I overcome leveling.[32]

The path to overcome the consequence of leveling is a path to overcome the self with its incessant desires—which, ceteris paribus, reminds us of the Buddhist path to release the self lost in *saṃsāra* or the realm of desire (*kāmadhātu*). Kierkegaard's self must undergo a "self-annihilation before God" that reduces its desires to relative significance deserving ultimate indifference:

> My absolute indifference to the satisfaction of my desires and needs allows me to live in a kind of eternal present.... I have an eternal present because I accept my past and my future unconditionally.... I can appreciate satisfaction and dissatisfaction equally.[33]

---

31. NISHITANI (1990, 16–21) considers Kierkegaard's alternatives to nihilism, but not in the context of the notion of history. DREYFUS AND RUBIN 1987 explicate Kierkegaard's and Heidegger's alternatives to nihilism as more or less adequate forms of the *Gelassenheit* and authenticity of the self.

32. DREYFUS AND RUBIN 1991, 288–9. My summary of their summary selects points relevant to the problem in Nishitani.

33. Ibid., 292. MARALDO (2017, 266–71) briefly presents the related notion of

11. History from a Buddhist Perspective | 283

The direct connection between Kierkegaard's stage of leveling and Nishitani's equivalence of historical moments is made in the leap from self to the *absolute—emptiness* in Nishitani's terms, *God* in Kierkegaard's:

> For God there is nothing significant and nothing insignificant.... In a certain sense the significant is for Him insignificant, and in another sense even the least significant is for Him infinitely significant.... In a manner eternally unchanged, everything is for God eternally present, always equally before Him.[34]

For Kierkegaard, this is precisely the situation of despair (or "what would be salvation for the Buddhist," Dreyfus and Rubin say). Relief from this condition, Kierkegaard argues, requires the stage beyond that overcomes leveling by committing to something concrete and specific outside oneself, as exemplified by the person of Jesus, the paradigm of someone with a world-defining commitment.

We note that Kierkegaard's journey through and beyond despair and the leveling of moments—beyond nihilism, in other words—is a movement from the self who makes ethical decisions to the possibility of a truly religious self who enters into a relationship with the absolute. Nishitani presents the absolute emptiness underlying selfhood as realized reality that requires recognition of the equivalence of moments. If ethical accountability is a problem with Nishitani's account, a similar problem would seem to arise in the case of Kierkegaard's individualized religiosity beyond the stage of ethics. Dreyfus and Rubin analyze Heidegger's early notion of authenticity as a secularized version of Kierkegaard's religious self, and present later Heidegger's critique as a plea for a culture released from blind technology. They do not men-

---

the absolute present in Nishitani and other students of Nishida, without mentioning Kierkegaard's notion.

34. DREYFUS AND RUBIN 1991, 294, cited from Kierkegaard's *Edifying Discourses*. Recently, the philosopher Willem DREES (1990, 74) has argued that the doctrine of *creatio ex nihilo* implies an equivalence of all moments for God: "all moments have a similar relation to the Creator. Either they are all just 'brute facts', or they are all equally created."

tion the problem of ethical responsibility that Heidegger, Kierkegaard, and Nishitani seem to bypass.

From accounting to accountability

Does not the demand for accountability contradict the conception of the equivalence of moments? When Nishitani offers a refreshing way to understand each and every moment of time as equally new and infinitely open, does he not undermine the discrimination among times that seems to be a necessary ingredient of history? He himself assumes that there is something particular about modernity when he presents nihilism as an historical problem. The solution to nihilism, that is, the "standpoint of emptiness," seems ironically to be a way of dissolving the problem by voiding the particularity of the modern era. The problem deepens when we seek to discern values in historical actions, moments, and events. The very possibility of value judgments based on the discrimination among times is in question.

Thomas Kasulis and Masao Abe have addressed the problem in their own illuminating discussions of Nishitani's philosophy of history. Their examination and criticisms focus on the problem particularly as it is relevant for theologians and buddhologists, but what they write is also relevant to the problem of accountability in history.

Kasulis takes a comparative approach that both clarifies Nishitani's challenge to Christian thinkers and presents a limit to Nishitani's Buddhist view:

> In the broadest terms, what Christians would assume and what Nishitani explicitly denies is this—spiritually speaking, some things are more important than others. The correlate of this principle for history is that some events are more important than others.[35]

Christian theologians are challenged to explain how the world can be self-determining or auto-telic, as the modern worldview prescribes,

---

35. KASULIS 1989, 273–4.

if a transhistorical source makes some things and events spiritually more valuable than others.[36] Nishitani contends that only the spiritual equality of all things, by virtue of their true emptiness, allows reality to be self-determining; yet his view cannot account for the orientation that lets some things count as intrinsically more valuable than others. While the possibility of an ethics based on *śūnyatā* deserves further investigation, we stay focused here on the question whether it makes sense at all to speak of history, and historical accountability, if no events are more important than others.

Abe Masao raises a similar question in his explication of Nishitani's philosophy of history, but attempts to show that *śūnyatā* ultimately can account for a difference in values. He notes that for Nishitani the origin of time and history lies in the infinite openness of the absolute present. Abe goes on to ask:

> Since [Nishitani's] standpoint is so strongly absolute-present oriented, do not his ontology and view of history tend to be weak in terms of an axiological approach (value judgment)?[37]

Abe finds that axiology or the study of values is underdeveloped in Nishitani's identification of *is* and *ought*:

---

36. My paraphrase of points that Kasulis makes, ibid., 276–7. Kasulis notes that process theologians with their systematic hierarchies, and Karl Rahner with his levels of explication in religious symbols, address similar problems independently of Nishitani's challenge, but that current theological dialogue would be greatly enriched by a direct confrontation with it. It seems to me, however, that for most Christian thinkers the world or reality is precisely not auto-telic, but rather the world (or human spirit at least) is given purpose by a higher order and teleology that orients it. Although it may seem that "postmodern" theology disillusions us of this orientation to a transcendent order, someone like Karl Rahner would contend that the differentiation between transcendent salvation history and ordinary history is precisely what is needed to establish a standpoint for judgment of a history that includes evil and events like the holocaust. On the difference between salvation history and ordinary history, see RAHNER 1984, 142–75: "The History of Salvation and Revelation as Coextensive [not identical] with the Whole of World History."

37. ABE 1989, 291. Abe's criticism elaborates a point made earlier by H. WALDENFELS 1980, 117.

In my view, however, the standpoint of *śūnyatā* must be realized not only ontologically but also axiologically. This means that the identity of *being* and *ought to be* of all phenomena—this is a *conditio sine qua non* for the realization of *śūnyatā*—must be realized by including a possibility of *will not do* although *ought to do*.[38]

Abe finds ultimately that the *equality* of things and the *distinctness* of things are both preserved in *śūnyatā*. He claims that distinctness entails axiological judgment, and therefore the standpoint of ontology and axiology go together. In his answer to Kasulis, Abe writes further that "each human being is more important in its distinctiveness than a rock," and the symbol of Buddha better preaches the Dharma than, say, refuse does. We are not told *why* some distinct things are more important than others, but Abe does tell us *to* or *for whom* they are more important: "Each human being is more important than a rock *not to God nor to the human self,* but *to absolute nothingness.*"[39] Talk of importance, in other words, implies what we may call a dative of evaluation, but it is not clear how absolute nothingness can function as a dative of evaluation.

Abe's implicit claim that distinctness entails axiological judgment seems questionable, for we can distinguish between things without imputing relative values to them. It is evident that difference is required for the notion of equality; think of the standard concept of equal rights, which entails distinctly different people. But distinctness does not entail a hierarchy of values, a "better" or "more," that is, a difference in quality. A difference in quality is something that Abe does recognize: Humans are distinct from things like mountains and water, in that humans necessarily confront and must overcome the problem of *oughtness* in order to be realized.[40] What is more, human beings are

38. ABE 1989, 297. See NISHITANI 1961, trans. 1982, 195.
39. ABE 1989, 297–8.
40. Ibid., 298. Neither Abe nor Nishitani alludes to the Buddhist mythology of the six realms of transmigration, in which humans are envisaged as the only beings capable of the aspiration to enlightenment. Abe might suggest that this is because only humans are

more important than things like rocks because they can realize the dynamic identity of *is* and *ought*, of the ontological and axiological dimensions.[41]

Abe's suggestion implies that the problem of "*will not do* although *ought to do*" exists precisely on the standpoint of will. In Nishitani's terms, it is the field of consciousness, not of *śūnyatā*, that would account for a discrimination of values, an axiology. Yet the field of consciousness, the standpoint of will, is precisely what must be overcome if humans are to realize their suchness. To take *oughtness* as a problem, and *will* as a mode of being that must be overcome, is to say that values are not basic, that the axiological dimension itself must be overcome.[42] From Nishitani's perspective, talk of its identity with the ontological dimension turns out to be otiose, and our original conundrum reappears. It would seem that, basically, nothing (no one thing) is more important than anything else. There is, in this view, no history conceived as a progression (or narration) of events with inherently different qualities or degrees of importance. Historical judgments that discern qualitative differences, values, and ranks of importance are

---

confronted with moral choice. Contrast this human distinction also with the Zen view explored in Chapter 8 that equates self (as activity, not as substance) with mountains, waters, and other phenomena.

41. Ibid, 299. Thus to awaken to one's own suchness by overcoming the problem of *oughtness*, Abe writes, is simultaneously to awaken to the suchness of mountains, waters, rocks, and plants. Dōgen writes differently, however; it is not that humans awaken to the suchness of all things, but rather: "the world and all sentient beings in it are awakened at the same time." "If we examine the matter closely, was it the layman [Su Dongpo] who awakened, or was it the mountains and streams which awakened?" "If you yourself, who are the valley streams and mountains, cannot develop the power which illuminates the true reality of the mountains and valley streams, who else is going to be able to convince you that you and the streams and mountains are one and the same?" (Adapting the translations of COOK 1999, 106, 103, and 114.)

42. Abe writes of overcoming not only the problem of karma [as understood in Buddhism] but also of original sin, by which he means, I think, the consciousness of good and evil. His profound reading of original sin here is reminiscent of Bonhoeffer's interpretation in his *Ethics*: "Already in the possibility of the knowledge of good and evil Christian ethics discerns a falling away from the origin" (BONHOEFFER 1955, 17).

rooted in human convention, culture, and caprice. This much resonates with postmodern theories, with the difference that, for Nishitani, historical discernment rests on human will. Without discernment, there is no particular meaning to be found in human history; meaning is vacated. Is this not precisely the problem of nihilism that Nishitani wants to overcome? His notion of the equivalence of all times seems to leave the problem intact. The same challenge is equally unanswered by much historical practice, and particularly by postmodernist theory, as well.[43]

Where, then, has this inquiry taken us? For Nishitani, the fulfillment of time in history, and the only possible ground for meaning in history, is the emptiness beneath each moment that ensures its absolute newness. The realization of this is the realization of historical reality. Does the realized human being simply appreciate a rock as a rock, and a person as a person—a being confronted with decisions? Does such appreciation itself require a discrimination of values, over and above a discernment of distinctness among equal but different things? Does historicity (that is, historical consciousness and history become conscious) require not only distinctness but also connection, and not only equivalence but also evaluation?

THE ELEMENTS NECESSARY FOR HISTORICAL CONSCIOUSNESS, AND REMAINING QUESTIONS

This chapter has made the following points regarding the significance of newness for Nishitani's conception of history:

1. In order for history to have meaning, it must be possible to create something absolutely new in time.

---

43. For Jean-François LYOTARD (1988), the preeminent theorist of the postmodern condition, the challenge appears in the form of the *differend* or disparity in rules of judgment, precisely when judgment is most called for—for example, in defining the victims of the Jewish Holocaust of the twentieth century.

2. History needs to be free of predetermination in order to allow "new, once-and-for-all" events. 3) Newness is needed if time and history are to be "actual."
3. The emptiness of time entails "newness without ceasing."[44]
4. The fulfillment of time in history, and the only possible ground for meaning in history, is the emptiness beneath each moment that ensures its absolute newness.

We have criticized this conception for leaving unclarified the possibility of understanding historical times and events in sequences connected to one another, and for precluding a qualitative discrimination of different times and events. Such a criticism becomes cogent, however, only if those missing elements are essential to the emergence of true historicity. The challenge of coming to terms with Nishitani's standpoint leads necessarily to the task of identifying the elements that are essential to historical consciousness.

Our examination suggests three such elements: historical memory, storytelling, and accountability. In order for a sense of history to emerge, we must be able to retain the past in the present and to anticipate a future. This sort of retention and anticipation do not presuppose that time is linear; but they do require a discrimination of what has happened from what is happening and what might happen. They require a retrieval of the past. In the activity of storytelling we give an account of the present in terms of the past, and toward the future; we thus lend a sense of continuity to human life. To the extent that our accounts recognize responsibility, that we hold ourselves accountable, our futures remain open. Indeed, we can recognize the possibility of different futures insofar as we recognize that the present is the way it is, in large part because of our actions in the past. Fatalist views do not allow for historical consciousness.

How does Nishitani's account accommodate these elements of history? First, where is the past retained, the future anticipated, in

---

44. NISHITANI 1961, trans. 1982, 221.

his conception? Secondly, where is there room for a sense of accountability, particularly where the field of karma, the effects of the past, is broken through? And thirdly, even if emptiness does not produce or provide for responsibility, we may ask what responsibility looks like from the standpoint of emptiness. These are the questions that Nishitani's account raises for us. One aspect, the element of absolute newness that Nishitani's standpoint requires, seem compatible with the possibility of history in a kind of account that he did not anticipate, a phenomenological account.

A PHENOMENOLOGICAL NOTE ON HOW HISTORY MIGHT REQUIRE ABSOLUTE NEWNESS

Husserl's phenomenology offers some support for the connection between the newness of each moment and the possibility of history. Historical memory is the point of convergence here. Both Husserl and Nishitani would, I think, agree that historicity requires that a sense of the past be retained in the present.[45] Phenomenologically speaking, historical consciousness of the past requires that a *present* consciousness recognize the past precisely *as* past, and not as something presently being experienced. This holding of the past in the *present* moment of consciousness is what we call remembering. The memory of something past is a kind of repetition of the past experience, however partial and perspectival that repetition might be. What is remembered *as* past is held over-against a stream of present consciousness, in order to be recognized precisely as past. The ever-present stream itself is never repeated; it is ever new. In other words, to have a sense of history, and of events as past, a retention or recollection of a

---

45. Nishitani makes this assumption explicit in an earlier essay, of 1949, 「批判の任務とファシズムの問題」 (The Duty to Criticize and the Problem of Fascism). There he writes that "the recent war must become a real question for us today. Otherwise we will not be able to think authentically about the present situation. In this sense, that past is a problem of the present" (NKC 4: 461, my translation).

part of conscious life must be layered on a temporal flow of unrepeated experience.[46] The unrepeating, living, flowing present is the dimension that may be akin to Nishitani's idea of "newness without ceasing."

Valuing, like remembering, is a mode of consciousness that for Husserl requires a layering. In the case of valuing, an object or event is perceived in a way that adds to its merely sensual presence. Taking an object or event as valuable is not necessarily a second act, added after the first act of apprehension. The event or object can be immediately experienced with or without the valuing act. I have suggested that historical consciousness goes beyond indiscriminate historical memory by assessing relative values to events. The problem with Nishitani's conception of historical consciousness would then be that it seems to acknowledge only indiscriminate historical memory.

A RESOLUTION TO THE PROBLEM?

Yunmen Wenyan's "Every day is a good day" intimates a plausible resolution. This saying appears is Case 6 of the kōan collection called the *Blue Cliff Record*. Yunmen says to his monks, "I don't ask you about before the fifteenth day; try to say something about after the fifteenth day." Yunmen then answers for everyone: "Every day is a good day."[47] Yunmen's *question* acknowledges a consciousness of succession in time, as well as a valuing of the special time that is the fifteenth of the month, when the moon became full, and the days leading up to this were increasing in importance. Yunmen's *answer* brings the focus back to the unrepeatable, ever-new present, day after day equally good. Taken alone, the phrase "every day is a good day" transcends historical consciousness. But taken together the question and answer present the two sides of historical memory: the recalled past (and anticipated

---

46. I owe this description of the phenomenology of memory to the account of SOKOLOWSKI 1974, 155. The application to history is my own.
47. CLEARY 1978, 37.

future), and the unrepeatable present right now. What is more, his answer, which transcends valuing, is given only after the question sets up the expectation of value.

Valuing requires a discrimination of parts—in the case of historical consciousness, of times or events. Historical consciousness necessarily discriminates and weighs the importance of one time or event against another. Although such valuing invariably and essentially characterizes this form of consciousness, the values that are assessed or assigned can vary from one occasion (of assessment) to another. It is said that we cannot change past history, but it is evident that *what* we select from passed time, and *how* we evaluate a selected event, do change; history gets written and re-written. What is more, conceptions of history change along with the range of things considered as factual or real. It may be that a Chan abbot named Yunmen never actually said such a thing to his monks, that the story is more legendary than "historical," according to modern measures of historicity.[48] For all that, interpretations and appropriations of Yunmen's saying do not necessarily depend on "the facts" behind the story. The story assumes, in my appropriation, a consciousness of succession in time, a valuing of a special time (the day/night of the full moon during the month). What is more, it makes a statement that brings to light the presupposed evaluation by neutralizing it. Evaluations work by advocating a difference of importance or relevance, a better and worse, a "should be" as opposed to a "just is." Yunmen's "every day: a good day" collapses the difference between "should" and "is" and calls for attention to the right here and now underlying all time.

For his part, Nishitani cites Yunmen's saying to illustrate "the absolute state" opened up by "the discernment of non-discernment."[49] The

---

48. MARALDO 2021 advocates the careful discrimination of notions of historicity, legend, and myth, particularly in the study of Chan/Zen Buddhist history.

49. NISHITANI 1961, trans. 1982, 182. Nishitani quotes Yunmen's saying alongside biblical sayings that illustrate this "bottomless non-discernment," such as "Let the day's own trouble be sufficient for the day (Matt. 6: 34)." He comments, "In Christian teach-

"absolute state" is the state of things as presented on the field of emptiness that realizes an equi-valence of times or events.

> Here "as it is" and "as it ought to be" are one and the same; the nature of the task of the *ought* is the other-directedness of the *is*.... And if, further, on the field of emptiness doing becomes manifest ecstatically as true doing, then it follows that in the doing in its elemental and original form comes to be as something that is directed toward all others and makes every other its master.[50]

And yet, if Yunmen's saying helps to resolve the problem with indiscriminate historicity, it elicits another, equally significant problem. If Nishitani's basis (or bottomlessness) for the equivalence of historical times invokes a convergence of *is* and *ought*, it would seem to undermine the normative basis of ethics that requires precisely the discrimination of good and evil, better and worse, should do and should not do. In fact, Nishitani does not obviate the ought at the basis of normative ethics. Just how his Zen vision might deal with normativity takes us to the next chapter.

---

ing, this bottomlessness seems to open up to the Kingdom of God and his righteousness (Matt. 6: 33)" (ibid.).

50. Ibid., 260. The allusion to a self that makes all others its master takes us back to the topic of Chapter 9 on alternative autonomy.

12
The Alternative Normativity of Zen

> "You became a monk—A commandment-breaker monk—
> because you killed the buddhas and the patriarchs"
> – Shidō Munan, about Rinzai

The question I begin with is a seemingly simple one: what is the nature of ethical norms in Zen? I am interested in this issue not only because Zen ethics has become a much-discussed topic today. Scholars and practitioners alike make claims about ethics in Zen as distinct from other Buddhist traditions, and many find ethics lacking in Zen. But I am also interested in its potential to present an alternative notion of normativity, and thus to expose long-entrenched assumptions and perhaps liberate us from them. The Kyoto School and other Japanese philosophers most likely recognized this potential in their adaptations of an alternative normativity.[1]

First a word about normativity. To put it roughly, normative ethics is supposed to us tell us what is good or bad, what is right or wrong to do, and to tell us why something is right or wrong. Normativity not only distinguishes between *what is* and *what ought to be*, between the descriptive form and the imperative, but also gives reasons for the distinctions. If we conflate the two, the real and the ideal, we commit the "naturalist fallacy." Yet we often hear that Zen teachings transcend the

---

1. Variations of an alternative to the standard opposition between normative and descriptive, without reducing one to the other, appear in Watsuji Tetsurō's *Ethics* (see MARALDO 2019, 40–4, 61–2), in Tanabe Hajime's metanoetics (ibid., 197), and in Kuki Shūzō's transformed imperative (ibid., 238–85), among other Japanese philosophers.

distinction. So the question is, just what sort of normativity is at work in Zen?

I called this question *seemingly* simple. As soon as we are aware of the assumptions behind the question, it begins to look quite complicated.

COMMON ASSUMPTIONS ABOUT ZEN AND ITS (LACK OF) ETHICS

For one thing, *the word* Zen *is problematic.* It conveniently gathers a vast array of practices and texts and teachers under one name to give them an identity that historical scholars today like to challenge.[2] My purpose here, however, is not to present an accurate historical picture of all the ethical variations and vagrancies in this set of traditions. Nor will I consider the question whether Zen ethics differs from other ethical approaches in Mahāyāna and Theravāda Buddhism. What is more, my examples of an ethical alternative are somewhat random. My point is not to present a particular sense of normativity in order to define Zen, and to exclude texts, practices or teachers from the name of Zen solely because they do not fit into the alternative. My purpose is to mine the ore for material that suggests an interesting and viable alternative to understanding normativity.

Assuming that there is a living, variegated tradition we can call Zen, we encounter other, more explicit assumptions that complicate the question. One is that *Zen ethics is basically Mahāyāna ethics* and has nothing distinctive to offer. This assumption seeks a mark of distinction; I will return to it briefly later. Another related assumption is that, historically, we can distinguish between two parts of Zen ethics: a set of rules and regulations governing monastic life and intended to facilitate Zen practice and awakening—call them house rules—and then a more encompassing but vague social ethics, derived primarily

---

2. MARALDO (2021, 10, 27–31, 101) discusses the ambiguity of the name *Zen*.

from Confucianism. This view ignores two things: the connections often explicitly made in Zen literature between monastic training and living in society, and the mutual influence of Zen and Neo-Confucian normative ideals. If, as is commonly understood, the rules regulating a monastic community are there to promote harmony and the awakening of the practitioners, that counts as a social ethic, all the more so when ideal behavior in the community is supposed to guide behavior in society at large.

It is true that Zen and other Buddhist institutions often adapted Confucian moral norms (and that they discarded parts of the Indian Vinaya they considered inappropriate); but it is also the case that Neo-Confucians sometimes adopted Buddhist rituals and ethical models. For example, Zhu Xi (1130-1200) adopted "quiet sitting" as an aid to intuit ethical principles, and in Japan Satō Naokata (1650–1719), referring to Zhu Xi, recommended quiet sitting as a way to expel selfishness and ground right activity. But let us suppose that there was a good deal of borrowing from Confucianism, in both Chinese and Japanese Zen.[3] The question remains: what was the Confucian normativity that was adapted by Zen, and what were the normative procedures for adapting it? The question of Zen normativity has not been answered by a reference to Confucian ethics.

One abbreviated answer is that *Zen ethics* (both house rules and the adapted Confucian social ethics) are *highly situational and with-*

---

3. Many factors in the formulation of Zen precepts were at work, in both China and Japan. CHU (2006, 23) summarizes the research of others:
> As expected, the previously outlined Chinese developments in preceptive model, such as the incorporation of Tantric elements, the reduction of myriad proscriptions to a single principle such as the "Mind" or the enlightenment experience, the conformity to Confucian values, and the flexibility in interpretation, without exception found expression in Tokugawa Buddhism. Concrete examples abound, including Kaibara Ekken's (1630–1714) Confucianized precepts, Jiun Sonja's (1718–1804) "Vinaya of the True Dharma" that subsumed specific precepts under the category of the "Mind," and Kokan Shiren's (1278–1346) invocation of buddhas/bodhisattvas in his "Zen Precept Procedures."

out normative principles. Only the context determines right behavior. Dōgen tells his monks, "From the outset, there is neither good nor evil in the human mind. Good and evil arise according to circumstance."[4] Of course I have taken the words of Dōgen out of context. But I do not want to address the role of context here, except to say that such statements do not necessarily entail relativism. They often are couched in a higher norm, a more encompassing ideal. The imperative that Dōgen gives in this passage is "Just follow the circumstances," but his words also point to the context of discovering one's true mind. The invocation of the higher ideal is even more problematic for normative ethics than is moral relativism, however, and leads to the next crucial assumption.

This is the claim that *there is no sense of normativity in Zen*. There is of course ample evidence of normative ethics in Buddhism. Think, for example, of the teachings that something is good if it is conducive to the liberation of sentient beings from suffering, and bad if it causes suffering; or the teaching that what is conducive to enlightenment is good. The implications here are that these things are good because suffering and delusion are bad. (We might say "undesirable" instead of "bad," but that wording would have to be reconciled with the teaching that desiring itself leads to suffering.) Now while Zen is a Buddhist tradition, we often hear that Zen undermines or transcends normative distinctions between right and wrong, good and bad. Zen is (said to be) beyond such discrimination. A capping phrase in Chinese kōan texts puts it this way:

来説是非者 便是是非人
Those who come expounding right and wrong
Are the very ones who are right and wrong.[5]

Dōgen once tells his monks, in the words of one translator, "To enter the Buddha Way is to stop discrimination between good and evil

4. DŌGEN 1971B, 89.
5. My translation of a phrase in the *Zenrin kushū* (禅林句集). HORI (2003, 384) translates: "One who approaches with 'right and wrong' talk is a 'right and wrong' person."

and to cast aside the mind that says this is good and that is bad." Other passages in the same collection of talks have Dōgen instructing the monks to practice "what we find to be really good" and discard "what we find to be really bad."[6] In general in these talks Dōgen instructs his monks to keep the precepts, but he also says (in the words of another translator), "it is wrong to insist upon them as essential, establish them as a practice and expect to be able to gain the Way by observing them."[7] Of course, if he says "it is wrong," he invokes a sense of normativity. When asked further about conduct, he says: "Practitioners of the Way certainly *ought* to maintain" monastic regulations, but then he adds the rhetorical question, "When we sit *zazen*, what precept is not observed?"[8] In a similar vein, Hakuin (1685–1768) once wrote:

> Observing the precepts, repentance, and giving, the countless good deeds, and the way of right living all come from *zazen*. Thus one true *samādhi* extinguishes evils; it purifies karma, dissolving obstructions.[9]

In fact, underlying the claim to transcendence in Zen texts is usually an invocation to practice and to awakening. One is called to practice and to awaken, one *should* practice. Often the invocation is put in an imperative form. Nishitani Keiji once quoted a seventeenth-century Zen master: "While still alive become a dead one, become completely dead; then do whatever you will; all your deeds are good."[10] Nishitani is commenting on Nietzsche's answer to the question of what one should do: "Be holy and then do whatever you want."[11] I do not mean

---

6. DŌGEN 1971, 29 and 71.
7. DŌGEN 1987, 21.
8. Ibid., 22.
9. In his "Chant in Praise of Zazen," LOW 1988, 89.
10. The reference may be to Shidō Munan's "live as if you were dead." See MALDONADO 2022, 46–7, for a reading of this phrase as an ethical imperative at work in Tanabe Hajime's metanoetics, referring to the continuous and paradoxical death of the self that still lives, through continuous metanoesis.
11. Cited in PÖGGLER 1995, 105. The Nietzsche quotation appears in Heidegger's 1934/35 Hölderlin lectures. NISHITANI (1961, trans. 1982, 280–5) discusses the connection between the "great death" of Zen and great compassion as well as the Christian "love

to say this imperative is the last word from Nishitani on the subject, but it is true that at least in later years he took the question of awakening as prior to political and social problems.

In any case, we should not overlook the normative imperative in such sayings as the Zen master's or Nietzsche's: be(come) like a dead person, die! Or "be holy!" The sayings set an ideal that differs from what one is, or from what one is presently manifesting. If we follow one possible Buddhist reading, the reading extrapolated from "original enlightenment" theory, then the normative injunction assumes that the seeming *ought* is inherent in the *is*; one is to become what one originally, at one's source, *is*, namely, selfless. Aside from the Buddhological assumptions at work in this theory, the relevant assumption here is that selflessness is the root of all good. Thus one "must" die to self—or awaken one's original no-self nature, in Hakuin's words. Selflessness, or no-self, is one formulation of the root of Mahāyāna ethics; wisdom and its concomitant compassion is another. But the assumption about Zen normativity here lies not so much in invoking the ideal as in claiming, seemingly, that awakening—or at least *zazen* (seated meditation) practice—is *all* that is needed to be ethical.

That assumption frequently conceals another one: *zazen* practice awakens wisdom (*prajñā*) and compassion follows from wisdom and in turn nurtures it.[12] But an ethics of compassion seems to be situational and without clear principles. This is why some scholars today argue that Zen needs to be complemented by critical, rational reflection to formulate an ethics,[13] and others propose that Zen ethics cannot be understood as normative ethics but (if developed) can offer a

---

of neighbor."

12. An alternative view sees wisdom and compassion in a creative tension with one another. This is the way PARK (2006) reads the Korean Zen master Chinul. In either interpretation, both wisdom and compassion are rooted in an originally pure *mind*.

13. See, for example, IVES 2006 and WRIGHT 2006. There, any connection between Zen meditative practice and rational reflection remains in the dark. See MARALDO 2008 for my reflections on their approaches.

critique of such ethics, similar to postmodernist critiques.[14] Insofar as both of these proposals make normative recommendations, they either apply external criteria to evaluate Zen ethics or try to develop new criteria out of old Zen. Instead of making normative recommendations, I want to take a close look at what old Zen normativity has been. Zen Buddhism is full of ideals, such as the bodhisattva ideal, and imperatives, such as the precepts.

THE ALTERNATIVE NORMATIVITY OF PRECEPTS

To simplify matters, I will focus on a single precept, the precept to abstain from taking life, and the judgment underlying it. I want to consider first the form of such judgments and the consciousness behind them. Then we will have a look at the form of imperatives like the precepts, both in usual moral theory and in its Zen variation.

Crucial to the moral judgment is the copula or link between subject and predicate. For example, in saying "It is wrong to kill [sentient beings]," there is a binding force, characteristic of moral judgments, between killing and wrongness. This force is a measure of how strongly killing and wrongness are connected. Notice that in all but the most literal of ethical approaches (in Jainism, for example), for all traditions the force of the connection varies according to different factors. Every tradition adds qualifications to the judgment, so that it is interpreted to mean "killing is wrong except when..." and then an exemption is made. The binding force is almost always taken as a variable. Granted the variation, we can still ask about the nature of the connection in normative judgments, and its possible alteration in Zen. Moral philosophers typically take the binding force of moral judgments to be different from that in descriptive judgments about how things are.

A description is supposed to reflect accurately the state of affairs described; the truth of the matter at hand determines the binding

---

14. PARK 2006, at the end of her article.

force. When we describe what we take to be an invariant natural necessity, such as a law of nature, then the binding force is stronger than if we are describing circumstances that are changeable or subject to interpretation. But in mainstream philosophy, the binding force is still determined by the actual state of affairs. This force both binds the predicate to the subject of the judgment, and binds the person making the judgment to state the truth as accurately as possible.

The second kind of binding here is itself a normative one: one *should* state the truth. The sciences *are supposed to* state the truth; the scientist has an obligation. Nishida Kitarō, following some Neo-Kantians, was one Japanese philosopher who noticed this connection between truth and normativity. Nevertheless, the binding force of truthful descriptive judgments is taken to be quite different from that at work in moral judgments such as "killing is wrong." Few philosophers today follow the attempt of A. J. Ayer to reduce moral judgments to descriptions of personal preferences and sentiments. Normative moral judgments seem to refer necessarily to an external standard that determines their binding force, that determines why killing is wrong, for example.

The discipline of ethics tries to discover, or to formulate, the rationale behind the binding force. This ethical consciousness is one of finding a rationale, usually a standard external to the terms of the judgment. The standard might simply be the authoritarian "because I said so" or "because God said so," or it might be a pragmatic principle like the preservation of social order. It might be a principle like non-contradiction at work in Kant's categorical imperative, or like the value of benefit in utilitarianism, or like the value of saving sentient beings in Buddhism. In Buddhism, for example, we might say that "killing is wrong" because it is detrimental to the liberation of oneself and others. No such external standard seems to be required in non-normative judgments, such as Newton's or Einstein's laws of gravitation. No further standard is required for determining why gravitation is as it is.

To summarize so far, in the usual understanding of normativity, the binding force of moral judgments depends upon a standard external to the particular judgment. The appeal to external standards is the first characteristic of the moral judgment's binding force. The binding force between subject and predicate in this kind of judgment requires more than a match between them, more than true predication. For the judgment to have force, to be true in the sense that a value judgment can be true, there is an implicit reference to an unexpressed value.[15]

Now what about moral judgments in Zen? Before we prematurely dismiss the question by claiming that Zen does not engage in moral judgments, we need to look at an indirect form in which they might appear. Granted that we seldom see explicit judgments or rationales in a form such as "Killing is wrong because it is detrimental to the liberation of oneself and others," we do find plenty of expressions that appear as moral imperatives.[16] Let us take now take a look at this form.

In general, imperatives, commandments, or precepts are a more common expression of normativity than moral judgments. We could make the case that imperatives imply moral judgments and moral judgments entail imperatives. That is, behind each moral imperative is a judgment about the relative value, the good or evil, of a matter, and the judgment is such that it calls for one to act in a manner that accords with that value. The call to action is an implication of the moral judgment's binding force; the imperative form of expression makes this explicit.[17] Here again we see that the link between subject and predi-

---

15. This implicit reference differs from that in descriptive judgments whose truth, for many philosophers, appeals to context (Wilfred Sellars) or conceptual scheme (Willard Quine), while for others, no such variable context determines the truth of the descriptive judgment. A further question is whether the implicit referent in moral judgments must ultimately be a final, definitive judgment or expression of value, some ultimate good.
16. For an extensive trans-lation of *zazen* practice (as expressed by Shunryū Suzuki) into Kantian terms, see OLSON 1993.
17. A Nietzschean variation on this connection would say that morality commands an action that makes the judgment true. I am commanded not to kill, to make it true that "killing is wrong."

cate in a moral judgment does not suffice to express its binding force, that is, the obligation it calls for.

What else may we say about the binding force of imperatives in particular? Again, let us focus on the imperative form, "Do not kill!" (in Japanese Zen: ものを殺すことなかれ). I am not concerned here with the possible exceptions to the imperative, the possible qualifications that determine the circumstances in which killing might be permitted. We formulate such exceptions and qualifications only where there is a standard rule with a binding force. One might take a behaviorist position and say that the threat of punishment is what determines the binding force of an imperative. "Do not kill, or else! Or else you will be punished." The threat can take a more subtle form when the punishment is conceived as internal, as in philosophies of karma. For example, "do not kill, or else you will be harming yourself." On the other hand, one might take the position that the binding force of the imperative depends only upon that of the implied judgment. "Do not kill because killing is wrong (and killing is wrong because...," where one appeals to an external standard or value). Alternatively, one might appeal to the transformation of such imperatives into what seem like descriptions such as "there is no killing," or simply "non-killing." We need to say more about such statements, but I think that a prior step is needed to make sense of any such transformation, lest it simply discard the normative dimension. Or lest one commit the naturalist fallacy, as Christopher Ives warns in his constructive critique of Buddhist ethics.[18]

The prior step I suggest also involves an alteration—from one imperative form to another, from "do not kill" to "I will not kill." In fact, the latter is the more common form historically found in communal Zen practice. I call it an imperative because I understand it as a self-imposed demand. One demands of oneself not to kill. Critics might say that self-demands have no ascertainable binding force: if I make a demand solely of myself, I answer to no one and no one ensures that

---

18. IVES 2008, 25–6.

the demand is carried out. A self-demand, however, can be understood as a promise, not to oneself, but to others.

The promise, or more precisely, the vow, is the common formulation of precepts in Zen. Taking vows, or receiving the precepts (*jukai* 受戒) is a frequent way to formally join a Zen community or to assume the identity of being a Buddhist. Receiving the precepts means accepting them, vowing to uphold them.[19] The vow is a formalized promise and would seem to have the same binding force as a promise. In its phenomenological structure, a promise is a kind of intention that explicitly recognizes a gap between a present reality and an ideal—this is why promises are normative acts—along with an explicit call to fulfill the ideal. The promise thus differs from other acts that explicitly recognize the gap, such as wanting to do something, in that promising obliges or binds one to (at least try to) fulfill the intention. There is a fundamental difference between vows as self-imposed (or self-decided) imperatives on the one hand, and commands of the form "thou shalt (not)" on the other. Such commands assume that one has—or demands—authority over others. The authoritarian structure is a factor if one is punished when a vow is broken. I think the vow is better seen as an on-going decision for oneself.

The placement of the bond differs in Zen vows (and perhaps vows in general) from the bond in other types of promising. It is common to think of a promise as binding the person to perform, or to not perform, some action in the future. The promise binds present and future.[20] Religious vows in Zen—and in other traditions, I think—bind one to each present moment, and their fulfillment is performed progressively,

---

19. In Japanese, the officiant of the ceremony says to the postulant, "*Mono o korosu koto nakare. Yoku tamotsu ya?*" The postulant responds, "*Tamotsu.*" The precepts also form the subject matter of the final stage of kōan practice in some communities, where an understanding of their content is supposed to be deepened, but I will limit my discussion here to a beginner's understanding of them.

20. The link to the future is considered crucial. ARENDT (1958, §33 and §34), for example, proposes that promising is our way of coping with the undecidable nature of the future, just as forgiveness is our way of dealing with the irrevocable nature of the past.

moment by moment, rather than being deferred to the future. The vow of the first precept, for example, takes the form "I will abstain from taking life." In English, the phrase "I will" can indicate the future tense or can express an act of willing; I suggest that the vow stresses the act of willing more than the future tense. I will to fulfill my vow; my willing is here and now and the fulfillment must be here and now. I must be able to say, "I am abstaining from taking life"; my vow binds me to be able to say that. The formulation, "I will abstain," lines up with "I am abstaining." But this abstaining or non-killing takes the form of an ongoing practice, performed for its own sake—in the alternative mode of practice sketched previously in this book. When practiced, when I become practiced or proficient in this acting, when it becomes "second nature to me," occurring naturally (自ずから) so to speak, there is no need for the explicit intention called willing, or for the reflective reference to "I." The thought of "I will," even of "I am... abstaining," drops out, and we are left with "not taking life." The imperative "I will not kill" lines up with the descriptive "there is no killing," or more briefly, into "non-killing."

Several other scholars have explicated this shift as it appears in Dōgen's *Shōbōgenzō Shoakumakusa*, for example, as Thomas Kasulis did many years ago in his book, *Zen Action/Zen Person*.[21] I would add to their expositions by proposing that Dōgen is not substituting a descriptive formulation for a prescriptive or normative one, but rather aligning the prescriptive with the descriptive in order to convey the sense of normative practice he consistently advocates.

---

21. KASULIS (1981, 94) explicates the more general imperative "Do no evil," and its shift into "the nonproduction of evil." He writes, "Dōgen's basic strategy is to regard this passage not as an ethical imperative but as a description of the ideal state of mind." My analysis takes the shift not as a substitution but an alignment of imperative and descriptive, and proposes that the ideal implied in the prescriptive is something constantly being realized through practice. If we are to speak of a transformation, it is of the practitioner as well as the imperative form.

Earlier I mentioned Dōgen's implied imperative: just do *zazen* and you will be keeping all the precepts. Hakuin implies something similar. Some have taken such comments to indicate an avoidance of the issue about the bounds of the precepts, and others see an affirmation of the absolute as epitomized in *zazen*, beyond good and evil. Either way, it is rather obvious from these writings that Dōgen and Hakuin did not suppose that formal *zazen* was the only activity their monks were to engage in. An alternative reading is to see them advocating *zazen* as the site where one learns to practice. For them, by practicing one learns how to continuously embody a precept such as non-killing.

Two Zen Teachers on Killing

My discussion so far has remained somewhat abstract and general, so I want now to look at two texts that illustrate the sense of normativity in Zen in more concrete terms. These examples will help us understand the connection between the imperative and the descriptive in Dōgen, as well as the passage from text to non-textual practice. The first text is the commentary of a contemporary Zen teacher influenced by Dōgen, and the second is a passage from Dōgen's informal conversation with a monk.

More than twenty years ago the late Zen teacher Robert Aitken, founder of the Diamond Sangha in Hawaii, published a book on Zen Buddhist ethics focusing on the precepts. Aitken writes that the

> First Precept plainly means "Don't kill," but it also expresses a social concern: "Let us encourage life," and it relates to the mind: "There is no thought of killing."[22]

As a teacher of an international community of students, Aitken faced the challenge of explaining how the ultimate "no thought of killing" connects to the imperative "do not kill." As an expression of the ulti-

---

22. Aitken 1984, 16.

mate, he quotes the Rinzai Zen abbot Takuan Sōhō (1573–1645): "There is no one killing, no killing, and no one to be killed." Aitken then warns students of the danger of divorcing this descriptive statement from its use.[23] He goes onto give an example that intimates his understanding of the consciousness behind moral judgments and their transformation, although we will need to pose some questions to bring out the points I want to make.

Writing about one current issue where the precept is relevant, he mentions that he is often consulted by women in his community who are thinking of undergoing an abortion. "...I get the impression that when a woman is sensitive to her feeling, she is conscious that abortion is killing a part of herself...." It is clear that Aitken approves of that consciousness. "Self-awareness is never more important," he says.[24] We may ask then, what is the relation between such self-awareness and "no thought of killing"? On the one hand, self-awareness here presumably means consciousness that reflects on the gravity of killing "a part of oneself" as well as another potentially sentient being. Aitken writes:

> if... I learn that the decision is definite, I encourage her to go through the act with the consciousness of a mother who holds her dying child in her arms, lovingly nurturing it as it passes from life.[25]

Now Aitken would presumably understand the statement "there is no thought of killing" as describing not the mind of a deluded killer oblivious of the morality of his acts, but rather an absence of any intention to kill, even of any act of imagining killing a sentient being. The thought of killing does not even cross one's mind. But the mind of no-killing seems to differ considerably from the mind of someone thinking of undergoing an abortion.

Let us consider two interpretations here. The first takes the "mind of no-killing," for Aitken at least, as a description of a normative ideal

23. Ibid., 17.
24. Ibid., 21.
25. Ibid.

that the person considering abortion has not yet attained, or not yet manifested. Whether or not Aitken understands it this way is not clear, but he does make it clear that there is no blame, no moral judgment on the person who thoughtfully and self-consciously considers and undergoes an abortion. If realization of the ideal mind of no-killing is lacking, Aitken does not consider the lack a culpable fault.

The second interpretation takes the position that the person can actually be manifesting the mind of no-killing in undergoing an abortion. Perhaps Aitken thinks that the self-aware woman is being aware of "the flow of life and death"—a phrase that Aitken uses—rather than selfishly committing an act of killing. His emphasis on the suffering of the would-be mother who deserves our compassion, and his phrase, "to go through the act," suggest a receptive side of a process more than simply an act committed on an other. To reflect the implied receptive and processive side of the action, I have spoken of "undergoing" rather than "committing" or "having" an abortion. In either interpretation, it is clear that Aitken considers the abortion a matter for the woman to decide and implies that the act of decision is irrevocable. He does not mention responsibility, and indeed the word "responsiveness"—to use Thomas Kasulis's alternative—better captures Aitken's attitude, as long as we keep in mind the implied normative imperative to be responsive. I noticed that Aitken once again uses a descriptive phrase to evoke the sense of the imperative: "the decision to prevent birth is made on balance with other elements of suffering"—he does not say *should* be made this way.[26]

I find the descriptive form of Aitken's statement more indicative of Zen normativity than the impression that it advances a utilitarian approach. It would be misleading, I think, to take it as advocating a utilitarian *calculation* that aims at a negative balance of suffering in all affected beings. Attempting to add up quantities and degrees of suffering does not seem part of the kind of mind that Aitken promotes here.

26. Ibid., 22.

He does not describe a procedure, utilitarian or otherwise, for making a moral decision. What he does instead is state descriptively a model for understanding and living the precept. (I am concerned here only to make sense of Aitken's presentation, not to advocate it or to judge its moral adequacy from external criteria.) Aitken's comments take us far in understanding the consciousness behind moral judgments in part of Zen, but not as far as Dōgen's comments.

Dōgen's conversation with a monk is fascinating because it similarly finds him challenged to connect what sounds like an ultimate statement to the imperative form of a precept. The conversation was recorded by the monk, Ejō, about 1233, in the *Shōbōgenzō Zuimonki*.[27] It concerns the famous kōan case of Chan master Nanquan killing a cat. According to the story, Nanquan's monks in the West Hall and those in the East Hall were arguing about a cat. Stopping the argument, Nanquan held up the cat and challenged the monks to say a saving word, or else he would kill the cat. No one is able to respond, and the master cuts the cat in two.

The twentieth-century Zen abbot Shibayama Zenkei comments that most people interpret the story "from the standpoint of ethics alone, or from a common-sense point of view, since they do not have the authentic Zen eye and experience to grasp the essence."[28] I will fol-

---

27. The most popular version of the *Zuimonki* was produced by Menzan Zuihō (1683–1769), edited among others by Watsuji Tetsurō in 1929. In 1942, an earlier version was discovered at Chōen-ji that often differs in both content and order of presentation and is considered closer to the original text. The case about Nanquan's cat is found in the kōan collections, *Gateless Gate* (C. *Wumen-kuan*, J. *Mumonkan*), case 14, and the *Blue Cliff Record* (C. *Biyan-lu*, J. *Hekiganroku*), cases 63 and 64. See MARALDO 2021, 133–5 for critiques of the story.

28. SHIBAYAMA 1975, 109–110. Robert Carter seems to follow this line of thinking by considering an enlightenment experience as the foundation or origin of all true ethics. But then he proceeds to play with the cat quixotically, as it were, at times advocating a direct response to Nanquan's question to show one's presence in the moment, and at times disavowing Nanquan's action by comparing it with Zen institutions' support of Japan's Pacific War: "and if the cat were not a cat [but a child, or one's enemy in wartime]?... The [morality of] killing the cat cannot be decided on the basis on the enlightenment

low Dōgen's disciple Ejō in pursuing the unenlightened, non-essential, ethical understanding. Following both Ejō and Dōgen, I also assume that killing the cat actually happened, and is not simply a metaphor, as some teachers have suggested. Robert Aitken's teacher Yamada Kōun, for example, considers the act a play-acting; Aitken speaks of the case as a folk story whose violence is similar to that in fairy tales; and Sekida Katsuki says the cat is a metaphor for your own ego.[29] Contemporary Chan scholars often comment that monastery abbots probably didn't walk around with big kitchen knives. In a very perceptive interpretation, Jin Y. Park deflects the question of whether cutting the cat is metaphorical or factual, and directs attention instead to the monks, whose attachment to some imaginary factual truth they cannot utter is itself a form of violence. Her reading advances a postmodernist ethics that sees fixed moral codes as an origin of violence.[30] That approach could also point to the "dead end" of oppositional arguments that cut mat-

---

experience alone." Yet again, "moral decisions are all too often kōan-like." CARTER 2001, 99–121; quotations 119–120.

29. YAMADA 2004, 70; AITKEN 1984, 6; SEKIDA 1977, 320. Here one might recall Linji's famous statement, "if you meet a buddha, kill the buddha," taken to refer to delusive ideals.

30. PARK (2008, 115) writes,

> The impasse of the monks and the consequent death of the cat contain an ethical message stronger than any ethical codes. Violence is not committed by Nanquan alone who killed the cat in a literal sense; instead, the monks who failed to respond to Nanquan and we, who thus failed to realize the meaning of Nanquan's question, became accomplices. Violence is not committed only by our active involvement with physically violent actions. The inchoate origin of violence lies in our non-action and failure to see the world as it is. Violence, then, begins with our thinking. The *physical* violence of killing a cat, be it actual or symbolic, was caused by the monks' inability to *think* [that is, to participate in the production of truth and meaning].

After the first layer of violence, articulation and naming, there arises a "second layer of violence from the institutionalized system such as moral codes, social regulations, and social laws. Out of this second layer emerges empirical and physical violence" (102). While I recognize Park's deep insight into the speechless behavior of the monks, her postmodernist reading deriving from Derrida invites the twin dangers of trivializing physical violence and, insofar as the reading ignores the historical role of monastic regulations in Zen institutions, of substituting an imaginary Zen for its historical forms.

ters in two, or to the impasse of conflicting binaries alluded to here by posing West Hall monks against East Hall monks, or by insisting on an imperative such as "do this or else...."

Dōgen himself, however, takes seriously Ejō's question whether Nanquan's action was a breach of normative ethics, the traditional ethics of the precepts. Dōgen calls *cutting the cat* (斬猫) a turning word (転語) that manifests the "great function of the buddha-dharma" and says it should immediately awaken those who hear it. He also explicitly says cutting the cat is none other than the action of a buddha. Ejō finds this confusing, as I do, and asks whether the action was an offense (a crime or sin 罪) that breaks the first precept (against killing living beings, 殺生), to which Dōgen unequivocally answers yes. "How is one to be released from such an offense," Ejō asks. Dōgen's answer apparently reverts to a different level of understanding that Ejō cannot follow. Texts vary as to his answer; the four English translations I have found all use a text considered older and closer to Ejō's version, but they add a lot of words to the Japanese original. Shohaku Okumura's translation put added words in brackets, and has Dōgen replying: "[The action of a Buddha and a crime] are different, yet both occur [in one action]."[31] The original is more cryptic: "Separate, yet coincident" (別, 並具).[32] What is Dōgen's saying here? Is he allowing for both

---

31. DŌGEN 2022, 71.
32. In choosing this possible translation, I am grateful for suggestions from Zuzana Kubovčáková, Steven Heine, and Christopher Ives. The phrase 別並具, read *betsu, narabini gusu*, is in the Chōen-ji version, DŌGEN 1974, 337. In a note the editors paraphrase it as: 仏行と罪相とは別である．しかし、斬る猫において、同時にそなわっている. The translation into modern Japanese of the Chōen-ji version, by Yamazaki Masakazu (DŌGEN 1972A, 71), has Dōgen saying,「...斬猫といってよいのだ」and Ejō responding,「それは、殺生の罪ではありませんか」. Dōgen:「その通り、罪である」, Ejō:「どうしたら、その罪から、のがれられますか」. Dōgen: 殺生罪と仏の行いとは別であって、しかも両者を並ね具えているのだ」. Reihō Masunaga (DŌGEN 1971, 9) translates: "The action of the Buddha and the crime are separate, but they both occur at once in one action." Masunaga uses the popular version for the most part, but the Chōen-ji version for Dōgen's reply here (DŌGEN 1971, 113 n.18). Yokoi (DŌGEN 1972B, 15) translates: "Sometimes the Buddha's deed is one thing, and a sinful one is another. And sometimes there is no gap between the

a conditional, "*if* that actually happened" and a descriptive "as it happened"? We might try to frame the issue in terms of karma and its turnabout or "conversion," as Nishitani called it, whereby the standpoint of emptiness releases an action from arbitrary will and it functions as a "non-doing."[33] But then how could *killing the cat* function as an transmoral "non-doing"? Once again we confront Ejō's perplexity and the very question of a Zen ethics. Is Dōgen perhaps invoking a Buddhist version of Thomas Aquinas's "double effect," whereby an action is justified if its intention was good even if its effects are bad, especially if the action is intended as expedient, a "skillful means" or *upaya*? But Dōgen soon explicitly advises against holding the view that killing the cat is a means of awakening others.[34]

Dōgen's own intent seems undecidable. In this conversation the received imperative, "I will keep [the precept of not-killing]," is lined up with the simple descriptive phrase *cutting the cat* (斬猫). It is evident that neither Ejō nor Dōgen takes the phrase to mean simply *cutting out the thought of killing*, or *cutting through delusions*,[35] or else the scandal

---

two." Shohaku Okumura (Dōgen 2022, 69, 71) translates: "This cutting of the cat is the action of a Buddha." Ejō then asks, "Is it a crime?" Dōgen: "It is a crime." Ejō: "How can we drop off [the causality of this action]?" Dōgen: "[The action of a Buddha and a crime] are different, yet both occur [in one action]." Cleary (Dōgen 1980, 5) translates: "[The activity of Buddha and the wrongdoing] are separate, without appearing to be so." In a note, Cleary (p. 25) writes:

> This is a difficult passage; the Chōen-ji text has it, "They are separate (different) but both contained (in the act)." Evidently it means that killing the cat as an act of Buddha (to teach) and killing the cat as a form of wrongdoing are separate, or different, yet contained in the same outward appearance.

Menzan Zuihō's version apparently misreads the characters 並具 as 無見 and has 別別無見 なり. His is the *rufubon* or popular version appearing in most editions today, for example, Dōgen 1932, 713 and Dōgen 1977, 15.

33. See Nishitani 1961, trans. 1982, 257.

34. Dōgen is referring to the *prātimoksa* precepts (別解脱戒):「但、如是料簡、直饒好事なりとも下如無」ただしかくの如きのれうけん、たとひこうじなりともなからんにはしかじ (Dōgen 1972a, 65; *kana* transcription by Watsuji Tetsurō, Dōgen 1977, 15).

35. Would the pun on *cutting* work in Japanese as well as English? Hakuin, referring to the scheme of eight levels of consciousness in Yogācāra Buddhism, uses a similar expres-

of the story would disappear for them. Rather, we might take both the descriptive and the imperative dimensions as separate but coincident. That is, "separate, yet coincident" could mean, to put it in an imperative form: "you should understand the matter both ways, as an offense and a buddha's action"; or in a descriptive form: "both liberation and transgression are contained within the story about the cat [and within life]."[36] Ejō continues to ask about precepts, and Dōgen warns against an abuse of teaching methods like killing a cat. He encourages repentance in those who break the precepts and says they should be given the precepts again. This too implies that receiving the precepts is a matter of constant practice, and when broken off, the practice is to be taken up again.

If we can say that Dōgen aligns the imperative with the descriptive, we must then show how the two are related. One way is to look at the language. Dōgen minces no words; he simply calls the action *cutting the cat*. He offers no vindication, no justification, no rationale. He does not excuse Nanquan; nor does he turn the words into an imperative: kill (殺せ) under such circumstances! He simply aligns the descriptive with the moral judgment "it is an offense" and its implied negative imperative. The statement and the judgment are separate, yet are expressed at the same time and occupy the same semantic space.

Another way to relate them is to break them down into two temporal phases. That is, the present description states an ideal that the practitioner is to strive for from now on in following the imperative. This leads us back to the view that Dōgen transforms the imperative into a description of an ideal.

---

sion, quoted by NISHITANI (1974, 23):「八識田中に一刀を下す」 "Slice right through the field of the eighth consciousness."

36. Yet another interpretation is inspired by Husserl's phenomenology, in which values are subsequent layerings on perceptions. Dōgen would be saying, "there's the act, and then there are the conflicting judgments: either it is an offense or it is the action of a buddha. Given act and subsequent judgment are two separable things." That interpretation, however, describes the issue in terms of mental acts, and ignores the dimension of the continual practice of vows and precepts.

THE REALIZATIONAL NATURE OF THE IDEAL

If we say that non-killing describes an ideal, we must keep in mind the way that Dōgen conceives the ideal. This differs from the usual understanding of ideals in normative theories. The usual understanding takes the ideal as removed from the real and the present, sometimes so removed that it belongs to a separate realm, as in Plato's theory. This sort of ideal has its own sort of separate existence that can be conceived and formulated; it is what we may call *pre-existent*. Dōgen takes the ideal differently.

In reading Dōgen and other Japanese philosophers, two assumptions concerning the achievement of ideals are undercut. The first concerns the relation between ideals and actuality, the second concerns the relation between the means needed to achieve the ideal and the end or ideal itself. One common assumption in normative ethics is that there is a clear distinction between what should be and what actually is, and as long as what should be is possible, as long as it *can* be, then one *ought* to try to achieve it. Ultimately, one ought to posit the *ought*. The implicit alignment of *is* and *ought* in Dōgen places their difference into a more encompassing space. The other common assumption is that the means is distinct from the end to be achieved. As the chapter about the alternative sense of practice argued, Zen teachings, along with much Buddhist and classical Confucian literature in general as well as Aristotle's virtue ethics, undermine the difference between means and end. They do so by enjoining a form of practice geared to realize an end that is not different in kind from the means to realize it. There are different senses in which this is the case. The sense of Aristotle's example of playing the flute to be proficient in flute-playing is different from Dōgen's sense of *zazen* as manifesting the end or goal of liberation. In both examples, the end to be achieved is not different in kind from the means; the "means" is an actualization of the end. But in Aristotle the relation is one of gaining proficiency, while in Dōgen it is a matter of manifestation: the "means" of *zazen* manifests the "end," the reality of enlightenment. Here a connection to Nishitani's equivalence of moments is evident (see Chapter 11): in this and every moment of practice, present and future are coincident (並具). (One meaning of the Chinese 並 is "at the same time.") Practice makes the ideal present.

In his talk "Not Doing Evils" (*Shoakumakusa*) of 1240, Dōgen writes, "At the very moment of doing good, every good comes into existence."[37] Dōgen's sense of the ideal is *realizational*, to adopt Hee-Jin Kim's phrase.[38] Practice realizes the good in the world; and what good *is*—what defines good—is realized in the body-mind of practitioners. Nishitani often deliberately puns on the English verb *realize*, meaning both objectively *actualize* and subjectively *recognize*. Dōgen makes abundantly clear in texts such as the *Bendōwa* that practice manifests realization, and he continually advocates practice in all his writings. Again, in the *Shoakumakusa* he writes, "Every good is not existent, is not non-existent, is not form, is not emptiness, nor anything else: it only is devoutly practicing."[39] Not doing [evil], not killing in our example, is the practice of not-killing, where the genitive "of not-killing" is subjective as well as objective, where it is not-killing's practice. In Dōgen's language, *not-doing* or *not-killing* becomes the subject that acts; it is not-killing's practice and not-killing's doing. The mind of "I will not kill" as well as of "I am practicing non-killing" seems to drop away to leave, simply, "non-killing." But the descriptive "non-killing" for Dōgen also *encompasses* the imperative rather than discards it. He says, "Even an admonishment not to act evil and even a recommendation to act good are fully apparent 'not doing.'"[40] To use our example, *even an admonishment not to kill is manifest in "not killing."* This understanding seems to be more encompassing than Aitken's reading, "there is no thought of killing," which can be taken to mean that the thought of killing simply does not cross one's mind, or even

---

37. An early translation by William Bodiford, in JPSB, 158.
38. KIM 2004, 61 and 67.
39. Ibid.
40. Ibid.

that one becomes incapable of killing. This understanding is also more fruitful than a reading that reverts to the view that the cat case is, after all, a kōan and therefore a paradox. Let us look briefly at these two readings.

The reading of Dōgen's response as a paradox plays on the duality of killing and non-killing, evil and good, and says that somehow the two are paradoxically equivalent (and as dualistic, mistaken). It questions the decision to call non-killing good and killing evil. It challenges ordinary views with questions such as, Why not killing? Why isn't killing a way to be? If killing is not a good way to be, why not? It suggests that whatever normativity is operative in Zen, it cannot answer this question, cannot appeal to an external standard telling us why something is good or not. For such an appeal would beg the question and imply simply that killing is not good because it is not good. The paradoxical reading would imply further that there is no ultimate good, and therefore any appeal to a superior good is ultimately otiose. This reading, however, does not necessarily imply a relativist position, to the effect that what is good or bad depends solely on some other variable or other, that "it all depends." And even if we cannot say ultimately that something is good and something else bad, the reading implies that discriminating good and bad, right and wrong—as absolutes or as relatives—is itself bad, itself an exercise of delusion. Whether this paradox can be resolved by the two-truths theory I will leave for future deliberations. Shall we say that discrimination is bad? Or simply that discrimination is? The paradoxical solution is hard to reconcile it with the more common approaches to ethics that we find in Dōgen and other Zen masters, who do not discard the precepts or the *pāramitās*. The realizational approach is more promising.

The other reading, "there is no thought of killing," reminds us of approaches to ethics in non-Buddhist traditions. The moral alternative of becoming incapable of doing wrong is not limited to East Asian philosophy, much less to Zen. Plato's translator, G. M. A. Grube, writes that the aim for Socrates was "not to choose the right but to become the sort of person who *cannot* choose the wrong and who no longer has any choice in the matter."[41] In the case of receiving the precepts in Zen, instead of "keep well [the precepts]" (*yoku tamotsu*) we would have "[I] cannot help but [keep the precepts]" (*tamarazaru o enai*). Aitken implies this ideal, the inability to choose the wrong, in his mention of the woman's decision to undergo or not undergo an abortion. He suggests that a good practitioner can morally choose an abortion, though not without thinking. This ideal, admirable as it is, does not go as far— or as near—as the formulation of Dōgen. In Dōgen, the imperative is not replaced by the descriptive; both are contained within the same space. *Imperative* and *descriptive* forms are grammatically separate, but inherently aligned. If we need a single word to express this space, I think the word *declarative* will do.

These considerations suggest an alternative, both to common views about Zen ethics and to the classical distinction between descriptive and normative, *is* and *ought*. They suggest that, in some Zen literature at least, normativity is not a preliminary stage ultimately transcended or undermined by something ultimate and absolute. The imperative form of Zen precepts is not ultimately replaced by a descriptive and non-normative form. Such a step would amount to a "naturalist" or "realist" reduction of ethics, an account that replaces normative statements with descriptions, as we find in Edward O. Wilson's statement:

> If the empiricist world view is correct, *ought* is just shorthand for one kind of factual statement, a word that denotes what society first chose (or was coerced) to do, and then codified....
> *Ought* is the product of a material process.[42]

Rather, the two forms of expression, descriptive and normative, *is* and *ought*, depend on one another for their sense.

If we use the word *declarative* to express their common space, we need to note one more feature of the alternative. Suppose we declare

---

41. GRUBE 1975, 2.
42. WILSON 1998, 251.

that killing is *not to be*. We implicitly describe but also advocate a *way to be*. No further appeal is given, no threat of punishment, no transcendent measure, no "just because." No ultimate answer to the question why is killing is wrong. Any such answer would refer to a further reason or ground. Instead of an appeal to a further ground, we find a pattern of manifestations, in this case, of suffering. Their connection is the ultimate equation of suffering and evil. It is not so much that suffering is considered an evil, as suffering is the meaning of evil. Some ultimate, absolute Zen understanding may say that it is only delusion that sees suffering in the world; the idea of suffering is itself a product of delusion, and so this evil is a matter of perspective, not an absolute. But Zen teachers like Dōgen also remind us that for deluded beings suffering and its causes are real and to be overcome. Even if overcoming calls for continuous, embodied practice.

Dōgen's Zen

13

The Study of Body-Mind
Dōgen's Alternative

> Mountains, rivers, and the great earth,
> the sun, moon, and waters—all are the mind.
> – Dōgen, *Body-Mind's Study of the Way*[1]

INTRODUCTION

Investigating an issue in light of intercultural philosophy poses questions that compel us to re-think the way we conceive of typical problems. One example is the traditional mind-body problem, which has been formulated as follows: if the mind is a spiritual thing and the body a material thing, how do they interact? Is the mind a thing, a substance, at all? Is the mind rather only a metaphor for what the brain does? What do words signifying mental events really mean?

There are, to be sure, alternative ways of posing the problem; there are even accounts which deny that a genuine problem exists, or which declare all its formulations to be themselves problematic.[2] Despite the controversy, however, or perhaps because of it and of recent findings in brain research, the burgeoning interest in the mind-body issue is greater than ever. The task of intercultural philosophy in addressing this issue is not so much to solve or dissolve the problem as to uncover the presuppositions that have traditionally nurtured it, perhaps for centuries. Philosophers working interculturally do not simply assume

---

1. KIM 1985, 98.
2. One of the most influential works about the status of the problem has been RORTY 1979. Allusions to Rorty in the present chapter refer to this work.

that a problem is perennial or universal, and then go on to compare approaches and solutions to it. Rather they attempt first and foremost to investigate the sets of guiding questions that cluster around an issue, to define the shifting boundaries of problems in differing traditions, and to raise new questions or propose new approaches that challenge those boundaries.

In the arguments of contemporary philosophers and cognitive scientists, the "mind-body problem" may be exposed as a whole cluster of problems, or as not a problem at all. But a contrast of arguments and their terms with the texts and contexts of a vastly different tradition or time can reveal a definable problem after all, one that is confined to modern European traditions.[3] This could happen if a jarring contrast revealed something that was utterly unthought of or forgotten in current argumentation, an aspect or dimension that offered a radical alternative to modern Anglo-European thinking. Whether anything so radically different turns up or not, such contrast can provide mutual illumination of the ways we read texts of divergent traditions.

We might, then, better gauge the bounds of the mind-body problem if we address the question of body and mind from the standpoint of an entirely different tradition, such as that conveyed by Dōgen. The Zen master's writing entitled *Shinjingakudō* (身心學道, "Body-Mind Studying the Way") is a paradigmatic text for an inquiry proceeding from contrast rather than from an assumption of parity.[4] What makes the contrast possible is a twofold translation, a trans-lation that renders the terms *mind* and *body*: *mind* as a variable signifier for both 心 and a range of European words, and *body* as a variable sig-

---

3. For a contrast with the ancient and early medieval Greco-European tradition, see the fascinating study of the Hebrew and Hellenistic notions of the body (but not of the "soul") by MILES 1981.

4. An indication of the contrast is the reading and order of sinographs in Dōgen's compound term 身心 (*shinjin*, body-mind), which reverses the order of the compound that names the contemporary "mind-body" (心身 *shinshin*) problem.

nifier for both 身 and another range of European words.⁵ This translation opens a space in which *mind* and *body* and their counterparts in Dōgen's Japanese can encounter one another. What is more, that space permits a disclosure of the formative questions of vastly different traditions: Anglo-European questions and the questions raised by Dōgen's text. It turns out that this thirteenth-century Sino-Japanese Buddhist text not only inherits certain questions, but also explicates and often transforms them. In turn, our investigation will suggest alternative formulations of the mind-body issue, new methods for intercultural philosophy, and new possibilities for the reading of ancient or alien texts.

To pursue this path of contrast, I propose to examine some of Dōgen's views on body and mind as expressed in his *Shinjingakudō* and to juxtapose these views with themes in Anglo-European philosophy of mind. In the following, I offer a tentative reading of Dōgen's text—more accurately, a series of tentative readings that take successive parts of the text as their anchor and use them as a foil to highlight the bounds of the mind-body problem. Reciprocally, I attempt to throw light (and shadows) on Dōgen's procedure from the stance of contemporary philosophy. I suggest that the phrase *shinjingakudō* has several senses that replace and transform one another, in dialectical fashion and, when applied to the European tradition, turn the mind-body issue inside out. Finally, I return to the question of our vantage point and hermeneutical procedure to comment on the open task of body-mind inquiry.

5. *Heart-mind* is another frequently used translation of 心; in Chapter 8 on Zen Landscapes, I suggest *mindful heart*. *Shintai* (身体) is another translation of *body*, and 身, when pronounced *mi*, can refer to oneself. The range of terms that the English *mind* is made to cover includes, for example, the German *Geist* and *Gemüt* and the French *L'esprit* and *le mental*. *Body* translates the German *Körper* as well as *Leib* and the French *le corps* that also means the *corporeal*.

Questions Raised by Context and Method

In 1242, shortly before Dōgen left his suburban temple Kōshōhōrinji for the remote mountains of Echizen, he composed *Shinjingakudō*. The text opens by echoing parts of earlier compositions: the beginning of the *Fukanzazengi* (普勸坐禪儀, "Universally Recommended Instructions for *Zazen*") and several passages in the *Bendōwa* (辨道話, "Discerning the Way"). The opening also offers a sample of the Japanese text's style and word plays:

> 佛道は、不道を擬するに不得なり、不學を擬するに轉遠なり。南嶽大慧禪師のいはく、修證はなきにあらず、染汙することえじ。佛道を學せざれば、すなはち外道・闡提等の道に墮在す。このゆゑに、前佛後佛かならず佛道を修行するなり。

I translate freely:

> The Buddha Way is not attained by aiming to waylay or silence it; it grows ever more remote by aiming to avoid study. As Dahui of Nanyue said, it is not that there is no practice and realization, just that they are not to be defiled. If one were not to study the Buddha Way, one would fall into heresy outside the Way and into talk of *icchantika*. For this reason, the buddhas of past and future practice the Buddha Way without fail.[6]

It can be said that the immediate context for these statements is Dōgen's reformist position vis-à-vis the eclectic practices of Zen during his day. They included the notion, prevalent in the Tendai sect on Mount Hiei, that no practice was necessary for enlightenment, as well as the opposing idea that some (the *icchantika*) were forever excluded from enlightenment.[7] Dōgen seems once again to be insisting solely on *zazen* practice and justifying the institution he is about to establish in Japan. But rather than take these historical circumstances to be the context of Dōgen's opening statements, I wish to consider the state-

---

6. All *Shinjingakudō* references are to Dōgen 1971a, 36–41.
7. Collcut 1981, 49–56 provides historical background to Dōgen's views.

ments themselves as the context of his views on body and mind, and to contrast that context with the typical framework of the modern mind-body problem.

In the *Shinjingakudō* (身心學道), the order in which Dōgen discusses topics is the reverse of that of the lexical elements named in the title: first comes the Way (道 *dō*), then study (學 *gaku*); and, although named together originally, mind (心 *shin*) will be discussed before body (身 *shin*). Study is specified as practice, and practice, as we learn in the passages to follow, is exemplified by the actions of the buddhas and ancestors. Dōgen's consideration of body and mind serves to elucidate the Buddha Way, something that is at once an ultimate reality and a path in need of realization. The opening lines of the text make it clear, then, that the primary concern and object of study is the Buddha Way; *shinjingakudō* first of all means to study the Way, not the body and mind. Dōgen's consideration of body and mind begins with a negation of their priority.

Arising as it does amidst medieval Sino-Japanese controversies about the nature and necessity of practice for accomplishment of the Buddha Way, the text's opening affirmation of the primacy of the Way has no strict counterpart in traditional European philosophy. Though the opening lines clearly intimate that this practice (修行) is a bodily accomplishment (the term connotes bodily endeavor), body and mind are not presented as central objects of study. This difference will prove to be heuristically significant for our reading of contrasting modern Anglo-European formulations as well as of Dōgen's text. The text forces not a detour around body-mind considerations, but a transference or transposition of the connotations these terms carry. Indeed, in an arena of contrast, the text will suggest that both terms *body* and *mind* in philosophical usage are already transpositions: they act more as metaphors than as names.[8]

8. I examine further terms and connotations relating to bodily practice in MARALDO 1981.

In traditional Anglo-European philosophy of mind, mind-body considerations have assumed the central position, from whose vantage point the bounds of human knowledge are to be fixed. Insofar as theories of knowledge were derived from considerations of body and mind, of sense and intellect, the latter were accorded primacy as objects of study. To be sure, intellect and senses were more often regarded as faculties or powers than as things, and it was their functions and functioning that interested philosophers. But this functioning was itself consistently taken as an object of reflection; the mind under investigation was more the mind thought-about than the mind thinking. Hence the epistemologies that were developed were epistemologies of representation. On the primary level, mind became mind-thought-about, and secondarily, all other things thought-about or known about became objects of that mind. In idealist positions, the mind comes to "represent"—to stand in for all the objects of the world. In realist and empiricist positions, the mind re-presents or reflects objects in the world as a mirror reflects whatever stands before it. "To know means to reflect accurately what is outside the mind," as Richard Rorty puts it in his critical study of the epistemologies of representation.[9]

Rorty's work shows that one need not read texts such as Dōgen's to link the mind-body problem with theories of knowledge based on representation. But when we do read traditional Anglo-European formulations in juxtaposition with Dōgen's text, their context and consequences emerge more clearly. Mind-body considerations that found theories of knowledge tend to focus on the nature, scope, and limits of reason as a mental power, on the ability of the mind to reflect and the nature of the world reflected, and on the question whether the mind is of a piece with all else in the world. We find a diversity of positions, ranging from idealism to empiricism to reductionism regarding the autonomy of mind and the foundations of knowledge. Yet in the most materialist positions as well as the most idealist, is not a predominant

9. RORTY 1979, 3.

objectivism apparent when we notice the focus on mind, embodied or not, precisely as an object of investigation? A contrast with Dōgen's emphasis on practice and exemplary human activities makes that objectivism quite apparent.

In the *Shinjingakudō*, Dōgen continues, "we may provisionally distinguish study by way of the mind and study by way of the body." Here the meaning of *gakudō* becomes "study by way of." Considering first study via the "mind" (心), Dōgen mentions its various aspects. Borrowing expressions from Tendai philosophy and old Chinese Zen records, Dōgen includes the reflecting or self-conscious mind (*citta*) and dimensions that transcend self-consciousness: ubiquitous mind and all-comprehending mind[10]; the aroused bodhi-mind, bits and pieces of straightforward mind, mind of ancient buddhas, ordinary mind, three worlds-one-mind. We may leave the interpretation of these various aspects of mind open for the time being, and proceed to the more important question of the methods of study.

Dōgen writes that "there is study of the Way by discarding or letting go of all these [aspects of] mind and study by taking up or employing them. There is, then, study by way of thinking (思量), study by way of not thinking (不思量), and study by "thinking of not-thinking," that is, non-thinking (非思量). Here any distinction between means of study and object of study dissolves, so that *shinjingakudō* also comes to designate the way of studying mind and body. The "thinking of not-thinking," or release of objects of thought, is also mentioned in the *Fukanzazengi* in the context of practical *zazen* instruction, but Dōgen goes a step further here when he connects it with various incidents in

---

10. The three terms Dōgen uses are almost as ambiguous as the English "mind." According to Nakamura S. 1975, 質多心, a transliteration of the Sanskrit *citta*, most likely denotes discriminating mind (慮知心). 汗栗駄心, Sanskrit *hṛdaya*, is probably equivalent to 草木心, the mind of plants and trees, connoting universal, omnipresent buddha-nature. 矣栗駄心, Sanskrit *vṛddha*, is probably 種聚精用心, the wisdom mind grasping and extracting the essence of the entire body or universe. Kim (1987, 127–35) discusses body and mind terms in Dōgen's works.

legendary Zen history. To illustrate "the study of mind with mind" (以心學心), he mentions (although with ellipsis of proper names) Shakyamuni's transmitting and Kashyapa's receiving the golden brocade robe, the Second Chinese Patriarch Huike's grasping the marrow of Bodhidharma's teaching, and the Sixth Patriarch's study by way of pounding rice and then receiving a robe.[11] Then, after citing such incidents, Dōgen makes the relevant connection: "To think of not-thinking is to enter the mountains [of practice], and non-thinking (非思量) is to discard the world [of attachments]."

Dōgen's appeal to legendary Zen history is significant because it takes something likely to be considered a mental technique and places it in the context of social practices. Even if one considers this way of thinking, not-thinking, and non-thinking as a method of engaging mind, the mind engaged is more than the conscious or reflecting mind, as Dōgen's list of the various aspects of mind makes clear. As the various expressions of mind illustrate, the mind totally engaged and totally disengaged is the pivot of study. Mental reflection, while not excluded, is not the only aspect of mind engaged in study; and its nature, scope, and limits are not the only objects of consideration. Dōgen will go on to imply that mind (心) is not merely "mental" and internal, much less essentially rational.

Let us shift back to Anglo-European philosophy of mind, bracketing the notion of body, as does Dōgen, for the time being. Rorty sums up the traditional stance: "To know is to represent accurately what is outside the mind, so to understand the possibility and nature of knowledge is to understand the way in which the mind is able to construct such representations."[12] But if we were to take this "mind" and place it within Dōgen's context, it would fit nowhere except under the category of *citta* or reflecting mind. Likewise, the method of under-

---

11. Does Dōgen's progression here from an aristocratic image ("the golden brocade robe") to a commoner's activity ("pounding rice") allude to a shift from an exclusive attainment to a practice available to all?

12. RORTY 1979, 3.

standing how the mind works would fall in the domain of study by way of thinking (that is, Dōgen's 思量). Specifically, this mind itself would appear an object of reflection or representation and the activity of representation would actually have a double object: first the world represented by mind and then mind itself represented as the power to represent. There is, then, a double process of externalization involved in reflecting accurately what is "outside the mind." Not only is world outside mind, but mind is outside mind. That is, not only is world outside, but mind itself, as an object of philosophical reflection is made to be "outside," or at least on the other side of, the invisible activity of reflecting. This is all the more true when mind is reduced to the brain or activities of the brain. Ironically, the view that placed mind inside ended up externalizing it, taking it as object or concept and forgetting it as living activity.

It is true that existential phenomenologists such as Heidegger, Sartre, and Merleau-Ponty criticize this tradition and place mind originally in the world, collapsing a rigid distinction between inside and outside. Heidegger's critique of representational or objectifying thinking reminds us of what had been forgotten and recalls some non-objectifying way of study: musing, poeticizing, questioning, conversing.[13] Sartre suggests that the thinker or ego as subject of thoughts is constructed post factum, after the act of thinking, and belongs to the world of objects.[14] Merleau-Ponty lets us see where mind and world are reversible: mind-thought-about and mind-thinking must be parts of an embodied whole, itself beyond objectification.[15] These philosophers break through the limits of representational theories of mind and stress its pre-reflective aspects. They approach Dōgen's primacy of

---

13. Although Heidegger does not address the "mind-body problem" as such, his insights concerning Being-in-the-World have laid the foundation for an alternative view of human be-ing. See especially HEIDEGGER 1927, §12. Critiques of representational or objectifying thinking are found in HEIDEGGER 1961 and in HEIDEGGER 1927–64, 22–33.
14. See SARTRE 1936–37.
15. See, for example, MERLEAU-PONTY 1964.

practice, in which mind as the way or method of study exceeds mind as object of study, where mind is a matter to be practiced and realized and not simply thought about. Heidegger in particular has implied that thinking is first and foremost a practice, and not a condition or an object of representation.[16]

But does Heidegger's thinking attain Dōgen's "thinking of not-thinking," either as a technique of practice or as an interpretation of exemplary human activity? I think not. The existential phenomenologists may "take up" in their study "various aspects of the mind" (as Dōgen has in part described "thinking"), including those that transcend reflective consciousness and incorporate the world. But their study does not include the practice that consists in letting go of thoughts, "discarding all aspects of mind" (as Dōgen has paraphrased "non-thinking"). Dōgen himself, however, never gives specific instructions on how to perform "non-thinking," either as mental technique or as exemplary action. Does he leave its meaning open because it is a meaning to be realized, a kōan like the expressions of the "transmission of mind" he cites from Zen history, or like "entering the mountains and discarding the world"? Do such statements serve a double grammatical function, proclaiming the nature of the study almost as a matter of fact, but at the same time enjoining upon the reader a task to be accomplished? Are they imperative as well as declarative statements (as was the case with his normative statements about Buddhist precepts)?

QUESTIONS POSED BY MANNER OF ARGUMENT AND ALLUSION

If we can answer yes to these questions, then the open, hortatory character of many of Dōgen's statements would temper the

---

16. A sustained attempt to practice thinking in his series of university lectures presented in HEIDEGGER 1961. Pages 127–38 in the present volume consider the question whether we can understand Heidegger's *Gelassenheit*, composure and releasement, as a practice.

13. The Study of Body-Mind | 331

authoritative, self-assured, even dogmatic tone one is likely to hear in them. To clarify this point and contrast it with Anglo-European modes of argument, let us turn to the main themes in the next part of Dōgen's text.

Echoing the *Awakening of Faith in the Mahāyāna* and innumerable Yogācāra and Zen texts, Dōgen proclaims mind to be "mountains, rivers, earth, sun, moon, and stars." Here Dōgen alludes to common Buddhist teachings and expressions concerning mind (心), as he has done previously in the text. But he does not simply repeat them without applying a kind of Mādhyamika logic and interpreting them from his own vantage point. "Mountains, rivers, earth," etc., "exceed the forms that appear to us; they are boundless phenomena of all the world [of Buddhist cosmology]; they appear differently to us than to other beings, according to different viewpoints; and therefore," as Dōgen twists ordinary logic,

> the view of one mind is one and the same. Are not all of these, mind in its universal form? Shall we construe this mind as inside or outside, coming or going, increasing with life or decreasing with death? As attained or not attained, known or not known?... Beyond our grasp, mind is such that we must resolve to let it study of itself, and must accept on faith or trust that this is *shinjingakudō*, the mind studying the way and the way the mind studies.

Leaving aside the task of tracing Dōgen's references and the question of how unique his interpretation might be, I want to comment on it as a mode of argument. A series of statements is given, and although their grammar at times suggests an interrogative, the questions seem rhetorical and the statements sound definitive. Allusions made in this passage and throughout the text, particularly when the alleged speaker is named, strengthen the impression that other, perhaps inaccessible sources are taken as authoritative. There is hardly a sense of a rational argument being developed, something that would consider various possible views of mind, raise objections, and defend one view against others for certain explicit reasons. Let us assume familiarity with the discursive, reason-based mode of argument characteristic of Anglo-European philosophy of mind. What, then, is the nature of Dōgen's argument, be it argument at all?

Dōgen does allude to various views concerning the nature of mind and does not always accept them uncritically. When he speaks of the mind neither increasing during life nor decreasing upon death, he refers implicitly to a view denounced by name in the *Bendōwa*, that is, to what he calls the "Senika heresy" of a personal, individual mind or soul that lives on after the death of the body. When he questions whether that mind (and mountains, rivers, earth, sun, moon, stars) are inside or outside, he implicitly criticizes those idealistic Yogācāra interpretations that would see phenomena as creations of the imagination (*parikalpita*), and he echoes sayings in his *Mountains and Waters Sutra* that we pondered in Chapter 8. Later in the *Shinjingakudō*, he directly implores young students not to concede to the mistaken view of innatism or naturalism (自然外道) that bodily practice is not necessary. But even there he cites as authoritative the words ascribed to Baizhang Huaihai, to the effect that liberation (解脱) itself is buddha, but attachment to liberation belongs to the heresy of naturalism or spontaneous enlightenment.[17] Dōgen offers no reasons against various views; he merely states that they are mistaken.

Yet we may ask whether this lack of reasons does not suggest a manner of argument that parallels the content of the text. Some criticisms are offered, just as consciousness and reason are included as part of mind, but not to the exclusion of other, universal dimensions. Authority is appealed to, just as acceptance by faith is invoked to complement a rational grasp of the dimensions of mind. Allusions

---

17. See KIM 1987, 155, for a discussion of innatism, also called naturalism and spontaneous enlightenment. I leave it an open question whether this innatism is synonymous with that criticized in Dōgen's "Disclosing Mind, Disclosing Nature" (説心説性) as the position of Dahui Zonggao, namely, the view that mind is only intellect and perception, Dōgen's *citta*.

interconnect the text with other texts in the tradition, just as mind and aspects of the world are said to be interdependent. Finally, attributes and descriptions of mind are consequently affirmed, negated, and emptied, just as non-thinking and release (放下) are named—and non-discrimination is implied—as ways of study. We are asking whether the *form* of Dōgen's "argument" recapitulates its content, whether what Dōgen is *doing* with words and statements reflects what he is saying (and not saying). But this question arises here by way of contrast to the discursive arguments, based on reasons and formal rules independent of content, that are typical of Anglo-European philosophy of mind.

QUESTIONS POSED BY METAPHOR

It is remarkable that Richard Rorty's own argument against the traditional mind-body problem concludes that "pictures rather than propositions, metaphors rather than statements, determine most of our philosophical convictions." He suggests, then, that something has been more persuasive than rational argumentation in the tradition, namely, the images and comparisons presupposed by the arguments. A few words are in order about metaphors for the mind and the mind that makes metaphors.

The controlling metaphor in the "Western tradition," Rorty finds, is this:

> The mind is a great mirror, containing various representations—some accurate, some not—and capable of being studied by pure nonempirical methods. Without the notion of the mind as mirror, the notion of knowledge as accuracy of representation would not have suggested itself. Without this latter notion, the strategy common to Descartes and Kant—getting more accurate representations by inspecting, repairing, and polishing the mirror, so to speak—would not have made sense. Without this strategy in mind, recent claims that philosophy could consist of "conceptual analysis" or "phenomenological analysis" or

"explication of meanings" or examination of the "logic of our language" or of "the structure of the constituting activity of consciousness" would not have made sense.[18]

We need not comment here on the mirror metaphor and the image of cleansing (versus sharpening) the mind by polishing the mirror that we find in Daoist and Zen literature.[19] Instead, let us add other, more recent comparisons to the list.

One controlling metaphor today is the mind as the brain. Three significant variations of this image are (1) The brain is a computer, the mind its software. One's behavior is determined by the way the brains have been "programmed." (2) The brain is a biosystem, not a machine, and the mind is the neural functioning of that system; one's behavior is the motor outcome of biological events in the central nervous system.[20] (3) The brain is a hologram, and the mind consists of interference patterns of waves encoded on it; one's behavior is a decoded and projected pattern.[21] Still another school would look in the mirror and see no mind at all; the brain is real enough, but the "mind" is nothing but behavior or dispositions to behave.[22]

18. RORTY 1979, 12.
19. The locus classicus of mirror imagery in Zen literature is the story of the verse competition to determine who the Sixth Patriarch would be. The verse of Shenxiu, the Fifth Patriarch's leading disciple, as translated by YAMPOLSKY (1967, 130–1) reads: "The body is the bodhi tree/The mind is like a clear mirror./At all times we must strive to polish it/ And must not let the dust collect." Huineng, who eventually became the Sixth Patriarch, replied, "Bodhi originally has no tree. / The mirror also has no stand. / Buddha nature is always clean and pure; / Where is there room for dust?" Compare the ancient Daoist metaphors in the *Daodejing* (trans. by LAU 1963, chapter 10): "Can you polish your mysterious mirror [i.e., your mind]?" and the *Zhuangzi* (trans. by WATSON 1968, 70): "... if the mirror is bright, no dust settles on it; if the dust settles, it isn't really bright" and "The Perfect Man uses his mind like a mirror—going after nothing, welcoming nothing, responding but not storing" (97).
20. One detailed defense of this position is BUNGE 1980.
21. Karl H. Pribram was the most energetic advocate of the holographic (or holonomic) theory; see e.g. PRIBRAM 2013 (1991). My statement of this metaphor is from PIETSCH 1981.
22. B. F. SKINNER (1972 and 1976) strongly advocated the behaviorist position.

Phenomenologists will resist such metaphors, take a more holistic approach, and insist on the irreducibility of consciousness and its intentional, intersubjective, and intramundane aspects. They will be less likely to forget that the program-mind, the neuron-mind, the hologramic mind and so forth, are parts of a whole that includes the very activities of programming computers, investigating the brain, observing behavior, proposing theories of mind, and creating metaphors. Thus, the metaphors they employ will cover more than what the term "mind" conveys in traditional philosophy of mind. Merleau-Ponty, for example, uses terms like "intertwining" and "chiasm" to indicate the intersection and reversibility of parts: you and I are of such a nature that we can both see and be seen, touch and be touched, etc.; as embodied consciousness each of us is a visible seer, an audible hearer, a tactile/tactual being. Merleau-Ponty chooses the term "flesh" to speak of something more elemental and relational, more concrete and yet universal, than what terms like "matter," "spirit," "body" and "mind" usually convey.[23]

For all that, Merleau-Ponty's metaphors seem abstract and recondite when compared with Dōgen's statement in the following phrase of the *Shinjingakudō*: "It is not three-worlds-mind only, it is not dharma realm-mind-only; it is fences and walls, tiles and stones."[24] Itself an allusion to a saying of Zen adept Sushan Guanren and unnamed others, this metaphor empties the metaphor of "the three worlds are mind only" of any remnant of idealism and abstraction. And just as "mountains, rivers, earth, sun, moon, and stars" open out mind, "fences and walls, tiles and stones" bring mind closer in.

We certainly cannot suppose that the term "mind" is univocal in all the descriptions I have mentioned. Yet I wonder if they do not share an underlying preconception of mind as something internal, invisible,

---

23. MERLEAU-PONTY 1964 (1968), 139–40.
24. This metaphor (牆壁瓦礫) is almost ubiquitous in Zen literature and appears again in fascicles of the *Shōbōgenzō* such as *Shinfukatoku* (心不可得, "Mind cannot be grasped").

and individual or individuated—even if that sense is to be dislodged. Thus, the metaphor of "three-worlds-mind-only" implies but turns against the sense of mind as internal and individual, and of world as external and independent. Likewise, Dōgen knows that we take things to be differentiated objects in the world, so his "fences and walls, tiles, and stones," like Zhaozhou's oak tree, turns around the presumption that mind can be differentiated, and reality objectified.[25]

Just as we cannot suppose that the term "mind" is used univocally, we cannot assume that the metaphors are used in the same sense. Indeed, some people will balk at calling the descriptions metaphors at all, and insist that they are to be taken literally. When Dōgen says mind is fences and walls, tiles and stones, he means just that.[26] And when the contemporary psychologist Mario Bunge says the mind is a set of brain

---

25. I allude to the legendary dialogue in the *Recorded Sayings of Zhaozhou*, as translated in GREEN 2001, 16:

> A monk then asked, "What is the mind that the Patriarch brought from the west?"
> The master said, "Oak tree in the front garden."
> The monk said, "Don't instruct by means of objectivity."
> The master said "I don't instruct by means of objectivity."
> The monk again asked, "What is the mind that the Patriarch brought from the west?"
> The master said "Oak tree in the front garden."

Ceteris paribus, ARISTOTLE (1942, 591-2), in *De Anima* III, 4: 429b, 29-30 and 430a, 14-15, suggests a remarkable parallel: " ...mind [νοῦς] is in a sense potentially whatever is thinkable, though actually it is nothing until it has thought.... it is what it is by virtue of becoming all things [το πάντα γενέσθαι] ...Mind ...is in its essential nature activity...." J. G. Hart proposes that that "mind" has null intension and infinite extension; thus Zhaozhou has to refer to an instantiation (extension) like the oak tree to present the (null) meaning of "the Patriarch's mind."

26. Dōgen is even more explicit in the *Zuimonki*, talks delivered in 1235-37 at Koshōhōrinji (DŌGEN 1971B, 65-6):

> Without knowing who taught them these things, students consider the mind to be thought and perceptions, and do not believe it when they are told that the mind is plants and trees. . . .Therefore, when the Buddhas and the Patriarchs categorically state that the mind is plants and trees, revise your preconceptions and understand plants and trees as mind. If the Buddha is said to be tiles and pebbles, consider tiles and pebbles as the Buddha. If you change your basic preconceptions, you will be able to gain the Way.

functions, he means this literally. But Bunge abandons this literalism when he goes on to develop formal definitions, postulates, and mathematical formulae to specify his sense of mind.[27] And Dōgen refuses a fixation of his meaning when he goes on to say (quoting Sushan): "Before the year Kantsū [Gantong of the Tang era] mind is built of fences and walls, tiles and stones; after the year Kantsū [Gantong] it is torn down." As if just to make sure, Dōgen later declares that "the mind of ancient buddhas is not fences and walls, tiles and stones, and these do not mean the mind of ancient buddhas."

In his talks to monks compiled as *Zuimonki*, Dōgen remarks that expressions like "mind—mountains, rivers and the great earth" are possible as *tengo* or turning words that evoke enlightenment.[28] This term may be a more appropriate word than "metaphor" to describe the expressions of mind in the *Shinjingakudō*. But perhaps these expressions also tell us that we ordinarily understand metaphors in a very restricted sense. We often define a metaphor as a comparison of two things, one thing standing for something else. This definition itself is an example of representational thinking. One thing ("mind," for example) is understood in terms of another, more basic or better-known thing (e.g., the brain), and the metaphor of comparison derives from the literal meaning of the base term (in this example, "we know what the brain really is, and we can say the mind is [like] the brain").

---

27. Compare one of his postulates on thinking, an activity mistakenly thought to be a property of "mind": "Postulate 7.4. A sequence of thoughts about propositions is (identical with) the sequential activation of the psychons whose activities are the propositions in the sequence" and "Definition 7.3. Two thoughts are equivalent if they consist in thinking of the same constructs. That is, $(\theta_a) \sim \theta_b(C')$ iff $C = C'$ for any animals a and b." BUNGE 1980, 159–61.

28. Turning words (転語), ubiquitous in Zen literature, find a parallel in *kakekotoba* or pivot words, a literary convention in classical Japanese, especially court poetry, where they function as a kind of pun. See the discussion in MINER 1968, 24–5. A potent example of the phrase "mind—no other than mountains, rivers and the great earth" functioning as a turning word is the enlightenment experience of Yamada Kōun Roshi, reported in KAPLEAU 1965, 205–6.

This manner of understanding metaphor does not work for "the mind is fences and walls, tiles and stones." Rather, expressions like this expose certain presuppositions and turn our sense of metaphor around. Might metaphors perhaps turn out to be connectives more basic than literally meant definitions—to be concrete expressions of an interconnected whole that outstretches a language of fixed concepts referring to independent entities? As such connectives, metaphors are particularly expedient when one element or reality (e.g. consciousness, or *ceteris paribus*, Dōgen's 心) is irreducible to anything more basic. Metaphors functioning fundamentally as connectives also straddle the difference between a differential transposition of oneself and one's surroundings, on the one hand, and one's full identification with the environment, on the other.[29] In this sense, mind as mirror, mind as brain, and mind as walls, tiles and stones would all be metaphors, whether meant "literally" or not. They are equivalent transpositions, as intimated at the beginning of our reading, which show the nature of mirrors, brains, and concrete pieces to be as relative as the nature of minds; they are transpositional equations in which both sides are essential for signification. One-sided views that objectify mind (or devalue metaphor) conceal the relativity of language and the reference to a sustaining whole. In contrast, Dōgen first asserts the primacy of the Way, then jolts the mind and dislodges the ordinary connotations of words. In the *Shinjingakudō*, "mind" (*shin*) becomes a cipher whose meaning is to be filled by expressing the Way via bodily practice.

Nor is it lost to us that Dōgen's talk begins by speaking of *Way* (道, *dō*) metaphorically, inter-connectively: the *Way* stands for a whole that can be signified by other words such as Dharma or Truth or—in modern parlance—"Buddhism" as authentically practiced. Signifying the path of realization, 道 functions as a nominal reference. At the same

---

29. Fayan's verse about self-identity, cited in Chapter 8 on Zen Landscapes, expresses this span of differentiation: "With reason exhausted, feelings and deliberations are forgotten/*How can it be likened to anything!* (如何んが喩斉有らん)/ Right here this frosty night's moon...."

time, 道 functions as a verb signifying the path's ever active expressing.[30] Yet the metaphor and double signification of *Way* do not lapse into mindless or endless ambiguity, for Dōgen explicitly tells us what the *Way* is not—not the aberrant ways (外道) and stymied speech (不道) of those who talk about *icchantika* and deny that the practice of realization is open to all. Dōgen's frequent, metaphoric reference to the "buddhas and ancestors" connects the practice engaging the individual to a whole continuum of practitioners.[31]

QUESTIONS POSED BY POINT OF DEPARTURE

The full sweep of metaphors at work in Dōgen's writing is a topic best left to other studies, but we can at least indicate the significance of the Way for a metaphorical understanding of mind. The opening passage of the *Shinjingakudō* asserts that the buddhas of past and future, so as not to fall into false views, have all practiced the Buddha Way, that is, have attained it bodily.[32] In our contrasts with Anglo-European philosophy so far, we have been following the bias of its pre-twentieth-century theorizing by isolating mind and relatively ignoring the role of the active body. Dōgen also postpones his discussion of the body until the last third of his piece. He has told us in the opening passage that there are, *provisionally*, two ways of study: via the mind and via the body. This simple remark, which suggests that the two will be taken up one at a time, is a tacit allusion to the doctrine of the "one-

---

30. Here I allude to Hee-Jin Kim's translation of 道得 (*dōtoku*) as *expression*, which should be understood nondualistically as the Way-gaining activity of all phenomena throughout the universe. See especially KIM 2004, 76–99.

31. I comment further on the communal nature of Dōgen's practice in MARALDO 2016.

32. In the *Zuimonki*, DŌGEN (1971B, 47) asks, "Is the Way attained through the mind or through the body?" He answers: "In Zen the Way is attained with both body and mind...," but then he emphasizes: "Therefore, if you cast aside completely the thoughts and concepts of the mind and concentrate on *zazen* alone, you attain to an intimacy with the Way. The attainment of the Way is truly accomplished with the body. For this reason, I urge you to concentrate on *zazen*."

ness of body and mind" (身心一如). We find this principle affirmed throughout Dōgen's works and discussed especially in the *Bendōwa* in connection with the "Senika heresy." The gist of the discussion there is that to believe the mind to be eternal or immutable and the body perishable, or indeed, to assume any real separation between then, is aberrant and self-defeating. From the perspective of perishability, all things are perishable; from the perspective of immutability, all things are immutable. Body and mind are not two.[33]

In the *Shinjingakudō*, Dōgen assumes that his followers already have in mind the concrete way of bodily practicing that he has described in other writings—the method of what we often call "meditation" and what he calls, in more somatic terms, *zazen*, "sitting meditation." Up to now, our explication has focused on words and their references, on what one might say is merely the way Dōgen and others think (and do not think) about body and mind. Our analysis has not given even a hint of verbal instruction, much less an ostensive demonstration, of how one is to go about, to embody, "thinking of not thinking"—as if that "non-thinking" truly left all words behind.

The text of *Shinjingakudō* may be silent about a *method* in the sense of a developed way (*meta-hodos*) to do something, but in the same year as its composition, 1242, Dōgen revised his *Fukanzazengi* that, as its title implies, recommends concrete generic instructions for doing *zazen*. Using very specific language, Dōgen describes in detail how to assume the lotus posture, how to place legs and hands, to position ears and nose and back, to adjust eyes and breathing. He describes the proper attitude and atmosphere: choose a quiet room; eat and drink moderately; cast aside all involvements and cease all affairs; do not think good or bad, pros or cons; cease all movements of the conscious mind; have no designs on becoming a buddha. Yet this *zazen*, he asserts, "has nothing whatsoever to do" with sitting or lying down [or standing or walking, the four classical postures] and is "not learning

33. Dōgen 2002, 146.

meditation. It is simply the Dharma gate of repose and bliss. It is the practice-realization of totally culminated enlightenment."[34]

I have come to think of Dōgen's *zazen* as the place—though not the only one—where practice is exemplified and "awakening" is made manifest. The Chapter 4 on alternative practice indicated how *zazen* functions as the exemplar of a practice not aiming for a goal extrinsic to it but actualizing it from the beginning.[35] Chapter 3 on hermeneutics suggested how such practice grounds an alternative understanding that exceeds the grasp of texts. Dōgen's text calls forth a specific, concrete way of practice that he proclaims, paradoxically, to be *the* way and yet not a way/a method at all. The *Fukanzazengi* opens with this conundrum:

> The Way is originally perfect and all-pervading. How could it be contingent upon practice and realization?... And yet if there is the slightest discrepancy, the Way is as distant as heaven from earth.[36]

The opening passage of the *Shinjingakudō* echoes this with its statement that nearly defies textual understanding and translation: "The Buddha Way is not attained by aiming to silence it"—as if it of itself spoke up[37]—and it becomes ever more remote if we aim to avoid study, to obviate body-mind practice.

---

34. My abbreviation and quotations follow the translation of Norman A. Waddell and Abe Masao in DŌGEN 2002, 3–4, who note that Dōgen uses the term *sanzen* (參禪) synonymously with *zazen* in giving these instructions.

35. See page 117 of the present volume, which quotes from Dōgen's *Bendōwa*: "The Dharma [the truth] is amply present in every person, but without practice, it is not manifested; without realization, it is not attained.... As it is from the first realization in practice, realization is endless. As it is the practice of realization, practice is beginningless" (DŌGEN 2002, 8 and 19).

36. Ibid., 2–3. DAVIS 2016A gives an insightful reading of the entire *Fukanzazengi* that also shows how Dōgen's situating of *zazen* practice does not obviate awakening experience. DAVIS 2023 introduces the *Shinjingakudō* in the context of renewed embodied spiritual practice.

37. KIM (1985, 97) translates 「佛道は、不道を擬するに不得なり」 as "The Buddha-Way is such that it is impossible not to say it."

I take the nonduality of body and mind to be the point of departure for the separate discussions of mind and body in the *Shinjingakudō*. Dōgen's approach cannot be said to be dualist in the sense that modern Anglo-European philosophies of mind presuppose. Fundamentally, practice (行) is oneness of body and mind, and practice-realization (or practice-authentication, 修證) does not pull them apart. Their separate treatment in the text, however, indicates that a provisional distinction between them is expedient not only for purposes of discussion, but also for bringing home the point that body and mind signify a unity to be practiced and achieved. They are neither merely conceptual opposites nor a pre-given identity.[38] Once again, an examination of Dōgen's text will show that its very form reflects this transposed unity. The later section of the text that begins with the phrase *shingakudō* ("body-studying Way") recapitulates the main points and procedures expressed previously. We can highlight part of its content by shuffling the order of presentation somewhat:

> *Shingakudō* (身學道) means... to study the Way with the body, with the whole naked flesh. What the body is emerges from the study of the Way, and what emerges from the study of the Way is the body. All worlds in the ten directions are this very human body; birth and death, coming and going, the four elements, the five aggregates[39] are this human body. To study with the body is to cut oneself off from the ten evils, uphold the eight precepts, convert to the three treasures, leave home, and renounce the world.

Here Dōgen expresses, in order, the concrete, universal, phenomenal, boundless, practical and social dimensions of the body (身), in parallel with expressions concerning the mind (心). And again, the manner of argument is to let the style or mode of presentation itself

---

38. For a contemporary Japanese philosopher's explication of the theme of mind-body unity accomplished through practice, see YUASA 1987.

39. Note that classical Buddhist classifications identify the body only with the first aggregate or *skandha*, *rūpa* or matter.

demonstrate the meaning of the content. Dōgen displaces more abstract metaphors ("the ten directions") with more concrete ones ("a grain of dust"); more static images ("a grain of dust") with more active, social ones ("to construct a practice hall is to incorporate the whole world in a grain of dust; this of itself is the true human body"). Even concepts signifying active practice-realization, such as liberation (解脱), become like broken furniture in an empty house when attachments to them form, when they become merely conceptual. Just as there is practice with the body and expressions of that practice, there is also practice by discarding the body and discarding expressions: "to drop the body is to raise the voice that stops all echoes."

As in the *mind* section of the text, the *body* section embeds numerous allusions and quotations. The image of practice by stopping the echo (perhaps itself an allusion) is followed by the phrase "cutting an arm and attaining the marrow," an allusion to the legend of Huike's devotion to study under Bodhidharma and his transmission, and hence to the practice of cutting off objectifications of mind, the "mind" that Huike cannot find.[40] The allusions refer to teachings that Dōgen sometimes affirms, sometimes criticizes, sometimes reinterprets: "Broken furniture in an empty house," for example, criticizes innatism, the heresy Dōgen identifies by quoting words ascribed to Baizhang about attachment to liberation. These allusions and quotations seem to make Dōgen's own contribution more elusive. In a sense they break down a strict distinction between his own position and that of others.[41] It becomes impossible at times to distinguish his originality—his self—from others, so that Dōgen's very style illustrates the

---

40. Huike's story forms the 41st case of the *Gateless Gate* (*Mumonkan*). Standing outside in the snow, the future Second Patriarch begs Bodhidharma to set his mind at rest. Bodhidharma replies, "Bring me your mind and I will put it at rest." Huike says, "I have searched for the mind but cannot find it anywhere." Bodhidharma: "I have now set it at rest for you."

41. MARALDO 2021, 215–29 shows how Zen legends often exemplify the transpositional nature of authorship.

message he alludes to and quotes: the true human body is beyond selfness and otherness.

What can Dōgen's starting point, the nondual, transposable nature of body-mind, tell us, then, about the mind-body problem in modern philosophy? It would seem that a starker contrast is unimaginable, both in content and style of thinking. I find that the juxtaposition brings to light two biases typical of current presentations of the mind-body problem. Most solutions and dissolutions presuppose dualism and mentalism, even when they are monist and materialist. In order to explain this strange accusation, it may be helpful to repeat a typical formulation of the problem. If the mind is a spiritual thing and the body a material thing, how can they interact? Is the mind a thing, a substance, at all? Is the mind, rather, only a metaphor for what the brains does? What do words of mental events ("feeling sad," "thinking about supper," etc.) really signify?

While other formulations of the problem occur, it is difficult to find one that does not initially *oppose* mind to body, even if the solution is to reduce one to the other.[42] The philosophical problem, then, concerns the relationship of two terms (or their cognates), taken as proposed realities or as realms of signification. Let us consider two philosophical positions that seem to dismiss the opposition outright: conceptual behaviorism and physicalism. Behaviorism avowedly rejects the term "mind" as meaningless. It admits only of publicly observable entities and events, assumes that the body belongs entirely to the public realm, and attempts to explain in terms of conditioned bodily responses the more private, hidden human experiences for-

---

42. An example of a current sophisticated dualist position is David Chalmer's naturalistic dualism, whereby mental states naturally supervene on physical systems such as the brain but are ontologically distinct from and irreducible to these physical systems. An example of an equally nuanced physicalist position is J. J. C. Smart's view that states and processes of the mind are identical to states and processes of the brain, even if ordinary language does not allow straightforward translations. The sophistication and detail of current positions do not diminish the degree of an initially conceived opposition, however.

merly attributed to "mind." But just this persistent attempt belies a mind-body opposition posited initially or implicitly in behaviorism, where "mind" *means* such and such, that is, it signifies events such as feeling emotions and thinking thoughts, or it mistakenly purports to signify the substratum of such events. But (it argues) these events can be explained in terms of verbal or non-verbal behavior, and no subject or substrate other than body is necessary for an adequate explanation. In behaviorism, the reality of mind may be dismissed, but a notion of mind opposed to body is not; otherwise there would be nothing to explain. Likewise, a mind-body opposition is presumed, before it is dissolved, by all the strong and weak forms of physicalism, ranging from the simple identification of mind with brain-events to the sophisticated view of mind as a qualitatively different "emergent property" of the brain. The position of psychoneural monists is that "mind" can be shown to be brain, or a product of the organization of the brain; "spirit" is shown to be matter-energy.[43]

Reductions of "mind" to brain, however, in whatever form they occur, presuppose a notion of mind whose functions can be shown to be identical with those of the brain. The conceptual terms and models in modern solutions may be changed (one may speak of covert verbal behavior instead of private thoughts, or of plastic neural systems instead of "mind"), but such solutions come in the wake of the historical oppositions of body and mind and derive their cogency from that opposition. They remain dualist solutions, then, insofar as a mind-body duality, to explained or explained away, remains their point of departure.

A glance at what mind and body denote in the *Shinjingakudō* suggests by way of contrast another bias in the modern philosophy of mind. In addition to terms signifying the universal, boundless, and formless dimensions of body and mind, there are expression that iden-

---

43. BUNGE (1980) declared himself to be a psychoneural monist. A classic defense of materialism in general is ARMSTRONG 1968.

tify the mind or body as a particular social action. "Leaving home and renouncing the world" (a description of a monk's vocation) is just as much a metaphor for mind (and body) as is "thinking" or "not-thinking"; "constructing a meditation hall" describes body (and mind) just as much as does "the four elements," just as much as does "a grain of dust."

One might interpret such actions merely as examples of behavior, and conclude that for Dōgen, too, mind is behavior. But surely no behaviorist would concur with Dōgen that "mind" (or whatever substitutes for "mind") can manifest in *one* concrete action, here and now. The behaviorist's position is actually mentalist insofar as "mind" is taken to refer to a set of *internal* functions explainable as covert and overt behavior, and it is representational insofar as "behavior" does not include the behaviorist's own activity of observing and testing the behavior of others. The behaviorist takes a different stance toward himself than toward others; somehow, he retains mind, whereas others exhibit behavior. Likewise, the physicalist, who demonstrates that what we call "mind" is identical with functions of the brain. The meaning of "brain" (its logical intension) and therefore of "mind" does not include for the physicalist the social *activity* of researching the properties of the physical organ. If such activity engages her "whole body and mind," to put it metaphorically, and cannot be reduced to neural occurrences in the brain, then the physicalist, too, remains paradoxically a "mentalist." She locates "mind" in the brain and excludes it from its sense activity in the world. Like the behaviorist, the physicalist permits evidence only from the realm of objects and objectifications: brains, object-bodies, and observable behaviors. But the functioning brain, after all, is not directly an object in the world; it is an organ hidden in a cavity enclosed in a skull beneath skin and hair. Physicalism, too, shares in the fundamental bias of the traditional philosophy of mind that we may call the mentalism of representational thinking. This is the mentalism that, ironically, has internalized mind by placing it inside and the world outside, indeed by *placing* it at all.⁴⁴ Contrary to Dōgen's deliberate practice of affirming, negating, and emptying the identities of mind and body, the tradition even in its current forms would fix the meaning of mind to *something definite*.

We have let Dōgen's *Shinjingakudō* turn solutions to the modern mind-body problem on their head. The behaviorist denial of mind is mentalist, and psychoneural monism presupposes a dualist starting point. I think it would be possible to see other solutions and procedures in the same light, that is, as representatives of representational thinking and reliant on an inner territory once called mind.

Once again, phenomenologists have come closer to Dōgen's approach to body and mind. Gabriel Marcel, Jean-Paul Sartre, and Maurice Merleau-Ponty resurrected the body as a theme of philosophical discourse, developed a terminology that did not initially presuppose a mind-body duality, and exposed some basic prejudices in the tradition.⁴⁵ They refused the language that implied I *am* my mind and I *have* a body, and sought alternatives to the metaphors of mind as self, body as property, and both as object. In particular, Merleau-Ponty spoke of the subject-body and the "flesh" that defied objectification. He intentionally spoke in metaphors and drew his examples from concrete activity in the world. But he also labored to overcome Cartesian dualism and chose his metaphors and examples in conscious opposition to the tradition. Universal dimensions of mind that had been thematized in pre-Socratic philosophy were as foreign to him as to most of the tradition,⁴⁶ so the idealism he opposed was that of Kant and

---

44. On the philosophical debate regarding semantic internalism and externalism, and Nishida's alternative to the distinction, see MARALDO 2017, 179–98. In a nutshell, that debate revolves around the question whether "mind" is self-contained and solely internal to the individual subject of experience, or whether its contents are entirely dependent on the environment and the world in general. The crucial question in the present chapter concerns where the reference to the word "mind" is located.

45. A summary and critical examination of the role of the body in these phenomenologists is Richard M. ZANER 1964.

46. The philosophy of A. N. Whitehead is an exception. See the discussion of mind

Husserl, not that of Yogācāra. And starkly concrete metaphors, like "fences and walls, tiles and stones," would not be able to express the total embodiment of mind or of world for Merleau-Ponty, who had no contact with the sort of thinking (and non-thinking) that is practiced in Dōgen's writings.[47]

Concluding Questions

For our investigation of Dōgen's *Shinjingakudō* in contrast with the problem of mind and body, we have employed the method of jarring contrast, pitting a thirteenth-century Sino-Japanese text and current Anglo-European formulations against one another. The contrast showed us remarkable divergencies in the priority of theme, forms of argument, status of language, and points of departure. But perhaps it also misled us into forgetting that the divergent texts arise from separate traditions and address quite different questions. This method escapes the danger of being ahistorical only upon recollection that the terms of contrast themselves relate metaphorically. They are deliberately dislodged from their comfortable home in history to confront one another in a contemporary arena of inquiry. They do take part in originally different questions, and any unification of themes or traditions must come, like Dōgen's unity of body and mind, as an achievement. That achievement, however, is likely to be not a fusion of traditions but a transposition of barriers.

Be that as it may, before the achievement or along its way, further historical retrieval and open questioning are called for. Let me point the way by recalling Richard Rorty's masterly summation of traditional "Western" philosophy of mind and my difference from it. Rorty discusses "solutions to the mind-body problem" not, he says, to propose

---

extending throughout the natural universe, in WHITEHEAD 1958.

47. On the other hand, LOUGHNANE 209, 176–7 finds innovative ways to bring Dōgen and Merleau-Ponty closer together by making explicit their common ontology of the expressibility that is shared by all beings, animate and inanimate.

one but to illustrate why he does not think there is a problem. The mind-body problem belongs to history for Rorty, in the sense both of being historically determined and of being obsolete. Specifically, our notions of the mental belong to a philosophical game that "links up with no issues in daily life, empirical science, morals, or religion."[48] Rorty intends his work to be therapeutic rather than constructive, and to restore conversations and not a tribunal of reason as the context of knowledge. Alluding to Aristotle's and Plato's "wonder" indirectly by way of Heidegger, he would evict from the great conversation of humankind technical and determinate questions that are poor substitutes for that "openness to strangeness which initially tempered us to begin thinking."[49]

Certainly, one would have to be open to strangeness to listen to a conversation between Dōgen and modern philosophy of mind. Like Rorty, I have offered no solution to the mind-body problem as I formulated it at the outset. I have not even attempted a reformulation. But perhaps by "playing" with that problem, by bouncing it against fences, walls, tiles, stones and other strange pivots, we have caught some bits and pieces of Dōgen's mind whole before they dissolved in our grasp. We turned the body and mind's study of the Way into a study by way of body and mind, into the way the body-mind studies, into a study of body-mind forgetting the Way. We found that a behaviorist and a physicalist have a mind of their own that they seem unwilling to share with mountains, rivers, and the great earth. We found the phenomenologists' body not exhausted by constructing metaphors, and not exhaustively embodied in any one grain of dust.

Unlike Rorty, I cannot renounce the practical and social consequences of the mind-body problem and view it as a retreat to the mountains of words better forgotten, as a remote language game long played out. Although I have not touched on these issues here, I think

---

48. RORTY 1979, 22.
49. Ibid., 9.

that other urgent problems hinge in part on conceptions of body and mind, their sameness and their difference Whether we insist on respect for all conscious animals and sentient beings, whether we find limits to behavioral modification, whether we divide responsibility for acts bodily committed under mental incompetence, even how we relate to our environment—as property or as self—these are social issues that depend on how we conceptualize, and how we practice, oneness of body and mind.

14
Negotiating the Divide of Death in Japanese Buddhism
Dōgen's Difference

> When you die, you want to die a beautiful death. But what makes for a beautiful death is not always clear. To die without suffering, to die without causing trouble to others, to die leaving behind a beautiful corpse, to die looking good—it's not clear what is meant by a beautiful death. Does a beautiful death refer to the way you die or the condition of your corpse after death? This distinction is not clear. And when you start to stretch the image of death to the method of how to dispose of your corpse as befitting your image of death, everything grows completely out of hand.
> – Aoki Shinmon, a Buddhist mortician[1]

The Question

Many of us consider Dōgen to be the most profound of philosophically-minded Japanese Buddhist teachers in the classical period. But what, if anything, does Dōgen have to teach us about the meaning of a "beautiful death"? Can he take this matter that so easily gets completely out of hand and place it within our grasp?

Divides

When it comes to the topic of death in Japanese Buddhism, it seems we encounter two disparate Buddhisms that rarely if ever meet.

---

1. Aoki 2002, 44–5.

On the one hand we find the Buddhism of the philosophers, including the Kyoto School and the Buddhist thinkers they quote, and on the other hand we encounter the Buddhism of the populace and of the scholars who study it.[2] The sense and significance of death differ so profoundly in these two approaches to Buddhist teachings and practices that one wonders whether death is a unequivocal phenomenon at all.

Philosophical Japanese Buddhism deals with the "great matter" of birth-and-death (*shōji* 生死, samsara) and focuses on liberation through either rebirth in a Pure Land, or the realization of one's birthless and deathless buddha-nature, or the transformation of one's own body-mind. In the esoteric tradition, Kūkai (774–835) taught that we attain buddhahood with our present body, and emphasized embodying to the (near) exclusion of dying. In the Zen tradition, Dōgen writes that seeking buddha outside of birth-and-death is as futile as trying to travel south by heading north,[3] and other philosophers cite his words frequently when they explain the non-separation of samsara and nirvana. Hakuin (1685–1768) wrote of the Great Death, the death of the illusions that sink one into the cycle of birth-and-death, and the Great Joy experienced at the awakening that frees one from this cycle.[4] The twentieth-century Zen teacher Hisamatsu Shinichi (1889–1980) exclaimed "I do not die" to proclaim his awakening from the delusion of being a self subject to birth and death.[5] In the Pure Land tradi-

---

2. A distinction in terms of philosophical Buddhism and the Buddhism of the populace is a tentative suggestion. Scholars have contrasted doctrinal with popular or folk Buddhism, and the Buddhism of the elites with that of non-elites, but these sets of distinctions pose historical problems of their own. See FORMANEK AND LAFLEUR 2004, 24–5 and 34. Whatever the terms, the point is to contrast a major difference in the two ways that Buddhists and scholars both have presented Japanese Buddhism, while recognizing that monk elites and illiterate laity shared many beliefs, and that the keepers of doctrine also performed rites for common folk.

3. *Shōbōgenzō Shōji*. See DŌGEN 2002, 106.

4. *Orategama Zokushū*. See HAKUIN 1971, 145.

5. "Speaking in an interview, Hisamatsu Sensei once said, 'I tell my family I do not die. I say that I am the formless Self. Therefore I do not die. In fact, death never even crosses my mind. I have some work to do.'" MERRILL 1981, 129.

tion, philosophers speak of birth and death or life and death together, on the same side, as opposed to the other side and the power of the Other to liberate the devotee. Hōnen (1133–1212) wrote that "The path to liberation from the cycle of birth-and-death at the present time is none other than birth in the Pure Land of Amida Buddha."[6] Shinran (1173–1263), contesting the view of the earlier Pure Land thinker Genshin (942–1017), wrote, "There is no need to wait in anticipation for the moment of death, no need to rely on Amida's coming. At the time true entrusting becomes settled, birth [in the Pure Land] too becomes settled; there is no need for the deathbed rites that prepare one for Amida's coming."[7] In the twentieth century, Kiyozawa Manshi (1863–1903) wrote that "Life, that is not only who we are. Death is also who we are. We have life and death, side by side. But we do not have to be affected by life and death. We are a spiritual existence outside life and death."[8] Philosophical Buddhism places birth and death (or life and death) together on one side of a divide that distinguishes both from nirvana, even where nirvana is considered nothing but awakening within birth-and-death.

The Buddhism of the populace, on the other hand, concerns itself with a death that divides the departed from the living, and focuses on the care of the corpse and of the spirit of the departed who often is thought to care for or to curse the survivors. This Buddhism recognizes the fear and the pain of death and offers rites of passage and of mourning. The depiction early in the *Tale of Genji* of the treatment of the death of Yūgao, Genji's lover, may be fictive but it is not far from the longstanding truth about this Buddhism: Outside the room where the body was laid out for the wake,

> two or three monks chatted between spells of silently calling Amida's Name.... A venerable monk, the nun's own son, was chanting scripture

---

6. HŌNEN 1974.
7. SHINRAN 1997, 523, cited in ŌMINE 1992, 26.
8. KIYOZAWA 2003, 270.

in such tones as to arouse holy awe. Genji felt as though he would weep until his tears ran dry.

Though the cause of his ailment is kept secret, the court has "rites, litanies, and purifications... in numbers beyond counting" performed for the grief-stricken Genji; and later Genji has "images made every seven days for [Yūgao's] memorial services." The translator, Royall Tyler, notes that these images depicting Buddhist divinities were newly painted for each memorial service, "held every seven days during the first forty-nine days after death and at widening intervals thereafter," "to guide the soul toward a fortunate rebirth."[9] The Buddhism of the people sees death as the departure of one who is born: it places the body of the departed in the care of clergy and family, and imagines the spirit of the departed somehow, somewhere, on the other side of life.

Far from being merely one topic among others in the complex known as Japanese Buddhism, the topic of death forms the core of what, for a great many scholars, actually defines Buddhism, what Buddhism is really about. If we may speak of two disparate Buddhisms in Japan (and elsewhere), then the divide between the two over the sense of death marks a significant difference in interpretations of the nature of Buddhism. On the one hand, philosophically inclined Japanese Buddhists have criticized the fact that their religion became "funeral Buddhism" and a religion of rituals at the expense of the true teaching of liberation and the core practices of morality (Sanskrit: *śīla*), meditation (*dhyāna*), and wisdom (*prajñā*) to attain liberation. Some lament the "decline" of Japanese Buddhism to the extent of deeming predominant practices not true Buddhism at all.[10] On the

---

9. MURASAKI 2001, 72, 73, and 75.

10. Watanabe Shōkō is an example of a scholar who documents but harshly criticizes the "decline" of Buddhism in Japan into formalized religious ritual and the loss of its true mission: the "seeking of *bodhi*-mind above (上求菩提) and the saving of beings below (下化衆生)." The religion that lacks these aspirations "is not [truly] Buddhism." WATANABE 1986, 207; trans., 1970,125.

other hand, scholars who would abstain from normative judgments argue that the practice of rituals for the dying and the dead, even if not confined to Japanese Buddhism, historically defines its most important social role.[11] Some find concern with death, the death opposed to life and the living, at its very core.

The eminent Buddhist scholar Sueki Fumihiko recently published a book that re-examines the history of Buddhism by focusing on death. He contends that arguments about the existence of the dead are irrelevant to what we can know about how the living relate to the dead, and what we know is that "the Japanese worldview allows for an ambiguous conceptual realm with an uncertain existence." The realm of the dead in this worldview includes deceased persons, Japanese and Buddhist deities, and even ghosts and spirits, to whom the living inevitably relate. For those living in the medieval period, this "other world" (他界) was dreamlike, not in the sense of being illusory but in its inherently ambiguous nature. Sueki argues that the relationship of the living to the dead defines the entire history of Buddhism, beginning with the passing of the Buddha and the consternation of his disciples over his absence. Practices of enshrining his relics were a way of keeping him present, as were practices of composing sutras. Pure Land sutras presented an Amida Buddha ever living in a realm into which one could be reborn, and the second half of the Lotus Sutra described how a rela-

---

11. WATANABE (1970, 41) considers rituals on behalf of the dead as a defining characteristic of what happened to Buddhism particularly in Japan. STONE AND WALTER (2008, 1) stress that services for the dead represent "the major social role of Buddhist priests and temples in Japan today." STONE 2016 significantly expands our knowledge of deathbed practices in medieval Japan, and SHINOHARA 2007 discusses those among Chinese monks. ROWE (2011, 2–3) presents the positive aspects of Japanese funerary Buddhism and argues that "the care of the dead has become the most fundamental challenge to the continued existence of Japanese temple Buddhism." Other scholars would extend that characterization to most of the history of Japanese Buddhism. SCHOPEN 1997 gives evidence of the central role of rituals and concern for the dead in Indian Buddhism from its very beginning. For evidence of the centrality of death in all Buddhism, see CUEVAS AND STONE 2007.

tionship with the dead Shakyamuni Buddha was possible. Buddhism preeminently is a religion of dealing with the dead.[12]

Whatever differences there are among traditions of Buddhism in Japan, practices of dealing with the dead seem to run through all of them like a common thread. Jacqueline Stone states that, despite differences in the understanding of postmortem liberation, "the notion that a person's last hours should be ritually managed, as well as the basic techniques for so doing, cut across all divisions of 'old' and 'new', 'exoteric' and esoteric', in which we are accustomed to thinking of medieval Japanese Buddhism."[13] For the most part, the great founders of various sects who did engage in philosophical reflection also paid special attention to the dying person and to deathbed rites. In general, they taught that what the dying person did, and what was done for him or her, was crucial to liberation. Genshin exhorted the dying person to concentrate on Amida Buddha as his last thought (念), to avoid rebirth in samsara. Kakuban (1095–1143) encouraged the dying to focus on union with the Buddha to realize, on the deathbed, buddhahood in this very body, which he considered synonymous with birth in a pure land. The "lotus *samādhi*" of Saichō (767–822), although not confined to the time of death, eventually came to define a rite for the dying. Nichiren (1222–1282) taught followers to recite, once again on their deathbed, the name of the Lotus Sutra as a bridge to reach the pure land (of Sacred Eagle Peak).[14] Their concern with the dying represents the norm, the ordinary practice.

The extraordinary philosophical position of Kūkai, Shinran, and Dōgen is apparent in their attitudes toward their own passing and their disregard for rites for the dead. Some legends depict Kūkai as never having died at all, as having simply entered *samādhi* in the Inner Shrine

---

12. See SUEKI 2009A and 2009B.
13. STONE 2008, 71.
14. Ibid. (61 and 70) presents the practices of Genshin and Kakuban. WALTER (2008, 252 and 259) discusses the practices of Saichō and Nichiren.

on Mount Kōya where he still sits.¹⁵ Although Shinran was probably cremated,¹⁶ he is reputed to have told his congregation, "When my eyes close for the last time, place my body in the Kamo River, so the fish can feed on it."¹⁷ Dōgen told his monks that the "body, hair, and skin are the products of the union of our parents. When the breathing stops, the body is scattered amid mountains and fields and finally turns to earth and mud. Why then do you attach to this body?"¹⁸ The utter disregard on the part of Kūkai, Shinran, Dōgen and later Zen philosophers was the exception, and a sign of a great divide between them and the teachers more representative of the Buddhism of the people. The messy matters of the deceased's body and the survivors' emotions are not taken into account in the Buddhism of the philosophers.

Several divides are discernible in this synopsis. The divide between Kūkai, Shinran, and Dōgen on the one hand and other Japanese Buddhist teachers on the other hand parallels the more general divide between the Buddhism of the philosophers and the Buddhism of the populace. The former side attends to liberation from birth-and-death, and the latter to death as a departure from life. Accordingly, the former divides birth-and-death from something beyond birth-and-death, even if found within it; and the latter divides death from life.¹⁹ But

15. G. TANABE 1999, 358–9. According to WALTER (2008, 253), Kūkai did compose and recite a text at the death of a close disciple, his sister's son. As far as I know, however, his writings pay no attention to such practices.

16. Teachers on both sides of the divide were evidently cremated. *Emaki* picture scrolls depict Hōnen's and Shinran's cremations, as well as Nichiren's, to name only a few figures. See the colored plates in GERHART 2009.

17. As translated by Wayne Yokoyama, in AOKI 2002, 45. In an unpublished manuscript, Yokoyama provides a more literal translation: "When the eyes of this fellow (某) [Shinran] close, let [his body] be committed to the Kamo river to be given over to the fishes." The source of this statement is Kakunyō's *Gaijashō* (改邪鈔) of 1337; see SHINRAN 1969, 4 and 2003, 937.

18. DŌGEN 1971B, 62. Dōgen makes it clear in other talks in the *Zuimonki*, as well as in the *Bendōwa*, that he is not opposing the mortal body to some supposedly eternal mind or spirit; body and mind (身心) are undivided in practice.

19. The divide between these two Buddhisms in Japan is not repeated throughout Asian Buddhism. The divides between life and death on the one hand, and samsara and

these divides are made visible by yet another, less studied division that throws them into relief. This is the more complicated divide of interests: the interests of historical scholars as distinct from those of philosophers past and present, and both these sets of interests as opposed to the interest of practitioner-devotees in their own death or the death of others close to them. Historical scholars are interested in explaining predominant patterns of practice and in documenting their details; philosophers' interests turn to doctrinal interpretation that, for many of them, entails a universal soteriology; and practitioner-devotees are concerned with what happens to them and those close to them when they die. While these three groups of people may at times overlap in the focus of their attention, we can, without undue exaggeration, distinguish three points of view on the sense and significance of death. If "death" means something different for these three groups, then death in Japanese Buddhism is a polysemous phenomenon.

POINTS OF VIEW

One heuristic for clarifying the different senses of death emerges from a grammatical distinction that is usually evident in English, the language in which I write, but is often obscure in Japanese, the language of the people I am writing about. I am writing now and you are reading; were we together we might discuss what they, the others, talked about. "I," "you," "we," "they" (and "she" or "he," etc.) name the "grammatical person." The category of grammatical person indicates the speaker, the addressee, or the other participants in an event. As a "deictic" reference, grammatical person requires a listener or reader to know the context of the situation in order to determine the referent. You the reader know that John Maraldo is the referent to "I" in

---

nirvana on the other, intersect in the *parinirvāṇa* of Shakyamuni depicted, for example, in early Indian Buddhist literature, since *parinirvāṇa* refers both to the final, definitive liberation of the Buddha and to his death as a departure from this world.

the sentence above (although what sort of self "John Maraldo" refers to may be a matter of philosophical debate). In English, grammatical person is often coded in personal pronouns like "I," "you," "we," "they"; and other Indo-European languages may code grammatical person in the form of verbal endings. As you may know, however, indicators of grammatical person are more complicated in Japanese. Personal pronoun equivalents are much less often used than in English and are derived from words indicating location. Such words indicate social status in a relationship as much as they identify a speaker or addressee. In the written language of the Buddhist teachers I have referred to, and in the *Tale of Genji*, such words are all but absent. When rendering Japanese into English, translators must interpret the context to generate the appropriate personal pronouns.

If grammatical person is so obscure in the language of Japanese Buddhists, why try to employ this category to clarify the senses of death? The reason is that death allows description from the perspectives of at least three grammatical persons—first-person, second-person, and third-person—and the distinctions and interplay among these three bring clarity to the meanings of death in its various divides. I shall return to the question whether yet another perspective is at work in some Buddhist philosophical accounts.

The *first-person perspective* presents the meaning and significance of death (and possibly liberation) for oneself. First-person perspectives on death are both a perennial concern of philosophical reflection and a matter of everyday anxiety for countless individuals. First-person perspectives imply some sense of self, of being oneself, that may be left ambiguous for the time being. We may note one remarkable parallel, however: the way that translators generate pronouns seems to mirror the way that a person's sense of self is generated to allow that person to refer to himself or herself. Although it is not a specific external agent like a translator that generates one's sense of self, that sense is discovered and (re)constructed out of a context wherein it did not previously exist as an experienced identity. Once a person's own point of view comes into being, it defines that person over against other individuals, and comes to articulate her own distinctive view of things. This is the point of view so central to phenomenological analysis, which seeks to clarify matters as experienced from a first-person perspective.[20] It is also crucial to any reflection on death, insofar as death poses a limit to personal experience and existence. What death is for me, what *my* death means to me, and just how *my own death* defines a divide in my own existence—these are matters articulated in the first-person, whether or not a grammatical indicator is evident. Since the "I", the "me" and the "my" refer to any and all of us in this case, we may shift to a more anonymous but less contextual formulation: what *one's own death* means *to oneself* and *for oneself*. The more anonymous formulation in terms of "oneself" is sometimes considered a third-person perspective, but I will define the third-person perspective on death as the viewpoint of commentators and observers who are more or less detached from what they describe or see.

One may of course imagine another person's first-person perspective on death, what death is to or for that person herself. A passage from Oe Kenzaburo's novel *A Personal Matter* provides an example both of a third-person perspective and of an imagined first-person perspective. The protagonist nicknamed "Bird" ruminates on the pending death of his infant child, who he is told was born with a brain hernia that renders it (in the words of the doctor) a "vegetable," unable to respond like a normal human being:

20. Philosophers of many persuasions have reflected on the meaning of death from the first-person, but probably none more thoroughly than phenomenologists. One of the most systematic and enlightening investigations is HART 2009, vol. 1, chapters VII and VIII, and vol. 2, chapters 1 and 11. Heidegger's *Being and Time* defines the authentic self as the self resolutely open to its own death. Paul Ricoeur considers death and birth as the limits of personal experience: as important as our birth and death may be to others, especially our family and friends, we do not experience them ourselves; for each of us birth is an "already happened" event and death a "not-yet occurred" event. "If 'learning finally how to live' is to learn to die, to take into account absolute mortality without salvation, resurrection, or redemption, I share all the negatives here" (RICOEUR 2009, 85).

14. Negotiating the Divide of Death in Japanese Buddhism | 361

Bird shuddered... and began thinking about the baby.... The death of a vegetable baby—Bird examined his son's calamity from the angle that stabbed deepest. The death of a vegetable baby with only vegetable functions was not [according to the doctor] accompanied by suffering. Fine, but what did death mean to a baby like that? Or, for that matter, life? The bud of an existence appeared on a plain of nothingness that stretched for zillions of years and there it grew for nine months. Of course, there was no consciousness in a fetus, it simply curled in a ball and existed, filling utterly a warm, dark, mucous world. Then, perilously, into the external world. It was cold there, and hard, scratchy, dry and fiercely bright. The outside world was not so confined that the baby could fill it by himself: he must live with countless strangers. But, for a baby like a vegetable, that stay in the external world would be nothing more than a few hours of occult suffering he couldn't account for. Then the suffocating instant, and once again, on that plain of nothingness zillions of years long, the fine sand of nothingness itself.[21]

In this passage, the novelist Oe depicts "Bird" in the third person, from the perspective of a more or less detached observer, albeit an "omniscient" observer that can read the mind of the protagonist. Bird's own mind tries to imagine the experience of a severely disabled infant, to imagine what birth, life, and death might be like for his infant son. Bird tries to imagine the infant's first-person perspective on life and death. The difficulties involved in doing so are staggering, and the novelist Oe has deliberately piled one difficulty on top of another. Oe implicitly acknowledges the general difficulty of imagining *another person's* experience: he has Bird asking himself questions and examining this "personal matter" from a particular angle. But Oe adds to this general difficulty two more limitations: any person's own limitation in imagining her own death, and the limitations of an infant, a brain-damaged infant at that, to imagine or experience anything at all. The omniscience of the novelist runs up against an utterly unknowable personal matter, which he describes as a "plain of nothingness zillions of

21. OE 1964, 45–50.

years long." This unknowability breaches the first-person perspective and necessitates an interplay with a third-person view of "the bud of an existence that appeared on the plain of nothingness."

If the first-person perspective commands the attention of all us mortals, philosophers or not, *the third-person perspective* presents things from the standpoint of an observer who is disengaged from the world that is described. It is the perspective Murasaki Shikibu takes in the *Tale of Genji*, and it defines the narrative stance of many works of fiction. It also represents the practice of most historical scholars who aim to be objective, disinterested, and purely descriptive as opposed to normative or ideological (despite postmodernist challenges to this aim). The scholarship on death and the afterlife in Japanese Buddhism generally employs the third-person perspective. The historical scholar usually assumes the viewpoint of a detached observer. Yet the scholar often links her research with more or less universal human interests, to show that the research has broader relevance, or to identify herself as one of us who have a shared interest in the matter of life and death. Karen Gerhart, for example, writes her enormously informative book, *The Material Culture of Death in Medieval Japan*, from the third-person perspective for the most part, but in her opening passage she makes the link to this sense of shared identity and uses the first person plural grammatical form: "Death is an event of cataclysmic separation," and for this reason "we use ritual and ritual objects to help bridge the gulf, suture the wound to the collective body of family and of community, and overcome a sense of powerlessness in the face of death."[22] Gerhart is commenting here about people of all cultures, to introduce her specialized study of medieval Japanese death rituals. Her study is an example of the kind of detailed historical research on Japan that is not found prior to the Meiji era, on a topic, death, that in earlier Japan was rarely if ever presented from the disinterested, third-person stance of the scholar. But she too initially speaks of the separation that death

---

22. GERHART 2009, 1,

means in a manner that connects this third-person perspective with concerns all of us have: "*we* use rituals and ritual objects to help bridge the gulf...." The third-person perspective on death gains relevance from its interplay with first-person experience, a point of view that historical scholars must recognize if they are to describe the meanings of matters like death for others.

In many languages the grammatical first person also comes in a plural form—as in the English words *we* and *us* and *our*. The plural form may indicate an extension of the singular first-person perspective to a community of people who share similar experiences or viewpoints, or it may define an "in group" as opposed to outsiders. In the matter of death, however, "our death" can only refer to the death of each of us, individually, whether that death means a departure from life or an entrance into nirvana. The philosophers who divide birth-and-death from something beyond it (yet possibly within it) often imply a first-person plural perspective insofar as liberation is conceived as universal, for all of us, but even there liberation comes by way of the work of, or on behalf of, the individual practitioner, each of us. When it comes to death, the first-person plural perspective derives from the first-person singular.

The *second-person* invokes the perspective of someone who can address me, hear me, respond to me, challenge me or engage me. The engagement with me can occur even when you are not at the moment speaking or writing; it may occur simply by your presence, or by the signs of your presence in your artifacts or your remains. The convention in English grammar of calling this perspective the "second" person may conceal a bias toward self-centered consciousness, but need not imply that the "second-person" is less important than the "first." As James G. Hart writes, this 'you' is "the second first person."[23] The imperative grammatical form implies the second-person: "[you should or must]

23. "The 'you' is a 'second first-person' made present by analogizing first-person experience." HART 2009, vol. 1, 213.

do this!" The person so addressed may be a general "anyone"; indeed in contemporary English, "you" often substitutes for the generic "one," meaning anyone. Here, however, I will confine the second-person to the forms of speech and speech acts that are directed at specific persons known to the speaker, rather than at anonymous others. My use of the term differs from so-called "second-person narratives," a form of literary fiction and nonfiction that also occurs in advertisements and musical lyrics, where second-person personal pronouns or other grammatical indicators are employed to address an anonymous reader. The novel *If on a winter's night a traveler*, by the Italian writer Italo Calvino, is an example of a (rather complex) second-person narrative. Invoking an anonymous, imagined reader, the book begins, "You are about to begin reading Italo Calvino's new novel, *If on a winter's night a traveler*. Relax. Concentrate. Dispel every other thought."[24]

The three major perspectives according to grammatical person may be summarized as follows:

- The first-person refers to "my" (one's own) perspective on matters, including my own experience and what is at the limit of my own experience: my own death. Japanese Buddhist philosophers often, though not always, take this perspective in reflecting about matters such as life and death. So do practitioner-devotees.
- The second-person refers to others known to and addressed by the writer or speaker. Buddhist teachers often invoke this form in performing rites and giving instruction to others they know, even if without explicit mention of the addressee (such as the mention of "you" in English).
- The third-person intends to give someone's perspective on others, their experiences, their activities, their practices, or on any-

24. CALVINO 1981, p. 3. In the original Italian, the second person is indicated by verb endings and the imperative form as well as by personal pronouns: "Stai per cominciare a leggere il nuovo romanzo Se una notte d'inverno un viaggiatore di Italo Calvino. Rilassati. Raccogliti. Allontana da te ogni altro pensiero" (CALVINO 1979, 3).

thing at all, from a detached and often unidentified viewpoint. Contemporary scholars of Buddhism usually use this perspective in presenting their work

It is important to keep two points in mind when applying the heuristic of the perspectives of grammatical person to clarify notion of death. First, although the use of personal pronouns in English explicates these perspectives, they are not limited to a language like English that requires personal pronouns for clear communication. First-person, second-person and third-person perspectives are present—are ways of presenting things—for speakers and writers of Japanese as well, and probably of most languages.

Dōgen's Japanese is a case in point. His writing is rarely marked by pronouns, referential nouns, or honorifics that might indicate the status of the speaker or the addressee. In autobiographical remarks, he uses the word *yo* to refer to himself as the present speaker or writer or as the protagonist of stories he tells about himself.[25] Dōgen also uses the word *ware*, sometimes as a personal pronoun, sometimes in the sense of the general noun "the I" or "das Ich."[26] He also uses grammatical terms that translate as imperatives and imply the grammatical second-person, such as *shirubeshi* (しるべし, "you should know") and *nakare* (なかれ, "do not..."). Moreover, Dōgen uses *ware* and the imperative

---

25. In the *Zuimonki* and the *Bendōwa*, for example. STEINECK 2009 gives a narratological analysis of Dōgen's references to himself in the *Bendōwa*.

26. In the *Shōbōgenzō Zenki*, Dōgen uses われ as a personal pronoun, e.g.: "われふね にのりて... riding a boat, I [or 'we']...." Most translations of the *Genjōkōan* interpret われ as 我, *ātman*, a substantial, self-subsisting self that has its own independent nature (自性). A few translations render われ more ambiguously, simply as "an I," which can refer to this kind of objectified, substantial self, or to a subject that can characterize or examine phenomena, in expressions like われにあらざる,われにあらぬ,自心自性は常住なるかとあやまる. KASULIS (2010, 24) argues that われ in Dōgen is solely a first-person reference, a personal subject who can take a standpoint; it does not refer to a self-subsisting *ātman* or 我. In my free interpretation I prefer the more ambiguous reading. In contrast, the word *jiko* (自己) in the *Genjōkōan* and other texts can refer simply to oneself as a self-conscious subject, as in the famous phrases 自己をならふといふは、自己をわするるなり ("to model the self is to forget the self").

forms in writings and talks concerned with death, in some sense of the word. The meaning of death for Dōgen will become clearer when the perspectives implied in his writing emerge more clearly. The second point to keep in mind is that the explicit or implicit use of grammatical person does not necessarily entail any particular philosophical concept of self. Dōgen's philosophy, for example, articulates a very specific notion of self and nonself, but he does not appeal to this notion every time he uses the word *jiko*, much less when he uses an imperative grammatical form that implies a "you," that is, the monks he is addressing. Perspectives according to grammatical person remain open-ended with regard to philosophical concepts of self.

With these grammatical perspectives in mind, it is possible to differentiate, at least tentatively, three senses of death.[27]

Autobiographical death is my death, in each case one's own death. It means death as the ending of my life, my departure or passing from life. It is independent of whatever beliefs I and others may have regarding an afterlife, a world beyond (*takai*), or a life before this present life, a repeated or re-incarnated life in a great cycle (*rinne*). I may imagine my death as the end of an interim, but this interim is still going on. Others may experience my death, but I myself cannot imagine or conceive this ending, for an end would stop the very act of imagining or conceiving. I may imagine myself continuing on in some form in an afterlife, but I cannot imagine or conceive my own death. Autobiographical death poses a limit to my experience. It is death in—and perhaps death of—a first-person perspective. This is the sense of death that the divide between birth-and-death (*shōji*) and liberation seems to entail, at least initially.

Biographical death refers to the death of an individual as perceived and conceived by other people in general. The dates on a gravestone

---

27. For a similar distinction among three perspectives regarding death, see the section "La mort en troisième, en seconde, en première personne," in JANKÉLÉVITCH 1966, 21–32.

mark one's biographical birth and death. Biographical death signifies the end to an interim that began with the individual's birth. It is the demise of persons that anonymous observers can witness and scholars can describe; it is death in the third-person. When we divide life from death, literally or metaphorically, we appeal to this sense of death.

Your death, death of the second-person, is the biographical death of someone personally known, someone in one's family, congregation, or community. It is death for those left behind, the survivors (*izoku, ide*). Two features characterize this sense of death: your death means your absence from the others who knew you, and it leaves your body for others to take care or dispose of. This is the death that is of central concern to the Buddhism of the people, to the priests who perform rites for the dying and the dead and the survivors. This in particular is the death of no concern to Kūkai, Shinran, Dōgen, and the philosophical Japanese Buddhist teachers. As we saw, they seemed to have little if any regard for death in the third person as well. (Dōgen for example frequently cites the patriarchs of old as models for the monks of his day; it is of no concern that they are no longer living. For Dōgen the patriarchs are still present insofar as their words and admonitions live.) The divide between "us survivors" and the death of "one of us" evokes the notion of the death of the second person.

In a crucial sense, the death of the second-person makes possible the sense of speaking of my death. I come to an awareness of death for me when I experience the death of others I know. My death approaches me—even if it never becomes accessible to me—via your death; the death of someone I personally know evokes in me the prospect of my own death. Death in its autobiographical sense, distinct as it is, derives from the death of the second-person. In this sense, the death of the second-person always comes first.

These distinctions are crucial if we are to understand the disparate ways that the matter of death is treated in Japanese Buddhism.

Yet something, some aspect, still seems missing when we try to understand what death means in the matter of birth-and-death (*shōji*), as the Buddhist philosophers think of it. Birth-and-death, life-and-death, touches on the matter of *my* death and the liberation of (or from) *me*, and thus has to do with autobiographical death more than with biographical death or with death for the second person. The Buddhist philosophers, however, might be speaking of the death *of* a first-person perspective. Not only that: it is as if their utter disregard were directed at all three perspectives, as if these perspectives were more or less equivalent. Insofar as they function equivalently, I will refer to all three perspectives as *personal death*.

The death of Dōgen

Biographically, Dōgen was born in 1200 and died in 1253. In his early twenties he went to China and experienced an awakening under the direction of the Zen master Rujing. After his return to Japan he taught monks that single-minded *zazen* (which could include sitting with a kōan) was the only practice that could realize buddhahood. But Dōgen also led lay worship ceremonies, reputedly often accompanied by miraculous events such as the appearance of flowers over the altar statuary, and he performed rituals of popular appeal such as precept recitation and worship of the sixteen arhats who protect Buddhism.[28] Whether or not his and his monks' performance of lay rituals was an increasing concession to gather financial support by patrons, it is evident that he continually used and adapted Chinese monastic rules and regulations for the monastic communities he led; in other words, that Buddhist practice for him meant a meticulously regulated and ritualized lifestyle that facilitates *zazen*. In the final period of his life, Dōgen devoted his writing to commentaries in Chinese on Chan monastic codes compiled as the *Eihei Shingi*.

---

28. BODIFORD 1993, 14, xii, 32.

Although these writings do stress proper attitude more than the outward form of rules and rituals,[29] there is no question that ritual was part and parcel of Dōgen's Zen.

Given all this attention to ritual, it is surprising that Dōgen left no record of performing services for the dead.[30] His monastic codes give no guidance for the treatment of deceased monks or laity, and his Japanese *Shōbōgenzō* and other writings do not deal with what I have called the death of the second person, marked by the dead body and the absence of the person, much less biographical death.[31] He appar-

29. Ibid., 31. For a translation of the *Eihei Shingi* see DŌGEN 1996. The translator Leighton (21) emphasizes Dōgen's intent to convey the proper attitude to benefit community practice.

30. BODIFORD 1993, 192. Dōgen did, however, memorialize the life and death of his mentor Myōzen, who went to China with him, in a Chinese poem in the *Eihei kōroku*, translated by HEINE (2022, 99), and by Shōhaku Okumura, <https://dogeninstitute.wordpress.com/2021/06/06/manifesting-the-true-body/>:
His everyday practice of the way was thorough and intimate.
When he passed into nirvāṇa his face was fresh.
Tell me, what is his affair today?
Since the vajra flame, he manifests his true body.

31. BODIFORD (1993, 191) writes that Dōgen's recorded sayings in Chinese include no funeral sermons. But Steven Heine reminds me that Dōgen did occasionally give memorial sermons, especially for his teacher in China, Rujing. The collection of formal sermons in the Sino-Japanese *Eihei kōroku* contains seven such sermons. See HEINE 2006, 182–3. The collection of Chinese verses Dōgen composed while in China also includes examples of mourning on behalf of lay followers—a common practice for Song Chan masters, sometimes done by writing letters. Dōgen apparently abandoned this practice after he returned to Japan (personal communication from Heine, July 29, 2013). Dōgen also occasionally refers to relics; HEINE (2006, 2 and 2022, 244) mentions Dōgen's text of 1226, put in writing shortly after he returned from China, called *Shari sōdenki*, on preserving his teacher Myōzen's relics. For all that, something Dōgen says in the *Zuimonki* removes the specialness of reverence for the dead and care for the grieving, and places these in a larger context:
The masses on mourning days and the good deeds done during *Chūin* [the seven weeks' mourning] are all employed by laymen. Zen priests must truly be aware of their deep gratitude to their parents. All my deeds should be like this. Do you suppose it is the Buddha's idea to practice prayer just on a special day to special people?
Cited in WATANABE 1970, 73; the original text seems to be "Shōbōgenzō Zuimonki," in *Jōyō Daishi shōgyō zenshū* [Collection of Great Teacher Jōyō's sacred teachings], ed.

ently was not concerned with the treatment of the deceased, and in any case would have rejected rites to transfer merit and ensure one's fortune in an afterlife.[32] Dōgen left it to his disciples to deal with his death when he died in Kyoto at the age of 54. He had been ill for nearly a year, and had already appointed his main disciple, Ejō, as abbot of Eiheiji, but we can imagine that the community was both distraught and at a loss as to its future direction. William Bodiford notes how little we know about the treatment of Dōgen's body. The body was cremated, and Ejō recited the *Shari raimon*, a verse on attaining all perfections through the power of the Buddha.[33] Otherwise the records are silent about the topic.

Eiheiji (Tokyo: Eiheiji shutchōjo, 1909), 84.

32. Dōgen was an exception in the history of Japanese Zen with regard to funeral rites and spirit cults. WILLIAMS (2008, 213) notes that the first Sōtō Zen funeral did not occur until the third generation after Dōgen, at the death of Gikai in 1309. Contrary to the myth of "traditional Zen," BODIFORD (1993, 1–2) characterizes Zen practices as mingled with spirit cults and rituals, notes the widespread performance of Zen funeral rites, and claims that these rites were the major source of all Japanese Buddhist funeral rituals. Using Bodiford's research, GERHART (2009, 17) summarizes the nine special rites typically used at a funeral for a Zen abbot:

> First the body was carefully bathed and dressed and then placed in the coffin (*nyūgan*). It was then transferred (*igan*) from the room where the priest had died to the Lecture Hall, and three rites were performed while the body lay in state in the hall: the coffin lid was closed (*sogan*), the deceased's portrait was hung above the altar (*kaishin*), and a wake in the form of a priest's consultation with the deceased was held (*tairyō shōsan*). The coffin was then moved to the cremation grounds (*kigan*), where libations of tea (*tencha*) and hot water (*tentō*) were offered. The final rite was the lighting of the funeral pyre (*ako, hinko*).

33. BODIFORD 1993, 192. Bodiford surmises that the "death of Dōgen presented the Eiheiji community with a loss from which it could not easily recover. Dōgen had been the community's source of spiritual authority. After Dōgen's death, his disciples faced the new task of directing their communal life without the external support of their master's supervision and guidance" (35). Wayne Yokoyama's research, based on that of Ishikawa Ryōiku who read records at Higashiyama Kōdaiji (高台寺), indicates that after Dōgen died Ejō went to the west gate of Kenninji where he read the *Shari raimon* at the altar niche (龕) where there was a tower erected in memory of Dōgen. See 石川良昱,「舍利礼文について」, 印度學佛教學研究 通号22 (1963-03-31), 272–6.

Dōgen did leave a few indications of his attitude toward the prospect of his imminent death in three poems he composed in his final days. Disciples had urged him to travel to his hometown Kyoto to seek medical help, and on the way there he composed two short Japanese poems (*waka*) that suggest a clear sense of his impending demise. It is possible to read in them a hint of a turn from a plaintive sense of passing to being absorbed in the presence of what was happening then and there. In one poem, Dōgen seems to feel frail and momentary as a blade of grass as he passes through the mountains, then is swept up by the presence of mounting clouds:

> A frail blade of grass I pass over Mount Kinobe,
> my feelings all a cloud adrift.
>
> 草の葉にかどでせる身の木部山
> 雲にをかある心地こそすれ

In another poem, Dōgen seems to long to see the autumn moon again—the celebrated moon of the fifteenth day of the eighth lunar month—which then leaves him sleepless in the presence of its beauty:

> Thinking to see it again in the fall,
> such a wistful time—
> the moon tonight
> robs me of sleep.
>
> また見むと思ひし時の秋だにも
> 今夜の月にねられやはする[34]

A third poem, composed in Chinese just before he died and alluding to the legendary abode of the dead, seems to explode all ambivalence; Dōgen's "entire body" or person (身) fully lives even at the brink of the abyss of death:

> Fifty-four years lighting up the sky
> A quivering leap smashes a billion worlds
>
> 五十四年照第一天
> 打箇勃跳觸破大千

---

34. DŌGEN 2010, 47 and 49. For other translations with commentary, see HEINE 1997, 26 and 94. The 1806 illustrated edition of Kenzei's 1472 biography of Dōgen (see note 35 below) contains a drawing of Dōgen being transported in a palanquin over Konomeyama (Mount Kinobe), alongside a drawing of Dōgen sitting hunched over in death, surrounded by disciples and with a brush and a sheet of paper on which he inscribed a death poem.

Hah!
Entire body looks for nothing
Plunging alive into Yellow Springs.³⁵

咦
渾身無覓
活陷黃泉.

Even in his own case Dōgen turns our attention away from thoughts of personal death as a coming to end of life.

Dōgen's relative lack of concern with personal death is all the more surprising when we recall stories of his childhood experience with death that motivated him to study the Buddha Way in the first place. His mother died when he was only seven. It is said that a profound sense of impermanence overcame the young Dōgen as he watched the smoke of incense rise during her funeral.³⁶ Dōgen never abandoned his concern with impermanence, even after identifying it as the place of awakening, and he frequently exhorted his monks to practice while they had the chance in this short life of ours, to practice as if their hair were on fire, casting aside body and mind.³⁷ Yet his own awakening had left personal death in the dust, had cast it into the realm of distractive and illusory concerns. The comment in the *Zuimonki* quoted earlier, about the folly of attaching to one's body-mind, reflects his seeming indifference toward the significance of personal death in his own case as well. If we take this stance as a sign of his own liberation from birth-and-death, then it does seem to pertain to his own death, death for the first person. But it is notable that this liberation took

---

35. Trans., slightly modified, by Philip Whalen and Kazuaki Tanahashi, in DŌGEN 1985, 219. The original Chinese is taken from DŌGEN 1993, vol. 7, 307. HEINE (2022, 29–30) offers another translation with illuminating commentary on Dōgen's alteration of his teacher Rujing's death verse. Wayne Yokoyama's research into the sources of this poem (personal communications October 2022) indicates that the poem first appeared in a biography of Dōgen by Kenzei called the *Eihei kaizan gyōjō kenzei-ki*, composed ca. 1472 and published in a popular illustrated edition in 1806. It reappeared at the An'yōji temple in Imono in Kyoto prefecture in 1926, and was reprinted in a modern edition in 1931. See also Shōhaku Okumura's translation and commentary in DŌGEN 2022, 380.

36. KIM 2004, 19.

37. In the *Gakudōyōjinshū* and *Zuimonki*. See, for example, DŌGEN 1971B, 83 et passim.

14. Negotiating the Divide of Death in Japanese Buddhism | 373

place during his lifetime, not at the end of it; that he had, so to speak, already died to personal death.

What precisely do Dōgen's teachings about life-and-death (*shōji*) have to do with death in the first person? Dōgen's directives and sermons to his followers make it abundantly clear that each must practice and manifest realization for himself, that the Buddha Way is a "personal matter," a matter of one's own life-and-death. Dōgen's teaching must pertain to autobiographical death, death in the first person, in some way. An examination of some passages in the *Shōbōgenzō* reveals some possible connections.

The fascicles of the *Shōbōgenzō* that treat of birth(or life)-and-death, composed over a decade,[38] display a remarkable consistency. We may begin with the earliest of these, the profound study of perspectives known as the *Genjōkōan*. Whether the perspectives in Dōgen's various studies coincide with those in the category of grammatical person, that is, whether they are perspectives on personal death, remains an open question at this point.

The *Genjōkōan* begins by stating three doctrinal perspectives and then returning them to an ordinary, everyday stance:

> 諸法の佛法なる時節、すなはち迷悟あり、修行あり、生あり死あり、諸佛あり。万法ともにわれにあらざる時節、まどひなくさとりなく、諸佛なく衆生なく、生なし滅なし。佛道もとより豐儉より跳出せるゆゑに、生滅あり、迷悟あり、生佛あり。しかもかうのごとくなりといへども、華は愛惜にちり、草は棄嫌におふるのみなり。[39]

---

[38]. *Genjōkōan* dates from 1233, but was revised as late as 1252; *Zenki* dates from 1242. Scholars have found no colophon for the piece titled *Shōji*; it is not included in the 75-fascicle version of the *Shōbōgenzō*, but I accept the Sōtō School's treatment of it as authentic. Ejō recorded Dōgen's talks collected in the *Zuimonki* between 1235 and 1237. In examining Dōgen's statements about death, we should keep in mind that they were made relatively early in his teaching career, perhaps before he would have had to deal with the deaths of disciple monks or lay patrons.

[39]. DŌGEN 1988, vol. 1, 2. My interpretations draw upon several excellent translations of the *Genjōkōan* and other chapters of the *Shōbōgenzō*, without adhering to any one published translation.

I interpret freely and extract from the relevant passages:

> A common Buddhist perspective on things posits birth and death—samsara—along with delusion and enlightenment. A contrasting, self-less perspective on things discovers neither birth/life nor death/cessation. These two perspectives converge in the Way that speaks of birth and death, delusion and enlightenment, in the first place. Be that as it may, the flowers we cherish will perish and the weeds we despise will arise.

The grammar of the original Japanese does not clearly indicate the perspective of grammatical person from which Dōgen's statements are expressed, but the three at the beginning seem closest to the third-person point of view. These three statements seem to be made by an anonymous authority taking up a kind of detached, meta-viewpoint on three perspectives. Yet a hint of a category other than grammatical person appears in the way Dōgen has phrased the matter, explicitly in the first two statements and by extension in the third: the three perspectives are taken up at different junctures in time (時節); they are perspectives held temporarily. Birth-and-death, and the enlightenment that liberates them, appear as temporal perspectives. Dōgen presents perspectives as temporal rather than spatial. The fourth statement of the everyday stance reflects the temporal, transitory occasions of our (yours and my) cherishing and despising transitory things. This concluding statement, even without the interpolated "we," suggests that the doctrinal temporal perspectives must connect to one's personal being in a deep sense. The attachments of cherishing flowers while despising weeds arise as personal matters, like one's own preference for life over death. Yet even there (or then) too they are temporal, transitory matters: Dōgen's language suggests that lovely flowers fall and despised weeds flourish "only" in our loving the one and hating the other.[40]

---

40. In a note to their translation of the *Genjōkōan*, Norman Waddell and Masao Abe (DŌGEN 1982, 40) point out that elsewhere, in chapter one of the *Eihei kōroku*, Dōgen

14. Negotiating the Divide of Death in Japanese Buddhism | 375

A latter passage makes more explicit Dōgen's view of the divide of life and death. An analogy with firewood and ashes recapitulates the temporal perspective.

たき木ははいとなる、さらにかへりてたき木となるべきにあらず。しかあるを、灰はのち薪はさきと見取すべからず。しべし、薪は薪の法位に住して、さきありのちあり、前後ありといへども、前後際断せり。灰は灰の法位にあり、のちありさきあり。かのたき木、はひとなりぬるのち、さらに薪とならざるがごとく、人のしぬるのち、さらßに生とならず。しかあるを、生の死になるといはざるは、佛法のさだまれるならひなり、このゆゑに不生といふ。死の生に成らざる、法輪のさだまれる佛転なり、このゆゑに不滅といふ。生も一時のくらゐなり、死も一時のくらゐなり。[41]

I interpret freely:

> We speak of firewood turning to ashes, and not returning again to firewood. But it is not quite right to say something is first firewood and afterwards ashes. There is a "before" the firewood and an "after." What is before is not firewood and what is after is not firewood. Firewood takes up its own temporal position, has its own phenomenal status. [Like every other phenomenon, firewood is "an existence for a time," an *uji*.[42]] While we speak of there being a "before" and an "after," for the

---

implied that "flowers fall *because of* our longing, weeds flourish *because of* our hatred" (my emphasis).

41. DŌGEN 1971A 8; DŌGEN 1988, vol. 1, 3–4. A translation more literal than my free interpretation would be:

> Firewood cannot return to being firewood once it turns into ash. Be that as it may, we cannot take ashes as "after" and firewood as "before." Firewood resides in its own phenomenal position, and while we speak of there being a "before" and an "after," a prior and a subsequent, for the time being "before" and "after" are divided. Ashes are in the phenomenal state of ashes and have an "after" and a "before," [yet for the time being "before" and "after" are divided]. Just as this firewood, turning to ash, does not become firewood again, a person after dying does not live again. That being so, it is an established teaching of Buddhism that life cannot be said to turn into death, and for this reason it is called non-born, non-arising. It is an established teaching that death does not become life, and for this reason it is called non-perishing. Life is one stage of time, and death too is one stage of time.

42. Dōgen's famous term *uji* 有時 is not used in this fascicle but is especially relevant for his presentation of birth and death. The term presents translators with numerous pos-

time being "before" and "after" are divided. The same is true of ashes. Analogously, after a person dies she does not return to life. But it is not quite right to put it this way. A person's life is just that, a person's life. It is not followed by the person's death. There is no such thing as a person who undergoes birth/life and then death, and then life again. The right way is not to say that life becomes death, that something that was alive is now dead. The right way is to say "all is arising"; there is nothing but arising, being born, living. To turn that around, there is nothing to which to contrast birth or life; there is "no birth or life, no arising." (And no life after death.) Life is its own existential moment, its own stage of time. The right way is to say that death does not become life, that something that was dead is not alive again. So we say "all is perishing"; there is nothing but perishing, dying. And again to turn that around, there is nothing to which to contrast death or perishing; there is "no perishing." [And no death after life.] Death is its own existential moment, its own stage of time.[43]

---

sibilities and challenges. At its simplest, 有時 straddles two meanings, given by its two readings as *aru toki*, "at one time," and *uji*, "being-time." For the latter sense, ELBERFELD (2004, 229–330) argues convincingly that *u* 有 designates a particular being, which he renders as *ein Gegebenes*, something (temporally) given. See his translation of a passage of the *Uji* fascicle in DŌGEN 2006, 94, which in English would read: "What [we call] 'at a time' means time is (always) already (a particular) given [thing], and every given [thing] is (a particular) time." In recent Anglo-European philosophy, however, "the given" and "givenness" are contested terms best avoided here. Rein RAUD (2012) argues for the translation of *uji* as "existential moment," which places the emphasis on time. I understand Dōgen to say that phenomena or dharmas (諸法) are not things that undergo change "through time" as if they were separable from time, but are rather are instances (instantiations) of time. All things in this sense are "moments," leaving aside the question of the duration of such moments. Where we refer to particular beings, then, we might translate *uji* as "an existence for a time," or perhaps as "temporal existent." I use several translations here, depending on the context.

43. A passage in *Shinjingakudō*, the writing we interpreted in Chapter 13, confirms this conviction in metaphoric terms: 「生はいまた死に礙せられさるかゆゑに學道なり、生は一枚あらす、死は兩匹にあらす、死の生に相對するなし、生の死に相待するなし...」. Tanahashi (DŌGEN 1985, 94) translates: "Birth and Death are the study of the Way. Birth is not like one sheet of cloth; death is not like two rolls of cloth. Death is not the opposite of birth; birth is not the opposite of death."

Consider again the question of grammatical person, the perspective from which these statements are made. Mention of "after a person dies" is made from the external third-person perspective of those who remain in this world talking about others who do not. But what perspective allows the view that there is no perduring person who undergoes birth and life? If no person perdures, it cannot be the perspective of an anonymous third-person who perdures throughout the lives and deaths of others. The view seems to be from a first-person perspective, my perspective of myself, in which (my own) conscious life is not something that can be extinguished, in which I can speak of my own not-being-born and not-perishing. Others experience someone dying (or being born); I cannot experience my own birth or death.[44] Yet a statement that immediately precedes this passage challenges the first-person perspective:

もし行李をしたしくして箇裏に歸すれば、萬法のわれにあらぬ道理あきらけし。

If fully engaged in daily activities we come back to this right here and now, the truth that there is no "I" accompanying things will be evident.

Evidently it is a conditional perspective that allows us to see life and death as independent temporal positions that are not states of a perduring self; and the necessary condition is a return of consciousness to the situation at hand, this right here (箇裏 = このところ), leaving self-consciousness behind.

Since this passage refers to the established teachings of Buddhism, Dōgen's words *fushō* (不生, unborn) and *fumetsu* (不滅, unperishing) here most likely allude to the Indian Buddhist doctrine of the non-arising (Sanskrit: *anutpanna*) and non-perishing (*aniruddha*) of

---

44. Note that if this "I" is not extinguished, then Dōgen's position on perishing is not nihilist, advocating the annihilation of the self. Similarly, "non-arising" does not entail an eternalist position, an eternal self. Dōgen makes no pronouncements about the survival of a perduring self. His concern is the manifestation and the erasure of a personal, position-taking ego.

all things, due to their fundamental emptiness, as stated in the Heart Sutra, the Nirvana Sutra, and other scriptures.[45] But there is a twist in Dōgen's interpretation. The negations *fushō* and *fumetsu* traditionally describe buddha-nature, the body of the Tathāgata, nirvana, or other names for unconditioned reality; in some texts *fushō* serves as a synonym for emptiness or for nirvana. The Heart Sutra applies the negative descriptions to proclaim the emptiness of the five skandhas and of all phenomena (all dharmas); all are non-arising and non-perishing (*fushō-fumetsu*). Likewise there is no aging and no death (無老死), and no extinction of aging and death (and suffering) (亦無老死盡).[46] The Nirvana Sutra proclaims that "non-arising and non-ceasing are precisely what liberation is" (不生不滅即是解脱).[47] But Dōgen turns around the sense of this statement. For him the unborn and the unperishing do not refer one-sidedly to unconditioned nirvana apart from arising and perishing (or to an unborn mind or buddha-nature as we find later in Bankei). In taking life and death as separate stages in time, and thus severing the link between them, Dōgen may be playing off of Nāgārjuna's teaching that since all phenomena are empty of self-nature,

45. We know that Dōgen was familiar with the Nirvana Sutra from his *Shōbōgenzō Busshō*, where he transforms the Sutra's statement, "All beings have Buddha-nature" to "All beings are Buddha-nature." The Sutra states that "All sentient beings universally possess Buddha-nature without exception" (一切衆生悉皆佛性), usually read in Japanese as *Issai shujō wa kotogotoku busshō o yusu*). Dōgen reads this as "All sentient beings, all existence, buddha-nature" (*Issai shujō shitsuu busshō*) (thanks to Victor Sōgen Hori for this translation). Dōgen also transforms the sense of *hō-i* (法位): in the Lotus Sutra and other scriptures it refers to the incomparable, necessary truth of the Dharma, according to Nakamura H. 1973, 1228. In the passage of the *Genjōkōan*, *hō-i* means the transitory status that defines a particular dharma or phenomenon.

46. Similarly, the Vimalakīrti Sutra speaks of the patient "recognition that nothing really arises or perishes" (*mushōbōnin*, Sanskrit: *anutpattika-dharma-ksanti*).

47. Mark Blum's translation of the phrase in the Chinese version of *Mahāyāna Mahāparinirvāṇa-sūtra*, Taishō 12.396a18. Blum (2004, 606) notes that the Nirvana Sutra not only negates the view that things arise and perish; it also complements this negation with an affirmation of "the permanence, joy, self, and purity" of "buddha, nirvāṇa, and by extension the buddha-nature within everyone." "Despite our experience, there is thus another 'great self' [大我] within us and the Sutra even uses the term *true ātman*."

14. Negotiating the Divide of Death in Japanese Buddhism | 379

causal links between them are undermined. More concretely, Dōgen applies the words *fushō* and *fumetsu* to conditioned dharmas, temporal phenomena like firewood and ashes, and like our life and death. It is not that nothing truly arises or perishes, but that when we see all things as arising, then arising exhausts the being of all things; and when we see all things as perishing, then perishing exhausts the being of all things. When it comes to our life and death, in other words, life is completely life, and death is completely death. Life does not become death; thus we speak of absolute life. And death does not become life; thus we speak of absolute death.[48] When we face the divide between life and death, Dōgen offers no passage.

The pronoun "we" and the temporal-conditional "when" in this restatement are not present in the original Japanese, of course, but reflect the conditional perspective introduced by the statement that immediately precedes the passage, "if... we come back to this right here and now... there is no 'I.'" This statement suggests that absorption in the "here and now" merges the first-person, the subject of the sentences ("When we face" and "when we see") with the object ("all things as arising" or "all things as perishing"). The grammar as well as the content of Dōgen's statements suggest that in this temporal condition the person who views her own life is absolved, liberated, into that life, into living. (The phrase "もし箇裏に帰すれば" could also be read as 若しこ こにまかせば... "if one yields to the present situation....") This perspective on life is "absolute" (絶対) in the sense that it absolves, or frees us from, any contrast or opposition (対を絶する), not only between life and death, but between the person living and that person's life. Yet

---

48. This interpretation of *fushō* (不生), literally "non-arising," may be controversial, but it is supported by the passage from the fascicle called *Shōji* cited in the following paragraph in this chapter. It is also supported by the entries for *fushō* and *fumetsu* (不滅) in NAKAMURA H. (1973, 1163 and 1173), which give "absolute" (*zettai*) for the meaning of 不 in these words in the *Genjōkōan*. According to these entries, *fushō* does not mean "unborn" or "non-arising" but rather "absolutely everything is arising" (全体は生であるこ と), and *fumetsu* means "absolutely everything is perishing" (全体滅ばかりで、生に対す るものがないこと), with precedents in the *Laṅkāvatāra Sutra*.

how is it possible to say that the person who "views" her own death is absolved or freed into that death, into dying? What meaning of death or dying lies here?

The fascicle of the *Shōbōgenzō* called *Shōji* approximates an answer. Dōgen begins by saying that seeking buddha apart from life-and-death is like facing south to see north, and this only intensifies the idea of samsara (*shōji*) and loses sight of the way of liberation. When we take to heart that our very life-and-death (*shōji*) itself is nirvana, and neither detest one as samsara nor desire the other as nirvana, then, for the first time, it is clear how to detach from life-and-death (and presumably from nirvana well):

> このときはじめて、生死をはなるる分あり
> Only at the time that you detach from life-and-death....[49]

Then, echoing a statement in the *Genjōkōan*, Dōgen says,

> 生より死にうつると心うるは、これあやまり也。生はひとときのくらゐにて、すでにさきあり、のちあり。故、佛法の中には、生すなはち不生といふ。滅もひとときのくらゐにて、又さきあり、のちあり。これによりて、滅すなはち不滅といふ。生とふときには、生よりほかにものなく、滅といふとき、滅のほかにものなし。かるがゆゑに、生きたらばただこれ生、滅来らばこれ滅にむかひてつかふべし。いとふことなかれ、ねがふことなかれ.

I interpret freely:

> To imagine there is a passage from life to death is a mistake. Be aware that, as its own stage of time, life has a "before" and an "after." (What is before is not one's life and what is after is not one's life.) So the right way is to say: in the time that is life there is nothing but living, and there is no (contrast to) living. Similarly, as its own stage of time, death has a "before" and an "after." Accordingly, we say: in the time that is death there is nothing but death, and there is no (contrast to) death. When

---

49. DŌGEN 1971A, 778; DŌGEN 1988, vol. 2, 528. Many translations have "free *from* life and death"; KIM (2004, 166) has "free *in* birth-and-death," which seems more appropriate. Thomas Cleary (DŌGEN 1986, 122) has "some measure of detachment (はなるる分) from birth and death."

it comes to living, just give yourself to life; when it comes to dying, just give yourself to death. Do not detest, do not desire.

In this passage Dōgen invokes the authority of the teachings of Buddhism (佛法) and implicitly includes himself as an authority, shifting grammatically from a third-person description of how things are, to a kind of first-person perspective indicated in my free interpretation by the word "we." He speaks to his followers, and at the end implicitly addresses them in the second-person: "[you should] not detest or desire." Although the Japanese text contains no words that translate as "I," "we," or "you," the imperative verbal form that Dōgen uses (いとふ ことなかれ、ねがふことなかれ) clearly implies a directive issuing from a first-person voice and addressed to some "you."

The category of grammatical person, however, is hermeneutically insufficient without the grammar and references related to time. Grammatically, Dōgen writes his words in the present tense; and now that they are written, a common hermeneutical practice is to interpret them as released from the particular time or occasion of their being written. Contrary to this common practice, we may place Dōgen's writing in the present that he invokes both in the tense of his statements and in his references to time. Here Dōgen's text evokes the "alternative understanding," discussed in Chapter 3, that surpasses textuality toward an ever-present call to practice.[50] There are two modes

---

50. The European practice of romanticist hermeneutics in the nineteenth century aimed to re-live the original occasion of the writing. In the twentieth century philosophers criticized this attempt as misguided, and the practice turned to liberating the text from any surmised intention of the author in his time. RICOEUR (1983, 191) writes, "Writing tears itself free of the limits of face-to-face dialogue and becomes the condition for discourse itself *becoming-text*. It is to hermeneutics that falls the task of exploring the implications of this becoming-text for the work of interpretation." A hermeneutics related to the romanticist practice is at work in current homilies by Zen teachers when they quote Zen masters like Dōgen as if the master's words were timeless, immediately applicable to the present audience. Scholars of Zen criticize this hermeneutics as part of a naïve "rhetoric of immediacy," a fabricated sense of spontaneity and immediacy found both in the original text and in its current use. While I too want to hear what Dōgen has

of referring to time in the passages I have quoted. In the last mentioned passage, for example, Dōgen is telling whoever his present audience is, to be aware (心える), now, of life or of death, each as its own time (生は ひとときのくらゐ, 生とふとき. 滅もひとときのくらゐ, 滅といふとき). One mode of reference here is to time (or temporal position, 時のくらい) for the first person, for me and each of us, even as each of us is to give ourselves over completely to the occasion of one time. Borrowing a word from the *Shōbōgenzō Uji*, we may interpret this part of Dōgen's message by restating: "this living moment (*nikon*) of being-time is all there ever is to life, and to death."[51] Another mode of reference is the conditional formulation, "only at this time when you detach from life-and-death..." (このときはじめて 生死をはなるる分...). These words occur near both the beginning and the end of the *Shōji* fascicle. The dimension of time, or better: the presencing of time, is necessary to understand the perspective from which Dōgen makes his pronouncements.

The *Zenki* fascicle offers some final clues that intimate the meaning of death for Dōgen and the perspective from which he speaks. Similar to the *Genjōkōan* and the *Shōji*, the *Zenki* often interprets the samsaric compound birth/life-and-death (*shōji*) by treating the lexical elements *shō* (life) and *shi* (death) separately but equally. What is said of one is also asserted of the other. To summarize some points: life completely liberates life and death completely liberates death; life is the presencing of the whole works (*zenki*) and so is death.[52] Life does not get in the way of death and death does not get in the way of life. All reality (the entire earth and the whole empty sky) is contained in life but is

---

to say to us here and now, in this day and age, concerning death, I appeal not to timeless words but rather to the temporal grammar of Dōgen's text that indicates an occurrence taking place within a present: the mutual presence to one another of the quoted speaker/actor and his audience. In Dōgen's writing that occurrence hardly seems fabricated. Be that as it may, Dōgen's writings are often based on his verbal Dharma talks that embodied a presence not fully captured by textual hermeneutics.

51. This is the restatement of DAVIS 2009, 255.
52. I use here Thomas Cleary's innovative translation of the word *zenki* (全機), the dynamic and interdependent activity of all phenomena. DŌGEN 1986, 43.

likewise contained in death. Life and death, like earth and sky, are not one but not different, not different but not the same, not the same but not many.[53] How then do they relate?

Scholars often claim that Japanese Buddhism emphasizes and values death equally with life, contrary to a Western emphasis on life.[54] According to this view of Japanese Buddhism, life and death entail one another so completely that in speaking of life, we may as well say death; in speaking of death, we may as well say life. There is life, if and only if there is death; there is death, if and only if there is life. Thus, to live in accord with the teachings of Buddhism, we should, while living, always keep death in mind as well. Dōgen seems to reflect this view at one point, when his equivalence of the terms "life" and "death" implies that in speaking of life, we may as well say death; in speaking of death, we may as well say life. But I think this view as a whole is the view of ordinary Buddhism, in contrast to Dōgen's relatively extraordinary perspective on life and death. Dōgen clearly implies that life and death are each complete in themselves—not that they are of equal value and entail one another.[55] Life and death interchangeably are samsara and are the occasion of nirvana.

I think of myself as alive, not yet dead—how could one think of oneself as dead? Dōgen encourages me to give myself over completely to being one existential moment (*uji*) of living at a time. In the *Zenki* he encourages me to investigate a time like this very one (この正當恁麼時を功夫參學すべし), and he writes of the "I that is life, the life that

---

53. 「一にあらざれども異にあらざれども即にあらず、即にあらざれども多にあらず。」 The order of contrasts here differs from the usual sequence, which is: not one and not many, not different and not same. Kyoto School philosopher TANABE (2011, 686) interprets this sentence as an example of a unity of opposites.

54. SUEKI (2009A, 3) writes that in the modern (post-Christian) Western worldview that determined the conventional understanding of Buddhism, "only 'life' was considered of value and with death all value is lost."

55. KIM 1985, 245 n. 7, interprets the *Zenki*. as saying that birth/life is all-inclusive, totally independent and self-sufficient. Presumably the same holds true for death as well.

is I " (生なるわれ、われなる生).⁵⁶ He does not follow this with a parallel comment concerning death, as if he could speak of "the I that is death"—how could he?—but he does follow it with a quotation from Song-era Zen master Yuanwu, to the effect that life is the presencing of "the whole works" and so is death.⁵⁷ Dōgen's formulation implies that there is no self separate from birth/life and no self separate from death. It is not that *I* am born, live, and die, as if there were some person undergoing these events separate from them. Rather this I *is* the being-born, living, dying—yet even that manner of speaking spreads the self over time. In practice I am to give myself over completely to each and every moment right now. (In some texts *nikon*, a common Chinese expression for *now*, is the word Dōgen uses).

A FOREGONE CONCLUSION

What then does Dōgen have to say about personal death? Nothing directly about biographical death, the death of others described by a detached, anonymous observer. Little about the death of the second person, the others he personally knows, save for a few words of admonition and encouragement, such as "do not detest death, do not desire life." These two perspectives already imply some divide between life and death, but Dōgen places between life and death an even deeper divide. As for autobiographical death, this death of oneself becomes for Dōgen the death *of* the first person and *of* a first-person perspective.⁵⁸ The sense of death that Dōgen defines absolves or liberates oneself into the moment. The divide between birth-and-death (生死) and liberation that initially characterizes autobiographical death in much of philosophical Buddhism is healed; there is no divide here.

56. DŌGEN 1971A, 203; DŌGEN 1988, vol. 1: 220. Buddhist dictionaries say 正當恁麼時 means 正如此時: "just like this time," or "truly like this very moment."
57. Dōgen quotes the line 生也全機現、死也全機現 from a poem by Yuanwu (Taishō 47.1997.793c6). See DŌGEN 2006, 183 n. 138.
58. DAVIS (2011) presents Dōgen's philosophy as one of "egoless perspectivism."

Several Mahayana traditions already identify samsara with nirvana; but Dōgen adds a difference: constantly practicing the perspective of the all-engulfing moment.[59]

Philosophically, what we may gain from this perspective is the insight that the meaning of personal death, that is to say, one's intentionality directed to death, is inevitably directed to another time, not this time, not now. When I speak of the death of anonymous others I mean a time past; when I speak of your death, I think of a future time; when I think of my own death, I intend a future time too, perhaps about to come, but not right now. Dōgen shifts these meanings, this intentionality, to a different sense of death, death in the right now. *Death, more clearly than anything else, makes present the element of time.* Practically, the practice of absorption into a momentary right now gives rise to serious ethical problems that Chapter 12 has addressed. When it comes to a beautiful death, in any case, attention to the moment at hand, in whatever degree possible, may be the only way to go.

---

59. Dōgen's concentration on the all-engulfing moment at any time thus differs from what was once the focus in much of Japanese Pure Land Buddhism on the moment of death as the particularly momentous time of liberation, when one should die with a fervent hope for birth in the pure land. We noted how Genshin exhorted the dying person to concentrate on Amida Buddha as his last thought (念). Carl Becker notes that this thought has precedents in many sutras, which stress the importance of wholesome thoughts at the moment of death. "Buddha declared that the crucial variable governing rebirth was the nature of the consciousness at the moment of death." BECKER (1990, 547) refers to texts from the Pali canon: the *Petavatthu* and the *Vimānavatthu* ("Stories of the Departed"), *Majjhima Nikāya* II, 91; III, 258; and *Samyutta Nikāya* V, 408.

Follow-up
Ante-Originality and the Alternative Creativity of Japanese Pathway Arts

> To model the Way is to model yourself.
> To model yourself is to forget yourself.
> To forget yourself is to be realized in all things.
> To be realized in all things is
> to let body-mind fall off,
> your own as well as that of others.
> – Dōgen, *Genjōkōan*[1]

Models and exemplary persons have featured in several chapters in this book. We noted the role of the exemplary person for both Confucius and Aristotle in the chapters about practice in an alternative mode and about alternative normativity. In our reflections on alternative autonomy, Zen teacher Linji recommended persons "of great resolve" who learn to respond to their circumstances and environs, to become a "great vessel" and "followers of the Way," and this idea is echoed in Nishitani Keiji's exhortation to become "subservient to *all* things." The chapter about text-based hermeneutics presented embodied practice as a model for an alternative sense of understanding. In the dialogue with Ueda Shizuteru, we saw how Japanese linked verse or *renku* models the language of alterity.

---

1. This paraphrase reads the verb *narau* (ならう) as 倣う, to follow or emulate—rather than as its homonym 習う, to learn or study. Both can connote training or learning under a teacher. The translation of *Genjōkōan* by Thomas P. Kasulis (JPSB, 145) also reads the verb this way. Most translations into English have "study": "to study the Way is to study the self...," but Dōgen frequently writes 學 for study, as we saw in Chapter 13, "The Study of Body-Mind."

While Dōgen's words about modeling in the epigraph above are best understood via embodied practice, we may notice already that the words do not end with an exhortation to emulate oneself. Even modeling by taking after others, following in their footsteps, must fall away to open us to a totality of phenomena that serve as models of how to be and what to do. Dōgen's words about forgetting and dropping away suggest a kind of breaking away—a pathbreaking practice—that happens to characterize a phase in the "ways" of various Japanese arts, such as the Way of Flowers, the Way of Tea, the Way of Writing, as well as the "ways" of many martial arts. And while these various "ways" have left clear tracks in the forest of Zen,[2] they have their own institutions and embodiments that deserve attention. We may distinguish them with their own name, "pathways." Their own kinds of trail-blazing can take us beyond the paths we have explored so far in this book. The "pathway arts" present examples of the continuity and the breaks that give rise to an alternative mode of creativity. And so they together serve as a model of the continuity and breaking-away (or branching out) that allow most alternatives to arise. Our "Follow-up" turns to some of these other-than-Zen ways.

Before Originals and Copies

In his 1935 essay, *The Work of Art in the Age of Mechanical Reproduction*, Walter Benjamin famously wrote that "the presence of the original is the prerequisite to the concept of authenticity."[3] This evaluation of the work of art is undermined by one common feature of traditional Japanese aesthetics: the esteem placed on modeling the work of an instructor who herself has learned by emulating the work

---

2. D. T. Suzuki's *Zen and Japanese Culture* is the classical and now controversial example of linking many pathway arts to the Zen tradition.
3. BENJAMIN 1968, 170. The original German emphasizes the "here and now" presence of the object: "Das Hier und Jetzt des Originals macht den Begriff seiner Echtheit aus" (BENJAMIN 2010, 13).

and actions of a model teacher. While other aesthetic traditions have also recognized the educational value of reproducing the styles and techniques of exemplary artists, several Japanese traditional arts prioritize the practice of modeling oneself and one's work after exemplars. Instead of striving from the start to become independent and original, the artist-in-the-making spends years incorporating the awareness and skills of teachers before she introduces variations and innovations. Teachers as well as beginners continue to embody forms that are not abstract but rather compliant with one's concrete situation. Authenticity in these traditions means appropriating a pliable model that has been refined through the practice of numerous predecessors. Emphasis is placed on perfecting an activity rather than producing a unique artifact. In contrast to prevalent notions of originality in art, the relevant notion might be called "ante-originality," for it is embodied in a model that precedes and takes precedence over the production of original works. We will illustrate this notion in the practice of floral arrangement, tea ceremony, and calligraphy—arts that among others are often called "pathways" (*dō* 道), as in *kadō* (花道), the Way of Flowers, or *shodō* (書道), the Way of Writing. Ante-originality is not unique to artistic practice in Japan, nor characteristic of all Japanese arts, but its prevalence there lets us better notice its working elsewhere.

Since Japan is often described as a "copy culture," it is important to distinguish the aesthetic practice of modeling from the practice of imitation noted throughout Japanese history. The ability of the Japanese to assimilate foreign technologies and artificially remake and automate the world around them is renowned.[4] A common stereotype (which itself is a kind of copy) depicts Japanese artists and engineers through the centuries as borrowing, copying, and sometimes improving upon products and methods of producing them. The notion of copying implies an original, but Japanese history reveals several modal-

---

4. See the introduction in Cox 2008, 4. Parts of this paragraph adapt descriptions from that introduction.

ities of originality and copying—from flawlessly tracing over a piece of Chinese writing and displaying it alongside the original, to adapting "quality control" in the production of automobiles and claiming it as Japan's invention. Traditional "arts of citation," including some calligraphy and poetic composition, "demonstrate the originality and creativity of the copy by identifying a process and particular persons by which the copy is made."[5] Copying can generate creativity by transforming the character of the copier and employing new materials and techniques. Calligraphic artists as well as painters in Japan often apply a stamp or seal to their work to signify its temporal origin, but each successive owner of the work may add a seal to indicate a provenance that extends its caretaking over time. Poetic composition may cite a verse (without credit) and then build new verses upon it. In short, what is often simplistically differentiated as either *original* or *copy* displays a wide variety of modes. But the arts that display ante-originality challenge that difference in all its modifications.

THREE PATHWAYS TO ANTE-ORIGINALITY

Imagine that an encounter with a Japanese floral arrangement has surprised and delighted you for its striking liveliness and way of configuring space. The space around it seems charged with electricity. You decide to begin formal instruction in *ikenobō*, the oldest school of *ikebana,* the art of displaying the momentary life of flowers.[6] In your first lesson, you watch as your teacher lays out three or four flowers alongside five or so branches of different lengths and holds each one up to notice its shape. She selects one to place in the pin holder in a vase or container with water, then the second, the third, and so on, trimming each in sequence and adding the flowers. Pausing to gaze at the com-

5. Ibid., 11.
6. This definition is inspired by a reading of Nishitani Keiji, "Ikebana," in JPSB, 1197–1200, which stresses the art's attention to the impermanence of flowers and plants.

position, she may make small adjustments, trimming here and there or coaxing a branch or flower to curve a bit more or a bit less. Finally, she sits back to appreciate the composition and its space. All the while you have been sitting slightly behind her to notice how she holds and turns the materials as she examines them and executes each step. You take advantage of the opportunity to see her seeing.

After a few moments, she motions you to remove all items from the container and then to recreate the arrangement with the very same materials and vase. What you imagined to be a simple act of replacing the materials soon proves to be a challenging assignment: your branches somehow stand differently, the flowers seem a bit misplaced, and the arrangement looks a bit askew even to your beginner's eyes. The teacher gracefully guides you through some adjustments that shape the arrangement closer to her model. She shows you how the branches display a shade (or *yin*) side and a sun (or *yang*) side in their natural growth, and how the arrangement forefronts their interaction with each other under a specific light source. She may clarify that this particular work exhibits the classical *shōka* style, with the tallest branch standing for *heaven*, the shortest branch representing the *earth*, and a mid-length branch standing in for the *human* as mediator in this mini-universe. The three elements with other "attendant" branches and the flowers together configure a space that now comes clearly into view. At the end of your lesson, you disassemble the arrangement, take it home, and put it back together again. And yet it is not exactly the same arrangement, for the shapes of materials have slightly changed, the vase or container is different, and the space in which it is placed is altogether distinct. After a few days, the flowers wither, following the natural way of all life forms, and the arrangement is gracefully discarded.

Over the following one or two years of weekly lessons, you repeat the pattern of watching the teacher compose and recreating her composition. There is variation enough. Even within the same style, *shōka* for example, the materials change according to the seasons; the number, shape, and color of branches and flowers vary; new placement techniques are required; and, in every re-creation of the teacher's model, your arrangement reflects your own level of active understanding. Further seasons of instruction gradually introduce other styles, each with its own guidelines, some styles simpler yet and some complex, some more regulated and others more free-form. Each lesson embodies your unique interaction with a manifold of factors. You learn to see cutting as shaping that expresses the temporal limits of every life form,[7] and for each arrangement you trim branches and flowers anew. It might take four spring seasons to learn to cut an iris leaf adeptly. A repertoire of practical solutions builds into a body of experiential knowledge. That knowledge, in turn, lets you see plant life differently, noticing the stage of a bud's blossoming, for example, the sun and shade sides of leaves, the ways that different plants grow precisely and compliantly in response to their surroundings and sources of light and water.

At some point in your training, your teacher instructs you to do an alteration (*henka* 変化) on a formal style while still remaining within that style. The set of rules that specifies a particular style, more or less, has guided your interactions with the material, and the teacher's actions have modeled appropriate interactions. If you have internalized the guidelines, you need not "bend the rules" but can now realize them in your own way. You come to see your teacher's arrangements not as originals that you copied but rather as models to which you learned to conform. "Once you learn the form," she tells you, "the flowers (the arrangement) become(s) *your* flowers (*your* arrangement)." This sounds like a contradiction: if all you are doing is applying rules that are not of your own making, how could you be creating something that is uniquely your own? But the form circumscribed by a set of rules is not a fixed and transcendent Platonic form whose instantiations are inevitably only imperfect copies. It is rather a compliant form

---

7. Ōhashi Ryōsuke, "Cutting," in JPSB, 1192–4.

that comes to life only through creating actual, unrepeatable arrangements. The contour and color of the branches and flowers will differ on each occasion, so the material immediately at your disposal serves as a guideline as much as do the rules. The teacher, too, has been modeling a form that comes to life only in virtually infinite variety. Just as natural things never repeat themselves exactly, your precise actions in arranging as well as the materials you use are singular, one time only. Your experience has not been a matter of learning to "do your own thing" and make something original, as is often stressed in art education focused on originality.[8] Your education in *ikebana* has been a matter of realizing a form over and over again by modeling the natural growth of plants as well as the actions of a teacher.

The Way of Tea (*sadō* 茶道) provides another example of a form that precedes the endeavor to produce something original. This example reveals further insight into the nature and origin of rules. Like *ikebana*, the art of tea produces no lasting artifact. As we shall see, however, that lack does not determine the form. In tea lessons one learns to model a master's movements and skill, to pay close attention to hands and gestures, and to follow the precise order of minutely prescribed steps in preparing and serving the tea. For example, one learns precisely how to lift the lid from the little iron pot of heated water and where to place it, how to lower the bamboo dipper into the pot and gently pour water into the tea cup, then replace the dipper on its stand and slide one's fingers along its handle before lifting the hand for the next move. We need not recount all the details here to make the point. To the beginner or the unfamiliar observer, the activity may seem an excessively rule-bound procedure. True, the implements used and the occasion provide some variation: the charcoal used to heat water will burn differently each time, the utensils and tea bowls as well as the

---

8. Theodore Adorno argues that, for all the originality we see in works of all eras of art, the focus on creativity or originality, and on art detached from religious functions, is a modern Western phenomenon. See ADORNO 1998, cited in NAKAMURA F. 2007, 80.

tea itself will vary, and the movements of the teacher and student will change to adapt to the situation. Despite these variations, however, the rules seem to take precedence. And they do—but only because they express a model that has previously emerged from extensive practice.

The tea master and philosopher Hisamatsu Shin'ichi explains their origin in relation to the performance. "The Way of Tea is unthinkable without conformity to the rules," he writes.[9] However, the rules do not represent some exterior mandate. They have been formulated from the proficient practice of making and serving tea. Their origin lies in the refined activity of tea masters, practitioners who sought the most efficient and elegant ways of preparing and appreciating an everyday refreshment. The rules that guide the movements of the body, the handling of the implements, and the attention to everything and everyone present express the forethought that paves a way to harmonious interaction. Each object and each person are treated with respect. Respect also entails seeing how a rule ensures the simplicity, elegance, and appropriateness of an action. The beginner might respond, "Of course, this makes perfect sense!" And because one is following the most direct, simple, and appropriate way to accomplish something, unfettered by distractions and extraneous matters, one is becoming free. The interiorized rules take the truism that "creativity thrives under constraints" to the next level.

Hisamatsu makes a comment that, taken out of context, seems contradictory: "Autonomous and free activity *becomes* the rule, so that conformity with it occurs naturally. For this reason, the practitioner is forever breaking away from the rules to work freely."[10] We once watched a student who had been taking lessons for about a year do "tea ceremony." Right afterwards, at age 79 Nishitani Keiji, who had learned decades earlier, prepared and served tea. It was obvious that the student had memorized the rules and was conscientiously, some-

---

9. Hisamatsu Shin'ichi, "The Way of Tea," in JPSB, 1195.
10. Ibid., translation adjusted.

what stiltedly, conforming to them. When the elder Nishitani sensei "did tea," the motions were fluid and the ambience relaxed; the rules, it seemed, had been interiorized and forgotten. Perhaps this is what Hisamatsu meant by "breaking away... to work freely." By freeing up a seemingly fixed form to comply with ever-changing situations, the rules are kept alive and adaptive. One learns to keep the rules alive and make this art one's own by modeling a teacher's performance and then releasing oneself from it and letting new performances live. Once again, a prior origin facilitates the "originality" of the artist.

The Way of Writing (*shodō* 書道) is another art form that exhibits ante-originality. It could also be called the Way of Drawing, for calligraphy in this guise is as much drawing as it is writing Sino-Japanese characters or kanji. The "Way of the Brush" in the broad sense includes both *shodō* and sumi-ink painting, both of which involve mastery by way of modeling. These arts differ from the ways of flowers and tea in that they leave a durable object in the world, the writing or the painting that can be displayed in a tokonoma, an exhibition, or a museum. Indeed, museums often collect Chinese, Korean, and Japanese calligraphic works as superlative examples of an individual artist's originality. The Way of Writing would seem to exemplify a pattern of originality commonly celebrated in modern Western cultures. It developed from distinct kanji that are intelligible because of their repeated usage, but it re-presents them in unique and unrepeatable patterns. Various styles have developed over the centuries, from very distinct writing resembling uniform printing to very cursive and nearly illegible flows. The artist may adhere to a relatively fixed number and order of brush strokes within each style, but the few styles depicted in writing manuals are patterns generalized and simplified from historical works. The *avant-garde* "calligraphy" that developed in the second half of the twentieth century transgressed historical patterns both by creating abstract images and by displaying works in exhibitions. As long as the "writing" is of ink brushed on paper or another surface, whether based on kanji or not, it is considered *sho*. In both traditional and *avant-garde* calligraphy, an unwritten rule constrains the way the brush is used: the brush never retraces its path.

What then is the place of modeling in this art form that seems geared toward originality? Of course, the beginner first learns to prepare the sumi ink and to brush kanji on the paper by closely watching the teacher's actions and then trying things out herself. But mere imitation will get the student nowhere. Far too many contingencies arise for straightforward copying to work. One usually already knows how to form the kanji, what stroke order to use, and what "radicals" or often-repeated elements to write. But writing with brush and ink is entirely different from writing from rote memorization with a pen. It demands constant attention and fluid bodily movement; it engages the whole body-mind at once. At the same time, it demands a willingness to let go of one's will and conform to the quirks of the material that may thwart one's initial intentions. The speed of the flow of the ink from the tip of the brush guides the speed of the brush moving along the paper as the writer intends. The surface of the paper eases and sometimes impedes the flow. It can seem as if the whole world becomes located in that tip, but it is crucial to widen one's vision and see the field of the entire paper, too. One's focus on a point of rolling ink expands to the space that takes shape with the developing contours of the inked image. The artwork is the space opened by the image as much as the inked image itself. The agency behind this art is the interaction of artist, brush, ink, and paper. The *avant-garde* calligrapher Morita Shiryū goes so far as to say that what is created is the artist as much as the artwork; the artist becomes the activity of writing.[11]

The model in Japanese calligraphic art is manifold. For the novice, the teacher who first demonstrates the method sketched above is a model. In the traditional practice called *rinsho* (臨書), artists take an example of classical Chinese calligraphy (or sometimes later Japanese calligraphy) as their model, which they copy as exactly as possible.

---

11. Morita Shiryū, "Calligraphy," in JPSB, 1200–02.

(Often, the model itself is one of several classical copies of a work no longer extant.) Yet artists who practice *rinsho* are already proficient writers of kanji, and what they are doing is more than producing a copy that a photographer could do better today.¹² They are modeling their movements after the movements their eyes trace in the exemplary work. In a sense, then, it is the performance captured in the exemplary writing and visible to the trained eye that serves as the model. While calligraphers want to conceal the effort required to achieve technical mastery, they cherish the way that their work makes spontaneity visible. There is no hiding the dynamic movement that created the work, and trained viewers try to trace in their mind or with their hand the choreography of the brush across the surface. The work is a record of an "expressive gesture"—still another way to define what it is that the artist models.¹³

As in the case of *ikebana* and the Way of Tea, creativity does not reduce to producing an original or independent work, but appears in the unique performance of the art. We will return to this idea, but for now note that a parallel between calligraphic art and the floral and

---

12. The crucial difference is captured in a passage from "Miscellaneous Discussions at Cold Mountain" (寒山箒談) by the Chinese writer and critic Zhao Yiguang (趙宧光, 1559–1625):

> Copying model-calligraphy [e.g. in rubbings from steles] as one's own is stealing, not learning.
> Referring to them for one's own is borrowing, not stealing.
> Transforming them for one's own is stone-stepping, not borrowing.
> Assimilating them for one's own is modeling, not stone-stepping.
> Only then does learning begin.

In other words, "assimilation is the key to perpetuating the heritage and arriving at transformation." "Reinvigorating the Past: Selected Calligraphy Works from the Museum Collection," 2008 Exhibit at the Hong Kong Museum of Art, <https://hk.art.museum/en_US/web/ma/resources/archive/exhibitions/2004-now.html>.

13. "Expressive gesture" is the anthropologist Tim Ingold's phrase to describe musical performance, and adapted by NAKAMURA F. (2007, 85) to describe calligraphic art. That article presents insights we have appropriated here as well as many details about Japanese calligraphic art that we have had to pass over. Our presentation differs from Nakamura's by emphasizing modeling in distinction from "imitating."

tea arts becomes apparent: the outcome is ephemeral. Some calligraphers liken their artistry to the performance of a musical composition, "an activity where one *performs* forms of words envisaged in mind."[14] The Western abstract painting that features nothing but the agency of the artist also served as a model for *avant-garde sho* artists (just as their work was a model for Western painters). It is remarkable, however, that *sho* artists often discarded a work as soon as it was created. They recognized that creativity truly lies in the performance, not in a durable "original" work to be hung on a wall. "Authenticity is not then directly linked to originality but to reproductive performance."[15] In other words, authenticity is achieved by reenacting an ante-original.

A WIDESPREAD PRACTICE OF MODELING

Adaptive modeling has, of course, been practiced in cultural forms in which originality has not been an issue. Practitioners of martial arts such as Taekwondo, aikido, and judo learn by modeling forms or *kata*. Apprentices in trades such as welding learn by modeling the techniques of experienced teachers and by conforming to the demands of the material. Learning a language requires its own modes of modeling. There is no premium placed on originality in these practices.

The notion of ante-originality reminds us that the practice of modeling is not something unique to Japan and is not its original invention. Nor is this practice characteristic of all Japanese art forms. We find it decisive for Japanese "pathway" (道) arts—those that present flowers, tea, and writing, for example—and for theatrical arts like *Noh*. In this limited sense, its presence in Japanese aesthetics is exemplary. However, precedents are apparent especially in classical aesthetic practices of China, the home of the pathway traditions.[16] Outside

---

14. Hidai Nankoku (1912–1999), in his book co-edited with UNO Sesson 1983, 26, cited in NAKAMURA F. 2007, 87.
15. Ibid.. 2007, 86.
16. BURNETT 2013 investigates concepts of originality in Chinese arts, focusing on

those traditions, modeling was a practice of artists who trained in institutions in Europe as well as in Japan—the Renaissance art academies of Italy, for example, or the Kanō school of painting that thrived from the fifteenth century to the Meiji Period.

What is more, subsequent interaction between modern Euro-American visual artists and Japanese calligraphers has erased imagined boundaries between "East" and "West." For some seventy years now, *sho* artists and Euro-American abstract painters have engaged in a virtual dialogue of images that transformed methods and objectives on both sides.[17] *Ikebana* and the Way of Tea, although adhering more closely to Japanese traditions, have become international practices, and the modern Sōgetsu School of *ikebana*, with its use of plastic, plaster, and steel in its arrangements, arose partially in response to Western cultural influence in the twentieth century. There is no monopoly on creativity.

Alternative creativity

Yet pathway arts in the broad sense have made visible a "different kind of creativity."[18] In initial modeling, the artist is neither reproducing the work of another nor attempting to express herself independently. Through patient practice, the expressive gestures become her own, and her personal style emerges. But that style remains a living "form"—something that lives by way of performance, *per forman*, rather than *pro-forma* in a fixed format.[19] What is creative is the living form, the form as performed ever anew, and not simply

---

seventeenth-century art criticism and the increasing reference to 奇 ("different," "original," "novel"). She refutes the contention that originality was devalued even while modeling was practiced.

17. For reflections on and further references to this interaction, as well as the issue of nationalism in Japanese *sho* art, see Maraldo 2018.
18. Nakamura F. 2007, 80.
19. I owe the Latin expressions, as well as the reference to the *shu-ha-ri* formula, to Heisig 2019, 28–9.

the artist as a subject who produces a supposedly unique object in the world. If we were to extract a pattern that describes this performance of creativity, we could speak of three phases: (1) embodying a form as it is exemplified in a teacher's performance; (2) then breaking away by adapting or varying the form, making it one's own, and finally (3) releasing the form from oneself, from one's control. To describe this adaptive pattern, pathway arts such as *sadō*, the Way of Tea, and martial arts such as aikido, sometimes make use of a pithy expression written with three sinographs: *shu* 守 *ha* 破 *ri* 離: protect, break, distance. *Shu-ha-ri* expresses a movement from appropriation to detachment that becomes apparent when we follow a work of art—a working of art—through its temporal performance. And the adept's temporal performance gains spatial dimension when it includes acts of receiving on the part of viewers or other participants. It is a cliché to say that art can be transformative for artists and viewers alike; it is refreshing to shift attention from artist and viewer to the forms that transcend them when they personally set them free. The liberated form is an expression of the self's freedom that has become a freedom from self. This process is progressively at work in each of the phases; artists are taken out of themselves in modeling the performance of others and then adapting to circumstances, in breaking their own mindless or automatic responses and letting a form live on its own.

What is more, the "breaking away" that Hisamatsu mentions works on two levels: in the history of the pathway arts as well as within performing individuals. Creative "breaks" occur historically when the new forms break away from established ones—when the *Sōgetsu* School floral arranging broke away from more traditional ways of *ikebana*, for example, or when avant-garde calligraphers released *kanji* into abstract forms and placed them in artistic exhibitions. Or when an artist constructs three-dimensional *kanji* and places them in an installation modeled after forms of *ikebana*, thus merging two traditional pathway arts. Their various "schools" have continued to adapt to changing circumstances, as if they were modeling Linji's alternative autonomy that "accords with all environing things." The very plurality of pathway schools and the development of new styles are evidence of the creative movement from inherited to transformed models. This process of creative performance has reached back in time as well as out to present conditions. In fact, one of the best examples of creative calligraphy occurred in 1945 at the end of the war, when the calligrapher Hidai Nankoku used ancient writing (古文) as a model to break an impasse in his own development:

> It was difficult to make a definite shape for the motif I had in mind.... This continued for some time, until I suddenly remembered my father's admonition, "If you come to an impasse, return to the origin." I remembered 古文 (ancient script) and began leafing through the Ku-chou Hui-pien, a dictionary of 古文. The character for lightning or thunder attracted me in a curious way and I began working it. The result was "Spirit Line Work No. 1," which turned out to be variations on 雷 (J. *den*).[20]

Hidai's performance disassembled the sinograph into lively, interacting but separate brush strokes that resemble fish swimming or birds flying. Critics debated whether his creation should count as *sho* or writing at all, and this very debate shows that the practice of working from models, ancient or contemporary, does not preclude creativity. Both viewers and artists continued the creative movement unleashed by the work: Hidai's creation is now considered "the first abstract work in the history of calligraphy,"[21] the beginning of the new movement that we have called *avant-garde* calligraphy. Other Japanese calligraphers like Nishikawa Yasushi more closely modeled ancient brushed writing on a piece of silk that was unearthed in China in 1934, again releasing an old style as a model for innovative work.[22]

20. "Until Spirit Line Work was born," 1955; cited on the web page < https://www.shodo.co.jp/nankoku_eng/>.
21. Ibid.
22. WORDS IN MOTION 1985, 89.

Innovation indebted to precedents without end is the generator of ante-original art work.

To recapitulate

Where an artwork is defined as "an original object that can be created only once,"[23] the role of modeling is undervalued and the extent of creativity is cut short. In the facet of Japanese aesthetics reviewed here, the "artwork" designates the one-time performance as much as the object of temporal duration, and the performance uniquely models what we may call the creative ante-originality of the art.

---

23. Alfred GELL 1998, 30; cited in NAKAMURA 2007, 80. Contemporary digital art erases the distinction between original and copy more than Walter Benjamin imagined, and yet art buyers still seek authenticity, as this newspaper article by E. Griffith indicates:
> In a fast-growing market for ownership rights to digital art, ephemera and media called NFTs, or "nonfungible tokens," the buyers are usually not acquiring copyrights, trademarks or even the sole ownership of whatever it is they purchase. They're buying bragging rights and the knowledge that their copy is the "authentic one."

"Why an Animated Flying Cat With a Pop-Tart Body Sold for Almost $600,000," *The New York Times*, February 22, 2021, <https://www.nytimes.com/2021/02/22/business/nft-nba-top-shot-crypto.html>.

Bibliography

Abbreviations

JPSB Heisig, James W., Thomas P. Kasulis, and John C. Maraldo, eds. *Japanese Philosophy, A Sourcebook* (Honolulu: University of Hawai'i Press, 2011).

NKC 『西谷啓治著作集』[Collected Works of Keiji Nishitani] (Tokyo: Sōbunsha, 1986–1995), 26 vols.

NKZ 『西田幾多郎全集』[Complete Works of Nishida Kitarō], 4th edition (Tokyo: Iwanami Shoten, 1978–1980), 19 vols.

Other sources

ABE Masao 阿部正雄
- 1985 *Zen and Western Thought*. Honolulu: University of Hawai'i Press.
- 1989 "Will, Śūnyatā, and History," in Taitetsu Unno, ed., *The Religious Philosophy of Nishitani Keiji*. Berkeley: Asian Humanities Press, 279–304.
- 1990 "Kenotic God and Dynamic Sunyata," in COBB AND IVES, 3–65.

ACKROYD, Joyce, trans.
- 1979 *Told Round A Brushwood Fire. The Autobiography of Arai Hakuseki*. Princeton: Princeton University Press.
- 1982 *Lessons From History: Arai Hakuseki's Tokushi Yoron*. St. Lucia, Queensland: University of Queensland Press.

ADDISS, Stephen, and Stanley LOMBARDO, trans.
- 1993 *Tao Te Ching*. Indianapolis and Cambridge: Hackett.

ADORNO, Theodore
- 1998 *The Culture Industry: Selected Essays on Mass Culture*, ed. J. M. Bernstein. New York: Routledge.

AGAR, Michael
- 1994 *Language Shock: Understanding the Culture of Conversation*. New York: William Morrow.

AGUILAR, Claudia
  2022 "Relational Autonomy in Spinoza. Freedom and Joint Action," *Comparative and Continental Philosophy* 14/1. <https://www.tandfonline.com/doi/abs/10.1080/17570638.2022.2091972>.

AITKEN, Robert
  1984 *The Mind of Clover: Essays in Zen Buddhist Ethics*. San Francisco: North Point Press.

AKIZUKI Ryōmin 秋月龍珉, trans.
  1972 『臨済録, 禅の語録10』[Record of Linji, Zen Recorded Sayings 10]. Tokyo: Chikuma Shobō.

AMES, Roger, and David L. HALL
  2003 *Dao De Jing: A Philosophical Translation*. New York: Ballantine Books.

AMES, Roger, and Henry ROSEMONT, Jr.
  1998 *The Analects of Confucius: A Philosophical Translation*. New York: Ballantine Books.

AOKI Shinmon 青木新門
  2002 *Coffinman: The Journal of a Buddhist Mortician*, trans. by Wayne S. Yokoyama. Anaheim, CA: Buddhist Education Center.

APP, Urs
  n.d. "Introduction to the Ten Oxherding Pictures. <https://terebess.hu/english/oxherd3.html>.

ARAI Hakuseki 新井白石
  1964 『戴恩記・折たく柴の記・蘭東事始』[*Daionki, Oritaku Shiba no Ki, Rangaku Kotohajime*], Odaka Toshirō and Matsumura Akira, eds. Tokyo: Iwanami Shoten, Nihon koten bungaku taikei 95.

ARAI, Paula
  2008 "Women and Dōgen: Rituals Actualizing Empowerment and Healing," in Steven Heine and Dale S. Wright, eds., *Zen Ritual: Studies of Zen Buddhist Theory in Practice*. New York: Oxford University Press, 185–204.
  2011 *Bringing Zen Home: The Healing Heart of Japanese Women's Rituals*. Honolulu, University of Hawai'i Press.

ARENDT, Hannah
  1958 *The Human Condition*. New York: Doubleday Anchor.
  1971 "Martin Heidegger at Eighty," *The New York Review*, October 21. A translation by Albert Hofstadter of "Martin Heidegger is achzig Jahre alt," *Merkur* 23/258 (October 1969): 893–902.

ARISTOTLE
1941 *The Basic Works of Aristotle*. Edited and with an introduction by Richard McKeon. New York: Random House.

ARMSTRONG, D. M.
1968 *A Materialist Theory of Mind*. London and New York: Routledge and Kegan Paul.

AUSTIN, J. H.
1998 *Zen and the Brain: Toward an Understanding of Meditation and Consciousness*. Cambridge, MA: MIT Press.

BARBERY, Muriel
2008 *The Elegance of the Hedgehog*, trans. by Alison Anderson. New York: Europa Editions.

BARNHILL, David Landis
2010 "Renga: The Literary Embodiment of Impermanence and Non-self," *Semantic Scholar*. Online journal: <https://www.uwosh.edu/facstaff/barnhill/244-japan/Renga.pdf>.

BARRETT, William
1956 "Zen in the West," in William Barrett, ed., *Zen Buddhism: Selected Writings of D. T. Suzuki*. New York: Doubleday (1996).

BASSO, Keith H.
1996 *Wisdom Sits in Places: Landscape and Language Among the Western Apache*. Albuquerque: University of New Mexico Press.

BECKER, Carl B.
1984 "Religious Visions: Experiential Grounds for the Pure Land Tradition," *The Eastern Buddhist* 17/1: 138–53.
1990 "Buddhist Views of Suicide and Euthanasia," *Philosophy East and West* 50/4: 543–6.

BEHUNIAK, James Jr.
2010 "John Dewey and the Virtue of Cook Ding's *Dao*," *Dao—A Journal of Comparative Philosophy* 9/2: 161–74.

BELLAH, Robert N.
1978 "Baigan and Sorai: Continuities and Discontinuities in Eighteenth-Century Thought," in Tetsuo Najita and Irwin Scheiner, eds., *Japanese Thought in the Tokugawa Period*, Chicago: University of Chicago Press, 137–52.

BENJAMIN, Walter
1968   *Illuminations: Essays and Reflections*, trans. Harry Zohn. New York: Schocken Books.
2010   *Das Kunstwerk im Zeitalter seiner technischen Reproduzierbarkeit.* Berlin: Suhrkamp Verlag, 1935.

BERGSON, Henri
1988   *Matter and Memory.* New York: Zone Books.

BESEMERES, Mary
2002   *Translating One's Self: Language and Selfhood in Cross-Cultural Autobiography.* Oxford: Peter Lang.

BIELEFELDT, Carl
1988   *Dōgen's Manual of Zen Meditation.* Berkeley: University of California Press.

BILLETER, Jean François
2002.   *Leçons sur Tchouang-tseu.* Paris: Allia.

BITTNER, Egon
1973   "Objectivity and Realism in Sociology," in G. Psathas, ed., *Phenomenological Sociology: Issues and Applications.* New York: John Wiley.

BLUM, Mark L.
2004   "Nirvāṇa Sūtra," in *Encyclopedia of Buddhism*, Robert Buswell et al., eds. New York: Macmillan Reference, 605–6.

BODIFORD, William M.
1993   *Sōtō Zen in Medieval Japan.* Honolulu: University of Hawai'i Press.
2012   "Textual Genealogies of Dōgen," in Steven Heine, ed., *Dōgen: Textual and Historical Studies.* Oxford and New York, 15–41.

BONHOEFFER, Dietrich
1955   *Ethics.* Eberhard Bethge, ed. New York: Macmillan.

BOURDIEU, Pierre
1990   *The Logic of Practice*, trans. by Richard Nice. Stanford: Stanford University Press

BRANDOM, Robert B.
2002   *Tales of the Mighty Dead: Historical Essays in the Metaphysics of Intentionality.* Cambridge, MA: Harvard University Press.

BROUGHTON, Jeffrey L., with Elise Yoko WATANABE, trans.
2013   *The Record of Linji: A New Translation of the* Linjilu *in the Light of Ten Japanese Zen Commentaries.* New York: Oxford University Press.

BUCHNER, Hartmut, ed.
1989   *Japan und Heidegger: Gedenkschrift der Stadt Meßkirch zum hundertsten Geburtstag Martin Heideggers.* Sigmaringen: Jan Thorbecke Verlag.

BUNGE, Mario
1980   *The Mind-Body Problem: A Psychobiological Approach.* Oxford and New York: Pergamon Press.

BURNETT, Katharine P.
2013   *Dimensions of Originality: Essays on Seventeenth-Century Chinese Art Theory and Criticism.* Hong Kong: The Chinese University of Hong Kong Press.

BUSS, Sarah, and Andrea WESTLUND
2018   "Personal Autonomy," in Edward N. Zalte, ed., *the Stanford Encyclopedia of Philosophy.* <https://plato.stanford.edu/archives/spr2018/entries/personal-autonomy/>.

BUTLER, Judith
1990   *Gender Trouble: Feminism and the Subversion of Identity.* New York: Routledge.

BYRD, Dustin J., ed.
2020   *The Critique of Religion and Religion's Critique: On Dialectical Religiology.* Leiden and Boston: Brill.

CALVINO, Italo
1979   *Se una notte d'inverno un viaggiatore.* Torino: Edizione Einaudi.
1981   *If on a winter's night a traveler,* trans. by William Weaver. San Diego, New York, and London: Harcourt Brace Jovanovich.

CAMPBELL, Neil
2005   *A Brief Introduction to the Philosophy of Mind.* Peterborough, Ont.: Broadview Press.

CARTER, Robert E.
2001   *Encounter with Enlightenment: A Study of Japanese Ethics.* Albany, NY: State University of New York Press.

CESTARI, Matteo
1998 "The Knowing Body: Nishida's Philosophy of Active Intuition," *The Eastern Buddhist* 31/2: 179–208.

CHAI, David, ed.
2022 *Daoist Resonances in Heidegger: Exploring a Forgotten Debt*. London and New York: Bloomsbury.

CHU, William
2006 "Bodhisattva Precepts in the Ming Society: Factors Behind Their Success and Propagation," *Journal of Buddhist Ethics* 13. <https://blogs.dickinson.edu/buddhistethics/2010/04/27/bodhisattva-precepts-in-the-ming-society-factors-behind-their-success-and-propagation/>.

CLASPER, Paul D. and Janet CLASPER
1979 *The Ox-herder Pictures: Zen Buddhism's Version of "The Pilgrim's Progress."* Hong Kong: The Lotus-Logos Press.

CLEARY, Thomas and J. C. CLEARY, trans.
1978 *The Blue Cliff Record*. Boulder: Prajñā Press.

COBB, John B. Jr.
1998 Review of IVES 1995. *Journal of the American Academy of Religion* 66/2: 436–9.

COBB, John B. Jr., and Christopher IVES, eds.
1990 *The Emptying God: A Buddhist-Jewish-Christian Conversation*. New York: Orbis Books.

COLLCUT, Martin
1981 *Five Mountains: The Rinzai Monastic Institution in Medieval Japan*. Cambridge MA: Harvard University Press.

COLLINS, Steven
1982 *Selfless Persons*. Cambridge: Cambridge University Press.

COMO, Michael
2008 *Shōtoku: Ethnicity, Ritual, and Violence in the Japanese Buddhist Tradition*. New York: Oxford University Press.

CONZE, Edward
1958 *Buddhist Wisdom Books*. New York: Harper Torchbooks.

COOK, Francis Dojun
1999 *How to Raise an Ox: Zen Practice as Taught in Zen Master Dogen's Shobogenzo*. Somerville, MA: Wisdom Publications.

CORNILLE, Catherine
2008   *The Im-possibility of Dialogue.* New York: Crossroad Publishing Co.

COX, Rupert, ed.
2008   *The Culture of Copying in Japan: Critical and Historical Perspectives.* New York: Routledge.

CUEVAS, Bryan J. and Jacqueline I. STONE
2007   *The Buddhist Dead: Practices, Discourses, Representations.* Honolulu: University of Hawai'i Press.

DAVIS, Bret W.
2007   *Heidegger and the Will: On the Way to Gelassenheit.* Evanston, IL: Northwestern University Press.

2009   "The Presencing of Truth," in William Edelglass and Jay L. Garfield, eds., *Buddhist Philosophy: Essential Readings.* Oxford: Oxford University Press, 251–60.

2011A   "The Philosophy of Zen Master Dōgen: Egoless Perspectivism," in Jay L. Garfield and William Edelglass, eds., *The Oxford Handbook of World Philosophy.* Oxford: Oxford University Press, 349–60.

2011B   "Das Innerste zuäußerst: Nishida und die Revolution der Ich-Du-Beziehung," *Allgemeine Zeitschrift für Philosophie* 36/3: 281–312.

2016A   "The Enlightening Practice of Nonthinking: Unfolding Dōgen's *Fukanzazengi*," in Tetsuzen Jason M. Wirth, Shūdō Brian Schroeder, and Kanpū Bret W. Davis, eds., *Engaging Dōgen's Zen: The Philosophy of Practice as Awakening.* Somerville, MA: Wisdom Publications, 199–224.

2016B   "Heidegger on the Way from Onto-Historical Ethnocentrism to East-West Dialogue," *Gatherings: The Heidegger Circle Annual* 6:130–56.

2019A   "Knowing Limits: Toward a Versatile Perspectivism with Nietzsche, Heidegger, Zhuangzi and Zen," *Research in Phenomenology* 49: 301–34.

2019B   Expressing Experience: Language in Ueda Shizuteru's Philosophy of Zen," in Gereon Kopf, ed., *The Dao Companion to Japanese Buddhist Philosophy.* Dordrecht: Springer, 713–38.

2020   "Heidegger and Daoism: A Dialogue on the Useless Way of Unnecessary Being," in CHAI, 161–96.

2022A   *Zen Pathways: An Introduction to the Philosophy and Practice of Zen Buddhism.* New York, Oxford University Press.

2022B "Ueda Shizuteru's Zen Philosophy of Dialogue: The Free Exchange of Host and Guest," *Comparative and Continental Philosophy* 14/2: : 162–77.
2023 "Shinjin Gakudō (Studying the Way with Body and Mind)," in Sarah Flavel and Chiara Robbiano, eds., *Key Concepts in World Philosophies*. London and New York: Bloomsbury, 167–80.

DE MAN, Paul
1979 *Allegories of Reading: Figural Language in Rousseau, Nietzsche, Rilke, and Proust*. New Haven: Yale University Press.

DENKER, A., S. KADOWAKI, R. ŌHASHI, G. STENGER, and H. ZABOROWSKI, eds.
2013 *Heidegger und das ostasiatische Denken*. Freiburg and Munich: Verlag Karl Alber.

DERRIDA, Jacques
1976 *Of Grammatology*, trans. by Gayatri Chakravorty Spivak. Baltimore: Johns Hopkins University Press.

DE VOS, George A.
1985 "Dimensions of Self in Japanese Culture," in MARSELLA, DE VOS, AND HSU, 141–84.

DICKMAN, Nathan Eric
2022 *Philosophical Hermeneutics and the Priority of Questions in Religion: Bringing the Discourse of Gods and Buddhas Down to Earth*. London and New York: Bloomsbury.

DILTHEY, Wilhelm
1900 "Die Entstehung der Hermeneutik," in Wilhelm Dilthey, *Gesammelte Schriften V*. Stuttgart: B. G. Teubner; Göttingen: Vandenhoeck and Ruprecht, 1964, 317–31. Translated by Fredric Jameson as "The Rise of Hermeneutics," in Gayle L. Ormiston and Alan D. Schrift, eds., *The Hermeneutic Tradition: From Ast to Ricoeur*. Albany, NY: State University of New York Press, 1990, 101–14.

DŌGEN 道元
1932 『道元禅師全集』[Complete works of Dōgen Zenji]. Ōkubo Dōshū 大久保道舟, ed. Tokyo: Shunjūsha.
1971A 『正法眼藏』[Treasury of the true dharma eye], Ōkubo Dōshū 大久保道舟, ed. Tokyo, Chikuma Shobō.
1971B *A Primer of Sōtō Zen: A Translation of Dōgen's Shōbōgenzō Zuimonki*, trans. by Reihō Masunaga. Honolulu: East-West Center Press.

1972A 『正法眼蔵隨聞記』[Shōbōgenzō Zuimonki], annotated trans. by Yamazaki Masakazu 山崎正一. Tokyo: Kōdansha.

1972B *The First Step to Dogen's Zen: Shobogenzo-zuimonki*, trans. by Yuho Yokoi. Tokyo: Sankibo Buddhist Bookstore.

1974 『正法眼蔵 正法眼蔵隨聞記』[Shōbōgenzō Shōbōgenzō Zuimonki]. Nishio Minoru 西尾實, Kagamishima Genryū 鏡島元隆, Sakai Tokugen 酒井得元, and Mizuno Yaoko 水野彌穂子, eds. Tokyo: Iwanami Shoten.

1977 『正法眼蔵隨聞記』[Shōbōgenzō Zuimonki]. Watsuji Tetsurō 和辻哲郎, ed. Tokyo: Iwanami Shoten.

1980 *Record of Things Heard. From the Treasury of the Eye of the True Teaching*, trans. by Thomas Cleary. Boulder: Prajñā Press.

1985 *Moon in a Dewdrop: Writings of Zen Master Dōgen*, Kazuaki Tanahashi, ed. San Francisco: North Point Press.

1986 *Shōbōgenzō: Zen Essays by Dōgen*, trans. by Thomas Cleary. Honolulu: University of Hawai'i Press).

1988–93 『道元禅師全集』[Complete works of Dōgen Zenji, 7 vols.]. Kawamura Kōda et al., eds. Tokyo: Shunjūsha.

1996 *Dōgen's Pure Standards for the Zen Community*, trans. by Daniel Leighton and Shohaku Okumura. Albany, NY: State University of New York Press.

2001 "Mountains and Waters Sutra (*Sansuikyō*)," trans. by Carl Bielefeldt, *Dharma Eye* 9: 11–17

2002 *The Heart of Dōgen's Shōbōgenzō*, trans. by Norman Waddell and Masao Abe. Albany: State University of New York Press.

2006 *Shōbōgenzō: Ausgewählte Schriften*, trans. by Ryōsuke Ōhashi and Rolf Elberfeld. Tokyo: Keio University Press.

2010 『道元禪師全集 原文對照現代語譯 第17卷 法語・歌頌等』[Complete works of Dōgen, Modern translation in contrast to original texts, vol. 17: Dharma talks and poems], Takahashi Bunji 高橋文二, Tsunoda Tairyū 角田泰隆, Ishii Seijun 石井清純, eds. Tokyo: Shunjūsha.

2022 *Dōgen's Shōbōgenzō Zuimonki: The New Annotated Translation, Also Including Dōgen's Waka Poetry with Commentary*, trans. by Shohaku Okumura. Somerville, MA: Wisdom Publications.

DÖLL, Steffen

2020 "Ueda Shizuteru: The Self That Is Not a Self in a Twofold World," in Bret W. Davis, ed., *The Oxford Handbook of Japanese Philosophy*. Oxford and New York: Oxford University Press, 485–99.

DREES, Willem B.
  1990   *Beyond the Big Bang: Quantum Cosmologies and God.* Chicago and LaSalle, IL: Open Court.
DREYFUS, Hubert L., and Jane RUBIN
  1991   "Appendix: Kierkegaard, Division II, and Later Heidegger," in Dreyfus, *Being-in- the-World: A Commentary on Heidegger's Being and Time, Division I.* Cambridge, MA: MIT Press, 283–340.
DUMOULIN, Heinrich
  2005   *Zen Buddhism: A History. Volume 2: Japan,* trans. by James Heisig and Paul Knitter. Bloomington: World Wisdom.
EAKIN, Paul John
  1985   *Fictions in Autobiography: Studies in the Art of Self-Invention.* Princeton: Princeton University Press.
EBERSOLE, Gary L.
  1983   "The Buddhist Ritual Use of Linked Verse in Medieval Japan," *The Eastern Buddhist* 16/2: 50–71.
ELBERFELD, Rolf
  2004   *Phänomenologie der Zeit im Buddhismus: Methoden interkulturellen Philosophierens.* Stuttgart-Bad Cannstatt: Frommann-Holzboog.
FITZGERALD, Timothy
  1997   "A Critique of 'Religion' as a Cross-cultural Category," *Method and Theory in the Study of Religion* 9/2: 91–110.
FORMAN, Robert K. C., ed.
  1990   *The Problem of Pure Consciousness: Mysticism and Philosophy.* New York and Oxford: Oxford University Press.
FORMANEK, Susanne, and William R. LAFLEUR
  2004   "Introduction," in *Practicing the Afterlife: Perspectives from Japan.* Vienna: Verlag der Österreichischen Akademie der Wissenschaften, 7–48.
FOULK, T. Griffith
  2012   "'Just Sitting'? Dōgen's Take on Zazen, Sūtra Reading, and Other Conventional Buddhist Practices," in Steven Heine, ed., *Dōgen: Textual and Historical Studies.* New York: Oxford University Press, 75–106.
  2015   "Dōgen's Use of Rujing's 'Just Sit' (*shikan taza*) and Other Kōans," in Steven Heine, ed., *Dōgen and Sōtō Zen.* New York: Oxford University Press, 23–45.

FOWLER, Edward
1988   *The Rhetoric of Confession: Shishosetsu in Early Twentieeth-Century Japanese Fiction.* Berkeley: University of California Press.

FUKUZAWA Yukichi 福澤諭吉
1960   *The Autobiography of Fukuzawa Yukichi,* trans. by Eiichi Kiyooka. Tokyo: Hokuseido Press.

FURUKAWA Tesshi 古川哲史
1967   "The Individual in Japanese Ethics," in Charles A. Moore, ed., *The Japanese Mind,* Honolulu: East-West Center Press, 228–44.

GADAMER, Hans-Georg
1965   *Wahrheit und Methode,* second edition. Tübingen: J. C. B. Mohr. Translated as *Truth and Method.* New York: Crossroad. 1984.

GEERTZ, Clifford
1973   *The Interpretation of Cultures.* New York: Basic Books.

GELL, Alfred
1998   *Art and Agency: An Anthropological Theory.* Oxford and New York: Clarendon Press.

GERHART, Karen Margaret
2009   *The Material Culture of Death in Medieval Japan.* Honolulu: University of Hawai'i Press.

GILLIGAN, Carol, Janie Victoria WARD, and Jill McLean TAYLOR, eds.
1990   *Mapping the Moral Domain: A Contribution of Women's Thinking to Psychological Theory and Education.* Cambridge, MA: Harvard University Press.

GILMORE, Leigh
1994   *Autobiographics: A Feminist Theory of Women's Self-Representation.* Ithaca: Cornell University Press.

GIMELLO, Robert M.
1983   "Mysticism in Its Contexts," in Steven T. Katz, ed., *Mysticism and Religious Traditions.* New York: Oxford University Press, 61–88.

GRANOFF, Phyllis, and SHINOHARA Koichi, eds.
1994   *Other Selves: Autobiography and Biography in Cross-Cultural Perspectives.* Oakville, Ontario: Mosaic Press.

GRANT, Beata
2003   *Daughter of Emptiness: Poems of Chinese Buddhist Nuns.* Somerville, MA: Wisdom Publications,

GREEN, James, trans.
2001 *The Recorded Sayings of Zen Master Joshu.* Boulder: Shambhala.

GREENE, Eric M.
2021 *Chan Before Chan: Meditation, Repentance, and Visionary Experience in Chinese Buddhism.* Honolulu: University of Hawai'i Press.

GRIFFITHS, Paul J.
1986A *On Being Mindless.* LaSalle, IL: Open Court.
1986B "On the Possible Future of the Buddhist-Christian Interaction," in Minoru Kiyota, ed., *Japanese Buddhism: Its Tradition, New Religions, and Interaction with Christianity.* Tokyo and Los Angeles: Buddhist Books International, 145–61.

GRUBE, G. M. A.
1975 "Introduction" to *The Trial and Death of Socrates: Euthyphro, Apology, Crito, Death Scene from Phaedo.* Indianapolis: Hackett Publishing Co., 1–2.

GUÉHENNO, Jean
1966 *Jean-Jacques Rousseau,* trans. by John and Doreen Weightman. London: Routledge and Kegan Paul.

GUTMAN, Huck
1988 "Rousseau's *Confessions*: A Technology of the Self," in Luther H. Martin, Huck Gutman, and Patrick H. Hutton, eds., *Technologies of the Self: A Seminar with Michel Foucault.* Amherst: University of Massachusetts Press, 99–120.

HAKUIN Ekaku 白隠慧鶴
1971 *The Zen Master Hakuin: Selected Writings,* trans. by Philip B. Yampolsky. New York: Columbia University Press.

HARE, Thomas W.
1979 "Linked Verse at Imashinmei Shrine: Anegakoji Imashinmei Hyakuin, 1447," *Monumenta Nipponica* 43/2: 169–208.

HAROOTUNIAN, H. D.
1985 "Review of *Told Round a Brushwood Fire: The Autobiography of Arai Hakuseki* by Joyce Ackroyd; *Lessons from History: Arai Hakuseki's Tokushi Yoron* by Joyce Ackroyd," *Journal of Japanese Studies* 2/1: 170–7.

HART, James G.
2009 *Who One Is. Book 1: Meontology of the "I": A Transcendental Phenomenology. Book 2: Existenz and Transcendental Phenomenology.* Dordrecht: Springer.

2020 "Transcendental pride and Luciferism: On being bearers of light and powers of darkness," *Continental Philosophy Review* 53: 331–53.

HARTLE, Ann
1983 *The Modern Self in Rousseau's Confessions*. Notre Dame: University of Notre Dame Press.

HASE Shōtō 長谷正當
1997 "Emptiness Thought and the Concept of the Pure Land in Nishitani: In the Light of Imagination and the Body," *Zen Buddhism Today* 14: 65–79.

HAVER, William
1992 "Review of *Nietzsche and Asian Thought*," *Journal of Asian Studies* 51/3: 629–30.
2012 "Introduction" to Nishida Kitarō, *Ontology of Production: 3 Essays*, trans. by William Haver. Durham, NC, and London: Duke University Press.

HEIDEGGER, Martin
1927 *Sein und Zeit*. Tübingen: Max Niemeyer Verlag, 1963. Translated by Joan Stambaugh as *Being and Time*. Albany, NY: State University of New York Press, 1996.
1927–64 *The Piety of Thinking: Essays by Martin Heidegger*. Translations with notes and commentary by James G. Hart and John C. Maraldo. Bloomington: Indiana University Press, 1976.
1954 "Das Ding," in *Vorträge und Aufsätze, Teil 2*. Pfullingen: Günter Neske.
1959 *Gelassenheit*. Pfullingen: Günter Neske.
1961 *Was heisst Denken?* Tübingen: Max Niemeyer Verlag.
1963 『放下』 (A translation, by Tsujimura Kōichi, of *Gelassenheit*. Pfullingen: 1959.) Tokyo: Risōsha.
1966 "Nur noch ein Gott kann uns retten," *Der Spiegel* 30 (Mai, 1976): 193–219. Translated by W. J. Richardson as "'Only a God Can Save Us': The *Spiegel* Interview (1966)" in T. Sheehan, ed., *Heidegger: The Man and the Thinker* (1981), 45–67.
1995 "Αγχιβασίη: Ein in Gespräch selbstdritt auf einem Feldweg zwischen einem Forscher, einem Gelehrten und einem Weisen," in *Gesamtausgabe Band 77: Feldweg-Gespräche (1944/45)*. Frankfurt am Main: Vittorio Klostermann.
2010 *Country Path Conversations*, trans. by Bret W. Davis. Bloomington: Indiana University Press.

HEINE, Steven
- 1994A *Dōgen and the Kōan Tradition: A Tale of Two Shōbōgenzō Texts*. Albany, NY: State University of New York Press.
- 1994B "History, Transhistory, and Narrative History: A View of Nishitani's Philosophy of Zen," *Philosophy East and West* 44/2: 251–78.
- 1997 *The Zen Poetry of Dōgen*. North Clarendon, VT: Tuttle Publishing.
- 2006 *Did Dōgen Go to China? What He Wrote and When He Wrote It*. Oxford and New York: Oxford University Press.
- 2022 *Wisdom Within Words: An Annotated Translation of Dōgen's Chinese-Style Poetry*. New York and Oxford: Oxford University Press.

HEISIG, James W.
- 2019 *Of Gods and Minds: In Search of a Theological Commons*. Nagoya: Chisokudō Publications.

HEISIG, James W. and John C. MARALDO, eds.
- 1995 *Rude Awakenings: Zen, the Kyoto School, and the Question of Nationalism*. Honolulu: University of Hawai'i Press.

HENRICH, Dieter
- 1967 "Einleitung," in Rehbert Gentz, ed., *Über Theorie und Praxis*. Frankfurt: Suhrkamp Verlag.

HERMAN, Jonathan R.
- 1996 *I and Tao: Martin Buber's Encounter with Chuang Tzu*. Albany, NY: State University of New York Press.

HEUBER, Fabian
- 2022 "The Politics of *Uselessness*: On Heidegger's Reading of the *Zhuangzi*," in CHAI, 225–42.

HICK, John
- 1989 *An Interpretation of Religion: Human Responses to the Transcendent*. New Haven: Yale University Press.

HOMANS, Peter
- 1987 "Psychology and Religion Movement," in Mircea Eliade, ed., *The Encyclopedia of Religion*, vol. 12. New York: Macmillan.

HŌNEN 法然
- 1974 "The Philosophy of Nenbutsu," trans. by Mark Blum, in JPSB, 242–4. The original text is 「浄土宗略抄」 [Summary of the Pure Land school], in 『昭和新修法然上人全集』 [Complete works of Hōnen Shōnin in a new Shōwa edition]. Kyoto: Heiraku-ji Shoten, 1974, 590.

HORI, Victor Sōge
2003   *Zen Sand: The Book of Capping Phrases for Kōan Practice.* Honolulu: University of Hawai'i Press.
2005   "Introduction," in DUMOULIN 2005, xiii–xxi.
HU Shih 胡適
1953   "Chan (Zen) Buddhism in China: Its History and Method," *Philosophy East and West* 3/1: 3–24.
HUNTINGTON, Patricia
2020   "Heidegger and Zhuangzi: The Transformative Art of the Phenomenological Reduction," in *Chai*, 197–218.
IRIYA Yoshitaka 入矢義高, trans.
1989   『臨済録』[Record of Linji]. Tokyo: Iwanami Shoten.
IVES, Christopher
1995   (ed.) *Divine Emptiness and Historical Fullness: A Buddhist Jewish Christian Conversation with Masao Abe.* Valley Forge, PA: Trinity Press International.
2006   "Not Buying into Words and Letters: Zen, Ideology, and Prophetic Critique," *Journal of Buddhist Ethics* 13. <https://blogs.dickinson.edu/buddhistethics/2010/04/27/not-buying-into-words-and-letters-zen-ideology-and-prophetic-critique/>.
2008   "Deploying the Dharma: Reflections on the Methodology of Constructive Buddhist Ethics," *Journal of Buddhist Ethics* 15. <https://blogs.dickinson.edu/buddhistethics/?s=Deploying+the+Dharma%3A+Reflections+on+the+Methodology+>.
2009   *Imperial-Way Zen: Ichikawa Hakugen's Critique and Lingering Questions for Buddhist Ethics.* Honolulu: University of Hawai'i Press.
JANKÉLÉVITCH, Vladimir
1966   *La Mort.* Paris: Flammarion.
JOHNSON, Mark
1987   *The Body in the Mind.* Chicago: University of Chicago Press.
JOSEPHSON, Jason Ānanda
2012   *The Invention of Religion in Japan.* Chicago: University of Chicago Press.
KANE, Leslie
1984   *The Language of Silence: On the Unspoken and the Unspeakable in Modern Drama.* Rutherford: Fairleigh Dickinson University Press; London and Toronto: Associated University Presses.

KANT, Immanuel
1773   Über den Gemeinspruch: Das mag in der Theorie richtig sein, taugt aber nicht für die Praxis. / Zum Ewigen Frieden: Ein philosophischer Entwurf. Heiner F. Klemme, ed. Hamburg: F. Meiner. 1992.
1785   Grounding for the Metaphysics of Morals, trans. James W. Ellington. Indianapolis and Cambridge: Hackett Publishing Co., 1981.

KAPLEAU, Philip
1965   The Three Pillars of Zen. Boston: Beacon Press.

KASULIS, Thomas P.
1981   Zen Action/Zen Person. Honolulu: University of Hawai'i Press.
1989   "Whence and Whither: Philosophical Reflections on Nishitani's View of History," in Taitetsu Unno, ed., The Religious Philosophy of Nishitani Keiji. Berkeley: Asian Humanities Press, 259–78.
2010   "The Ground of Translation: Issues in Translating Premodern Japanese Philosophy," in James W. Heisig and Rein Raud, eds., Classical Japanese Philosophy (Frontiers of Philosophy 7). Nagoya: Nanzan Institute of Religion and Culture, 7–38.

KATZ, Steven, Huston SMITH, and Sallie B. KING
1988   "On Mysticism," Journal of the American Academy of Religion 56/4: 751–61.

KASZA, Justyna Weronika
2022   "Autofiction and Shishōsetsu: Women Writers and Reinventing the Self," in Alexandra Effe and Hannie Lawlor, eds., The Autofictional: Approaches, Affordances, Forms. Cham, Switzerland: Palgrave Macmillan, 247–66.

KELLER, Catherine.
1990   "Scoop Up the Water and the Moon is in Your Hands: On Feminist Theology and Dynamic Self-Emptying," in COBB AND IVES, 102–15.

KIM, Hee-Jin
1985   Flowers of Emptiness: Selections From Dōgen's Shōbōgenzō. Lewiston, NY; Queenston, Ont.: Edwin Mellen Press.
2004   Eihei Dōgen: Mystical Realist, revised, third edition. Boston: Wisdom Publications.

KING, Richard
1999   Orientalism and Religion: Post-Colonial Theory, India, and the Mystic East. New York; London: Routledge.

KING, Sallie B.
1988 "Two Epistemological Models for the Interpretation of Mysticism," *Journal of the American Academy of Religion* 56(2): 257–79.

KING, Winston, Jocelyn KING, and TOKIWA Gishin, trans.
1972 "The Fourth Letter from Hakuin's 'Orategama,'" *The Eastern Buddhist* 5/1: 81–114.

KIYOZAWA Manshi 清沢満之
2003 "Absolute Other Power," trans. by Mark Blum, in JPBS: 270–2. The original text is 「絶対他力の大道」[The great path of absolute Other-power], in 『清沢満之全集』[Collected Works of Kiyozawa Manshi] 6. Tokyo: Iwanami Shoten, 2003, 110–13.

KLEIN, Anne Carolyn
1995 *Meeting the Great Bliss Queen: Buddhists, Feminists, and the Art of the Self.* Boston: Beacon Press.

KOSTA, Barbara
1994 *Recasting Autobiography: Women's Counterfictions in Contemporary German Literature and Film.* Ithaca: Cornell University Press.

KRAUT, Richard
2022 "Aristotle's Ethics," in Edward N. Zalte, ed., *The Stanford Encyclopedia of Philosophy.* <https://plato.stanford.edu/archives/sum2022/entries/aristotle-ethics/>.

KUHN, Thomas S.
2012 *The Structure of Scientific Revolutions.* Chicago: University of Chicago Press (1970).

LAKOFF, George
1987 *Women, Fire, and Dangerous Things: What Categories Reveal about the Mind.* Chicago; London: University of Chicago Press.

LAU, D. C., trans.
1963 *Tao Te Ching, by Lao Tzu.* London: Penguin Classics.

LAWLOR, Robert
1991 *Voices of the First Day.* Rochester, VT: Inner Traditions International.

LEDER, Drew
1990 *The Absent Body.* Chicago: University of Chicago Press.

LEGGE, James
  1962 *Texts of Taoism: The Tao Te Ching of Lao Tzu, The Writings of Chuang Tzu.* New York: Dover.

LEVERING, Miriam, ed.
  1988 *Rethinking Scripture: Essays from a Comparative Perspective.* Albany, NY: State University of New York Press.

LEIGHTON, Dan Taigen, and Shohaku OKUMURA, trans.
  2010 *Dōgen's Extensive Record: A Translation of the Eihei Kōroku.* Somerville, MA: Wisdom Publications

LOCKE, John
  1924 *An Essay Concerning Human Understanding.* A. S. Pringle-Pattison, ed. Oxford: Clarendon Press.

LOPEZ, Donald S., Jr., ed.
  1988 *Buddhist Hermeneutics.* Honolulu: University of Hawai'i Press.
  1995 *Curators of the Buddha: The Study of Buddhism Under Colonialism.* Chicago: University of Chicago Press.

LOUGHNANE, Adam
  2019 *Merleau-Ponty and Nishida: Artistic Expression as Motor-Perceptual Faith.* Albany, NY: State University of New York Press.

LOW, Albert
  1988 "Master Hakuin's Gateway to Freedom," in Kenneth Kraft, ed., *Zen: Tradition and Transition.* New York: Grove Press, 88–104.

LYNN, Richard John
  1987 "The Sudden and the Gradual in Chinese Poetry Criticism: An Examination of the Ch'an-Poetry Analogy," in Peter N. Gregory, ed., *Sudden and Gradual: Approaches to Enlightenment in Chinese Thought.* Honolulu: University of Hawai'i Press: 381– 427.

LYOTARD, Jean-François
  1988 *The Differend: Phrases in Dispute.* Minneapolis: University of Minnesota Press.

MA Lin 马琳
  2008 *Heidegger on East-West Dialogue: Anticipating the Event.* New York and London: Routledge.

MACINTYRE, Alasdair
  1970 "Is Understanding Religion Compatible with Believing?" in Bryan R. Wilson, ed., *Rationality.* New York: Harper and Row, 62–77.

MANSINI, Guy
1985 *"What is a Dogma?": The Meaning and Truth of Dogma in Edouard Le Roy and His Scholastic Opponents.* Rome: Editrice Pontificia Università Gregoriana.

MALDONADO, Rebeca
2022 "Pensar con John Maraldo," *European Journal of Japanese Philosophy* 7: 30–51.

MARALDO, John C.
1974 *Der hermeneutische Zirkel: Untersuchungen zu Schleiermacher, Dilthey und Heidegger.* Freiburg: Karl Alber Verlag, Symposion.
1976 "Some Heideggerian Pathways to Technology and the Divine," in HEIDEGGER 1927–64, 152– 67.
1981 "The Hermeneutics of Practice in Dōgen and Francis of Assisi: An Exercise in Buddhist-Christian Dialogue," *The Eastern Buddhist* 14/2: 22–46.
2001 "Views from Somewhere: Local Lore and Global Knowledge." *Dokkyo International Review* 14 (2001): 37–50.
2008 "Saving Zen From Moral Ineptitude: A Response to Zen Social Ethics: Historical Constraints and Present Prospects," *Journal of Buddhist Ethics* 13. <https://blogs.dickinson.edu/buddhistethics/2010/04/27/saving-zen-from-moral-ineptitude-a-response-to-zen-social-ethics-historical-constraints-and-present-prospects/>.
2016 "*Shushōgi* Paragraphs 11–14," in Wirth, Schroeder, and Davis, eds., *Engaging Dōgen's Zen: The Philosophy of Practice as Awakening.* Somerville, MA: Wisdom Publications, 115–20.
2017 *Japanese Philosophy in the Making 1: Crossing Paths with Nishida.* Nagoya: Chisokudō Publications.
2018 "The Aesthetics of Emptiness in Japanese Calligraphy and Abstract Expressionism," in A. Minh Nguyen, ed., *New Essays in Japanese Aesthetics.* Lanham, MD: Lexington Books, 335–52.
2019A *Japanese Philosophy in the Making 2: Borderline Interrogations.* Nagoya: Chisokudō Publications.
2019B "Nishida Kitarō," in Edward N. Zalta, ed., *The Stanford Encyclopedia of Philosophy.* <https://plato.stanford.edu/archives/win2019/entries/nishida-kitaro/>.
2019C "The 'Philosophy' in Japanese Buddhist Philosophy," in Gereon Kopf, ed., *The Dao Companion to Japanese Buddhist Philosophy.* Dordrecht: Springer, 53–70.

2021　*The Saga of Zen History and the Power of Legend.* Nagoya: Chisokudō Publications.

MARCUS, George E., and Michael M. J. FISCHER
1986　*Anthropology as Cultural Critique: An Experimental Moment in the Human Sciences.* Chicago: University of Chicago Press.

MARSELLA, Anthony J., George A. DE VOS, and Francis L. K. HSU, eds.
1985　*Culture and Self: Asian and Western Perspectives.* New York: Tavistock Publications.

MARRA, Michael
2011　"Overview of Aesthetics," in JPSB: 1167–72.

MARTIN, Russell
1994　*Out of Silence: A Journey into Language.* New York: Henry Holt and Co.

MATSUNAGA, Daigan and Alicia MATSUNAGA
1974　*Foundation of Japanese Buddhism*, vol. 1. Los Angeles and Tokyo: Buddhist Books International.

MAY, Reinhard
1989　*Ex Oriente Lux: Heideggers Werk unter ostasiatischem Einfluss.* Stuttgart: Franz Steiner.

1996　*Heidegger's Hidden Sources: East-Asian Influences on His Work.* Translated with a complementary essay by Graham Parkes. London and New York: Routledge.

MAYO, Bernard
1952　*The Logic of Personality.* London: Jonathan Cape.

MCCARTHY, Erin
2010　*Ethics Embodied: Rethinking Selfhood through Continental, Japanese, and Feminist Philosophies.* New York: Rowman and Littlefield.

MCCLELLAN, Edwin
1971A　"Tōson and the Autobiographical Novel," in Donald H. Shively, ed., *Tradition and Modernization in Japanese Culture.* Princeton: Princeton University Press, 347–78.

1971B　*Two Japanese Novelists: Sōseki and Tōson.* Tokyo: Charles E. Tuttle.

MCCUTCHEON, Russell T.
1999　(ed.) *The Insider/Outsider Problem in the Study of Religion: A Reader.* London; New York: Cassell Books.

2003   *Manufacturing Religion: The Discourse on Sui Generis Religion and the Politics of Nostalgia*. Oxford and New York: Oxford University Press.

MCMULLEN, Ian James
1979   "Kumazawa Banzan and Jitsugaku: Toward Pragmatic Action," in Wm. Theodore de Bary and Irene Bloom, eds., *Principle and Practicality: Essays in Neo-Confucianism and Practical Learning*. New York: Columbia University Press, 337–73.

MCRAE, John R.
1986   *The Northern School and the Formation of Early Ch'an Buddhism*. Honolulu: University of Hawai'i Press.
2000   (trans.) *The Platform Sūtra of the Sixth Patriarch*. Berkeley: Numata Center for Buddhist Translation and Research.
2003   *Seeing through Zen: Encounter, Transformation, and Genealogy in Chinese Chan Buddhism*. Berkeley, University of California Press.

MERLEAU-PONTY, Maurice
1964   *Le Visible et l'invisible*. Paris: Editions Gallimard. Ed. by Claude Lefort and trans. by Alphonso Lingis as *The Visible and the Invisible*. Evanston, IL: Northwestern University Press, 1968.

MERRILL, Sally
1981   "Remembering Hisamatsu Sensei," *The Eastern Buddhist* 14/1 (1981): 128–9.

MIKI Kiyoshi 三木清
1926   「パスカルに於ける人間の研究」[The Study of the Human Being in Pascal] in 『三木清全集』[Complete Works of Miki Kiyoshi]. Tokyo: Iwanami 1966, 1: 1–191. Partially translated in David Dilworth, Valdo H. Viglielmo, and Águstin Jacinto Zavala, eds., *Sourcebook for Modern Japanese Philosophy: Selected Documents*. Westport, CT and London: Greenwood Press, 1998, 298–315.
1927   「解釈学的現象学の基礎概念」[Basic Concepts of Hermeneutical Phenomenology] in *Complete Works of Miki Kiyoshi* 3: 186–220.

MIKKELSON, Douglas K.
1997   "Who Is Arguing About the Cat? Moral Action and Enlightenment According to Dōgen," *Philosophy East and West* 47/3: 383–97.

MILES, Margaret R.
1981   *Fullness of Life: Historical Foundations for a New Asceticism*. Philadelphia: Westminster Press.

MINAMI Hiroshi 南博
- 1971 *Psychology of the Japanese People*, trans. by Albert R. Ikoma. Toronto: University of Toronto Press. Tokyo: University of Tokyo Press.

MINAMOTO Ryōen 源了円
- 1995 "The Symposium on 'Overcoming Modernity,'" in HEISIG AND MARALDO, 197–229.

MINER, Earl
- 1968 *An Introduction to Japanese Court Poetry*. Stanford: Stanford University Press.

MINH-HA, Trinh T.
- 1989 *Woman, Native, Other*. Bloomington: Indiana University Press.

MIYOSHI Masao 三好将夫
- 1974 *Accomplices of Silence*. Berkeley: University of California Press.
- 1991 "Against the Native Grain: The Japanese Novel and the Postmodern West," in Masao Miyoshi, *Off Center: Power and Culture Relations between Japan and the United States*. Cambridge: Harvard University Press, 9–36.

MORI Tetsurō 森哲郎
- 1997 "Religion in the Early Thought of Nishitani Keiji: The Bottomlessness of Nature," *Zen Buddhism Today* 14: 1–18.

MORITA Shiryū 森田子龍
- 1970 「書と抽象絵画」[Calligraphy and Abstract Painting], in *The Works of Shiryū Morita, Selected by the Artist*. Kyoto: Bokubi Press: 120–33.

MOYAERT, Marianne
- 2010 "Absorption or Hospitality: Two Approaches to the Tension between Identity and Alterity," in Catherine Cornille and Christopher Conway, eds., *Interreligious Hermeneutics*. Eugene, OR: Cascade Books, 61–88.

MÜLLER, Ralf
- 2015 "Die Artikulation des Schweigens in der Sprache. Zum Sprachdenken des Philosophen Ueda Shizuteru," *Asiatische Studien— Études Asiatiques* 69(2): 391–417.

MURASAKI Shikibu 紫式部
- 2001 *The Tale of Genji*, trans. by Royall Tyler. New York: Viking.

MURPHY, Jeffrie G.
1998   *Character, Liberty, and Law: Kantian Essays in Theory and Practice.* Dordrecht and Boston: Kluver Academic Publishers.

NAGATOMO Shigenori
2020   "Japanese Zen Buddhist Philosophy," in Edward N. Zalte, ed., *The Stanford Encyclopedia of Philosophy.* <https://plato.stanford.edu/archives/spr2020/entries/japanese-zen/>.

NAKAI, Kate Wildman
1988   *Shogunal Politics: Arai Hakuseki and the Premises of Tokugawa Rule.* Cambridge, MA: Harvard University Asia Center.

NAKAMURA Fuyubi 中村冬日
2007   "Creating or Performing Words? Observations on Contemporary Japanese Calligraphy," in Elizabeth Hallam and Tim Ingold, eds., *Creativity and Cultural Improvisation.* Oxford and New York: Berg.

NAKAMURA Hajime 中村 元
1973   『仏教語大辞典』[Dictionary of Buddhist Terms]. Tokyo: Tōkyō Shoseki.

NAKAMURA Sōichi 中村宗一
1975   『正法眼蔵用語辞典』[Dictionary of Terms in the *Shōbōgenzō*]. Tokyo: Seishin Shobō.

NEARMAN, Hubert
2007   Translator's Introduction, *Sansuikyō,* "On the Spiritual Discourses of the Mountains and the Water," in Eihei Dōgen, *Shōbōgenzō: The Treasure House of the Eye of the True Teaching. A Trainee's Translation of Great Master Dōgen's Spiritual Masterpiece.* Mount Shasta, CA: Shasta Abbey Press.

NEUSNER, Jacob
1990   *The Christian and Judaic Invention of History.* Atlanta: Scholars Press.

NIHON SHOKI 日本書紀
720   *Nihongi: Chronicles of Japan from the Earliest Times to A.D. 697,* vol. 2. Trans. W. G. Aston. Rutland, VT and Tokyo: Charles E. Tuttle Co., 1972.

NISHIDA Kitarō 西田幾多郎
1990   *An Inquiry into the Good,* trans. by Masao Abe and Christopher Ives. New Haven: Yale University Press.

2012 *Ontology of Production: Three Essays*, trans. by William W. Haver. Durham, NC, and London: Duke University Press.

NISHITANI Keiji 西谷啓治
1961 『宗教とは何か』[What is religion?]. Compiled in NKC 10. Translated by Jan Van Bragt as *Religion and Nothingness*. Berkeley: University of California Press, 1982.
1974 「禅の立場」in 『禅の立場』, Nishitani Keiji, ed., Tokyo: Chikuma Shobō. Translated by John C. Maraldo as "The Standpoint of Zen," *The Eastern Buddhist* 17/1 (1984): 1–26.
1990 *The Self-Overcoming of Nihilism*, trans. by Graham Parkes and Setsuko Aihara. Albany, NY: State University of New York Press.

OE Kenzaburō 大江健三郎
1969 *A Personal Matter*, trans. by John Nathan. New York: Grove Press.

O'FLAHERTY, Wendy Doniger
1973 *Siva: The Erotic Ascetic*. New York: Oxford University Press.

O'LEARY, Joseph Stephen
1996 *Religious Pluralism and Christian Truth*. Edinburgh: Edinburgh University Press.

OLSON, Phillip
1993 *The Discipline of Freedom: A Kantian View of the Role of Moral Precepts in Zen Practice*. Albany, NY: State University of New York Press.

ŌMINE Akira 大峯顯
1992 "The Genealogy of Sorrow: Japanese View of Life and Death," trans. by Taitetsu Unno. *The Eastern Buddhist* 25/2: 14–29.

ORTIZ Alfonso
1972 *The Tewa World: Space, Time Being and Becoming in a Pueblo Society*. Chicago: University of Chicago Press.

PANDIAN, Jacob
1991 *Culture, Religion, and the Sacred Self: A Critical Introduction to the Anthropological Study of Religion*. Englewood Cliffs, NJ: Prentice Hall.

PARK Jin Y.
2006 "Wisdom, Compassion, and Zen Social Ethics: the Case of Chinul, Sŏngch'ŏl, and Minjung Buddhism in Korea," *The Journal of Buddhist Ethics* 13. <https://blogs.dickinson.edu/buddhistethics/2010/04/27/wisdom-compassion-and-zen-social-ethics-the-case-of-chinul-songchol-and-minjung-buddhism-in-korea/>.

2008 *Buddhism and Postmodernity: Zen, Huayan, and the Possibility of Buddhist Postmodern Ethics*. Lanham, MD, and Boulder: Lexington Books.

PARKER, Joseph D.
1999 *Zen Buddhist Landscape Arts of Early Muromachi Japan (1336–1573)*. Albany, NY: State University of New York Press.

PARKES, Graham
1987 (ed.) *Heidegger and Asian Thought*. Honolulu: University of Hawai'i Press, 105–44.
1997 "The Putative Fascism of the Kyoto School and the Political Correctness of the Modern Academy," *Philosophy East and West* 47/3: 305–36.

PARRY, Richard
2008 "Episteme and Techne," in Edward N. Zalte, ed., *the Stanford Encyclopedia of Philosophy*. <https://plato.stanford.edu/archives/win2021/entries/episteme-techne/>.

PIETSCH, Paul
1981 *Shuffle Brain: The Quest for the Hologramic Mind*. Boston: Houghton Mifflin.

PIKE, Kenneth L., and Marvin HARRIS, eds.
1990 *Emics and Etics: The Insider/Outsider Debate*. London: Sage Publications.

PÖGGLER, Otto
1987 "West-East Dialogue: Heidegger and Lao-tzu," in PARKES 1987, 47–78.
1995 "Westliche Wege zu Nishida und Nishitani," in Georg Stenger and Margarete Röhrig, eds., *Philosophie der Struktur—"Fahrzeug" der Zukunft?* Freiburg: Verlag Karl Alber.

POLLACK, David
1985 *Zen Poems of the Five Mountains*. New York: Crossroad Publishing Co. and Scholars Press.

POLT, Richard
1999 *Heidegger: An Introduction*. Ithaca: Cornell University Press.
2013 *The Emergency of Being: On Heidegger's "Contributions to Philosophy."* Ithaca, NY: Cornell University Press.

POWERS, John
 1993 *Hermeneutics and Tradition in the Saṃdhinirmocana-sūtra*. Leiden: Brill.

PREUSS, J. Samuel
 1987 *Explaining Religion: Criticism and Theory from Bodin to Freud*. New Haven: Yale University Press.

PRIBRAM, Karl H.
 2013 *Brain and Perception: Holonomy and Structure in Figural Processing*. New York and London: Psychology Press, 1991.

PROUDFOOT, Wayne
 1985 *Religious Experience*. Berkeley: University of California Press.

RAHNER, Karl
 1984 *Foundations of Christian Faith*. New York: Crossroads.

RAPPAPORT, Roy A.
 1971 "The Sacred in Human Evolution." *Annual Review of Ecology and Systematics* 2: 23–44.

RAUD, Rein
 2012 "The Existential Moment: Rereading Dōgen's Theory of Time," *Philosophy East and West* 62/2: 153–73

RED PINE (Bill Porter)
 2006 *The Platform Sūtra: The Zen Teaching of Hui-neng*, translation and commentary. Berkeley: Counterpoint.

RICOEUR, Paul
 1969 *Le conflit des interprétations: essais d'herméneutique*. Paris: aux Éditions du Seuil. English translation edited by Don Ihde, *The Conflict of Interpretations: Essays in Hermeneutics*. Evanston: Northwestern University Press, 1974.
 1976 *Interpretation Theory: Discourse and the Surplus of Meaning*. Fort Worth: Texas Christian University Press.
 1983 "On Interpretation," trans. by Kathleen McLaughlin, in Alan Montefiore, ed., *Philosophy in France Today*. New York: Cambridge University Press.
 1992 *Oneself As Another*, trans. by Kathleen Blamey. Chicago: University of Chicago Press.
 2009 *Living up to Death*, trans. by David Pellauer. Chicago: University of Chicago Press.

ROBERTSON, Roland
1988 "Modernity and Religion: Towards the Comparative Genealogy of Religion in Global Perspective," *Zen Buddhism Today: Annual Report of the Kyoto Zen Symposium* 6: 125–33.

RORTY, Richard
1979 *Philosophy and the Mirror of Nature.* Princeton: Princeton University Press.

ROSSETTI, D. G.
1870 *Poems.* Boston: Roberts Brothers.

ROUSSEAU, Jean-Jacques
1953 *The Confessions of Jean-Jacques Rousseau*, trans. J. M. Cohen. London: Penguin Books.

ROWE, Mark Michael
2011 *Bonds of the Dead: Temples, Burial, and the Transformation of Contemporary Japanese Buddhism.* Chicago: University of Chicago Press.

RUNZO, Joseph
1986 *Reason, Relativism, and God.* New York: St. Martin's Press.

RUNZO, Joseph, and Craig K. IHARA, eds.
1986 *Religious Experience and Religious Belief.* Lanham, MD and London: University Press of America.

RUPP, George
1979 *Beyond Existentialism and Zen: Religion in a Pluralistic World.* New York: Oxford University Press.

SAEKI Shōichi 佐伯彰一
1981 『近代日本の自伝』[Modern Japanese Autobiography]. Tokyo: Kōdansha.
1985 "The Autobiography in Japan," trans. by Teruko Craig, *Journal of Japanese Studies* 11/2: 357–68.

SAFINA, Carl
2020 *Becoming Wild: How Animal Cultures Raise Families, Create Beauty, and Achieve Peace.* New York: Henry Holt and Co.

SARTRE, Jean-Paul
1936–37 "La transcendance de l'ego: Esquisse d'une description phénoménologique," *Recherches Philosophiques* VI. Translated by Forrest Williams and Robert Kirkpatrick as *The Transcendence of the Ego.* New York: Hill and Wang, 1960.

SASAKI, Ruth, trans.
    1975   *The Record of Lin-chi*. Kyoto: The Institute for Zen Studies.

SASAKI, Ruth Fuller, and Thomas Yūhō KIRCHNER, trans. and ed.
    2009   *The Record of Linji*. Honolulu: University of Hawai'i Press.

SATŌ Naokata 佐藤直方
    1717   「静坐集説」[Quiet sitting], in 『佐藤直方全集3』[Collected Works of Satō Naokata 3]. Tokyo: Perikansha, 1979, 465–71.

SAVIGNON, Sandra J.
    1997   *Communicative Competence: Theory and Classroom Practice*, second edition. New York: McGraw-Hill.

SAVITA, Ma Satyam
    1987   『さがしてごらんきみの牛: 詩画・十牛図』[Search for Your Own Bull]. Kyoto: Zen Bunka Kenkyūjo, Hanazono College.

SCHAMONI, Wolfgang
    2016   *Erinnerung und Selbstdarstellung: Autobiographisches Schreiben im Japan des 17. Jahrhunderts*. Wiesbaden: Harrassowitz Verlag.

SCHLEIERMACHER, Fr. D. E.
    1805–33 *Hermeneutik. Nach den Handschriften neu herausgegeben und eingeleitet von Heinz Kimmerle*. Heidelberg: Carl Winter Universitäts Verlag, 1959. Trans. by James Duke and Jack Forstman, *Hermeneutics: The Handwritten Manuscripts*. Missoula, MT: Scholars Press, 1977.

SCHLÜTTER, Morten
    2008   *How Zen Became Zen: The Dispute Over Enlightenment and the Formation of Chan Buddhism in Song-Dynasty China*. Honolulu: University of Hawai'i Press.

SCHOPEN, Gregory
    1997   "Archaeology and Protestant Presuppositions in the Study of Indian Buddhism," in Schopen, *Bones, Stones, and Buddhist Monks*. Honolulu: University of Hawai'i Press, 1–22.

SEARLE, John R.
    2004   *Mind: A Brief Introduction*. New York and Oxford: Oxford University Press.

SEKIDA Katsuki 関田一喜
    1977   *Two Zen Classics: Mumonkan and Heikiganroku*. New York: Weatherhill.

SHIBAYAMA Zenkei 柴山全慶
1975   *Zen Comments on the Mumonkan*. New York: New American Library.
SHIMAZAKI Tōson 島崎 藤村
1974   *The Broken Commandment*, trans. by Kenneth Strong. Tokyo: University of Tokyo Press.
1976   *The Family*, trans. by Cecilia Segawa Seigle. Tokyo: University of Tokyo Press.
1978   「ルウソオの『懺悔』中に見出したる自己」[The Self I Discovered in Rousseau's *Confessions*] in 『島崎東村全集6』[Complete Works of Shimazaki Tōson 6]. Tokyo: Chikuma Shobō.
SHINOHARA Koichi
2007   "Writing the Moment of Death: Chinese Biographies of Eminent Monks," in Phyllis Granoff and Koichi Shinohara, eds., *Heroes and Saints: The Moment of Death in Cross-Cultural Perspectives*. Newcastle-upon-Tyne: Cambridge Scholars Publishing, 47–72.
SHINRAN 親鸞
1969   『定本親鸞聖人全集』[Critical edition of the collected works of Shinran]. Kyoto: Hōzōkan.
1997   *The Collected Works of Shinran*, Gadjin M. Nagao, ed. Kyoto: Jōdo Shinshū Hongwanji-ha.
2003   『浄土真宗聖典』[Sacred texts of True Pure Land Buddhism]. Kyoto: Jōdo Shinshū Hongwanji-ha.
SILKO, Leslie Marmon
1999   "Landscape, History, and the Pueblo Imagination," in David Landis Barnhill, ed., *At Home on the Earth: Becoming Native to Our Place*. Berkeley: University of California Press, 30–44.
SKINNER, B. F.
1972   *Beyond Freedom and Dignity*. New York: Bantam Books.
1976   *About Behaviorism*. New York: Vintage Books.
SMART, Ninian
1986   *Concept and Empathy: Essays in the Study of Religion*. New York: New York University Press.
1989   *The World's Religions*. Englewood Cliffs, N.J.: Prentice Hall.
SMITH, Huston
1987   "Is There a Perennial Philosophy?" *Journal of the American Academy of Religion* 55/3, 553–68.

SMITH, Wilfred Cantwell
  1967   *Questions of Religious Truth*. New York: Scribner.
  1978   *The Meaning and End of Religion*. San Francisco: Harper and Row.

SNYDER, Gary
  1990   "Blue Mountains Constantly Walking," in *The Practice of the Wild: Essays by Gary Snyder*. San Francisco: North Point Press, 97–115.

SOKOLOWSKI, Robert
  1974   *Husserlian Meditations*. Evanston: Northwestern University Press.

STANTON, Donna C.
  1987   *The Female Autograph: Theory and Practice of Autobiography from the Tenth to the Twentieth Century*. Chicago: University of Chicago Press.

STAROBINSKI, Jean
  1988   *Jean-Jacques Rousseau: Transparency and Obstruction*. Chicago: University of Chicago Press.

STEINECK, Christian
  2009   "Das Bendōwa von Dōgen: Narratologische Analyse eines doktrinären Textes," *Asiatische Studien: Zeitschrift der Schweizerischen Asiengesellschaft* 63/3: 571–95.

STEINER, George
  1967   "The Retreat from the Word," in Steiner, *Language and Silence: Essays on Language, Literature, and the Inhuman*. New York: Atheneum.

STONE, Jacqueline I.
  2008   "With the Help of 'Good Friends': Deathbed Ritual Practices in Early Medieval Japan," in STONE AND WALTER, 61–101.
  2016   *Right Thoughts at the Last Moment: Buddhism and Deathbed Practices in Early Medieval Japan*. Honolulu: University of Hawai'i Press.

STONE, Jacqueline I., and Mariko Namba WALTER, eds.
  2008   "Introduction," in *Death and the Afterlife in Japanese Buddhism*. Honolulu: University of Hawai'i Press, 1–26.

STRENG, Frederick J.
  1967   *Emptiness: A Study in Religious Meaning*. Nashville and New York: Abingdon Press.
  1987   "Truth," in Mircea Eliade, ed., *The Encyclopedia of Religion* vol. 15, 63–72.

SUEKI Fumihiko 末木文美士
2009A "Rethinking Japanese Buddhism," *Nichibunken Newsletter* 76: 3–4.
2009B 『仏典を読む—死からはじまる仏教史』 [Reading Buddhism: Buddhist history beginning from death]. Tokyo: Shinchōsha.

SUZUKI D. T. (Teitarō) Daisetsu 鈴木(貞太郎)大拙
1953 "Zen: A Reply to Hu Shih," *Philosophy East and West* 3/1: 25–46.
1960 *Manual of Zen Buddhism*. New York: Grove Press.
1969 *The Zen Doctrine of No Mind*. London: Rider and Co.

SWANSON, Paul
1996 "Absolute Nothingness and Emptiness in Nishitani Keiji: An Essay from the Perspective of Classical Buddhist Thought," *The Eastern Buddhist* 39/1: 99–108.

TANABE, George J., Jr.
1999 "The Founding of Mount Kōya and Kūkai's Eternal Meditation," in George J. Tanabe, Jr., ed., *Religions of Japan in Practice*. Princeton: Princeton University Press, 354–9.

TANABE Hajime 田辺元
2011 "The Philosophy of Dōgen," trans. by Ralf Müller, in JPSB, 683–8. The original text is 「正法眼蔵の哲学私観」 (My views on the Shōbōgenzō]), 1939, in 『田辺元全集』 [Complete Works of Tanabe Hajime, vol. 5]. Tokyo: Chikuma Shobō, 1963, 443–94.

TAYLOR, Douglas
1977 *Languages of the West Indies*. Baltimore: Johns Hopkins University Press.

TAYLOR, Mark C.
1987 *Altarity*. Chicago: Chicago University Press.

TEDLOCK, Barbara
1992 *The Beautiful and the Dangerous: Dialogues with the Zuni Indians*. New York: Penguin Books.

TILLICH, Paul, and HISAMATSU Shin'ichi 久松真一
1971–3 "Dialogues East and West: Conversations between Paul Tillich and Hisamatsu Shin'ichi," *The Eastern Buddhist* 4/2: 89–107 (Part One); 5/2: 107–28 (Part Two); 6/2: 87–114 (Part Three).

TIMM, Jeffrey R.
1992 *Texts in Context: Traditional Hermeneutics in South Asia*. Albany, NY: State University of New York Press, 1992

Tōson Shimasaki 島崎 藤村
- 1974 *The Broken Commandment*, trans. Kenneth Strong. Tokyo: University of Tokyo Press.
- 1976 *The Family*, trans. by Cecilia Segawa Seigle. Tokyo: Tokyo University Press.
- 1978 「ルウソオの『懺悔』中に見出したる自己」[The Self I Discovered in Rousseau's *Confessions*] in 『島崎東村全集6』[Shimazaki Tōson Complete Works 6]. Tokyo: Chikuma Shobō.

Tracy, David
- 1990 "Kenosis, Sunyata, and Trinity: A Dialogue with Masao Abe," in Cobb and Ives, 135–154.

Trainor, Kevin, ed.
- 2001 *Buddhism: The Illustrated Guide*. Oxford: Oxford University Press.

Tucker, John
- 2018 "Japanese Confucian Philosophy," in Edward N. Zalte, ed., *the Stanford Encyclopedia of Philosophy*. <https://plato.stanford.edu/archives/win2022/entries/japanese-confucian/>.

Uchiyama Kōshō 内山興正
- 1993 *Opening the Hand of Thought:* Approach *to Zen*, trans. by Shōhaku Okumura and Tom Wright. New York: Arkana, Penguin Books.

Ueda Shizuteru 上田閑照
- 1982a "Emptiness and Fullness: Śūnyatā in Mahāyāna Buddhism," trans. by James W. Heisig and Frederick Greiner, *The Eastern Buddhist* 15/1: 9–37.
- 1982b "Das Erwachen im Zen-Buddhismus als Wort-Ereignis," in Walter Strolz, ed., *Offenbarung als Heilserfahrung im Christentum, Hinduismus und Buddhismus*. Freiburg: Herder, 209–34.
- 1982c 「禅思想と宗教哲学：西田哲学の場合に即して」[Zen thought and philosophy of religion: The case of Nishida philosophy] in Mitsuyoshi Saigusa, ed., 『講座仏 教思想5』[Lectures on Buddhist Thought 5]. Tokyo: Risōsha, 173–235.
- 1989 "The Zen Buddhist Experience of the Truly Beautiful," trans. by John C. Maraldo, *The Eastern Buddhist* 22/1: 1–36.
- 1991 "Experience and Language in the Thinking of Kitarō Nishida," trans. by T. Nobuhara, *Bulletin of Zen Culture Research Institute* 17: 91–154.

1993 "Pure Experience, Self-Awareness, 'Basho,'" *Études phénoménologiques* 18/4): 63–86.
1994 "Gelassenheit im Zen-Buddhismus," in Ernesto Grassi and Hugo Schmale, eds., *Arbeit und Gelassenheit: Zwei Grundformen des Umgangs mit Natur.* Munich: Wilhelm Fink Verlag, 207–30.
1995 "Silence and Words in Zen Buddhism," *Diogenes* 43/2: 1–21.
2001 『禅：根源的人間』[Zen: Originary Human Being], vol. 4 of 上田閑照集 [Ueda Shizuteru Collection]. Tokyo: Iwanami.
2011 *Wer und was bin ich? Zur Phänomenologie des Selbst im Zen-Buddhismus.* Freiburg: Verlag Karl Alber.

UEDA Shizuteru 上田閑照 and YANAGIDA Seizan 柳田聖山
1982 『十牛図』[The Ten Oxherding Pictures]. Tokyo, Chikuma Shobō.

UEDA Yoshifumi 上田義文
1977 「仏教学の方法論について」[On the method of Buddhist studies], in Ueda, 『大乗仏教の思想』[The thought of Mahayana Buddhism]. Tokyo: Daisan Bunmeisha, 63–86.
1985 "Reflections on the Study of Buddhism," *The Eastern Buddhist* 18/2: 114–30.

UNO Sesson 宇野雪村 and HIDAI Nankoku 比田井南谷, eds.
1983 『現代書』[Contemporary calligraphy], vol. 1. Tokyo: Yūzankaku.

VAN BRAGT, Jan
1995 "Kyoto Philosophy—Intrinsically Nationalistic?" in HEISIG AND MARALDO, 233–54.
1998 "Nishitani Revisited," *Zen Buddhism Today* 15: 77–95.
2002 "Multiple Religious Belonging of the Japanese People," in Catherine Cornille, ed., *Many Mansions? Multiple Religious Belonging and Christian Identity.* Maryknoll, NY: Orbis Books.
2014 *Interreligious Affinities: Encounters with the Kyoto School and the Religions of Japan.* Nagoya: Chisokudō Publications.

VATTIMO, Gianni
1997 *Beyond Interpretation: The Meaning of Hermeneutics for Philosophy.* Stanford: Stanford University Press.

VEDDER, Ben
2000 *Was Ist Hermeneutik?: Ein Weg von der Textdeutung zur Interpretation der Wirklichkeit.* Stuttgart: Kohlhammer.

VIVEIROS DE CASTRO, Eduardo
2015 *The Relative Native: Essays on Indigenous Conceptual Worlds*. Chicago: Hau Books.

WADDELL, Norman, trans.
1982–3 "Wild Ivy: The Spiritual Autobiography of Hakuin Ekaku," *The Eastern Buddhist* 15/2 (1982): 71–109; and 16/1 (1983): 107–39.
1984 *The Unborn: The Life and Teachings of Zen Master Bankei, 1622–1693*. San Francisco: North Point Press.

WALDENFELS, Bernhard
2004 *Phänomenologie der Aufmerksamkeit*. Frankfurt: Suhrkamp.

WALDENFELS, Hans
1980 *Absolute Nothingness: Foundations for a Buddhist-Christian Dialogue*. New York: Paulist Press.

WALKER, Janet A.
1979 *The Japanese Novel of the Meiji Period and the Ideal of Individualism*. Princeton: Princeton University Press.

WALTER, Mariko Namba
2008 "The Structure of Japanese Buddhist Funerals," in STONE AND WALTER, 247–92.

WATANABE Shōkō 渡辺照宏
1968 『日本の仏教』. Tokyo: Iwanami Shoten. Translated as *Japanese Buddhism: A Critical Appraisal*. Tokyo: Kokusai Bunka Shinkōkai, 1970.

WATSON, Burton
1968 *The Complete Works of Chuang Tzu*. New York: Columbia University Press.

WEBB, Mark
2017 "Religious Experience," in Edward N. Zalta, ed., *The Stanford Encyclopedia of Philosophy*. <https://plato.stanford.edu/archives/fall2022/entries/religious-experience/>.

WHITEHEAD, Alfred North
1958 *Modes of Thought*. New York: Capricorn Books.

WILLIAMS, Duncan Ryūken
2008 "Funerary Zen: Sōtō Zen Death Management in Tokugawa Japan," in STONE AND WALTER, 207–46.

WILSON, Edward O.
1998 *Consilience: The Unity of Knowledge*. New York: Alfred A. Knopf.

WIRTH, Jason M.
2017   *Mountains, Rivers, and the Great Earth: Reading Gary Snyder and Dōgen in an Age of Ecological Crisis*. Albany, NY: State University of New York Press.

WITTGENSTEIN, Ludwig
1953   *Philosophical Investigations*, trans. by G. E. M. Anscombe. Oxford: Basil Blackwell, 1968.

WORDS IN MOTION: Modern Japanese Calligraphy
1985   (An exhibition catalogue). The Yomiuri Shinbun.

WRIGHT, Dale
2006   "Satori and the Moral Dimension of Enlightenment," *Journal of Buddhist Ethics* 13. <https://blogs.dickinson.edu/buddhistethics/2010/04/27/satori-and-the-moral-dimension-of-enlightenment/>.
2008   "Introduction: Rethinking Ritual Practice in Zen Buddhism," in Steven Heine and Dale S. Wright, eds., *Zen Ritual: Studies of Zen Buddhist Theory in Practice*. New York: Oxford University Press, 3–19.

YAMADA Kōun 山田耕雲
2004   *The Gateless Gate: The Classic Book of Zen Koans*. Somerville, MA: Wisdom Publications.

YAMPOLSKY, Philip B.
1967   *The Platform Sutra of the Sixth Patriarch*. New York: Columbia University Press.
1971   *The Zen Master Hakuin: Selected Writings*. New York: Columbia University Press.

YANAGIDA Seizan 柳田聖山, trans.
1972   『臨済録, 仏典講座 30』[Record of Linji, Lectures on Buddhist scriptures, 30]. Tokyo: Daizō Shuppan.

YU, Lan 喻岚
2021   "Relational autonomy: Where Confucius and Mencius stand on freedom," *Asian Philosophy* 31/3: 32–35.

YUASA Yasuo 湯浅泰雄
1987   *The Body: Toward an Eastern Mind-Body Theory*, trans. by Nagatomo Shigenori and T. P. Kasulis. Albany, NY: State University of New York Press.

ZAHAVI, Dan
　1999　*Self-Awareness and Alterity*. Evanston, IL: Northwestern University Press.

ZANER, Richard M.
　1964　*The Problem of Embodiment: Some Contributions to a Phenomenology of the Body*. The Hague: M. Nijhoff.

ZHANG Longxi 張隆溪
　1992　*The Tao and the Logos: Literary Hermeneutics, East and West*. Durham, NC: Duke University Press.

Index

Abe Masao 阿部正雄, 19–21, 39–41, 43, 49, 50, 54–7, 79, 100, 164, 284–7, 341, 374
abortion, 307–8, 317
Abrahamic traditions, 99
absence, 142, 177, 186, 238, 251, 258, 307, 355, 367, 369
absolute nothingness, 252, 259, 269, 286
absolute, 4, 32, 33, 46, 218, 228, 243, 252, 259, 269, 272–3, 282–3, 285, 286, 288–90, 292–3, 306, 317–8, 360, 379
abstract painting, 148, 398,
abyss, 252, 371. *See also* chasm
accordance, 118, 226–7, 229, 235–6, 302, 401
accountability, 10, 219, 266, 279, 283–5, 289, 290
Ackroyd, Joyce, 180–3, 187
act, 15–16, 72, 77, 86–7, 108–11, 118–9, 121, 147, 149–51, 178, 220–2, 227, 232, 234, 236, 243, 250, 257, 259, 280, 291, 302, 305, 307–8, 310–11, 313, 315, 325, 329, 366, 391
action, 6–7, 85, 105, 107–8, 110–12, 114–15, 118–19, 121–3, 130–1, 135–6, 139, 142, 151, 156, 177–8, 185, 220–3, 229, 234, 279, 302, 304–5, 308–9, 311–13, 330, 346, 394
actuality, 85, 278, 314; actualization, 277, 314
Addiss, Stephen, 142
Adorno, Theodore, 393
aesthetics, 203–4, 210, 264, 388–9, 398, 402
afterlife, 362, 366, 370

Agar, Michael, 66
agency, 1, 143, 223, 246, 396, 398
Aguilar, Claudia, 219,
aikidō, 121
Aitken, Robert, 306–10, 315, 317
Akizuki Ryōmin, 秋月龍珉, 228
alienation, 219, 250
alterity, 9, 10, 237–40, 245–7, 254, 257–62, 264–5, 387
alternatives, 2–7, 9–12, 39, 45, 56, 58–9, 61–3, 67, 69, 70, 78, 80, 85–92, 94, 98, 101, 105, 107–11, 114–24, 127, 135, 137–40, 143–4, 199, 218–9, 223–9, 233–7, 259, 262, 265–6, 272, 275, 281, 293–5, 299–300, 305–6, 308, 314, 316–7, 321–3, 329, 341, 347, 381, 387–8, 399, 400
Ames, Roger, 110, 142, 230, 232–4
Amida Buddha, 21, 353, 355–6, 385
Analects, 109–11, 224, 231–3
analogy, 39, 150, 154, 193, 375
animal, 23–4, 134, 239, 337, 350
ante-originality, 3, 12, 387, 388–90, 395, 398, 402
anthropology, 23–4, 36, 44–6, 48, 78, 102
antinomianism, 11
Aoki Shinmon 青木新門, 351
Apache, 215–17
App, Urs, 258
application, 2, 4, 56, 86, 94, 100, 102, 105, 108–9, 111, 121–2, 131, 154–5, 291
appropriation, 77, 126, 240, 269, 272, 292, 400
Arai Hakuseki 新井白石, 180–8. *See also* Hakuseki

Arai, Paula, 46, 53, 58
Arendt, Hannah, 107–8, 125, 304
Aristotle, 6, 112–16, 119–20, 314, 336, 349, 387
Armstrong, D. M., 345
art, artistic, 12, 30, 72, 92–6, 119–21, 121, 126, 134, 137, 138, 145–9, 151, 178, 179, 184, 197, 205, 254, 259, 261, 387–90, 393, 395–400; a. creation, 120, 127; a. practice, 389. *See also* pathway arts
Ast, Georg Anton Friedrich, 91
ātman, 365, 378
attention, 60, 62, 70, 83, 85, 89, 111, 117–8, 126–7, 129, 132–6, 138, 143, 146–7, 150–3, 158, 171, 184, 189, 262, 266, 292, 310, 356–8, 362, 369, 372, 385, 388, 390, 393–4, 396, 400
Augustine, 49, 190
Austin, James H., 209
Australian aboriginals, 201, 216
authenticity, 219, 224, 282–3, 388–9, 398, 402
authority, 42, 219, 220, 226, 232, 234, 304, 332, 370, 374, 381; authoritative, 64, 113, 220, 232–4, 331, 332; authoritative person, 232–3; authoritarian, 234, 301, 304
autobiography, 8, 172–3, 180–4, 186–8, 190–2, 196–8, 365–8, 373, 384
autonomy, 3, 8, 9, 139, 200, 218–38, 248, 263–4, 259, 272, 293, 326, 387, 394
Avalokiteśvara, 155
Awakening of Faith, 211, 331
awakening, 7, 40–1, 84, 165–6, 182, 194–5, 211, 249, 260, 264, 295–6, 298–9, 312, 331, 341, 352–3, 368, 372
awareness, 3, 22, 28, 89, 118, 135, 152, 166, 173–4, 178–9, 182, 213, 275, 277, 367, 389
axiom, 244; axiology, 285–7

Baizhang Huaihai 百丈懷海, 332, 343
Bankei Yōtaku 盤珪永琢, 188, 258, 378
Barbery, Muriel, 152,

Barrett, William, 125–6
Basso, Keith, 215–6
Becker, Carl, 26, 385
behaviorism, 303, 334, 344–7, 349
Behuniak, James Jr., 135, 137
being, 68–70, 73–4, 99, 130, 160–5; Being-in-the-world, 68, 329; b.-time, 376, 382
Being and Time, 68. 70, 27–8, 138–9, 145, 360
belief, 23, 25, 32–3, 44–6, 50–1, 56–7, 59–60, 175, 273
Bellah, Robert, 185
Bendōwa 辨道話, 54, 117, 315, 324, 332, 340–1, 357, 365
Benedictine, 80– 6
Benjamin, Walter, 388, 402
Bergson, Henri, 85, 130
Besemeres, Mary, 180
biblical, 67, 91, 99, 292
Bielefeldt, Carl, 157, 200, 212
biology, 24, 37, 246, 334
bioregionalism, 214–5
birth, 12, 148, 183, 192, 308, 342, 352–3, 356, 360–1, 367, 373–7, 380, 382–5; b./life, 361, 374, 376, 382–4; b.-and-death, 352–3, 357, 363, 366, 368, 372, 374, 380, 384
Bittner, Egon, 46
Blue Cliff Record 碧巖錄, 202, 291, 309
Blum, Mark, 378
Bodhidharma, 211, 328, 343
bodhisattva, 155, 159, 256, 296, 300
Bodiford, William M., 188, 315, 368–70
body, 6, 11, 18, 52–4, 63–4, 66–7, 70, 72, 74, 82, 85, 87, 91, 117–8, 120–3, 130, 136, 138–40, 146, 150, 152–3, 159, 165, 187, 189, 192–3, 211–13, 216, 321–3, 325–8, 332, 334–5, 338–40, 342–50, 352–4, 356–7, 362, 367, 369–72, 378, 392, 394, 402; b. of the Tathāgata, 159, 378; b.-mind, 11, 315, 321–3, 325, 341, 344, 349, 352, 372, 387, 396

Bonhoeffer, Dietrich, 287
Bourdieu, Pierre, 89, 118
Bragt, Jan van, 79, 156
brain, 66, 189, 209–10, 321, 329, 334–8, 344–6, 360
Brandom, Robert B., 123
breaking, 133, 161, 195, 258, 388, 394–5, 400
Broughton, Jeffrey L., 225, 228
brush 395–7, 401
Buber, Martin, 134, 137
Buchner, Hartmut, 126
Budai 布袋, 256, 259
Buddha, 11, 15–17, 21, 26, 149, 158–9, 165, 208, 211, 256, 260, 272, 277, 286, 297, 310–11, 313, 324–5, 332, 334, 336, 339–41, 352–3, 355–7, 369, 370, 372–3, 378, 380, 385; b.-nature, 163, 192, 256, 327, 352, 378; B. Way 仏道, 11, 297, 324–5, 339, 341, 372–3; b.-dharma, 311; Buddhas, 165, 294, 296, 324–5, 327, 336, 337, 339
Buddhism, 6, 12, 15–21, 26–7, 37, 39–41, 51–4, 56, 79, 80, 89, 100, 122, 126–7, 149, 159, 192, 201–2, 209–10, 239, 249, 254, 258, 266, 269, 281, 287, 295–7, 300–1, 312, 338, 351–8, 362, 365, 367–8, 375, 377, 381, 383–5
Bunge, Mario, 334, 336–7, 345
Burnett, Katharine P., 398
bushidō 武士道, 186
Buss, Sarah, 220, 221
Busshō 仏性, 378
Butler, Judith, 238
Byrd, Dustin J., 37

Calligraphy, 120–1, 147–9, 152, 389–90, 395–7
Calvino, Italo, 364
Carter, Robert E., 309
Cartesian dualism, 347; C. privileged access, 176; C. self-certainty, 175
cat, 309–13, 316, 402

causality, 95, 140, 221, 223, 276, 279–80, 311, 318, 354, 379
Celan, Paul, 244
cessation, 159, 374
Cestari, Matteo, 121
Chai, David, 134,
Chalmer, David, 344
Chan 禪, 40–2, 80, 157, 163, 201, 203, 206, 212, 214–5, 224, 281, 292, 309–10, 368–9
chanting, 52, 78, 82–6, 353
China, 116, 122, 126, 157, 188, 203, 212, 296, 368–9, 398
Chinese, 40, 110, 121–2, 134, 137, 143, 147, 149–50, 153, 189, 200–1, 205, 207, 209–12, 214, 219, 224, 226, 230–1, 296–7, 315, 327–8, 355, 368–9, 371–2, 378, 384, 390, 395–8
Chinul, 299
Christ, 19, 20, 56, 57
Christianity, 18, 19, 27, 61, 267, 270, 273; Christian, 4, 18–20, 30, 36, 56–7, 62, 80–1, 84, 91, 100, 186, 229, 254, 266–7, 284–5, 287, 292, 298
Chu, William, 296
Chuang Tzu, 134. *See also* Zhuangzi.
citta, 327–8, 332
Cleary, Thomas and J.C., 201, 291, 311, 380, 382
cleaver, 7, 134–8, 147, 149–52
Cobb, John B. Jr., 19, 5
cognitive science, 51, 119, 322
Cold Mountain, 214, 397
Collcut, Martin, 324
Collins, Steven, 258
commandment, 195, 197, 302
community, 5, 10, 30, 44–5, 53, 73, 101, 109–10, 113, 196, 232, 234, 296, 304, 306–7, 362–3, 367–9, 370; communal, 303, 339, 370
Como, Michael, 16
compassion, 229, 261, 269, 298–9, 308

442 | Index

concentration, 7, 17, 134, 150–60, 163, 165, 192, 234, 385
conceptuality, 20, 276
conditioning, 10, 25, 28, 98, 274, 277
confession, 171, 181–2; confessional, 44, 171, 180, 197
Confessions, The, 8, 171–2, 174–80, 183, 187–8, 194, 196
Confucianism, 18, 185, 187, 296; Confucian, 111, 113, 122, 173, 180–6, 190, 193, 197, 219, 230–5, 296, 314
Confucius, 6, 9, 109–11, 116, 224, 231–2, 236, 387
conscience, 18, 196
consciousness, 53, 65, 68, 89, 105, 119, 151, 159, 162, 171–2, 175, 177–9, 186–7, 210, 240, 242, 245, 268, 276–9, 287–92, 300–1, 307, 309, 312, 330, 332, 334–5, 338, 361, 363, 377, 385
contradiction, 33, 35, 109, 247–9, 392; contradictory self-identity, 243
control, 17, 55, 128, 133, 136, 138, 146, 182, 185, 221–2, 226–8, 234, 236, 257, 390, 400
conversation, 9, 19, 56, 71–3, 78–9, 81–2, 91, 110, 127, 130, 134, 138–41, 144–5, 180, 194–5, 239, 240, 260–1, 306, 309, 312, 349
conversion, 17, 90, 126, 312
Conze, Edward, 155
cook, 134–8, 147, 150, 152, 215
Cook, Francis, 211, 287
Cornille, Catherine 61–2, 82
Cosme de Torras, 18
Cox, Rupert, 389
creation, 77, 120–1, 127, 149, 175, 216–17, 246, 264, 267, 275; creativity, 3, 12, 251, 387–8, 390, 393–4, 397–402; creator, 48, 283
Cuevas, Bryan J., 355
cultivation, 155, 157
culture, 6, 23–6, 28, 29, 32, 37, 44–7, 51, 65–7, 85, 102, 172–3, 232, 251, 267, 271, 283, 288, 362, 388, 389 ; cultural, 4, 16, 18, 23–5, 27–8, 32–3, 37, 43, 45, 52, 65, 75, 101–2, 178, 180, 196–7, 237, 250–1, 398–9

Da Vinci, Leonardo, 96
Dahui Zonggao 大慧宗杲, 324
Dao De Jing 道德經, 224, 334
dao 道, 16, 121, 135–7, 141; Daoist, 6, 134–5, 142, 234, 334. See also *dō*
Dasein, 68–70, 101, 139
Davis, Bret W., 53, 126, 130, 134, 139, 141, 214, 247, 249, 251, 253–4, 262, 341, 382, 384
De Man, Paul, 175
De Vos, George A., 87
death, 11–12, 28, 57, 109, 182–3, 191–2, 194–5, 248, 270, 298, 308, 310, 33–2, 342, 351–85; Great D., 298, 352
deconstruction, 10, 97–8, 175, 196
delusion, 297, 316, 318, 352, 374
dependence, dependency, 144, 219, 223–6
Derrida, Jacques, 68, 97, 98, 310
Descartes, René, 177, 179, 333. *See also* Cartesian
DeVos, George, 45
devotion, 21, 81, 343
dharma, 18, 86, 117, 157, 188, 190–3, 211, 215, 224, 226, 235, 286, 296, 335, 338, 341, 378, 381; dharmas, 167, 225, 375, 378–9
dhyāna, 159, 354
dialectics, 76; dialectic, 71, 77, 226; dialectical, 72, 76–7, 106, 144, 243, 260, 323
dialogue, 4, 9, 19–21, 41, 55–63, 71–2, 74, 75, 77–85, 100, 109–10, 114, 163, 237, 239, 253, 259–62, 264, 270, 285, 336, 381, 387, 399
Diamond Sutra, 20, 149
Dickman, Nathan Eric, 91
difference, 4, 9, 10, 12, 22, 24, 40, 45, 47, 51, 54–5, 62, 65, 78–9, 81, 87, 91, 94,

98, 106, 108, 112, 116, 117, 120, 124, 127, 131, 158, 165, 175, 195, 197, 204, 211, 218, 237–41, 243, 246–7, 250, 252–4, 258, 260, 262, 264–5, 274, 285–6, 288, 292, 304, 314, 325, 338, 348, 350–2, 354, 385, 390, 397
differentiation, 239, 246, 252, 285, 338
dignity, 3, 235
Dilthey, Wilhelm, 68, 75, 91, 95, 96
discourse, 63, 68, 75–7, 92–4, 108, 110, 112, 124, 184, 211–12, 214, 224–5, 237–9, 261, 280–1, 283, 347, 381 ; d. analysis, 281; discursive, 6, 39, 52–3, 55, 58, 79, 81, 85, 91, 109–10, 117–8, 280, 332–3
discrimination, 202, 267, 280–1, 284, 287–9, 292–3, 297, 316, 327
distance, 5, 39, 43, 75–6, 126, 130, 138, 178–9, 198, 212, 221, 241, 400; distanciation, 77
distinctions, 1, 3, 41, 51, 90, 114, 120, 239, 294, 297, 352, 359, 367
diversity, 5, 23–4, 34, 36–7, 62, 326
divine, 16, 33, 57, 261, 273; divinities, 142, 354
dō 道, 16, 121, 137, 325, 338–9, 389, 398. See also *dao*, Way
doctrine, 17, 21, 23, 29–31, 35, 57, 64, 79, 83–5, 116, 191, 272, 277, 283, 339, 352, 377; doctrinal, 17, 21, 27, 31–2, 36, 79, 352, 358, 373–4
Dōgen 道元, 2, 6–8, 11–12, 54, 58, 117–18, 155–8, 164–7, 188, 200, 211–15, 246, 281, 287, 297–8, 305–6, 309–19, 321–33, 335–44, 346–9, 351–2, 356–7, 365–85, 387–8
dogma, 23, 30, 84; dogmatic, 30, 331; dogmatism, 11
Döll, Steffen, 254
Dostoevsky, Fyodor, 175
Dreyfus, Hubert L., 282–3
dualism, 194, 344, 347; dualist, 342, 344–5, 347; duality, 316, 345, 347
Dumoulin, Heinrich, 17–18

Dürckheim, Karlfried Graf, 126

Earth, 8, 11, 36–7, 135, 142, 151, 211, 213, 215–17, 230, 321, 331–2, 335, 337, 341, 349, 357, 383, 391
Ebersole, Gary L., 262
effort, 63, 231, 397; effortless, 135, 152
efforts, 192, 270, 280
ego, 77, 161, 177–9, 185, 194, 206, 229, 260, 310, 329, 377; egoless perspectivism, 214, 384
Eiheiji 永平寺, 369–70
Einstein, 301
Ejō 懷奘, 309–13, 370, 373
Elberfeld, Rolf, 375
Eliade, Mircea, 36–7
embodied, 6, 7, 30, 51–3, 55, 57, 63, 66, 74, 85, 89, 91, 112, 118, 120–1, 201, 204, 209, 212–13, 246, 318, 327, 329, 335, 341, 349, 381, 387–9
emic, 44–6, 49
emotions, 176, 207, 210, 249, 345, 357
empathy, 84, 86, 92
empiricism, 317, 326
emptiness (空), 9, 20, 140–3, 147, 151, 154–7, 161, 267–9, 271–8, 283–5, 288–90, 293, 312, 315, 378
enaction, 119; enactive intuition, 119, 246
engi 縁起, 278. See also *pratītya samutpāda*
enlightenment, 7, 27, 31, 34, 84, 86, 89, 117, 158–9, 163, 185, 188, 205–6, 209, 211, 256, 266, 273, 278, 286, 296, 297, 299, 309, 315, 324, 332, 337, 341, 374
Enomiya-Lassalle, Hugo, 35
environnent, 36, 80, 121, 127, 132, 134, 139, 146, 152, 200–6, 215–16, 226–8, 246, 338, 347, 350
epistêmê, 42, 114, 121
epistemology, 33, 59–60, 90, 121, 258, 326
equality, 80, 258, 272, 285–6
equivalence, 10, 21, 46, 267, 269, 281–4, 288, 293, 315, 383

Ernaux, Annie, 198
eternal Being, 174; e. mind, 357; e. recurrence, 273, 280; e. *samādhi*, 162; eternalist position, 377
ethics, 3, 5, 9–11, 16–17, 30–2, 101, 108, 110, 112, 114, 116, 183–5, 188, 219, 228–9, 235–6, 260, 271, 279. 281, 283–5, 287, 293–301, 303, 305–6, 309–12, 314, 316–17
ethnology, 23, 198
etic, 44, 45, 49
eudaimonia, 113–14
Euthyphro, 109
every day is a good day, 281, 291
evidence, 2, 23, 36, 62, 95, 122, 163, 186, 297, 346, 355, 401
evil, 18, 33, 111, 285, 287, 293, 297, 302, 305–6, 315–16, 318
existence, 11, 32, 36, 51, 75, 96, 114, 143, 153, 156, 162, 183, 199, 270, 273, 275, 282, 314–5, 353, 355, 360–2, 375, 378
existential moment, 375–6, 383
existentialism, 33; existentialist, 218, 276; existential phenomenologists, 329, 330
experience, 4, 25, 26, 28, 30–1, 35, 40–1, 53–4, 62, 82–4, 87, 89–91, 94–5, 97–9, 127, 138–40, 153, 164, 166, 172, 176, 178, 184, 191–3, 198, 209–10, 212–13, 248–53, 258–9, 267, 279, 290–1, 296, 309, 337, 341, 347, 360–1, 363–4, 366–7, 372, 377–8, 393; experiential, 31, 45, 113, 166, 247, 392; pure e., 9, 240–6, 248, 251–3, 264
expression, 30, 34, 57, 59, 60, 65–6, 84, 86–7, 96, 139, 178, 181–6, 195, 200–1, 204–5, 210, 212, 225, 226, 229, 233, 241, 246–7, 296, 302, 306, 312, 317, 339, 345, 384, 400; expressive, 62, 74, 186, 221, 246, 247, 397, 399; expressivity, 95, 246–7
external world, 206, 361

Fabian (Fukansai Habian), 18
faith, 5, 18, 28, 33, 35, 59–60, 211, 331–2

family, 16, 128, 182–3, 185, 187, 195, 352, 354, 360, 362, 367
Fayan Wenyi 法眼文益, 201–2, 338
Feuerbach, Ludwig,, 107, 229
Fichte, Johann Gottlieb, 243
fiction, 172, 175, 197, 362, 364
field, 156–7, 161, 276, 287, 293, 313; f. of consciousness, 287, 312; f. of emptiness, 156, 271–2, 276, 293; f. of karma, 276, 290; f. of nihility, 161
filial piety, 110, 181
final cause, 140–3, 274
first-person, 150, 171, 359–66, 368, 377, 379, 381, 384
Fischer, Michael M. J., 102
Fitzgerald, Timothy, 60
Five Mountains, 203–4, 206, 208
flesh, 335, 342, 347
folk Buddhism, 35; f. religion, 61
Forman, Robert K. C., 240, 399
Formanek, Susanne, 352
formless, 154, 157, 161, 164, 194–5, 345, 352
Foulk, T. Griffith, 158
Fowler, Edward, 188, 197
Francis of Assisi, 58, 230; Franciscan, 230
Francis Xavier, 17, 21
freedom, 9, 10, 29, 148, 187, 196, 218–9, 222, 225, 230, 232–4, 236, 265, 271–2, 275, 279, 400
Frege, Gottlob, 77
Fujiwara no Teika 藤原定家, 210
Fukanzazengi 普勧坐禪儀, 324, 327, 340–1
Fukuzawa Yukichi 福澤諭吉, 182, 187–8
funeral, 354, 369, 370, 372
Furong Daokai 芙蓉道楷, 212
Furukawa Tesshi 古川哲史, 186

Gadamer, Hans-Georg, 57, 65, 68, 71–4, 87–8, 94, 99, 101, 264–5
Gateless Gate 無門関, 309, 343
Geertz, Clifford, 27

Index | 445

Gelassenheit, 126–7, 130, 133–4, 138–9, 141, 143–5, 147, 151, 282, 330
gender, 4, 24–5, 29, 67
Genji 源氏, Prince, 353–4, 359, 362
Genjōkōan 現成公按, 166, 365, 373–4, 378–80, 382, 387
genre, 174, 179, 184, 196–7
Genshin 源信, 353, 356, 385
Gidō Shūshin 義堂周信, 208
Gilligan, Carol, 32
Gilmore, Leigh, 196
Gimello, Robert, 53
Giyō Hōshū 岐陽方秀, 205
Glassman, Bernard Tetsugen, 35
goal-oriented, 6, 106, 127, 135–7, 151, 157
God, 15–16, 18–20, 36, 51, 55–7, 86, 99, 139, 144, 227, 235, 273, 282–3, 286, 292, 301; gods, 16–17, 21, 36, 142, 151
gospels, 30, 91
grammar, 66, 87, 94, 208, 224, 331, 363, 374, 379, 381; grammatical, 87, 92–4, 161, 198, 330, 358–60, 362–6, 373–4, 377, 381; grammatology, 97, 98
Granoff, Phyllis, 196
Grant, Beata, 207
gravity, 228, 301, 307
Greek, 73, 107–8, 111, 113–15, 123–4, 178, 219, 250
Green, James, 40
Greene, Eric M., 40,
Griffiths, Paul J., 53, 159, 166
Grube, G. M. A., 316–17
Guéhenno, Jean, 175
Gutman, Huck, 175

Habit, 113, 144, 187; habituality, 116; habituation, 118
Hagakure 葉隠, 186
Hakuin Ekaku 白隠慧鶴, 2, 7, 155–8, 171, 188–97, 281, 298–9, 306, 312, 352
Hakuseki 白石, 7, 171, 180–7, 196–7. *See also* Arai Hakuseki
Hamlet, 95, 203

hammer, 70, 128–30, 131–2, 147, 149–52; hammering, 128–30, 132, 150–1
Hani Gorō 羽仁五郎, 182
Harada Shōdō 原田正道, 261
Hare, Thomas W., 263
Harootunian, H. D., 180
Hart, James G., 37, 336, 360, 363
Hartle, Ann, 174–5, 180
Hase Shōtō 長谷正當, 268
Haver, William, 120, 246, 271
Heart Sutra, 155, 378
heart, 8, 11, 200–17, 380; heart-mind 11, 200, 203, 256, 323; mindful heart, 8, 200–17
Hegel, Georg Wilhelm Friedrich, 226, 234; Hegelian, 260, 277
Heidegger, Martin, 6–7, 63, 65, 68–71, 73, 75, 88, 98–9, 101, 115, 125–34, 152, 167, 249–51, 269, 282–4, 298, 329–30, 360
Heine, Steven, 158, 212, 215, 280–1, 311, 369, 371–2
Heisig, James W., 36, 399
Henrich, Dieter, 105
heresy, 324, 332, 340, 343
Herman, Jonathan R., 137
hermeneutics, 5, 6, 56–102, 209, 341, 381, 387
Hick, John, 34
Hidai Nankoku 比田井南谷, 398, 401
Hisamatsu Shin'ichi 久松真一, 8, 126, 145, 149, 194–5, 352, 394–5
historical consciousness, 268, 276–9, 288–92
historicism, 76, 280
historicity, 267–8, 276–81, 288–90, 292–3
history, 10, 266–93, 355
Homans, Peter, 28
Hōnen 法然, 353, 357
Hori, Victor Sōgen, 42, 261, 297, 378
horizon, 65, 67–8, 71–3, 129, 139, 143, 213
Hu Shih 胡適, 41–3

Huangbo Xiyun 黃檗希運, 206
Huike 慧可, 328, 343
Huineng 惠能, 162, 334. *See also* Sixth Patriarch
human being, 48, 101, 145, 154, 194, 216, 229, 234, 240, 279, 286, 288, 260
human rights, 3, 272
Huntington, Patricia, 134
Husserl, Edmund, 68, 77, 119, 290–1, 313, 348; Husserlian, 143

I-novel, 171, 197
icchantika, 324, 339
Ichikawa Hakugen 市川白弦, 278
ideal, the, 294–317
idealism, 156, 166–7, 237, 326, 332, 335, 347
identity, 4, 8, 25, 40, 51, 83, 177–8, 216, 239, 256, 260, 270, 286–7, 295, 304, 342, 359, 362
ideologies, 19, 62, 180
Ienobu 家宣, 181
Ihara, Craig K., 31
ikebana 生け花, 121, 390–3, 397, 399–400
ikenobō 池坊, 390–3
imitation, 389, 396
immediacy, 240, 245, 381
impartiality, 181, 258
imperative form, 298, 302–3, 305, 309, 313, 317, 363–4, 366, 381
impermanence, 250, 274, 372, 390
Inatomi Eijirō 稲富英次郎, 186
independence, 9, 186, 219, 236
Indian, 215–6, 296, 355, 357, 377; I. Buddhism, 355
individualism, 173, 183, 186–8, 197
individuality, 92, 172–3, 176, 186–8, 195
infinity, 73, 74
Ingold, Timm, 397
innatism, 332, 343
insider, 5, 39, 42, 49, 83
insider/outsider Problem, 5, 39–55

instrumentality, 106, 123, 127, 130–3, 135–9, 142–3, 151–2, 155–6, 228
intentionality, 89, 210, 385
intentions, 75–7, 89, 128, 136, 147, 152, 220, 222, 236, 396
interaction, 2, 24, 37, 48, 59, 61, 63, 66–7, 106, 121, 127, 130, 139, 147, 161, 230, 236, 246, 391–2, 394, 396, 399, 401
intercultural philosophy, 3, 321, 323; interculturally, 321
interdependence, 26, 161, 163, 219, 225, 236. See also *engi*
intermonastic dialogue, 80–5
interpretation theory, 75, 77
interreligious, 6, 19, 55–63, 78–82, 85, 87, 90–1
intuition, 6, 119–22, 143, 243, 246
Irigaray, Luce, 238, 260
Iriya Yoshitaka 入矢義高, 228
Ishida Baigan 石田梅岩, 185
Islam, 27, 61
Ives, Christopher, 19, 56, 278, 299, 303, 311
Izutsu Toyoko 井筒豊子, 210

Jainism, 300
Jameson, Fredric, 95
Jankélévitch, Vladimir, 366
Jaspers, Karl, 126
jiriki 自力, 158
Jiun Sonja 慈雲尊者, 296
Johnson, Mark, 37, 51–2
Josephson, Jason Ānanda, 60
jūdō, 121
jug, 138, 140–3, 145–7, 151–2, 224
justice, 53, 235

Kaibara Ekken 貝原益軒, 231–2, 296
Kakuban 覺鑁, 356
kami 神, 15–16
Kane, Leslie, 250
Kanō school, 399
Kant, Immanuel, 105, 119, 218–19, 228–9,

234, 301, 333, 347; Kantian, 218–19, 228–9, 302
Kapleau, Philip, 337
karma, 275–6, 287, 290, 298, 303, 312
Kasulis, Thomas P., 117, 284–6, 305, 308, 365, 387
Kasza, Justyna Weronika, 196
Katz, Steven, 44
Keller, Catherine, 19
Keisei Sanshoku 谿声山色, 211
kenosis, 19, 56–7
kenshō 見性, 157, 193, 194
Kenzei 建撕, 371–2
Ki no Tsurayuki 紀貫之, 210
Kierkegaard, Søren, 229, 282–4
killing, 11, 111, 300–3, 305–13, 315–18
Kim, Hee-Jin, 165, 315, 321, 327, 332, 339, 341, 372, 380, 383
Kimura Rihito 木村利人, 219
Kindai no chōkoku 近代の超克, 271
King, Richard, 62
King, Sallie, 240
King, Winston 193
Kirchner, Thomas Yūhō, 224, 226
Kisei Reigen 希世霊彦, 204
Kiyō Hōshū 岐陽方秀, 205
Kiyozawa Manshi 清沢満之, 353
Klein, Anne Carolyn, 261
know-how, 70, 108, 123, 130
knowledge, 18, 21, 48, 59, 90, 92, 95, 97, 106, 109, 114–15, 119, 121–2, 130, 163, 175, 216, 287, 326, 328, 333, 349, 355, 392, 402
kōan, 35, 81, 83, 118, 153, 157–8, 163, 166, 192, 202, 291, 297, 304, 309, 316, 330, 365, 368, 373–4, 378–80, 382, 387
Koizumi Shinzō, 小泉信三, 187
Kokan Shiren 虎關師錬, 296
Kokinshū 古今集, 210
kokoro 心, 8, 185, 196, 210, 215
Korea, Korean, 15, 82, 147, 299, 395
Kraut, Richard, 112–13
Kuhn, Thomas S., 173, 196

Kūkai 空海, 352, 356–7, 367
Kuki Shūzō 九鬼周造, 21, 294
Kumārajīva, 149
Kumazawa Banzan 熊沢蕃山, 185
Kuoan Shiyuan 廓庵師遠, 254, 256, 161
Kyoto School, 9, 149, 294, 352, 383
Kyūō's Moral Discourses (鳩翁道話続), 184

LaFleur, William R., 352
Lakoff, George, 37, 51–2
landscape, 8, 10–11, 200–13, 215–17, 323, 338
language, 3–4, 6–7, 9, 16, 23–6, 29, 39, 44, 46–7, 51, 57, 59, 63–7, 70–9, 81, 84–97, 99–102, 109, 111, 126, 146, 154, 156, 158–9, 161, 191, 200, 202–3, 209, 216, 240–54, 260, 264–5, 313, 315, 334, 338, 340, 344, 347–9, 358–9, 365, 374, 387, 398
Laṅkâvatāra Sutra, 379
Laozi 老子, 141–2, 236
Lau, D. C., 334
Law of the Buddha, 16–17, 21
law, 16–18, 21, 29, 218, 219, 224–5, 232–5, 301; laws, 96, 234, 236, 238, 278, 301, 310
Lawlor, Robert, 216
Leder, Drew, 122
Legge, James, 137
Leighton, Dan Taigen, 211, 369
legalism, 110
legend, 162, 280, 292, 343, 356; legendary, 42, 180, 328
Legge, James, 137
Leighton, Dan Taigen, 211, 369
Levering, Miriam, 60, 128
Levin, David Michael, 139, 152
li 禮, 109, 232, 233
liberation, 39, 86, 148, 160, 209, 269, 297, 301–2, 313–14, 332, 343, 352–4, 356–7, 359, 363, 366, 368, 372, 378, 380, 384–5
limit, 57, 61, 81, 89, 122, 284, 304, 360, 364, 366
limitation, 4, 61, 131, 234, 361
linguistic, 23, 25, 52, 59, 67, 68, 75, 87,

92–4, 102, 115, 180, 248, 251–3, 280; linguisticality, 99
Linji 臨濟, 9, 139, 200, 224–6, 228, 310, 387, 400
Livingston, Julia, 147
Locke, John 177–9, 223
logic, 24, 33, 54, 77, 118, 161, 235, 250, 278, 331, 334; l. of *soku-hi* 即非, 161; logical, 33–5, 60, 109, 112, 123, 243, 346
logos, 86, 100, 113–15, 119–20, 250
Lombardo, Stanley, 142
Lopez, Donald S., Jr., 37, 100
Lotus Sutra, 355, 356, 378
Loughnane, Adam, 348
love, 20, 56, 68, 207, 229, 232, 298
Low, Albert, 298
Lynn, Richard John, 203, 224
Lyotard, Jean-François, 288

Ma Lin 马琳, 126, 134, 146, 397
MacIntyre, Alasdair, 49–51
Mādhyamika logic, 331
Mahāyāna, 10, 12, 211, 254, 258, 295, 299, 331, 378
Mallarmé, Étienne, 244
Mansini, Guy, 85
Maraldo, John C., 21, 28–9, 40, 42, 46, 48, 58, 67, 92–3, 101, 119, 133, 161, 214, 217, 223, 235, 243, 246, 262, 265–6, 269–70, 281–2, 292, 294–5, 299, 309, 325, 339, 343, 347, 358, 359, 399
Marcel, Gabriel, 347
Marcus, George E., 36, 45, 102
marketplace, 9, 138, 215, 261
Marra, Michael, 210
marriage, 27, 182, 236
martial arts, 121, 388, 398, 400
Martin, Russell, 251
Marx, Karl, 107, 229; Marxist, 102
mastery, 226, 228, 235, 395, 397
Masunaga, Daigan and Alicia, 311
materialism, 156, 345; materialist, 326, 344

McCarthy, Erin, 260
McClellan, Edwin, 173, 183
McCutcheon, Russell T., 44, 60
McMullen, Ian James 185
McRae, John, 42, 162, 163
means-end, 123, 135
meditation, 17, 35, 39–41, 52, 54, 78, 80–1, 85, 89, 117, 134, 145, 160, 163, 189, 195, 214, 299, 340–1, 346, 354
Mencius 孟子, 116, 232
mentalism, 344, 346; mentalist, 346, 347
Menzan Zuihō 面山瑞方, 309, 311
Merleau-Ponty, Maurice, 3329, 335, 347–8
Merrill, Sally, 195, 352
metanoetics, 3, 235, 294, 298
metaphor, 8, 206, 208–10, 214, 227–8, 249, 310, 321, 325, 333–9, 343–4, 346–9; metaphoric, 66, 163, 193, 200, 212, 274, 339, 376
metaphysics, 51, 164, 222–3, 230; metaphysical, 156, 163, 191, 222–3, 269
method, 11, 31, 67, 73, 95, 101, 109, 131, 137, 156, 174, 176, 178, 197, 233, 235, 324, 328, 330, 340–1, 348, 351, 396
methodology, 36–7, 100
Miki Kiyoshi 三木清, 101, 229
Miles, Margaret R., 212, 322
Minami Hiroshi 南博, 185, 187
Minamoto, Ryōen 源了円, 270–2
mind-body, 11, 321–3, 325–6, 329, 333, 342, 344–5, 347–9
mind, 7–8, 11, 12, 52, 82–3, 85, 86, 95, 117–19, 159–65, 185, 189, 194–5, 200–17, 256, 299, 305–8, 315, 321–50, 357, 378
mindful heart, 8, 200, 201, 204, 206–7, 209–11, 217, 323
mindfulness, 118
Miner, Earl, 337
Minh-ha, Trinh T., 238, 260
mirror, 31, 95, 326, 333–4, 338, 359
Miyoshi Masao 三好将夫, 188, 197

modeling, 3, 12, 70, 121, 388–9, 393, 395–400, 402
models, 32, 102, 116, 123, 173, 197, 237, 240, 252–3, 262, 264–5, 296, 345, 367, 387–8, 392, 397, 401–2
modernity, 28, 37, 270–2, 284
monastic, 81, 83, 191, 295–6, 298, 310, 368–9
monk, monks, 10, 17, 18, 80–6, 189–92, 197, 206, 208, 211–2, 291–2, 294, 297–8, 306, 309–11, 336–7, 346, 352–3, 355, 357, 366–9, 372, 373
Mononobe clan 物部氏, 15–16
moral, 4, 18, 22, 105, 113, 135, 171, 176–7, 182, 184, 196, 218, 229, 231, 234–6, 280, 286; m. law, 18, 235; m. theory, 105, 135, 300; m. relativism, 297
morality, 105, 294–318, 354
Mori Tetsurō 森哲郎, 229
Morita Shiryū 森田子龍, 120–1, 148, 396
mountain, 8, 200–6, 209, 211–17
Mountains and Waters Sutra (山水經), 200, 212, 332
Moyaert, Marianne, 77
mu 無, 2, 192
muga 無我, 193
Mugan Soō 夢巖祖應, 204
Mūlamādhyamakakārikā, 276
Müller Ralf, 249
Mumonkan 無門関, 309. See also *Gateless Gate*
Murasaki Shikibu 紫式部, 354, 362
music, 30, 82; musical performance, 397
Myōzen 明全, 369
mysticism, 80, 214
myth, 30, 37, 50–1, 280, 292, 370

Nāgārjuna, 276, 278, 378
Nagatomo Shigenori, 239
Nakai, Kate Wildman, 181
Nakamura Fuyubi 中村冬日, 393, 397–9
Nakamura Hajime 中村元, 378
Nakamura Sōichi, 中村宗一, 327, 397

Nakatomi clan, 中臣氏, 15–16
Nanquan 南泉, 309–11, 313
narration, 281, 287; narrative, 30, 77, 180, 196, 198, 281, 362, 364–5
nation, 44, 184, 271; nationalism, 37, 399
native American, 201, 216
naturalism, 188, 332; naturalist, 281, 294, 303, 317
nature, 3, 48–9, 129–30, 185, 203, 209–10, 270, 278
Nearman, Hubert, 214
nenbutsu 念仏, 158
Neo-Confucian, 10, 121–2, 180, 183, 231, 296
Neusner, Jacob, 29
Nichiren 日蓮, 189, 246, 356–7
Nicomachean Ethics, 112, 114, 116
Nietzsche, Friedrich, 10, 249, 269, 273, 280, 298–9, 302
nihilism, 10, 98, 269, 270, 272–3, 276–7, 279, 282–4, 288
nihility, 161, 166, 269
Nihon shoki 日本書紀, 16
Nirvana Sutra, 378
nirvana, 12, 39–41, 155, 352–3, 357, 363, 369, 378, 380, 383, 385
Nishida Kitarō 西田幾多郎, 2, 3, 6, 9, 28, 117–22, 149, 153, 167, 240–8, 252, 282, 301, 347
Nishitani, Keiji 西谷啓治, 2, 7–10, 20, 117, 126, 149, 153–67, 171–2, 175, 198, 200–2, 210, 213, 218, 226, 228–30, 235, 266–93, 298–9, 312, 315, 387, 390, 394–5
no-mind, 89, 185, 210, 256
no-self, 180, 184–5, 188, 191, 193, 299
non-action, 156, 310
non-discrimination, 10, 229, 333
non-doing, 280, 312
non-objectifying, 164, 329
nondual, 11, 54, 157, 163, 251, 260, 344; nonduality, 204–6, 216, 253, 259, 342
nonself, 239, 366

norm, 63, 92, 131, 297, 356; norms, 30, 294, 296
normative, 1, 10, 29–32, 35, 111, 115, 226, 265, 275, 277–8, 293–7, 299–301, 303–5, 307–8, 311, 314, 317, 330, 355, 362
normativity, 10, 275, 293–302, 306, 308, 316–17, 387
not-killing, 312, 315
not-thinking, 327–8, 330, 346
nothingness, 3, 142, 154, 160, 229, 245, 252, 259, 267, 269, 271–2, 286, 361–2
nuns, 46, 81

O'Flaherty, Wendy Doniger, 30
O'Leary, Joseph Stephen, 98
objectification, 96, 164, 329, 343, 346–7; objective stance, 52, 130
objectivism, 37, 51, 327
objectivity, 43, 46, 76–7, 156, 172, 174, 336
obligation, 5, 18, 79, 265, 301, 303
observation, 46, 52, 82, 85, 118, 129, 131, 198, 215; observant participation, 46, 78
Oe Kenzaburō 大江健三郎, 360–1
Ogyū Sorai 荻生徂徠, 122, 185
Ōhashi Ryōsuke 大橋良介, 139, 392
Okumura Shōhaku 奥村正博, 211–12, 215, 311, 369, 372
Olson, Phillip, 302
ontology, 78, 99, 167, 285, 286, 348; ontological, 158, 161, 163–5, 277, 287
openness, 80, 83, 274–5, 285, 349
opposition, 1–2, 5, 6, 40, 43–4, 51–2, 99, 105–7, 110–11, 115, 123, 144, 237, 258, 294, 310, 344–5, 347, 379
Orategama 遠羅天釜, 190, 192–4, 352
orientalism, 237
originality, 343, 389–90, 393, 395–6, 398
Oritaku shiba no ki 折りたく柴の記, 180–8
other-power 他力, 21
otherness, 9, 39, 237–40, 246–7, 259–60, 265, 344

Otto, Rudolf, 26
outsider, 5, 39, 42, 46–8, 88
Ouyang Xiu 歐陽修, 209
Oxherding Pictures, 9, 253–4, 256–61, 264

Pacific War, 278, 309
Pali canon, 385
Pandian, Jacob, 30
paradigm, 172–4, 176, 178–9, 186–8, 195–6, 198–9, 251–2, 283
paradox, 145, 198, 242, 316; paradoxical, 298, 316
pāramitās, 316
Park, Jin Y., 281, 299–300, 310
Parker, Joseph D., 203, 205, 209
Parkes, Graham, 126, 134, 139, 270, 280
Parmenides, 133
Parry, Richard, 114, 119
Pascal, Blaise, 101
pathways, 80, 121, 388–90; p. arts, 12, 387–402
performance, 12, 52, 86, 88–9, 105, 118, 119–22, 243–4, 254, 368, 370, 394–5, 397–402
performative intuition, 119–22
personal Autonomy, 8–9, 139, 218–23, 227, 230–2, 235–6
personal identity, 178, 270
personalists, 258
phenomenology, 68, 73, 76, 102, 129, 133, 143, 290–1, 313, 329–30, 335, 347, 349, 360; phenomenological, 57, 134, 151, 210, 290, 304, 333
physicalism, 344–6; physicalist, 344, 346, 349
Platform Sutra of the Sixth Patriarch (六祖壇經), 162
Plato, 71, 110–11, 114, 261, 314, 316, 349
poetics, 201, 203, 206, 210
Pöggler, Otto, 134, 298
poiesis, 114–15, 119, 120

political, 60, 105, 108, 181, 214, 219, 232, 236–9, 269–73, 299; politics, 37
Pollack, David, 203–4, 208
Polt, Richard, 139, 251
Polyani, Michael, 90
postmodern, 10, 34, 63, 237, 279–80, 282, 285, 288; postmodernist, 266, 280–1, 288, 300, 310, 362
Powers, John, 100
practical reason, 112–13; practical reasoning, 113, 119–21
practice, 4, 6–8, 12, 21–2, 30, 34, 36, 38–40, 52–4, 60, 79–91, 97, 105–6, 171–2, 195–6, 198, 214, 235, 253, 280, 295, 324, 328, 352, 354–7, 364, 370, 398–9
pratītya samutpāda, 225, 274, 277–8. See also *engi*
praxis, 105, 114–15, 119–20, 131, 156, 229
prayer, 78, 85, 369
pre-reflective, 3, 130, 150, 242, 243, 329
Pre-Socratic philosophy, 347
precepts, 10, 11, 296, 298, 300, 302, 304, 306, 311–13, 316–17, 330, 342; *prātimokṣa* p., 312
presence, 15, 66, 67, 125, 200, 248, 261, 291, 309, 363, 371, 381, 388, 398; presencing, 69, 249, 382, 384,
present, 274–8, 278, 280, 289–92, 304, 314–15, 353, 366, 379, 381–2, 385; absolute p., 283, 285; eternal p., 282
Preuss, J. Samuel, 27–8, 31
Pribram, Karl H., 334
principle, 1, 25, 94, 100, 105, 108–9, 111, 118, 154, 185, 244–5, 273, 280, 284, 296–7, 299, 301, 340
process philosophy, 244, 285
propositional language, 245, 247–8; p. logic, 77
propriety, 109, 116, 231–3, 235. See also *li*
Proudfoot, Wayne, 31
psychology, 141, 165, 172
Puggalavādin, 258

Pure Land 淨土, 21, 26, 158, 352–3, 355–6, 385

Quine, Willard, 302

Rahner, Karl, 30, 285
rationality, 119, 273, 299; rational argumentation, 333; rational knowledge, 106
Raud, Rein, 376
realism, 167; realist, 317, 326
realization, 6–7, 10, 11, 39–41, 43, 54, 73, 79, 117, 132, 153, 155, 157, 164–7, 258, 269, 273, 276–8, 286, 288, 308, 315, 324–5, 338–9, 341, 352, 373; realizational, 314–6
reason, 202, 326, 332, 338, 349; practical r., 112–13
reasoning, 34, 86, 109–13, 118–23, 267, 268, 274
rebirth, 191–2, 352, 354, 356, 385
reciprocity, 119, 200, 225–6, 228–9, 232–6; reciprocal, 46, 139, 226, 234, 236, 259
recollection, 176, 178, 180, 189, 290, 348
Red Pine (Bill Porter), 162
reductionism, 26, 166, 326, 345
referential, 64, 66, 68–70, 101, 129, 136, 143, 365
reflection, 59, 90–1, 95, 102, 111, 118, 127, 136, 138, 153, 165, 178–9, 195, 242–4, 246, 250, 299, 326, 328–9, 356, 359, 360
relativism, 4, 15, 20–2, 24, 29–37, 47, 100, 110, 297
relics, 355, 369
religion, 4–6, 16, 19, 21–2, 25, 27–37, 41, 50–1, 55, 57–62, 79–81, 86, 88, 90, 154, 160, 166, 229, 239, 244, 267, 269–72, 349, 354, 356
religiosity, 17, 271, 283
renga 連歌, 262–3
renku 連句, 10, 262–5, 387
repentance, 298, 313
representation, 37, 326, 329, 330, 333;

representational, 138–40, 144, 164, 329, 337, 346–7
responsibility, 3, 9, 35, 177, 219, 226, 234–5, 279, 284, 289, 290, 308, 350
Ricoeur, Paul, 65, 68, 71, 75–8, 198, 260, 360, 381
Rilke, Rainer Maria, 9, 247–9, 251–2, 262, 264–5
Rinzai 臨済, 254, 262, 294, 307
rites, 352–4, 356, 364, 367, 370
ritual, 15, 30, 46, 60, 78–9, 109, 232–3, 354, 362–3, 369
Robertson, Roland, 28
Roman Catholic, 19, 30, 61–2
Rorty, Richard, 321, 326, 328, 333–4, 348, 349
Rosemont, Henry, 110, 230, 232–4
Rossetti, D. G. 207
Rousseau, Jean-Jacques, 7–8, 171–7, 179–81, 183, 187–8, 190, 194, 196–7
Rubin, Jane, 282–3
Rujing. *See* Tiantang Rujing
Runzo, Joseph, 26, 31, 33
Rupp, George, 33
Russell's paradox, 242

Sadō 茶道, 30, 344, 393, 400. *See also* tea ceremony
Saeki Shōichi 佐伯彰一, 180, 184
Safina, Carl, 23
Saichō 最澄, 356
Sakabe Megumi 坂部恵, 101
salvation, 17, 34, 62, 84, 86, 267, 278, 283, 285, 360; salvation history, 267, 285
samādhi, 7, 153, 158–65, 298, 356
Saṃdhinirmocana-sūtra, 100
Sammai Ō Sammai 三昧王三昧, 164
samsara (生死), 12, 282, 352, 356–7, 374, 380, 382–3, 385
samurai, 186–8
Sartre, Jean-Paul, 329, 347
Sasaki, Ruth, 224, 226
Satō Naokata 佐藤直方, 296

satori 悟り, 40, 89, 189, 191–2, 209
Savignon, Sandra J., 87
Schamoni, Wolfgang, 184
Schleiermacher, Fr. D. E., 68, 71, 75, 91–5, 101
Schlütter, Morten, 42
scriptures, 60, 83, 84, 100, 378; sacred s., 60, 96, 100
second-person, 359, 363–5, 367, 381
Seigle, Cecilia Segawa, 183
Sein und Zeit, 125
Sekida Katsuki 関田一喜, 310,
self-identity, 20, 173, 178, 184, 216, 243, 246, 270, 338
self-mastery, 226, 228–30, 235–6
self-negation, 20, 218, 229, 259, 261, 271
self-power, 158. *See also jiriki*
self-realization, 7, 166–7, 205
self, 7–11, 41, 45, 75–8, 96, 119, 121–2, 148, 150–2, 154–6, 158–61, 163, 166–7, 169, 171–80, 218, 220, 222–3, 225, 228–9, 235–9, 243, 248, 252–3, 256–62, 282–3, 286, 293, 298–9, 343–4, 347, 350, 352, 359–60, 365–6, 377–8, 384, 387, 400; s.-investigation 己事究明, 2, 171
selfhood, 2, 7, 9, 195, 236, 260, 283
selfishness, 185–6, 230–1, 296
selflessness, 7, 154, 163, 184, 187, 229, 253, 259, 299
Sellars, Wilfred, 302
semantics, 66, 72, 74, 87, 347
Senika heresy 先尼外道, 332, 340
service, 130, 182, 184–8, 272, 354
Shakyamuni, 15, 212, 328, 356
Shibata Kyūō 柴田鳩翁, 185
Shibayama Zenkei 柴山全慶, 309
Shidō Munan 至道無難, 294, 298
Shimazaki Tōson 島崎藤村, 8, 172–8, 180, 183, 186–8, 194–8
Shingaku 心學, 184–5
Shinjingakudō 身心學道, 321–50
Shinohara Koichi, 196
Shinran 親鸞, 158, 246, 353, 356–7, 367

Shintō 神道, 16–18, 34
Shōbōgenzō 正法眼蔵, 117, 157, 212, 305, 335, 373, 380, 382
shōji 生死, 352, 366, 368, 373, 379, 380, 382
Shōju Ryōjin 正受老人, 190, 192–3
Shōtoku, Prince, 聖徳太子, 16–17
shu-ha-ri 守破離 formula, 399
signification, 69, 338–9, 344
silence, 3, 9, 17, 82, 101, 183, 190, 243, 247, 249–53, 256, 264–5, 324, 341
Silko, Leslie Marmon, 216
Simpson, Peter, 115
sin, 227, 278, 287, 311
Sixth Patriarch, 162–3, 328, 334. See also Huineng
Skinner, B. F., 334
slavery, 219; slave, 226, 234
Smart J. J. C., 344
Smart, Ninian, 36–7, 39–41, 43, 49, 50, 54–5
Smith, Huston, 34
Smith, Wilfred Cantwell, 27, 31
Snyder, Gary, 212–5, 217
Socrates, 108–11, 114, 118, 177–8, 316; Socratic, 71, 109, 111
Soga clan 蘇我氏, 15–17
Sōgetsu School 草月流, 399–400
Sokolowski, Robert, 291
Song Di 宋迪, 203
soteriological, 34, 52, 86, 165, 258
Sōtō 曹洞, 35, 370, 373
speech, 64–5, 73–4, 82, 98, 154, 339, 364; s. acts, 65, 364
Spinoza, Baruch, 219
Spivak, Gayatri Chakravorty, 97
Starobinski, Jean, 175
Steineck, Christian, 365
Steiner, George, 250
Stone, Jacqueline I., 355–6
storytelling, 77, 289
Streng, Frederick J., 36
Su Shi 蘇軾, 203, 205–7, 211

subjectivity, 156–7, 166–7, 210, 218, 229, 272
substance, 176–7, 197, 287, 321, 344
Sueki Fumihiko 末木文美士, 355–6, 383
suffering, 177, 191, 278, 297, 308, 318, 351, 361, 378
Suiko, Empress 推古天皇, 16
Suzuki Shunryū, 鈴木 俊隆, 302
Suzuki, D. T. (Teitarō) Daisetsu 鈴木(貞太郎)大拙, 41, 43, 125–6, 161–2, 278, 388
svabhāva, 154, 202
Swanson, Paul, 269
symbol, 27, 29, 31, 36, 75, 248, 285, 310
syntax, 66, 72, 74, 189

Taihaku Shingen 太白真玄, 206
Tale of Genji, 353, 359, 362
Tanabe Hajime 田辺元, 3, 21, 235, 294, 298, 357, 383
Tanahashi Kazuaki 棚橋一晃, 372, 376
Taylor, Douglas, 25
Taylor, Mark C., 238
tea, 121, 217, 370, 388–9, 393–5, 397–400; t. ceremony, 389, 394. See also sadō
technology, 16, 128, 130, 133–4, 145, 152, 270, 273, 278, 283
Tedlock, Barbara, 46, 78
teleology, 279, 281, 285
telos, 76, 113, 218, 230
Tendai 天台, 210, 324, 327
Tenshō Shūbun 天章周文, 254
Tesshū Tokusai 鉄舟徳済, 208
text, 57–102; textuality, 62, 67–8, 71, 96, 99, 101, 381
theology, 19, 33, 60, 62, 102, 285; theological, 34, 36, 44, 56, 60, 62, 98–9, 285
theory, 1, 6, 24, 64, 67, 73–5, 77, 92, 94, 98, 101, 105–9, 111, 114, 118–9, 121, 124, 131, 135, 154–7, 219, 237, 280, 288, 299, 300, 314, 316, 334
theory-practice opposition, 106, 123
Theravada, 80, 89, 258

third-person, 12, 60, 118, 150, 171, 359, 360, 362–5, 367, 374, 377, 381
Tiantang Rujing 天童如淨, 188, 368–9, 372
Tillich, Paul, 194–5,
time, 10–12, 68–9, 217, 266–8, 273–7, 279–81, 284–5, 288–93, 315, 371, 374–6, 378, 380–5; temporality, 69
Timm, Jeffrey R., 60, 101
Told Round A Brushwood Fire, 180–8. See also *Oritaku shiba no ki*
tools, 23, 69–70, 73, 105, 109, 133, 139, 147, 149
Tracy, David, 20, 56, 100
tradition, notion of, 44–7, 50, 58
training, 52, 81, 83, 111, 173, 185, 212, 214, 296, 387, 392
Trainor, Kevin, 254
trans-lation, 3–4, 218, 223, 302, 322–3
transcendence, 36, 298; transcendent, 6, 20–1, 25, 84, 235, 269, 285, 318, 392
transhistorical, 270, 273, 279, 285
truth, 4, 18, 21, 22, 30–6, 40, 51, 54, 57, 59–60, 79, 80, 84, 98–9, 108, 114, 117, 133–4, 143, 145, 166, 174–6, 180, 224, 259, 269, 300–2, 310, 338, 341, 353, 377, 378
Tsujimura Kōichi 辻村公一, 126,
Tucker, John A., 122, 231
Tucker, Mary Evelyn, 231
turning word 転語, 311, 337
two-truths theory, 316
Tyler, Royall, 354,

Uchimura Kanzō 内村 鑑三, 186
Uchiyama Kōshō 内山 興正, 146
Ueda Shizuteru 上田閑照, 2, 9–10, 139, 145, 237–66, 387
Ueda Yoshifumi 上田義文, 43
Uji 有時, 375, 382–3
Unborn 不生, 191, 377–9
understanding, types of, 5–6, 56–105

universe, 20, 122, 163, 195, 236, 327, 339, 347
uselessness, 107, 134, 136
utilitarianism, 301; utilitarian, 108, 308–9

Validity, 4, 5, 22, 33, 36, 60, 95, 109–10, 184
Van Bragt, Jan, 79, 156, 268, 270
Vattimo, Gianni, 68, 97–9
Vedder, Ben, 92
Vimalakīrti Sutra, 378
violence, 4, 310
virtue, 112–14, 116, 119, 176, 184, 187, 314
Viveiros de Castro, Eduardo, 46
vow, 85, 188, 191–2, 304–5, 313

Waddell, Norman, 54, 164, 188–3, 341, 374
Waldenfels, Bernard, 133
Waldenfels, Hans, 285
Walker, Janet A., 173–4, 176, 188, 196, 197
Wang Yangming, 陽明子, 121–2
war, 219, 270, 278, 290, 309, 401
Watanabe Shōkō 渡辺照宏, 354–5, 369
Watson, Burton, 134, 137, 334
Watsuji Tetsurō 和辻哲郎, 101, 235, 294, 309, 312
Way, the, 16–17, 117, 121, 137, 224, 226, 235, 298, 322, 324–7, 338–42, 349, 374, 376, 387–9, 393–400. See also *dō, dao*
Webb, Mark, 26
Westlund, Andrea, 220–1, 232
Whalen, Philip, 372
Wild Ivy (*Itsumadegusa*, 壁生草), 188, 190–4, 197
will, 135, 139, 144, 152, 218, 221, 227, 234, 273; willful, 7, 136, 142, 154–6
Williams, Duncan Ryūken, 370
Wilson, Edward O., 317
Wirth, Jason, 214
wisdom, 155, 299, 327, 354

Wittgenstein, Ludwig, 63
women, 176, 198, 215, 238, 307
wonder, 158, 177, 272, 335, 349
world, notion of, 65, 69, 75, 121, 129–31, 139, 143, 151, 156, 167, 202, 205–6, 214, 244, 246, 250, 264–5, 284–5, 329
worldview, 270–1, 284, 355, 383
worship, 15–16, 29, 60, 368
Wright, Dale, 78, 299
wu-wei 無爲, 135, 234

Xavier, Francis, 17–18, 21

Yamada Kōun 山田耕雲, 310, 337
Yamaga Sokō 山鹿素行, 231–2
Yamamoto Tsunetomo 山本常朝, 186
Yampolsky, Philip B., 191–2, 334
Yanagida, 227, 254, 259,
Yogācāra, 53, 158, 202, 206, 312, 331–2, 348
Yokoyama, Wayne S., 137, 357, 370, 372
Yōmei, Emperor 用明天皇, 16–17, 21
Yuasa Yasuo 湯浅泰雄, 117, 342,
Yunmen Wen 雲門文偃, 281, 291–3

Zahavi, Dan, 239
Zaner, Richard M. 347
zazen 坐禅, 41, 79, 81, 84, 89, 117, 145, 157–8, 275, 298–9, 302, 306, 314, 324, 327, 339–41, 368
Zen 禅, 2, 4–11, 17–19, 21, 29, 33, 35, 39–42, 45–6, 49, 53–4, 56, 79–84, 86, 89, 91, 117–18, 125–7, 132, 145, 153, 157–8, 161, 163, 171, 180, 185, 188–91, 195, 197, 200–3, 205–6, 209, 214–15, 219, 224, 228, 238–9, 249–50, 253–4, 258, 260–2, 275, 278, 280–1, 286, 292–300, 302–10, 312, 314, 316–19, 322–4, 327–8, 330–1, 334–5, 337–9, 343, 352, 357, 368–70, 381, 384, 387, 388
Zenki 全機, 365, 373, 382–3
Zhao Yiguang 趙宦光, 397
Zhiyi 智顗, 210, 269
Zhu Xi 朱熹, 296
Zhuangzi 莊子, 134–6, 138, 334. *See also* Chuang Tzu
Zola, Émile, 188
Zuimonki 隨聞記, 309, 336–7, 339, 357, 365, 369, 372–3